IoT Protocols and Applications for Improving Industry, Environment, and Society

Cristian González García
University of Oviedo, Spain

Vicente García–Díaz
University of Oviedo, Spain

A volume in the Advances in Web
Technologies and Engineering
(AWTE) Book Series

Published in the United States of America by
    IGI Global
    Engineering Science Reference (an imprint of IGI Global)
    701 E. Chocolate Avenue
    Hershey PA, USA 17033
    Tel: 717-533-8845
    Fax: 717-533-8661
    E-mail: cust@igi-global.com
    Web site: http://www.igi-global.com

Library of Congress Cataloging-in-Publication Data

Names: Gonzalez Garcia, Cristian, 1985- editor. | García Díaz, Vicente,
  1981- editor.
Title: IoT protocols and applications for improving industry, environment,
  and society / Cristian Gonzalez Garcia and Vicente Garcia-Diaz, editors.

Description: Hershey, PA : Information Science Reference, an imprint of IGI
  Global, [2021] | Includes bibliographical references and index. |
  Summary: "This book studies how daily life operates using many objects
  with Internet connections such as smartphones, tablets, Smart TVs,
  micro-controllers, Smart Tags, computers, laptops, cars, cheaper
  sensors, and more, commonly referred to as the Internet of Things. To
  accommodate this new connected structure, readers will learn how
  improved wireless strategies drive the need for a better IoT network"--
  Provided by publisher.
Identifiers: LCCN 2020023245 (print) | LCCN 2020023246 (ebook) | ISBN
  9781799864639 (hardcover) | ISBN 9781799864646 (paperback) | ISBN
  9781799864653 (ebook)
Subjects: LCSH: Internet of things.
Classification: LCC TK5105.8857 .I697 2021 (print) | LCC TK5105.8857
  (ebook) | DDC 004.6/2--dc23
LC record available at https://lccn.loc.gov/2020023245
LC ebook record available at https://lccn.loc.gov/2020023246

This book is published in the IGI Global book series Advances in Web Technologies and Engineering (AWTE)
(ISSN: 2328-2762; eISSN: 2328-2754)

British Cataloguing in Publication Data
A Cataloguing in Publication record for this book is available from the British Library.

For electronic access to this publication, please contact: eresources@igi-global.com.

Advances in Web Technologies and Engineering (AWTE) Book Series

ISSN:2328-2762
EISSN:2328-2754

Editor-in-Chief: Ghazi I. Alkhatib The Hashemite University, Jordan David C. Rine George Mason University, USA

MISSION

The **Advances in Web Technologies and Engineering (AWTE) Book Series** aims to provide a platform for research in the area of Information Technology (IT) concepts, tools, methodologies, and ethnography, in the contexts of global communication systems and Web engineered applications. Organizations are continuously overwhelmed by a variety of new information technologies, many are Web based. These new technologies are capitalizing on the widespread use of network and communication technologies for seamless integration of various issues in information and knowledge sharing within and among organizations. This emphasis on integrated approaches is unique to this book series and dictates cross platform and multidisciplinary strategy to research and practice.

The **Advances in Web Technologies and Engineering (AWTE) Book Series** seeks to create a stage where comprehensive publications are distributed for the objective of bettering and expanding the field of web systems, knowledge capture, and communication technologies. The series will provide researchers and practitioners with solutions for improving how technology is utilized for the purpose of a growing awareness of the importance of web applications and engineering.

COVERAGE

- Data and knowledge validation and verification
- Metrics-based performance measurement of IT-based and web-based organizations
- Web user interfaces design, development, and usability engineering studies
- IT education and training
- Quality of service and service level agreement issues among integrated systems
- Web Systems Architectures, Including Distributed, Grid Computer, and Communication Systems Processing
- Human factors and cultural impact of IT-based systems
- Strategies for linking business needs and IT
- Integrated user profile, provisioning, and context-based processing
- Software agent-based applications

IGI Global is currently accepting manuscripts for publication within this series. To submit a proposal for a volume in this series, please contact our Acquisition Editors at Acquisitions@igi-global.com or visit: http://www.igi-global.com/publish/.

Titles in this Series

For a list of additional titles in this series, please visit:
http://www.igi-global.com/book-series/advances-web-technologies-engineering/37158

Design Innovation and Network Architecture for the Future Internet
Mohamed Boucadair (Orange S.A., France) and Christian Jacquenet (Orange S.A., Fance)
Engineering Science Reference • © 2021 • 478pp • H/C (ISBN: 9781799876465) • US $225.00

Challenges and Opportunities for the Convergence of IoT, Big Data, and Cloud Computing
Sathiyamoorthi Velayutham (Sona College of Technology, India)
Engineering Science Reference • © 2021 • 350pp • H/C (ISBN: 9781799831112) • US $215.00

Examining the Impact of Deep Learning and IoT on Multi-Industry Applications
Roshani Raut (Pimpri Chinchwad College of Engineering (PCCOE), Pune, India) and Albena Dimitrova Mihovska (CTIF Global Capsule (CGC), Denmark)
Engineering Science Reference • © 2021 • 304pp • H/C (ISBN: 9781799875116) • US $245.00

Result Page Generation for Web Searching Emerging Research and Opportunities
Mostafa Alli (Tsinghua University, China)
Engineering Science Reference • © 2021 • 126pp • H/C (ISBN: 9781799809616) • US $165.00

Building Smart and Secure Environments Through the Fusion of Virtual Reality, Augmented Reality, and the IoT
Nadesh RK (Vellore Institute of Technology, India) Shynu PG (Vellore Institute of Technology, India) and Chiranji Lal Chowdhary (School of Information Technology and Engineering, VIT University, Vellore, India)
Engineering Science Reference • © 2020 • 300pp • H/C (ISBN: 9781799831839) • US $245.00

For an entire list of titles in this series, please visit:
http://www.igi-global.com/book-series/advances-web-technologies-engineering/37158

701 East Chocolate Avenue, Hershey, PA 17033, USA
Tel: 717-533-8845 x100 • Fax: 717-533-8661
E-Mail: cust@igi-global.com • www.igi-global.com

Table of Contents

Detailed Table of Contents

Chapter 1
Challenges in Advanced Visualization in Industry 4.0: New Ways of Working ... 1
Manuel Pérez-Cota, University of Vigo, Spain
Miguel Ramón González-Castro, University of Vigo, Spain

Today's advanced visualization systems will revolutionize the way information is perceived in industrial environments. This will help the different industrial workers to interact more efficiently with the machines, equipment, and systems installed in the industrial plant. The display devices will provide operators with all the information they need to perform their work more efficiently, as well as inform them of all the hazards and safety in their environment. Also, screen operators, thanks to the use of a single 2.5D/3D screen, will possess an exhaustive knowledge of the state of the industrial process. This increases the amount on quantity and quality of information that is offered to the operator, and it avoids the superfluous navigation between operation screens.

Chapter 2
Non-Mobile Software Modernization in Accordance With the Principles of
Model-Driven Engineering 29
Liliana Maria Favre, Universidad Nacional del Centro de la Provincia
de Buenos Aires, Argentina & Comisión de Investigaciones
Científicas de la Provincia de Buenos Aires, Argentina

Smartphones are at the core of new paradigms such as cloud computing, pervasive computing, and internet of things. Frequently, the development of mobile software requires adaptation of valuable and tested non-mobile software. In this context, most challenges are related to the diversity of platforms on the smartphones market and to the need of systematic and reusable processes with a high degree of automation that reduce time, cost, and risks. To face these challenges, this chapter presents an analysis of non-mobile software modernization through an integration of MDE (model-driven engineering) with cross-platform development. Two approaches are analyzed. One of them is a lightweight process that combines MDA (model-driven architecture) with traditional static and dynamic analysis techniques of reverse engineering. The other approach is based on ADM (architecture-driven modernization) standards. A scenario for the migration of C/C++ or Java software through the multiplatform Haxe language is described.

Chapter 3

In the information age, activities and business models have become different. Factors such as new technologies and social media influence consumer behavior due to the variety of choices/channels. Companies are making a difference in consumers' minds by connecting with them active and creatively. Also, customers contribute with ideas and experiences, not only for products and services, but also for platforms and brands. Cyber-physical apps together with mobile media tend to revolutionize business models across multiple industries. This is important for tourism due to a contribution to link some still weakly linked activities across tourism sub-sectors in Portugal. The present work reflects on how Portugal is in terms of internet of things adoption (IoT) and digital transformation facing the challenges of sustainable and smart cities. It also explores which impacts this transformation can have through its platforms and processes in tourism and future services.

Chapter 4

The internet of things comprises billions of devices, people, and services and entitles each to connect through sensor devices. These sensor devices influence the real world by administering critical network infrastructure and sometimes may collect sensitive private information about individuals. Managing this data authentication of who can access the device data and under what circumstances it can be found and used by others is one of the major threats for consumers and businesses. So, the internet of things services deliver new privacy challenges in our day-to-day lives. Though information systems discipline addressed research in privacy to a great extent, there still prevails no robust approach for the inspection of privacy breaches in the internet of things services. This chapter provides a detailed view on the privacy concerns in various aspects and scrutinizes the challenges to be addressed to ensure that the internet of things becomes true in near future.

Chapter 5

The internet of things, popularly known as IoT, is intelligent sensors working together to accomplish a task. These devices are used in innumerable applications, and they are aiming to minimize human efforts. These unsupervised devices require some amount of security. Hence, the previous systems use blockchains to enhance security. The hashing system used in this technology preserves the security and confidentiality among the stakeholders. Medchain is a system that communicates between the personnel and insurance dealings securely. To enhance reliability of the previous work, the proposal is proposed. The methodology used in the contribution enhances the reliability by 2.89% compared to the previous proposal.

Chapter 6

The internet of things is a versatile technology that helps to connect devices with other devices or humans in any part of the world at any time. Some of the researchers claim that the number of IoT devices around the world will surpass the total population on the earth after a few years. The technology has made life easier, but these comforts are backed up with a lot of security threats. Wireless medium for communication, large amount of data, and device constraints of the IoT devices are some of the factors that increase their vulnerability to security threats. This chapter provides information about the attacks at different layers of IoT architecture. It also mentions the benefits of technologies like blockchain and machine learning that can help to solve the security issues of IoT.

In the last five years, we witnessed the shift from the vision of the internet of things (IoT) to an actual reality. It is currently shifting again from specific and single applications to larger and more generic ones, which serves the needs of thousands of users across borders and platforms. To avoid losing the personification of applications, on account of genericity, new approaches and languages that use generic knowledge as a steppingstone while taking into consideration users and context's specific and evolutive needs are on the rise. This chapter aims to provide a framework to support the creation of such approaches (DSPL4IoT). It is later on used to assess notable IoT specification approaches and extract conclusion of the trends and persistent challenges and directions. An approach for the specification of natural language (NL) requirements for IoT systems is also provided to assist domain and application engineers with the formulations of such requirements.

Chapter 8

Ambika N., Department of Computer Applications, Sivananda Sarma Memorial RV College, Bangalore,, India

The internet of things is the technology that aims to provide a common platform to the devices of varying capabilities to communicate. Industrial internet of things (IIoT) systems can perform better using these devices in combination with SDN network and blockchain technology. The suggestion uses random space learning (RSL) comprising three stages. The random subspace learning strategy is a troupe learning procedure called attributes bagging. It improves forecast and order errands as it utilizes group development of base classifiers rather than a solitary classifier, and it takes arbitrary subsets of properties rather than the whole arrangement of attributes. The system uses the blockchain methodology to secure the system. SDN networks aim to better the transmission of data in industrial IoT devices. Misrouting and forged attacks are some of the common attacks in these systems. The proposal provides better reliability than the previous contribution by 2.7%.

Chapter 9

Jerin Geo Jacob, Mount Zion College of Engineering, India
Siji A. Thomas, Mount Zion College of Engineering, India
Bivin Biju, Mount Zion College of Engineering, India
Richarld John, Mount Zion College of Engineering, India
Abhilash P. R., Mount Zion College of Engineering, India

This chapter discusses the design of a quantitative controlled pesticide sprayer and the development of an efficient algorithm for plant identification. The whole system is controlled using the raspberry pi and convolutional neural networks (CNN) algorithm for training the proposed model. Once the algorithm identifies the plant by processing the image, it is captured by using a pi camera, and it determines the pesticide and its dosage. The sensors will collect the information related to the plant condition such as humidity and surrounding temperature, which is simultaneously sent to the farmers/agriculture officers through the internet of things (IoT), for the purpose of live analysis, and they are stored using cloud services, making the system suitable for remote farming. The proposed algorithm is trained mainly for three types of plant leaves, which include tomato, brinjal, and chilly. The CNN algorithm scores accuracy of 97.2% with sensitivity and specificity of 0.94 and 0.95, respectively. The robot is intended to encourage the agriculturists for next-level farming to facilitate their work.

Chapter 10

   Dominik Hromada, FBM, Brno University of Technology, Czech Republic
   Rogério Luís de C. Costa, CIC, Polytechnic of Leiria, Portugal
   Leonel Santos, CIIC, ESTG, Polytechnic of Leiria, Portugal
   Carlos Rabadão, CIIC, ESTG, Polytechnic of Leiria, Portugal

The Internet of Things (IoT) comprises the interconnection of a wide range of different devices, from Smart Bluetooth speakers to humidity sensors. The great variety of devices enables applications in several contexts, including Smart Cities and Smart Industry. IoT devices collect and process a large amount of data on machines and the environment and even monitor people's activities. Due to their characteristics and architecture, IoT devices and networks are potential targets for cyberattacks. Indeed, cyberattacks can lead to malfunctions of the IoT environment and access and misuse of private data. This chapter addresses security concerns in the IoT ecosystem. It identifies common threats for each of IoT layers and presents advantages, challenges, and limitations of promising countermeasures based on new technologies and strategies, like Blockchain and Machine Learning. It also contains a more in-depth discussion on Intrusion Detection Systems (IDS) for IoT, a promising solution for cybersecurity in IoT ecosystems.

Chapter 11

   Kamalendu Pal, City, University of London, UK

The manufacturing industry tends to worldwide business operations due to the economic benefits of product design and distribution operations. The design and development of a manufacturing enterprise information system (EIS) involve different types of decision making at various levels of business control. This decision making is complex and requires real-time data collection from machines, business processes, and operating environments. Enterprise information systems are used to support data acquisition, communication, and all decision-making activities. Hence, information technology (IT) infrastructure for data acquisition and sharing affects the performance of an EIS significantly. The chapter highlights the advantages and disadvantages of an integrated internet of things (IoT) and blockchain technology on EIS in the modern manufacturing industry. Also, it presents a review of security-related issues in the context of an EIS consisting of IoT-based blockchain technology. Finally, the chapter discusses the future research directions.

Preface

The Internet of Things, also known as the IoT, is the interconnection of heterogeneous and ubiquitous objects between themselves. Currently, people have things to make an IoT network. People's daily life has a lot of objects with Internet connection like smartphones, tablets, Smart TVs, micro-controllers, Smart Tags, computers, laptops, cars, cheaper sensors, and the improved wireless connections. With these things, people have heterogeneous objects because these are of different type and people have ubiquitous objects because objects are installed in different places and some of these objects can be moved round the world. If we think about this, we could already think that we have the Internet of Things.

With the Internet of Things, we can create an enormous network to interconnect objects and facilitate our daily life. Some examples: to improve the tracking of deliveries, objects' situation, to improve the factory's production, or security in the industry; to prevent natural disasters, to automate actions in farms, or to obtain data about the ecosystem in order to protect fauna and flora according to certain situations, this is known as Smart Earth; the improvement of Smart Cities to help citizens in their daily life, for instance, to park, to avoid traffic jams, to automate traffic lights, to change the public transport in real-time or so on; to improve people's life with Smart Homes using of a Smart Fridge to help ill people or facilitating the garden maintenance.

This book contains different topics about the most important areas and challenges in the Internet of Things. In this book, you will be able to read about the different subparts which compose the Internet of Things and the different ways to create a better IoT network or IoT platform.

For instance, it is very important to know about the next step in the industry, in which people will use more technology and they will have to work very closely with it. Besides, these technologies need access to the Internet, then, reliability, security and privacy take a very important role to create good communications and do not have security breaches in which the information of people could reach anyone.

Furthermore, the Internet of Things is a very big field with a lot of subfields, which are very important such as Smart Homes to improve our daily life, Smart Cities to improve the citizens' life, Smart Towns to recover the livability and traditions, Smart Earth to protect our world, and Industrial Internet of Things to create safer and easier jobs.

These improvements can be applied in different ways. We can use different technologies and create different applications, or we can use the research of other fields like Big Data to process the massive data of the devices, Artificial Intelligence to create smarter objects or algorithms, Model-Driven Engineering to facilitate the use of it to any people, Cloud Computing to send the computation and the applications to the cloud, and Cloud Robotics to manage and interconnect the Robots between themselves and with other objects.

In our humble opinion, currently, the publications about the Internet of Things are very confusing because sometimes they are in journals with a different main subject, and they are very disseminated. This is why we are trying to join under a book the most important topics in this field.

We think that this could be very good to improve the understanding of what is the Internet of Things and what are the different ways that any researcher or student can choose to create or research in this field.

This is why we have edited a book which could be a reference to introduce people to what is the Internet of Things and what are the different parts of it. From researchers to practitioners and students to help others to understand the current state of the art on the Industrial Internet of Things.

We firmly believe that this publication could also be of interest for:

- Thousands of readers such as professors, researchers, and people who want to start in this world.
- Thousands of people who read and write about the IoT.
- Thousands of computer science students: PhD. students and college students.
- People interested in the Internet of Things related conferences all around the world.
- People working on the Internet of Things related research groups in Universities and other research institutions.
- People working on the Internet of Things in a large number of companies in the world.

In this book, readers can find information about the Industrial Internet of Things, also known as the Industry 4.0, software modernization, Smart Tourism, medical systems, software specification using a framework, reliability in Industrial Internet of Things systems, application of the Internet of Things in industry, and security, privacy, and different ways to secure the Internet of Things.

In the first chapter, the reader can find an example of the use of the Internet of Things in the industry. It is also known as Industry 4.0 or Industrial Internet of Things. Here, Manuel Pérez-Cota and Miguel Ramón González-Castro talk about the new tools and advances in the industry and how the competencies of an operator can fit in the new technologies. Some of these new technologies are Mixed Reality, Augmented Reality, and Virtual Reality. Very important because these will be the next changes in some industry, and we have to be prepared for them.

The second chapter shows an analysis of the software modernization using the Model-Driven Engineering principles. Using it, Liliana Maria Favre, the author, integrates the Haxe language with Model-Driven Engineering to migrate software to new technologies, like the Internet of Things. It is very important to have quick and safe changes at the same time that we update the technologies.

Silvia Fernandes presents Chapter 3. In this chapter, she shows the changes of the Internet of Things in tourism, from accommodation and travel agencies to food and transports and more. This is why the new technologies have changed and created a new way of tourism, the Smart Tourism in which the Internet of Thing is involved. These changes and opportunities are shown from the point of view of Portugal and will allow the reader to know how they affect the economy and why it is important to do them.

Chapter 4 is a survey about privacy on the Internet of Things. Here, K. Jayashree and R. Babu explain the data access and the importance of this access. The Internet of Things has new privacy challenges, and these are shown here. Exactly, they show the concerns from different aspects and the challenges to be addressed like the consent, the context-based privacy, the customization and anonymity and others. This is very important because every day we use services and applications which manage personal data that are very important and need to be treated correctly.

In the next chapter, the reader can see information about Medchain explained by Ambika N. Ambika explains how Medchain is a decentralized system to associate the different medical services like suppliers, emergencies, centres, and social insurances, and the reliability of the system. As we can see, the Internet of Things is everywhere and can help us. Here, it connects different services to help users and the government in medical aspects.

Njum Nazir Qureshi Sheikh, Asha Ambhaikar, and Sunil Kumar are the authors of Chapter 6. In this chapter, they present the challenges, attacks, and prevention of security on the Internet of Things. This is important because every day we have more devices connected to the Internet and they have a lot of security threats. Besides, they show the benefits of Blockchain and Machine Learning in this field. Something very important because we can see security breaches with millions of personal data every week. Furthermore, the Internet of Things devices access personal data, which is very important and contain very close information about us.

Chapter 7 is about Smart Cars and the guidelines for the specification of requirements on the Internet of Things. Here, Asmaa Achtaich, Camille Salinesi, Nissrine Souissi, Raul Mazo, and Ounsa Roudies show a framework called DSPL4IoT. This framework assists in the reusability, adaptation, and specification of the requirements for the engineers. This allows helping engineers giving them a natural language approach to the requirements of an Internet of Things application in the specification process. They explain the framework and its utility using Smart Cars as a case.

The next chapter shows the improvement of the reliability of a system. To achieve this, Ambika N. proposes an architecture and improves a previous system and the reliability in the Industrial Internet of Things systems. This is very important because, every day, we can see new attacks and security problems in different devices, sometimes with an expensive cost for industry and people.

Jerin Geo Jacob, Siji A Thomas, Bivin Biju, Richarld John, and Abhilash P. R. wrote Chapter 9. In this chapter, the authors explain how using robots the Internet of Things can detect the pesticide and the dosage to use over the plants. Then, this can help people to avoid the problem of working with pesticides like immune malfunction, neurological impairments, dermal problems, cancer, and vision-related issues, and relegate this work problem using the technology.

In Chapter 10, Dominik Hromada, Rogério Luís de C. Costa, and Leonel Santos explain different security concerns about the Internet of Things in its different layers. In addition, they explain the advantages, challenges, and limitations of the countermeasures. These countermeasures are Fog Computing, Blockchain, Edge Computing, Machine Learning, and Intrusion Detection Systems as a possible solution. All of these are important to try to avoid the possible breach of this new technology, and everyone is a different possibility in this field.

Kamalendu Pal, who is the author of Chapter 11, discusses how to secure the Internet of Things applications using Blockchain. First of all, the author shows the different layers and different attacks on each one. Next, the reader can see what is a Blockchain and information about it, terms, and uses as an introduction of the use of Blockchain to secure the Internet of Things.

In conclusion, we think that the book can be used to learn the new challenges related to the Industrial Internet of Things and different applications of the use of the Internet of Things. Besides, the book has different chapters about privacy and security in this field, something that is very important nowadays than before. Moreover, the chapter provides great background and a state of the art to learn and go more in depth about the different aspect of the Internet of Things. Besides, it has different use cases of frameworks and the impact in economy, in this last point, in Portugal. Besides, the chapters have future works and challenges for next years, which can provide a little background about the future of this technology in the coming years.

Acknowledgment

We would like to thank all the authors that have sent a chapter to this book, who have done their best effort in writing good chapters.

We would like to also thank all authors who have reviewed other chapters of the book and other external reviewers. Both parties have done a great job reading and suggesting improvements for each chapter:

Silvia Fernandes, K. Jayashree, Anjum Sheikh, Camille Salinesi, Liliana Favre, Manoj Devare, Ambika N, Jerin Geo Jacob, Siji A Thomas, Kamalendu Pal, Ashutosh Kumar Dubey, and Daniel Meana Llorián.

Chapter 1
Challenges in Advanced Visualization in Industry 4.0:
New Ways of Working

Manuel Pérez-Cota
ⓘD https://orcid.org/0000-0003-0471-6981
University of Vigo, Spain

Miguel Ramón González-Castro
University of Vigo, Spain

ABSTRACT

Today's advanced visualization systems will revolutionize the way information is perceived in industrial environments. This will help the different industrial workers to interact more efficiently with the machines, equipment, and systems installed in the industrial plant. The display devices will provide operators with all the information they need to perform their work more efficiently, as well as inform them of all the hazards and safety in their environment. Also, screen operators, thanks to the use of a single 2.5D/3D screen, will possess an exhaustive knowledge of the state of the industrial process. This increases the amount on quantity and quality of information that is offered to the operator, and it avoids the superfluous navigation between operation screens.

DOI: 10.4018/978-1-7998-6463-9.ch001

INTRODUCTION

The nowadays "industry (steel, cement, paper, car, etc.) is characterized because it has a critical production process in which any failure or stop can create very dangerous situations, for both, the environment and for people" (Pérez-Cota, González-Castro, & Díaz-Rodríguez, 2018). The use of new visualization tools and how the workers are applying them is being a big challenge, for actual enterprises, to maintain their presence in markets.

The appearance of a new entertainment industry and tools for sound, image, movement and sense can be applied to the industrial environments to enhance the way they can carry out their work.

The new advanced visualization systems are a key part of the development of other technologies in Industry 4.0. Here using critical techs as Big Data, Additive manufacturing, Simulation and Modelling, Digital Twins, Collaborative robotics, Enhanced Visualization, Computer Vision and Advanced Operator Site.

This paper explains how and operator should fulfil his/her competences to fit with the current and future technologies that are and will be used in Industry.

The first section of this document details the historical evolution of the DCS operating screens. The following section examines the uses of "Mixed Reality" (MR) and "Augmented Reality" (AR) in industrial environments. The next section describes the immersive "Virtual Reality" (VR) in today's industrial world. The penultimate section examines some innovative industrial management applications in 2.5D/3D environments. This type of interface increases the quantity and quality of information that is perceived by the operator; as it displays on a single 2.5D/3D graphic display the contents of a set of old 2D DCS operator displays. The last section describes the experiences of the operators who tested this interface.

IMPORTANCE OF THE DCS OPERATOR SCREENS

DCS are devices that manage several thousands of analogic and digital signals; and have a distributed architecture, which increases considerably their reliability and availability. However, its essential feature is the intensive interaction with the operator, since he/she is the one who has to do the key decisions about the operation of the process under his/her control.

Then, they are an Information System (IS) of extremely important characteristics, because from it depends the success or fault of an enterprise of any type. From a general conceptual perspective, an IS have suffered multiple evolutions over time. Still, despite this development, most authors continue to consider IS as technological solutions aimed at supporting organizations in their daily business activities and addressing the constant challenges imposed by their own environment (Chaparro-Peláez, n.d.). Supporting is the key word, because what we do in an DCS is to serve as a support of the way the enterprise should do all changes in its environment. In addition, nowadays, visualization is one of the highest challenges enterprises must face. We should remember that the principal idea is to earn money from the activity of the enterprise.

The first DCS in 1975 by Honeywell and called TDC 2000. The operator interface, of the DCS of this time based on a CRT (Cathode Ray Tube), which allowed a very elementary representation of the data of the industrial process. The monitor was connected directly to the DCS or was connected via a serial communication port. This operator display showed the information in textual format and through bar diagrams, which limited the amount of process data that could be viewed. In addition, the format was very unintuitive and forced the operator to do an effort to interpret the numerical values he/she perceived. Finally, the operator had a keypad and/or keyboard to send commands to the DCS.

The 1980s began with the birth of the IBM PC in 1981, which became a turning point in the world of computing, as it promoted the universalization of computers at a reasonable cost. This led to the generalization of the mouse or the increased performance in microprocessors, memories, peripherals and graphics cards. This resulted in the appearance of DCS screens that included elementary diagrams of the process chart, which grouped in a hierarchical structure to facilitate the visualization of the different stages of the industrial process. However, the screens still had too much information in numerical format, which the operator had to decipher and understand in order to have an exact situation awareness of the process. The operator's command input interface transformed into the keyboard and mouse.

The 1990s began with the commercialization of the "Windows 3.0" operating environment in 1990, as well as the launch of the "Windows NT 3.1" operating system in 1993. Also in this decade the use of LAN and multimedia systems got popular. All these advances resulted in the use of personal computers or workstations as DCS operator consoles. This led to the appearance of complex graphic figures, which allowed the state of the industrial process to be shown through textual, numerical and graphic information. This graphic information used colours, levels, animations, etc., which was complemented by the use of pop-up windows that informed in more detail of the selected component. Likewise, graphic O. S. allowed operators to display several process screens (windows) on the same monitor. The industrial process of these screens was a quasi-copy of the flowcharts used in the piping and instrumentation planes. The use of high-speed data networks provided greater transfer of information between the operator and the DCS. All this allowed the operator to increase the ability to understand the instantaneous state of the industrial process; since the visual information is easier to assimilate than the numeric or textual one.

Finally, it should be noticed that this graphic representation format remains almost unchanged until now.

The optimum operator interface must provide an accurate and thorough "situation awareness" in all industrial process conditions (normal, abnormal and emergency). Therefore, the best DCS screen designs are the ones that optimize the quantity and quality of information of the industrial process, which must be assimilated by the operator, in order to have an optimal knowledge of the situation of the process and thus, be able to make the best decision (Reising, 2010). For this reason, institutions such as the ASM (Abnormal Situation Management Consortium) have developed guidelines or recommendations with best practices, which can be applied in the design of the operator's screens (ASM, 2017). These guides or recommendations were created to be applied only on 2D screens.

Figure 1. Honeywell Experion Orion Console (Year 2020)

The DCS operator interfaces that are currently marketed have 2D monitors and, in addition, the screens contain diagrams or process diagrams in 2D format (Honeywell Corporation, 2020), (Honeywell Corporation, 2006), (Siemens GMBH, 2017), (Emerson, 2020), (ABB, 2020), (Pérez-Cota & González-Castro, Interfaz avanzado de operador de DCS, 2011-06). This implies that if you want to have different views of the process, it is imperative to create new screens. The DCS alarms are indicated on the operation screen, with a change in the colour of the component that generates it and, also, they are listed in a table sorted by priorities and/or areas, which is accessible from different places on the screens. Likewise, the appearance of an alarm causes the emission of an audible signal, composed by several tones.

All operation screens show the status of the components using a colour code; but some facilitate access to programming manuals, instrument manuals (valve, motor, etc.), block logic programs, electrical diagrams, piping diagrams or link to other management applications (Maximo, SAP ...). The typical input interface of the DCS is the keyboard and the mouse, although in some cases a touch screen as an advanced device is used. This is because it supports configurations predefined by the user, which facilitate the execution of complex tasks.

DCS screen operators typically manage up to fifty operation screens, with several thousand associated I/O signals; so there may be I/O screens or signals that are not accessed by them, for several work shifts or until an alarm is triggered. This forces to create summary screens with the most critical information of the process and/or forces the operator to navigate through all the existing screens in the DCS.

ABB and Umea's Interactive Institute have developed a prototype of a business management tool which facilitates tracking of any KPI (Key Process Indicator) (Breibvold H. P., 2010). This management tool has a touch screen monitor, which displays the building of the production plant and/or industrial equipment in a 2.5D environment. The touch screen facilitates the rotation, movement and/or zoom of the scene. An overview of the plant only shows high-level KPIs; but a view of a section of the factory presents KPIs specifically related to that area, which may not be visible at the top level. The data (KPI, multivariate, historical ...) are shown in a rectangular box containing the data name, its numerical value and a colour bar indicator with variable length. The application designed to convert the graphic display into a tool that would replace the classic projection screen, or portfolio. Thus, virtual drawings and annotations can be inserted, which remain fixed to the element and not to a physical position of the screen.

The Siemens Comos-Walkinside application facilitates management and engineering tasks throughout the lifecycle of an industrial plant (Siemens GMBH, 2020). This tool keeps all the technical documentation of the industrial plant up to date from the project phase to the operation phase, including detailed engineering, the execution project, the process design, etc.. Likewise, the 3D visualization of the equipment of the industrial plant favours the work of learning and maintenance. This 3D environment is complemented with tabular and textual information in 2D.

ABB software and the Siemens Comos-Walkinside software were not intended to become a DCS operator interface, as they do not allow interaction with industrial devices to examine or modify their status.

Some entities performed various works on the use of advanced visualization systems in business, commercial and recreational activities. Thus, M.R. Dickey described the nine activities (GPS, video-recording, transportation, construction, health, travel, education, safety and advertising), where Google Glasses could have a great impact (M.R., 2015). The educational field is one of the areas where more is being innovated in the use of advanced systems of visualization. Thus, the Glassist prototype was created to facilitate the work of teachers, by displaying in a Google Glass the data of the profile of the student, which is recognized by the use of facial recognition algorithms (Silva, 2014). Likewise, I. Malý developed a prototype that using an AR glasses show relevant information to operator over the robot he/she is watching (Malý I., 2016, July). Then, tele-operation and tele-inspection tasks allow the use of Google Glass, so that the operator sends orders to the drone that was controlling and receive the images sent by the camera of that drone (Teixeira & Ferreira, 2014).

Let's analyse, then in the next paragraphs how the different types of information that can be visualized:

- Manuals of the productive process. These documents contain the exhaustive technical information of all industrial processes that exist in the company. This information is usually consulted for the complex technical calculations on which the production process of a large industry is based. Operators or managers need to promptly access this information to help them solve complex and unusual breakdowns
- Operation manuals. Operators of the production process will have access to the operational procedures that indicate what actions need to be performed to properly manage the stage of the process they are managing
- Disassembly of equipment. This documentation contains schemas that show the parts and/or parts in which a complex device is decomposed. This information is critical for maintenance technicians to perform proper repairing
- Electrical or mechanical plans at various scales. These plans contain general information of the entire factory and/or details of each of the sections of the industrial plant
- Factory floor maps. The smart glasses screen can show the operator the priority paths to move inside a factory. This will allow him/her to avoid closed ways as well as unsafe or dangerous ways
- Real-time operation screens. Operation screens show the status of an installation or equipment. The lens frame shows the contents of an operation screen, as this information makes it easier for the operator to perform a job more safely. This allows him/her to check the status of the equipment before proceeding to repair or overhaul
- Work Orders and Work Permits. These documents indicate to the maintenance personnel the tasks that must be performed, as well as the assurances that must be activated so that the task is carried out with full security guarantees

- Check list. The list of tasks of maintenance of an equipment or an installation, facilitates the commissioning of a facility; as it ensures that the operator followed all the steps indicated in its repair or revision procedure
- Connection with ERP. The ERP indicate to the operator which are the work orders that must be attended and he/she can consult the state of the warehouse. This allows he/she to know if the material, which he/she needs for repair, is in store or even make an order request for the Purchasing Department to take steps to acquire it
- Dangerous areas. The operator receives information from hazardous locations/places; as well as indicating the type, duration, origin and possible consequences of that danger
- Information in noisy environments. Signalling or visualization of alarms in very noisy environments. The fact that the information can always be present in the field of view of the operator, prevents the user from needing to feel a vibration or to hear an alarm signal
- Emergency information. The user/operator receives information about the location and the ways that must follow to go to the emergency exits. This prevents users from having to consult documentation on paper or looking at symbols or signs indicating the outputs; because in environments with a lot of smoke or without visibility it is very confusing to determine which is the correct way to the exit
- Retransmission of works. The operator can retransmit in video the works that are being done, without having to carry any uncomfortable or annoying device. This allows him/her to record him/her task to analyse it at another time or to collect advice and indications from experts that a group of experts to analyse the task he/she is doing. This last task is of great help in repairing complex equipment in which the long distance experts can't move to check the fault in-situ
- Video surveillance. Real-time video showing the status of a restricted area or even images of security cameras to security personnel
- Locations of equipment/merchandise in the warehouse. This allows guiding the operator through the map of the warehouse, to direct it to the exact location of the material he/she is looking for
- Reading of bar-codes or labels for identification of equipment, materials or products
- OCR tools. The use of OCR tools facilitates the capture of texts that the operator is visualizing. Also, the captured text can be translated and displayed on the screen to the operator. This process is usually critical in repair tasks, where the equipment manuals are not translated into the operator's language

- Meetings. One of the most important tasks of any industrial officer is reporting at meetings. This task is improved if the user has the most relevant information on the screen of his smart glasses. This helps to make a more fluid presentation in which the critical data are within reach a slight rotation of the eye

In Spain the legislation of Prevention of Industrial Risks in the industry requires the use of Personal Protective Equipment (PPE), which are adapted to the hazardous that is being done. These PPE's may be made up of specific protections for some parts of the body or complete suits that fully protect the worker. Next, we will analyse the various benefits and damages that are derived from the use of ARM-G, depending on the PPE's that an industrial worker should use for each job:

- Full protective suit. Jobs that require the use of workers' comprehensive protective clothing are often used for tasks performed in hostile environments (chemical, nuclear, high temperatures, paint, mines, fire...). In these environments, the use of information on paper or shown on a tablet is completely inadequate; because paper or electronic devices would degrade very quickly if they were not properly protected. Likewise, the protective equipment, worn by the operator, drastically limits his/her field of vision; So it is very difficult to visualize any information that he/she has to hold with his/her hands, whether it is represented on paper or on an electronic screen. ARM-G (Augmented Reality Binocular Glasses) is an excellent option for the operator to receive information, since the protective suit he/she wears, protects both him/her and the glasses he/she carries. In addition, the user has no obstruction in his/her visual field that prevents him/her from accessing the information he/she needs to consult, since the glasses are located inside his/her protective suit
- Hearing protectors. The works, which run in very noisy environments, require the use of hearing protectors; but this makes it difficult to establish verbal communications. Thus, the exchange of information between operators deteriorates or even disappears. The use of smart glasses would allow the transmission of indications in text format, to be represented on the device's screen. He/she could even hear the messages transmitted verbally thanks to the bone induction system. Orders to ARM-G should be transmitted verbally through a microphone very close to the mouth or by the touch of a device similar to the one located on the temples of the glasses
- Special protective goggles. The welding or cutting tasks require the operator to wear special glasses. The use of Google Glass together with the welding glasses depends on the design of the latter, since ARM-G must be protected

by goggles, to prevent deterioration. Their joint use allows the operator to receive information regarding the task, while performing the welding. This action is not feasible without the ARM-G, because the opacity of the welding crystals prevent the operator can read or perceive any other type of visual information

- No protection required. The works, which do not require any protection, allow the operator to carry the ARM-G without any difficulty.

With these facts we can assume that IS with advanced visualization systems can "affect the manner in which business managers make decisions, plan and manage the available resources. The importance of IS and their complexity make them extremely pivotal for organizations. Considering the fact that IS are a critical part of organizations we cannot deny the importance of implementing and effectively managing Information Systems (Otim, 2012-29(1)) (Shatat, 2015 (18-1)). With the addition of effective visualization tools.

AUGMENTED REALITY AND MIXED REALITY

Smart glasses can also be divided into "Mixed Reality" (MR) and "Augmented Reality" (AR) depending on the type of computer-generated images, which are superimposed on the real scene seen through the lenses of the glasses. Augmented reality (AR) overlays computer-generated images on top of the real world, whilst Mixed Reality (MR) superimposes virtual interactive images on the glasses lenses.

AR overlays digital information on real-world elements, but it is focus on the real world central and enhances it with some other digital data. MR brings together real-world and digital objects in the same scene, so the user to interact and manipulate physical and virtual elements and environments. Therefore, smart glasses can be used to generate AR or MR depending on the type of overlaid digital images on the lenses of the glasses. Industry 4.0 uses above all AR instead of MR, because user needs to see the real information when it is working in the factory real.

Nowadays the use of these kind of glasses depends on the necessity of the user about the work he/she is doing. In the field of industrial management, this will be connected to the activity of the user. This means in the case of monocular vision, that he/she doesn't need to have a whole field of view of what he/she has in front of them, but a binocular view of the screens gives them some other characteristics that will be analysed later. Therefore, there are ARB-G (Augmented Reality Monocular Glasses) and ARB-G (Augmented Reality Binocular Glasses).

The first case (ARB-G) is only used to show overlapping images on a lens area of his/her field of view, and this doesn't affect the rest of the user's work area. However, in the case of ARB-G binocular views, the images overlap fully or partially on both lenses of the glasses and may totally or partially block the user's work area.

The ARB-G are a visualization device that permits the user to visualize over both sides of glasses an artificial image that it is superimposed on his/her field of view (FOV). The ARB-G are devices that really offer a full sensation of augmented or mixed reality, because they add virtual information to the whole field of view of the user. Then these devices add virtual information to the physical information that is been viewed in that moment. Technological devices of augmented or mixed reality facilitate the superposition of computer data on the real scene that the user is perceiving. The enlarged image is composed simultaneously of a real and an artificial image. The latter is added to the original image to improve the interpretation of the real scene that the user is perceiving.

Augmented or mixed reality devices can be grouped into two large families, depending on the method used to perceive the actual image. A group of devices superimpose an artificial image onto the lenses, through which the user perceives the actual image. However, the other group capture the actual image with an embedded camera within a (Head Mounted Display) HDM helmet and next it is fused with the artificial image. This aggregated image is shown on the HDM screen that it is in front of the user's eyes and gives a FOV of 37°.

The ARB-G devices are suitable for superimposing information relative to the image that the user is perceiving, without having to rotate the eyes of the point to which they are focusing. This allows the information to flow naturally to the user and does not require an additional effort to understand the information perceived.

Microsoft has created a new release of glasses "HoloLens" (2017), call "HoloLens 2" (2019) (Microsoft Corporation, 2020), figure 2, which blend augmented reality and 3D imaging and it raises FOV from 35° to 53°. These glasses have translucent lenses on which holograms or 3D images are projected (visualized) and give the user the feeling that they are really inside the real scene that he/she is also perceiving. The visualization of the holograms gives the user a sensation of volume in the figures that he/she perceives and this increases the conviction that these artificial figures are a part of the real scene. Likewise, these glasses have an internal support of circular form that facilitate that the weight of the set is distributed evenly on the head and not on the nose and the ears. They have also several microphones, cameras, speakers with surround sound and Wi-Fi connection.

Visualizations of the HoloLens 2 glasses can be carried to the extreme of only containing a single image of virtual reality, without any part of the real scene being perceived. This would transform them into an immersive virtual reality device. However, the great advantage of using these glasses in any type of industrial environment is because the user, in addition to seeing the holograms also observes the real environment of the scene in which he/she is. Thus, the user is aware of the innumerable dangers that exist around him/her. Likewise, in critical situations, an operator, who wears these glasses and wears a protective suit, can re-acquire his/her entire field of vision with a simple disconnection/shutdown of the device. These characteristics allow this device to be very suitable for introducing augmented reality to the industrial world.

"Epson Moverio BT-300" are glasses with transparent lenses that allow the sensorial perception of an almost augmented reality and/or 3D images (Epson, 2017). These glasses have dual screens of 1280x720 pixels, in each lens, which allow 3D visualization. In addition, the screens are centred in the middle of the user's field of vision and provide a 23° FOV. Therefore, the augmented reality sensation in 3D is limited, since the FOV of humans is 180°. Likewise, these glasses also have headphones, video camera, gyroscope, microphone, GPS, accelerometer, Wi-Fi

The "Meta 2" glasses allow the visualization of 3D images, with a FOV of 90° (Metavision, 2017). This is achieved by the use of 2560 x 1440 pixels projectors located at the top and the images emitting images on the glasses. It also has an integrated camera, speakers and position sensors.

Figure 2 . HoloLens 2. Retrieved from https://www.microsoft.com/en-us/hololens/

"C-Thru Smoke Diving Helmet" is a helmet prototype, which helps firefighters improve their vision in smoky areas (Omerth, 2017). This helmet has a thermal camera that captures the image of the environment, and once it is processed, it is projected onto the helmet glasses/screens. This information is composed of alphanumeric data and geometric figures that delimit the edges of objects. Also, the helmet has a technology that suppresses background noise, so that the fireman can perceive more clearly the sounds (screams) of a person, structural weaknesses of the building in flames or any other sound critical to his mission.

The augmented reality in industrial environments is a field that is still at the dawn of its development. However, augmented reality devices will have a strong development in the very near future. At present, the first prototypes are already being designed, but their use in industrial plants will soon be universalized (Omerth, 2017) (Draqui, 2017). The following is a summary of the tasks where augmented reality will facilitate and improve the quality and safety of the work being performed by the operators:

- Showing hidden structures behind or inside a wall, equipment or bulky structure. For example, this allows the user to know which is the ideal place to drill a wall, without fear of drilling a pipe that exists inside.
- Disclosing the values of the physical quantities of the equipment or components that are being perceived by the user. Thus, he/she can visualize the flow rate (m3/h, l/min) of a pipe, the current (Amperes) or voltage (Volts) of an electric line, etc.
- Including information about the objects in the scene that the user is watching. This allows the operator to indicate what he/she is perceiving on the scene. Thus, he/she can add arrows to the scene that point to the device, along with a text box that contains the component name or any other important information for the user. For example, it would be possible to know the name of the fluid (water, steam, oil, diesel, ...) circulating inside a pipe
- Identifying keys or buttons on a keyboard, keypad or any other user interface. The scene could include arrows that point to each key or button, to inform the user of the function performed by each element of the user interface
- Tracing, on the scene being watched by the user the route that he/she must follow to go from a source to a destination. This is similar to one of the features provided for Google Glass. However, augmented reality glasses indicate by arrows on the scene, which is the way the operator should follow. While, Google Glass show a plane on the lens and it is the path that must be followed from the source to the destination
- Indicating what data the operator must complete in a document. The augmented reality device must recognize and identify the document being viewed; warn of the text that should be written in each of the blank spaces or clarify the meaning of each of the boxes that must be marked
- To warn the danger of a device or installation through a colour code, so the operator intuitively perceives the risk that exists in their environment. For

example, the red colour may be superimposed on hazardous equipment or the yellow colour on medium risk equipment

- Superimposing infrared or thermal images to the actual scene the user is viewing. This allows, in environments with a lot of smoke, the user observes an infrared image about the reality that is perceived by him/her. This option is similar to another that is available for Google Glass, but in them, the image is displayed exclusively in a quadrant. However, augmented reality enables the infrared or thermal scene to overlap over the entire real scene. This allows us to intuitively reveal a reality that remained hidden from the operator.

The augmented reality allows the data superimposed on a real scene to complement and help to understand the image shown, since it improves the visual information of the scene that is perceived. Thus, the user next to the visual image also perceives an interpretation of reality, which is due to the written information that appears on the screen.

Likewise, if the information is not strictly complementary with the actual scene that is perceived, it should not be shown or overlaid on the entire surface of the lens. For example, it would be inappropriate to superimpose a spreadsheet or chart over a real scene, where a pipeline distribution is being observed. This type of information causes a lot of confusion for the user, since texts or graphics become unintelligible in some areas, as well as blurring the details of the actual scene. This information is best suited to be shown in the Google Glass box.

Much of the information, shown on augmented reality devices, can be adapted to be displayed on Google Glass (Google, 2017); since in its projection frame can be shown the real scene together with an artificial image superimposed. However, very little information specially adapted for Google Glass can be viewed on augmented reality devices.

Augmented reality glasses, which instead of lenses have LCD screens, are not suitable for use in all industrial environments. This is because the operator must remove the glasses he carries, to recover the entire visual field of the real scene; since the LCD screens only show a portion of the existing reality. In addition, this action would be impossible to carry out if the operator was inside a protective suit. Likewise, the fortuitous shutdown of this device would blind the operator, in an environment that could be dangerous to his/her physical integrity. Therefore, these glasses should only be used where there are no risks or hazards near of the industrial operator.

INMERSIVE VIRTUAL REALITY

Virtual reality is a visual and sensorial environment, where artificial scenes or objects, which are generated by computer technology, acquire real appearance and the user has the sensation of being immersed in this virtual world. This implies that the user's senses are feeling artificially created sensations, but the user interprets them as if they are real. This causes the user to feel that he/she is in a virtual world to which he/she is transported by his/her own senses.

Figure 3. Digital Mockup, Virtual Reality. Retrieved from www.plm.automation. siemens.com

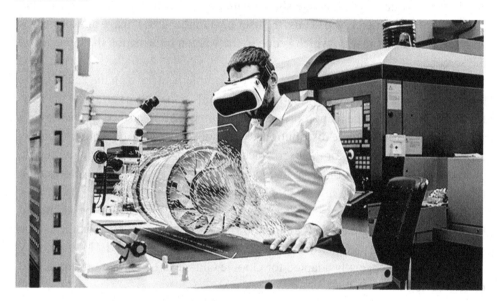

At the very least, virtual reality equipment must have a helmet that generates 3D images. Also, gloves that capture hand movement, omnidirectional platforms (Cyberith Virtualizer, Virtuix Omni), etc. can be added. The virtual reality gloves capture the hands movement and transfer it to the virtual world in which the user is immersed. Omni-directional platforms detect user movement without actually moving from location. There are brands, as Samsung (Samsung Corporation, 2017), that facilitates positioning the mobile phone within an adapted HMD, in order that each screen zone shows to each eye their correspondent 2D image, once fused inside the brain the user perceives a 3D image.

Next, the different types of information that can be visualized with the virtual reality systems are shown:

- Review of industrial structures. Visualization of industrial constructions or structures (beams, columns, tanks, etc.) while they are being designed allows for the early detection of problems that were not initially foreseen. For example, this makes it easier to see if there is any difficulty walking around the new structure. Likewise, it can be detected if it presents an anomaly that was not foreseen initially

- Analysis of problems when repairing an industrial equipment. Thus, he/she can examine the tasks that should be performed by an operator, to repair a device in the least possible time. This task is very critical if the operator does not physically know the equipment to be repaired; because with it reduces the time of repair and increase their physical security. For example, the repair of critical equipment such as a nuclear reactor, a boiler or a turbine must be carried out in the shortest time possible, while ensuring the minimum occupational risk of the operator. These immersive devices facilitate the operator's knowledge of the installations; allow to test the different methods of repair, to optimize the task; and check the dangers of certain actions taken during such repair

- Design of new products. The preview of the new industrial and/or consumer products, which are in the design phase, allows a better analysis of the technical characteristics that they must meet; since they can easily be observed from other approaches. Likewise, the designer can decompose each product in the parts that form it, to verify the difficulties that can arise in the stage of assembly. Likewise, it is possible to analyse the difficulties that will exist when making a repair or replacement of some piece of the product. For example, engineers can check if a car is accessible for repairs or how to facilitate the tasks that are performed in the repair shops

- Showing the industrial facilities to the new operators, indicating how to reach the different areas of the factory. It also indicates the location of the different equipment or machines in the factory and how to get there. Likewise, it can be shown to some operators as it will be the future industrial plant in which they are going to work. Thus, when these users reach their new plant they will know it completely and can start working from the first day, minimizing their adaptation time to the new working environment

- Training of process technicians. Virtual reality equipment allows process technicians to test the essential manoeuvers that must be performed on critical or complex industrial equipment. Some equipment or industrial machinery has such an extremely high cost that it is important to train technicians in how to perform certain tasks in the minimum time and with the highest quality. For example, the connection of a turbine, the heating of a boiler, etc.

- Actual views with superimposed operation data. The overlapping of virtual data of the industrial process with the actual images of the machines or instruments, allows the process operators to know the state of the industrial plant and even get to operate it. Thus, an operator can open/close valves, start/stop motors, etc. This operation is suitable for industrial equipment that is in the virtual surroundings of the place where the operator is located. If the actual equipment he/she had to deal with was far apart from one another, the operator would have to travel a virtual path to go from one to the other industrial device, which must operate. These operator paths, although virtual, are critical to the real time that this invests in that virtual displacement. This would be inadmissible in critical situations, where the operator's speed to activate/deactivate suitable equipment is critical to solving this problematic condition. Also, the visualization of the actual images of the process make it difficult for the operator to have a complete situation awareness of the entire industrial process that he/she is managing; Therefore, there are teams that are hidden or small teams, which although they are critical are not shown with sufficient definition. Finally, a visualization of real images of the industrial process prevents the creation of summary screens, containing the main data of the process.

Virtual reality transports the user to a world of illusions that, in some cases, can correspond to an existing reality, which may be relatively close or far from its physical location. This sensory illusion can be complemented with information about the virtual scene being shown. This will generate virtual scenes that are a hybrid between virtual reality and augmented reality.

The use of virtual reality in industrial environments is being postponed because of the need to use haptics and glasses. In addition, it is not very appropriate to be immersed in a world of virtual illusions, while being near of innumerable risks existing in industrial plants. This demonstrates the need to use virtual reality equipment in closed premises, which is isolated from any risk near its location. Even this closed places must be completely safe, since any incident in its vicinity can happen, that compromises the security of that place. In this case, the virtual user would not be aware of the immense danger that exists outside the place where he/she is, because he/she is inside a world of illusion that prevents him/her from knowing the surrounding reality.

DCS OPERATION SCREEN IN 3D

As it is going to be shown, IS industrial systems are composed by a set of sub-systems, each one responsible for a subset of organizational information and operational requirements and with its own data flows. Currently, IS has outperformed traditional management tasks supported by paper, and is thus becoming one of the most strategic resources of organizations (Peppard, 2018 (1)), but this being present is past, tele-control of systems trying to avoid the use of any kind of document is one of the most important part of the decision process. In fact, it can be seen that the idea is to transfer the control to systems in which the human in only a piece of control, observing like a watch dog what's happening in the process, with a minimum of intervention. This forces to create visualization structures that simplify the way those operators control the system, next it is shown a real example on how this was done in a real enterprise.

The usual operating screens of large industrial automation systems have a 2D flow chart format, Figure 4. However, this format has very restricted the amount of information it may contain. This information must be, also very well structured to facilitate the operator can understand it intuitively and with a single glance. This implied that new 2.5D and 3D operation screens have been developed to contain more information and make it more understandable to the operator (Pérez-Cota & González-Castro, Usability in a new DCS interface, 2013). This application can display 3D operation screens; but you can also display 2.5D displays on computers that do not have the necessary peripherals to view 3D images. Each of these new 2.5D and 3D operation screens may contain information that was previously displayed on various operation screens.

For example, this operation screen, Figure 5, manages to replace a set of 10 old 2D-format DCS screens. The old screen corresponding to digester number 8 is shown in Figure 4. Each digestion line, Figure 6, is composed of a digester, an exchanger, a condensate tank, a recirculation pump, steam valves, liquor valves and all associated pipes. The steam distribution screen shows a set of common facilities for all these lines.

Figure 4. 2D image of a DCS Screen. Digestion line.

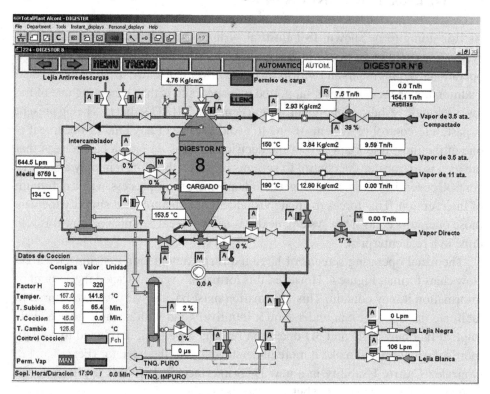

The navigation along the graphic scene is carried out by means of a Joystick, while the selection of a graphic element is done with the mouse and/or Joystick. Likewise, these peripherals facilitate the tasks of rotation, displacement and zoom of the graphic of the industrial process to achieve to visualize the scene from infinite points of view (frontal, lateral, rear, near, far...).

This operating environment also reports the occurrence of an alarm or warning by sending a voice message with emotion. The emission of the vocal messages with emotion facilitates the immediate compression by the operator, of the incidences that are happening; because the emotional intensity indicates the criticality of the alarm and the message indicates exactly which is the component that has generated it. The graphical scene also shows, in textual format, all the physical magnitudes of the process, as well as the state of all industrial apparatuses and equipment (valves, motors, switches, etc.).

The application includes a 2D window of information and command on the components of the process, that have been selected by means of the mouse or the joystick-3D. This window shows in text format the status of the selected component and allows its operation (change of state), by pressing buttons.

Figure 5. Oblique view of the Industrial Process 2.5D

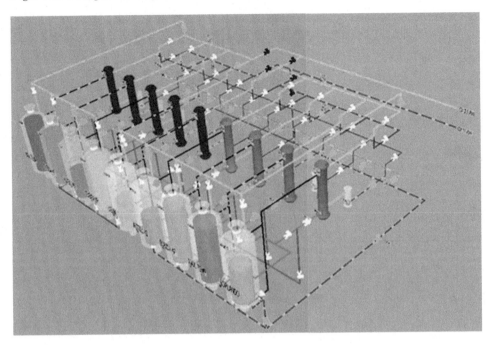

Figure 6. View of one of the industrial process lines

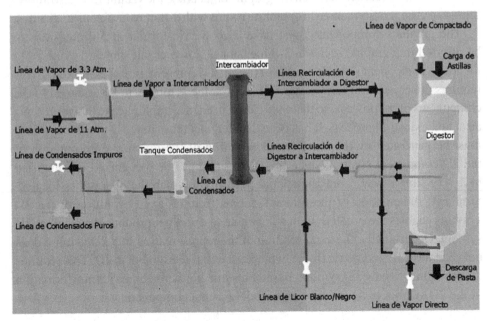

Figure 7. Partial view of the industrial process

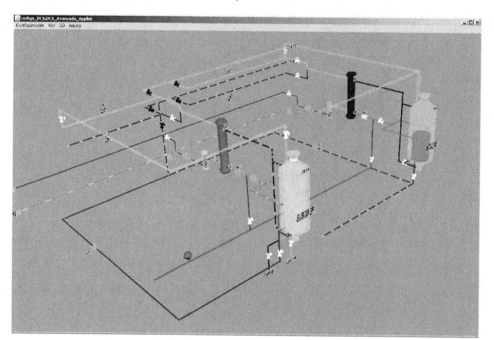

The background colour of the graphic scene is decided to be the grey colour, as it is the colour recommended by ASM for the operation screens. The grey colour intensifies the difference between the graphic objects and the vacuum and also allows the use of the operation screen in operating rooms with different luminous intensities.

The graphics components must have a geometric format in 3-dimensions to be inserted in a graphic scene in 3-dimensions. However, all standard symbols to identify a component were designed for use in 2D representations (ISO, 2017). This requires the creation of new designs of 3D graphic symbols, to be assigned to the components of the process, so that they can be used in a graphic scene that represents an actual industrial process. It has been decided that these new 3D graphic symbols must be generated by the axial round evolution of the graphic representation of the 2D component symbol; since this allows them to be recognized or identified in a very simple way, from any spatial position in which the operator is located. Similarly, the creation of these new symbols from an axial evolution of the 2D symbols enables the projection on a 2D plane to exactly reproduce the original 2D symbol. Occasionally, the axial rotation of the representation of a 2D symbol does not generate a 3D geometric figure, which resembles the symbol in 2D. This requires the creation of a new 3D symbol, based on some kind of geometric transformation of the 2D symbol or a new reference model for that component.

Figure 8 . Frontal view of the industrial process, with the command window

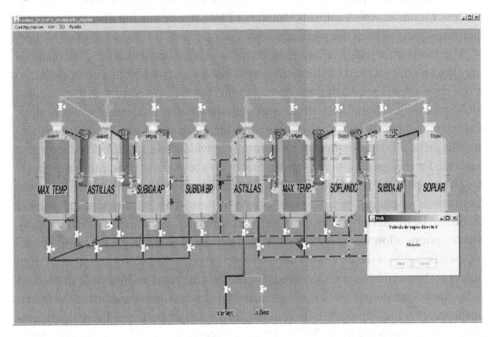

The red colour is used only to signal an alarm status; the yellow colour is used to display a warning state and the violet colour is identified with an undefined state of the component. The green and white colours are used to indicate the different states of operation in which there is a physical component of the industrial process. Green indicates that a pump is running/active or that a valve is open. The white colour warns that a pump is halted/stopped or that a valve is closed.

The pipes have several colours depending on the fluid they carry inside, while a change in a physical characteristic of that fluid is noticed with a variation in its colour shade. The graphic representation of the pipe has an animation to symbolize the flow rate of the liquid it transports.

The graphic scene is contained in a window, which has several menus or tabs, which are used to select different options for modification of the graphic scene. The application allows the individual or grouped display and/or hiding of the digester lines or the common line to all the digesters, Figure 7; as this allows the operator to focus exclusively on a limited group of lines. The pipeline animation is activated/deactivated in a menu option; since its activation is very advisable in tasks of simulation or learning process, as it shows the flow of the different matters involved in the industrial process.

Some components or sections of the circuit must display numeric data or messages to the operator, since a colour code only provides a very limited amount of information. This requires the display of information with information about the process Figure 8, which informs the state of the digester or the different physical quantities used to keep the process within limits.

The moment in which an alarm or warning of a component arises, the operator may not be concentrated on the display or the colour change of that component; so a voice message is send to tell the operator that there is a circumstance that requires his/her attention. Therefore, whenever a component enters an alarm or warning state, a voice message is send, which contains the unambiguous name of the component and the critical condition (alarm or warning) in which it is present. The menu also has a tab for the operator to activate or deactivate these alarm or warning messages.

The graphic scene, which shows the industrial process, has several options that facilitate its visualization from other points of view. This implies that the graphic scene can be moved to any position, rotated on any axis or modified in size (zoom). These options allow the operator to navigate the inside of the process, to concentrate on specific areas of the process. This facilitates the visualization of the process from other positions and ensures that no part of the process remains hidden or disfigured by another element in front of it. Consequently, the scene can be seen from the lower, posterior, oblique, Figure 8, enlarged, etc. The operator performs these operations using a mouse or a 3D joystick. The latter peripheral is the only device that can be used to interact with scenes shown in 3D, since the graphics card prevents the use of the mouse. Likewise, a menu option or a Joystick button allows you to place the graphic scene in its initial position and thus, make this task easier for the operator.

The components (digesters, valves and pumps) of the industrial process can be selected so that their information is displayed in a small command window, Figure 8. This window provides a more detailed information about the component, including its full name and operating state. Also, this window can also be used to modify the operating state of the component, as this option was excluded in the requirements of the application. The selection of the component is done with the mouse pointer or by means of an advanced pointer. The advanced pointer is represented on the screen with the geometric octahedron figure and its movement is controlled through the keyboard or the 3D Joystick. This advanced pointer is the only one available in 3D scene visualization.

It was observed on these last paragraphs, that the IS represent a fundamental part of organizational production engines. Their role in the organization can be divided into three main areas of focus: 1) support for business strategies aimed at generating competitive advantage; 2) support for the organization's decision making process; and 3) support for both the operational tasks and the existing business processes. As a result, managers understand the strategic implications of an economy drawn on Information, hence recognizing that adaptability speed, flexibility and constant innovation are fundamentals for an organization's success (Branco, 2019).

Then, Information presented in a clear and simple way is now a vital resource to take any kind of decision, remembering that DCS operators are only "watch dogs" of the process success, but from their decisions depends the way the business is going to fulfil the expectations, because they ward the effectiveness of the processes, not the control system.

An important part of errors can be attributed to normal error of malfunctions, then it is important to assure that operators are receiving information in the most accurate way and the simplest form, with shapes that need no interpretation, that can be seen as if the DCS operator is in the middle of the process being part of it. With this in mind it is possible to talk about 3D Visualization.

3D Visualization

Stereoscopic-3D visualization implies that the operator uses his two eyes to quasi-simultaneously perceive a 3D scene. Since, the eyes are separated by a few centimetres between them, causes each eye to perceive the scene from a different angle. The result is that viewing a real scene with both eyes implies a greater perception of the visual information of this scene than if it were perceived exclusively by one eye. This causes that the information that an operator perceives of a 3D screen is greater than if it were contemplating the same information in 2.5D.

If a valve or pump is hidden behind a bulky display object (digester, tank), it could be partially visible by performing a small rotation of the graphic scene. This small rotation would be the equivalent of perceiving the scene from the viewing angle provided by the operator's other eye. This determines that the visualization of graphical scenes in 3D increases the amount of information that the operator perceives, as to whether this maximum scene is shown in 2.5D.

Visualizing 3D scenes forces the use of 3D devices in the panel operator positions. These 3D devices can be 3D glasses or auto-stereoscopic monitors. The 3D glasses should be of the active type, since the operator must perceive the colours and details of the graphic scene in extraordinary detail. The self-stereoscopic monitors force the user to be positioned exactly in the centre of the screen. However, this is not always possible, as the operator often changes his position during his shift.

OPERATORS' EXPERIENCES WITHIN 3D ENVIRONMENTS

The application was tested by the DCS display operators of the Digesters Department of the company "ENCE, Energía y Celulosa" in Pontevedra (Spain), as well as by technicians from the Engineering Department of this company. This company has installed a DCS Honeywell TPA that has 2D screens, where each operator is responsible for several operation monitors, in which various operating screens are shown.

It is observed that the application shows an exceptional quantity and quality of information to the visual range of the operators, because in a single screen the same information is presented as in 10 of the old 2D screens of DCS. This prevents the operator from having to navigate between all the screens and ignores what happens on one screen, by watching another different screen. The process chart has a visual representation, which is more natural and intuitive for the user; as it has a great similarity with the actual process and allows it to resemble the augmented reality.

The symbols and colours used in the 3D graphic scene are immediately recognized by the DCS operators; since the symbols used to represent 3D components are an evolution of 2D designs, proposed by international standards. This graphic scene transforms hundreds of status signals from physical devices (valves, pumps, etc.) into visual colour-based information. Formerly, this information is shown in numerical and textual format.

It is observed that the operator requires less mental effort to understand the complete state of the industrial process. The operation screen complies with the key concepts of usability; as it is "easy to use" and "easy to learn". This is reflected in the fact of "how" the operator visualizes all the components of the graphic scene.

In addition, the use of different colours in the representation of figures 2.5D or 3D, which are visualized in the graphic scene, should not be considered strictly incompatible with the application of the principle of usability in computer systems. This is because the "risk assessment" of the workplace of a screen operator indicates that such a position can't be performed by people with colour blindness or other visual or physical impairments. This assessment would also apply to electricians, since an electrician with colour blindness would not be able to perform his job correctly, as he would not differentiate all coloured cables from a cable hose.

It is appreciated that operators and users need a period of adaptation to the new 3D environment, as they are initially surprised by the original presentation format of the process. Also, some people over 55 years or with vision problems are unable to visualize 3D images and indicate that they continue to visualize 2D images; However, some young people are extremely receptive to such 3D images. The position of the user, the distance to the monitor and the angle of distance of the images of each eye decisively influence the perception of the 3D image by the operator; since the presentation has been designed so that it is centred in front of the screen and at a distance of 60 cm.

It is verified that it is dangerous to have the animation of the pipes activated during the process control tasks; since it saturates the operator with an immense amount of visual information, which causes a decrease of its concentration. Likewise, it is detected the convenience of deactivating the sending of the voice warning messages (no alarms) during periods of crisis (for example a start (boot strapping) of the process), so as not to stun the operator.

CONCLUSIONS

The new advanced visualization systems will drive a great transformation in the way of performing the current maintenance, operation and design tasks in the industrial world. Thus, industrial operators will have at their disposal a universe of information, which will allow them to optimize the work they are doing. Even the operator can retransmit the task that he is executing, to receive help from a group of specialists, who are observing and analysing it from a very distant place.

As is written in many documents the structuring and integration of information is essential to obtain results. The correct integration of various technologies has a clear advantage for the organization as it is possible to follow business processes in real time and thus increase the appropriate information-sharing to support an increasingly knowledge-based economy (Verdouw, Robbemond, Verwaart, Wolfert, & Beulens, 2018 - 12(7)).

This group of display devices showed that they should not be used interchangeably for any job; since each of them is more adapted to a specific set of tasks. In addition, it was found that some of these display equipment should not be used inside a factory; because in some situations they increase the occupational risks of the operator who carries them. Likewise, the compatibility of carrying these devices together with personal protective equipment or full protective clothing.

The ARM-G are devices, which are more adapted to tasks where the operator requires information, which does not overlap over their entire field of vision. Likewise, ARB-G are convenient to display information that can be superimposed easily, on the actual scene that the operator is perceiving. However, virtual reality equipment is appropriate for training, teaching and design tasks. In addition, the operator must be located in a very safe place, since he is in a virtual world that distances him/her from the real world that surrounds him/her.

The DCS operation screens are designed to drastically increase the amount and quality of process information that the operator has at his/her disposal. This new environment brings together in a single 2.5D or 3D screen the equivalent of 10 of the old 2D screens of DCS. Also, the use of 3D peripherals allows the rotation or displacement of the process on the screen, facilitating their analysis from different angles and positions (front, back, side, oblique, interior, etc.). Likewise, it is verified that there are some functionalities of operation, that are hardly translatable to environments 3D. Finally, it is observed that some methods of design of 2D screens are unassuming in 3D environments, so they have to be adapted to the new environment, but trying to preserve its essence.

REFERENCES

ABB. (2020). *System 800xA Extended Automation.* https://new.abb.com/control-systems/system-800xa

ASM. (2017). *ASM.* http://www.asmconsortium.net

Branco, F. M.-Y.-O. (2019). *Conceptual Approach for an Extension to a Mushroom Farm Distributed Process Control System: IoT and Blockchain. In WorlCIST. A Toxa.* AISTI. doi:10.1007/978-3-030-16181-1_69

Breibvold, H. P. (2010). El Operario eficaz. *Revista ABB*, 6-11.

Cámara de Ópticos. (2013). *Salud y tendencias visuales de los españoles.* https://camaraopticos.com/salud-visual-y-tendencias-de-los-espanoles/

Chaparro-Peláez, J. P.-R.-M. (n.d.). Inter-organizational information systems adoption for service innovation in building sector. *Journal of Business Research*, 673-679. doi:10.1016/j.jbusres.2013.11.026

Draqui. (2017). *Smart Helmet.* https://daqri.com/products/smart-helmet: https://daqri.com/products/smart-helmet

Emerson. (2020). *Delta V.* https://www.emerson.com/en-us/automation/deltav: https://www.emerson.com/en-us/automation/deltav

Epson. (2017). *Epson Moverio BT-300.* https://epson.com/moverio-augmented-reality-smart-glasses?pg=3#sn

Google. (2017). *Google Glass.* https://developers.google.com/glass/

Honeywell Corporation. (2006). *TotalPlant Alcont and Printa. Configuration Manual & Application planning guide.* Author.

Honeywell Corporation. (2020). *Honeywell Experion.* https://www.honeywellprocess.com/en-US/pages/default.aspx

J., E. (2005). *Establishing Human Performance Improvements an Economic Benefit for Human-Centered Operator Interface.* Human Factors and Ergonomic Society.

Malý, I. E. A. (2016, July). Augmented reality experiments with industrial robot in industry 4.0 environment. In *IEEE 14th International Conference on Industrial Informatics (INDIN)* (pp. 19-21). Pointiers, France: IEEE.

McMahon. (2015). *Three decades of DCS technology.* https://www.controlglobal. com/articles/2005/227.html

Metavision. (2017). *Meta 2.* https://www.metavision.com

Microsoft Corporation. (2020). *Hololens.* https://www.microsoft.com/en-us/hololens/

M.R., D. (2015). *How Google Glass Will Revolutionize 9 Industries.* https://www. businessinsider.com/google-glass-will-totally-disrupt-these-tktk-industries-2013- 3?op=1

Olausson M., L. M. (2012). Colaborando en una nueva dimensión. *Revista ABB,* 6-11.

Omerth. (2017). *C-Thru.* http://www.omerh.com/c-thru#0

Otim, S. D. (2012). The Impact of Information Technology Investments on Downside Risk of the Firm: Alternative Measurement of the Business Value of IT. *Journal of Management Information Systems,* 159-194. doi:10.2753/MIS0742-1222290105

Peppard, J. (2018). Rethinking the concept of the IS organization. *Information Systems Journal, 28*(1), 76–103. doi:10.1111/isj.12122

Pérez-Cota, M., & González-Castro, M. R. (2013). DCS 3D Operators in Industrial Environments: New HCI Paradigm for the Industry. In Virtual, Augmented and Mixed Reality. Systems and Applications (pp. 271-280). Springer.

Pérez-Cota, M., & González-Castro, M. R. (2013). Usability in a new DCS interface. In Human-Computer Interaction. Design Methods, tools and interaction Techniques for inclusion (pp. 87-96). Academic Press.

Pérez-Cota, M., & González-Castro, M. R. (2011). Interfaz avanzado de operador de DCS. In *6° CISTI* (pp. 37-41). Chaves, Portugal: AISTI.

Pérez-Cota, M., González-Castro, M. R., & Díaz-Rodríguez, M. (2018). Advanced Visualization Systems in Industrial Environments: Accessible Information in Any Factory Place. In *C. G. García, V. García-Díaz, B. C. García-Bustelo, & J. M. Lovelle (Eds.), Protocols and Applications for the Industrial Internet of Things (pp. 1-34).* IGI Global. doi:10.4018/978-1-5225-3805-9.ch001

Reising D. V. L. J. (2010). Supporting Operator Sitation Awareness With Overview Displays: A Series of Studies on Information vs. Vitualization Requeriments. In *ICOCO,* (pp. 188-198). Academic Press.

Samsung Corporation. (2017). *Gear VR.* https://www.samsung.com/global/galaxy/gear-vr/

Shatat, A. S. (2015). Critical success factors in enterprise resource planning (ERP) system implementation: An exploratory study in Oman. Academic Press.

Siemens, G. M. B. H. (2017). *Simatic PCS7.* https://w3.siemens.com/mcms/process-control-systems/en/distributed-control-system-simatic-pcs-7/Pages/distributed-control-system-simatic-pcs-7.aspx

Siemens, G. M. B. H. (2020). *Siemens Comos-Walkinside.* https://new.siemens.com/global/en/products/automation/industry-software/plant-engineering-software-comos/virtual-reality-training.html

Silva, M. F. (2014). Glassist: Using Augmented Reality on Google Glass as an Aid to Classroom Management. In *XVI Symposium on Virtual and Augmented Reality (SVR)* (pp. 37-44). IEEE. 10.1109/SVR.2014.41

Teixeira, J., & Ferreira, R. E. (2014). Teleoperation Using Google Glass and AR, Drone for Structural Inspection. In *XVI Symposium on Virtual and Augmented Reality (SVR)* (pp. 28-36). IEEE. 10.1109/SVR.2014.42

Verdouw, C., Robbemond, R. M., Verwaart, T., Wolfert, J., & Beulens, A. J. (2018). A reference architecture for IoT-based logistic information systems in agri-food supply chains. *Enterprise Information Systems*, 755-779.

Vuzix. (2017). *Smart Glasses.* https://www.vuzix.com/Products/Series-3000-Smart-Glasses

Chapter 2
Non–Mobile Software Modernization in Accordance With the Principles of Model–Driven Engineering

Liliana Maria Favre

iD https://orcid.org/0000-0003-1370-1861

Universidad Nacional del Centro de la Provincia de Buenos Aires, Argentina & Comisión de Investigaciones Científicas de la Provincia de Buenos Aires, Argentina

ABSTRACT

Smartphones are at the core of new paradigms such as cloud computing, pervasive computing, and internet of things. Frequently, the development of mobile software requires adaptation of valuable and tested non-mobile software. In this context, most challenges are related to the diversity of platforms on the smartphones market and to the need of systematic and reusable processes with a high degree of automation that reduce time, cost, and risks. To face these challenges, this chapter presents an analysis of non-mobile software modernization through an integration of MDE (model-driven engineering) with cross-platform development. Two approaches are analyzed. One of them is a lightweight process that combines MDA (model-driven architecture) with traditional static and dynamic analysis techniques of reverse engineering. The other approach is based on ADM (architecture-driven modernization) standards. A scenario for the migration of C/C++ or Java software through the multiplatform Haxe language is described.

DOI: 10.4018/978-1-7998-6463-9.ch002

INTRODUCTION

The adoption of new software technologies in organizations such as Cloud Computing, Pervasive Computing and the Internet of Things, offers competitive advantages and performs like a market differentiator.

Pervasive Computing, also called Ubiquitous Computing is the idea that almost any device can be embedded with chips to connect the device to a network of other devices. The goal of Pervasive Computing, which combines current network technologies with wireless computing, voice recognition and Internet capability, is to create an environment where the connectivity of devices is unobtrusive and always available. Cloud Computing is an Internet-based computing for enabling ubiquitous, on-demand network access to a shared pool of configurable computing resources (e.g., networks, servers, storage, applications and services) that can be rapidly supplied with minimal management effort. Cloud Computing has long been recognized as a paradigm for Big Data storage and analytics providing computing and data resources in a dynamic and pay-per-use model. Finally, there is no single universal definition for the IoT which could be defined as the interconnection via the Internet of computing devices embedded in everyday objects, enabling them to send and receive data. The IoT is becoming so pervasive and several studies predict that, in 2021, the number of mobile devices integrated to IoT is expected to exceed 1.5 billion.

Pervasive Computing, Cloud Computing and the IoT face similar problems related to similar use cases, including smart cities, environmental monitoring, agriculture, home automation, and health. These technologies are possible thanks to the advances in mobile computing and electronic miniaturization that allow cutting-edge computing and communication technology to be added into very small objects. On the one hand, Mobile Computing promoted the globalization of networks (3G, 4G and 5G) facilitating the development of distributed processing to create a network of billions of devices.

The IoT is arriving at our every life. Smart objects such as smartphones through Wifi and 5G will handle all kind of objects including sensors that collect date, interact with the environment and communicate over the IoT, the network of these connected objects. For instance, IoT is being optimized to fit smartphones that can be viewed as a service center for different platforms in science, medicine, education, and the media. Just as smartphones have already displaced the camera, the GPS, the music player and the wallet, they will be on-ramp for a new IoT revolution. In this scenario, people are at the center of these paradigms through their smartphones that allow sensing their activities, location and consulting them to define interactions with the surrounding environment. Miranda et al. (2015) state that in a more desirable

IoT scenario, technology would take the context of the people into account moving from the IoT to the Internet of People (IoP).

Frequently, the development of software component and applications aligned to these new paradigms requires adapting existing non-mobile software to mobile platforms. For instance, there exist valuable software components and libraries implemented in C/C++ or Java that need to be adapted for mobile applications. Most challenges in this kind of software migration are related, on the one hand, to the proliferation of mobile platforms that makes mobile development very difficult and expensive and, on the other hand, to the need to define systematic, reusable processes with a high degree of automation that reduce risks, time and costs.

With respect to the first challenge, the ideal situation is to use multiplatform development. New languages are emerging to integrate the native behaviors of the different platforms targeted in development projects. In this direction, the Haxe language is an open-source high-level cross-platform programming language and compiler that can produce applications and source code for many different platforms from a single code base (Haxe, 2020; Dasnois, 2011).

With respect to the systematic modernization process, novel technical frameworks for information integration, tool interoperability and reuse have emerged. Specifically, Model- Driven Engineering (MDE) is a software engineering discipline which emphasizes the use of models and model transformations to raise the abstraction level and the degree of automation in software development. Productivity and some aspects of software quality such as maintainability or interoperability are goals of MDE.

In the context of MDE, a particular form of reengineering for the functional and technological evolution of software systems is called Model-Driven Software Modernization (MDSM). In this approach, models representing the legacy software are discovered semi-automatically through a reverse engineering process. Next, they are transformed into models that satisfy the modernization requirements which are the input to forward engineering processes that generate new modernized software. The most relevant and disseminated proposals under the MDSM are MDA (Model-driven Architecture) and ADM (Architecture Driven Modernization) (MDA, 2020) (ADM, 2020).

This chapter presents an analysis of software modernization in line with the MDE principles. In this context, to achieve modernization, two approaches are analyzed. One of them is a lightweight process that integrates MDA with traditional static and dynamic analysis techniques. The other approach is based on ADM standards such as KDM (Knowledge Discovery Metamodel) and ASTM (Abstract Syntax Tree Metamodel) (KDM, 2016) (ASTM, 2011). To exemplify the analysis, a specific case study scenario for the migration of C/C++ or Java software to different mobile platforms through the integration of MDE with Cross-Platform Development is described. In particular, the chapter shows how it is possible to integrate cross-platform developments in Haxe with MDE through the integration of a metamodel of a source language with a metamodel of Haxe and not necessarily with the metamodels of all the platforms it supports. The proposal is being validated in the Eclipse Modeling Framework (EMF) considering that some of its tools and environments are aligned with MDE standards (Steinberg et al., 2009) (Eclipse, 2020) (EMF, 2020).

The structure of the chapter is as follows. The section "Background" provides definitions and discussion emphasizing on MDE and multiplatform development. It also presents some relevant literature review related to our approach. The next two sections describe different MDE approaches to modernizing desktop software with the goal of adapting it to different mobile platforms. The section "Lightweight Modernization" describes an MDA-based framework for software modernization and different realizations of the framework for the migration of C/C++ or Java code to applications deployed on different mobile platforms. The section "ADM Modernization" describes an integration of ADM standards with cross-platform development to address the same problem. The section "Discussion" discusses the two approaches focusing in their advantages and limitations in relation to ad-hoc software migration. A comparative analysis of both approaches is also included. Finally, in the section "Conclusion" general conclusion and future work are included.

BACKGROUND

The adaption of non-mobile software to new technologies can be achieved by combining model-driven engineering and multiplatform developments. This section describes the bases of both lightweight and ADM modernization. Besides, it includes a summary of related work.

Model-Driven Engineering

Model-driven Engineering is a software development methodology that focuses on the use of models and model transformations to raise the level of abstraction and automation in software development. Different acronyms are associated with model- driven developments: MBE (Model Based Engineering), MDE (Model-driven Engineering), MDD (Model-driven Development), MDA (Model-driven Architecture), MDSM (Model-driven Software Modernization) and ADM (Architecture Driven Modernization) (Favre, 2018).

MDE can be viewed as a subset of MBE. It is the branch of software engineering in which processes are driven by models, i.e. models are the primary artifacts of different software processes. MDE has emerged as a new software engineering discipline which emphasizes the use of models and model transformations to raise the abstraction level and the degree of automation in software development. Productivity and some aspects of the software quality such as maintainability or interoperability are goals of MDE.

Model-driven principles can be summarizes as follows: all artifacts involved in a MDE process can be viewed as models that conform to a particular metamodel, the process itself can be viewed as a sequence of model transformations and, all extracted information is represented in an standard way through metamodels. Then, model, metamodel and transformations are crucial in MDE.

Model-driven Developments (MDD) refer to forward engineering processes that use models as primary development artifacts. A specific realization of MDD is MDA proposed by the Object Management Group (OMG) (MDA, 2020). The outstanding ideas behind MDA are separating the specification of the system functionality from its implementation on specific platforms, managing the software evolution from abstract models to implementations. Models play a major role in MDA, which distinguishes at least Platform Independent Model (PIM) and Platform Specific Model (PSM). An MDA process focuses on the automatic transformation of different models that conform to MOF (Meta Object Facility) metamodel, the standard for defining metamodels in the context of MDA. It provides the ability to design and integrate semantically different languages such as general-purpose languages, domain specific languages and modeling languages in a unified way (MOF, 2016). MOF can be considered the essence of MDA allowing different kinds of artifacts from multiple technologies to be used together in an interoperable way. The modeling concepts of MOF are classes, which model MOF meta-objects; associations, which model binary relations between meta-objects; Data Types, which model other data; and Packages, which struct the models. Consistency rules are attached to metamodel components by using OCL (OCL, 2014). MOF provides two metamodels EMOF (Essential MOF) and CMOF (Complete MOF). EMOF favors simplicity of implementation over expressiveness. CMOF is a metamodel used to specify more sophisticated metamodels. The OMG standard related to model transformation is the MOF 2.0 Query, View, Transformation (QVT) metamodel (QVT, 2012).

A particular form of reengineering for the technological and functional evolution of legacy systems begins to be identified in the early 21st century under the designation of Model-driven Software Modernization (MDSM) (Brambrilla et al., 2017). It is based on model-driven processes of reverse engineering, restructuring and forward engineering. In MDSM, models representing legacy software are semi-automatically discovered through a reverse engineering process and then transformed into models that meet the modernization requirements from which it is possible to forward engineering a new modernized software. The OMG Architecture-Driven Modernization Task Force (ADMTF) is developing a set of specifications and promoting industry consensus on modernization. (ADM, 2020). A set of standards (metamodels) to facilitate interoperability between modernization tools are associated to ADM. KDM (Knowledge Discovery Metamodel) is a central metamodel for knowledge discovery in software that allows representing information related to existing software assets, their associations, and operational environments regardless of the implementation programming language and runtime platform (KDM, 2016).

The success of MDE depend on the existence of tools that make a significant impact on software processes such as reverse engineering, restructuring and forward engineering. The Eclipse Modeling Framework (EMF) was created for facilitating system modeling and the automatic generation of Java code (EMF, 2020). EMF started as an implementation of MOF resulting Ecore, the EMF metamodel comparable to EMOF. EMF has evolved starting from the experience of the Eclipse community to implement a variety of tools and to date is highly related to MDE, and particularly with MDA and ADM. In this context, the subproject Model to Model Transformation (MMT), hosts model-to-model transformation languages. Transformations are executed by transformation engines that are plugged into the Eclipse Modeling infrastructure. For instance, Atlas Transformation Language (ATL) is a model transformation language and toolkit that provides ways to produce a set of target models from a set of source models (ATL, 2020). Another subproject is Acceleo, which is an implementation of the Model-to-Text (M2T) transformation standard of the OMG for EMF-based models (Acceleo, 2020). Acceleo is used in forward engineering processes.

Today, the most complete technology that support ADM is MoDisco, which provides a generic and extensible framework to facilitate the development of tools to extract models from legacy systems and use them on use cases of modernization. As an Eclipse component, MoDisco can integrate with plugins or technologies available in the Eclipse environment (Modisco, 2020) (Bruneliere et al., 2014). Modisco provides among other artifacts metamodels to describe existing systems such as KDM and ASTM and discoverers to create models. In particular, one of the specifications of ASTM is Generic Abstract Syntax Tree Metamodel (GASTM), a generic set of language modeling elements common across numerous languages that establish a common core for language modeling.

Multiplatform Development

Today, one of major challenges for software developers is dealing with the rapid proliferation of mobile platforms that entails the high cost, technical complexity and risk of targeting development to a wide spectrum of platforms. Software applications can take full advantage of platforms only when they are built using native codebase. To address this problem a possible solution is to have different teams of developers who are fluent in specific programming language to port an application to a specific platform. Instead of this traditional approach, organizations can use multiplatform or multi-paradigm cross-compiler based languages. In this context, the term *"multiplatform"* is used to refer source-source compilation, that is to say, the source code of these languages can be compiled into source code of other programming language.

Haxe is a good example of multiplatform languages. It allows using the same code to deploy an application on multiple platforms such as iOS and Android. In this direction, the Haxe language emerges as an open-source high-level multiplatform programming language and compiler that can produce applications and source code for many different platforms from a single code-base.

The Haxe principles are summarizes at (Cannase, 2014) as follows: "support mainstream platforms", "write once, reuse everywhere", "always native, no wrapper", "generated but readable" and "trust the developer". The Haxe programming language is a high level programming language that mixes features of object oriented languages and functional ones. It is similar (but not pure) to object-oriented languages. Haxe includes a set of common functions that are supported across all platforms, such as numeric data types, text, arrays, binary and some common file formats.

The compiler supports novel features such as type inference, enforcing strict type safety at compile time. To date, Haxe supports nine target languages which allow for different use-cases: JavaScript, Neko, PHP, Python, C++, ActionScript3, Flash, Java and, C#. It provides support for creating interfaces using popular libraries such as OpenFL, HAXEUI and ScableUI (Haxe, 2020). For instance OpenFL is a framework built on Haxe that provides Flash Api on several mobile platforms, and tooling to help compile and test your app on each platform.

In summary, the idea behind Haxe is to allow developers choose the best platform for a specific development. To achieve this, it provides a standardized language, a standard library that works the same on all platforms and platform specific libraries that allow us accessing the full API for a given platform from Haxe.

A detailed description of the Haxe language may be found at (Haxe, 2020).

Related Work

Several works highlight research directions and challenges on the IoT. The spectrum of research needed to achieve IoT on a large scale requires research along with many different directions. Stankovic (2015) identifies five prominent research communities that involve the smart vision of the world: IoT, mobile computing, pervasive computing, wireless sensors, networks and cyber-physical systems. A basis for discussing open research problems in the IoT and a vision for how the IoT could change the world in the next years are presented.

Gonzalez Garcia et al. (2015) define a domain-specific language (DSL) that allows specifying the coordination and communication between different types of smart objects. Their approach focuses on the IoT as a paradigm that promotes a smart world in which different smart objects, sensors and in general devices are integrated to perform tasks.

Zanella et al. (2014) present a discussion of the IoT for smart cities. The authors describe a general reference framework for the design of an urban IoT. An implementation of an urban IoT that has been realized in the city of Padova is described. Key research topics are enumerated and research problems within these topics are discussed.

A user-oriented language to enable user specifying when or under what conditions the interconnections between heterogeneous objects in the Internet of Things occurs, is presented at (González García, Zhao, and García Díaz, 2019).

The business world is being influenced by IoT which allows collecting and analyzing technical system data to identify and optimize the performance of many things in in daily life is analyzed in (Ploennings,Cohn and Stanford-Clark, 2018). In this context, authors analyze the pro and cons of new challenges and issues related to new technologies such as Artificial Intelligence, Blockchain or 5G.

Ciccozzi, et al. (2017) analyze mission-critical IoT systems which run applications whose failure might have several consequences. To address this challenge, the authors propose an MDE-based approach.

Next, existing approaches for the development of mobile applications related in some way with our approach are described.

Various authors describe challenges of mobile software development, for example, Dehlinger and Dixon (2011) highlight creating user interfaces for different kinds of mobile devices, providing reusable applications across multiple mobile platforms, designing context aware applications and handling their complexity and, specifying requirements uncertainty.

Kramer and Clark (2010) describe a DSL (Domain Specific Language), named MobDSL, to generate applications for multiple mobile platforms. They perform the domain analysis on two cases in the Android and iPhone platforms. This analysis allows inferring the basic requirements of the language defined by MobDSL.

ANDRIU, a reverse engineering tool based on static analysis of source code for transforming user interface tiers from desktop application to Android, is described in (Pérez Castillo et al., 2013). ANDRIU has been developed for migrating traditional systems to Android applications although it was designed to be extended for different migrations to others mobile platforms.

Islam (2014) describes six major trends affecting future smartphone design and use: personal computers, the IoT, multimedia delivery, low power operation, wearable computing and context awareness.

Acerbis et al. (2015) describe a comprehensive tool suite called WebRatio Mobile Platform for model-driven development of mobile applications. It is based on an extended version of OMG standard language called IFML (Interaction Flow Modeling Language) empowered with primitives tailored to mobile systems that enable specification of mobile specific behaviors.

Joshi et al (2015) bring out the findings of the experiments carried out to understand the impact of application characteristics, cloud and architecture and the android emulator used, on application performance when the application is augmented to cloud.

Ejarque, Miccsik and Badia (2015) present a solution for facilitating the migration of applications to the cloud, inferring the most suitable deployment model for the application and automatically deploying it in the available Cloud providers.

A reverse engineering approach that fits with MDD is described in (Favre, 2010). This book explains a framework to integrate different techniques that come from compiler theory, metamodeling and formal specification.

A survey of MDD approaches for mobile application is presented in (Umuhoza and Brambilla, 2016). A systematic literature review on model-driven reverse engineering approach may be found at (Raibulet et al., 2017). An analysis of the state in the research in model-driven engineering is presented at (Bucchiarone, Cabot, Paige and Pieroantonio, 2020).

Thramboulidis, Bochalis and Bouloumpasis (2017) describe a MDE approach and a framework to address challenges in the development of IoT-based manufacturing cyber-physical systems (a composition of cyber-physical and cyber-components with IoT).

A reengineering process that integrates traditional reverse engineering techniques such as static and dynamic analysis with MDA is presented at (Améndola & Favre, 2013). The article describes a case study that shows how to move CRM (Customer Relationship Management) applications from desktop to mobile platforms. The proposal was validated in the open source application platform Eclipse, EMF, EMP, ATL and Android platform. Diaz Bilotto and Favre (2016) describe a migration process from Java to mobile platforms through the multiplatform language Haxe. A migration process from C++ to mobile platforms based on ADM standards such as GASTM and KDM is described at (Martinez, Pereira, & Favre, 2017).

LIGHTWEIGHT MODERNIZATION

We propose a framework for the modernization of non-mobile software to new technologies. According to the three crucial concepts of MDE, the framework provides sets of models, metamodels and transformations. Figure 1 depicts the main components of the framework.

Figure 1. Modernization Framework

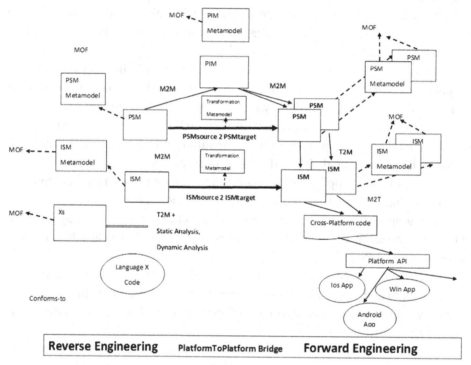

Three different types of models are distinguished: Platform Independent models (PIM), Platform Specific Model (PSM) and Implementation Specific Model (ISM). A PIM is a model with a high level of abstraction that is independent of an implementation technology. A PSM is a tailored model to specify a system in terms of specific platform. PIM and PSM are expressed in UML and OCL. The subset of UML diagrams that are useful for PSM includes class diagram, object diagram, state diagram, interaction diagram and package diagram. On the other hand, a PIM can be expressed by means of use case diagrams, activity diagrams, interactions diagrams to model system processes and, state diagrams to model lifecycle of the system entities. An ISM is a specification of the implementation (source code) in terms of models.

The framework includes PSMs and ISMs related to the source and target platform. The target PSM and target ISM are related to a cross-platform language that allows writing mobile applications that can be deployed on all major mobile platforms.

Metamodeling is a powerful technique to specify families of models. A metamodel is a model that defines the language for expressing a model, i.e. "a model of models". A metamodel is an explicit model of the constructs and rules needed to build specific models. It is a description of all the concepts that can be used in a model. MOF metamodels use an object modeling framework that is essentially a subset of UML 2.5.1 core. The modeling concepts are metaobjects, data types which model other data, and packages to struct the models. At this level MOF metamodels describe families of ISM, PSM and PIM. Every ISM, PSM and PIM conforms to a MOF metamodel.

The framework includes different kinds of transformations: T2M (Text-to-Model), M2M (Model-to-Model) and M2T (Model-to-Text).

T2M transformations allow representing the source code of the program in terms of a model compatible with MOF. They require to have a metamodel that describes the grammar of the source language. First, a representation of the original code in terms of an Abstract Syntax Tree (AST) is built. The next step in the reverse engineering process involves applying traditional techniques for static and dynamic analysis. The basic representation of the static analysis is a direct graph that represents all data flow. Static analysis can be complemented with dynamic analysis that analyses traces of execution for different test cases.

Model-to-model (M2M) transformations provide a mechanism for automatically creating target models based on information contained in existing source models.

The framework distinguishes vertical and horizontal model-to-model transformations. Vertical transformations occur when a source model is transformed into a target model at a different abstraction level. They are useful in reverse engineering processes (ISM-to-PSM, PSM-to-PIM transformations) or forward engineering (PIMtoPSM, PSMtoISM). Horizontal transformations involves transforming a source model into a target model that is at the same abstraction level. They are bridges between different platforms at the same abstraction level (ISM or PSM), for instance *ISMsource2ISMtarget* and *PSMsource2PSMtarget*.

M2T transformations focuses on the generation of textual artifacts from models. In our context, M2T transformations are the processes to extract code from models following the MDE principles.

The framework shows different scenarios of modernization to adapt software to diverse mobile platforms. In the most general form, reverse engineering processes extract PIM models from the code, which are transformed into code through MDD processes for forward engineering. Reverse engineering processes can also recover PSMs that can be restructured at the same level of abstraction through a migration between different platforms. Different realizations of this framework were analyzed. Next we will describe the realizations of the framework for the migration of C / C ++ and Java code to mobile platforms and the reverse engineering of Java code to UML models.

Analyzing Different Realizations of the Framework

This section is about customization of the framework. First, we partially show the metamodels that had to be defined in order to realize the objectives of our project: the C/C++ metamodel and the Haxe metamodel. The section "*From C/C++ to mobile platforms*" describes a realization of the framework for migrating (at ISM level) C/C++ code to Haxe and the generation of mobile applications that run over different platforms. The section "*From Java to mobile platforms*" describes a realization of the framework for migrating Java to Haxe. Finally, the section "*Reverse engineering Java Code to UML Models*" describes other customization for reverse engineering Java code to PIMs models expressed on UML.

The proposal was validated in the open source application platform Eclipse considering that some of its frameworks and tools are aligned with MDE standards. For example, EMF has evolved starting from the experience of the Eclipse community to implement a variety of tools and to date is highly related to MDE. Ecore is the core metamodel at the heart of EMF that can be considered the official implementation of MOF. The subproject M2M supports model transformations that take one or more models as input to produce one or more models as output. ATL is a model transformation language and a toolkit that provides ways to produce a set of target models from a set of source models develop on top of the Eclipse platform.

The Haxe and C++ metamodels were developed from the grammars of the languages using the Ecore metamodeling graphical language and the OclInEcore textual representation of them that allows us greater readability, modifiability and integration with versioning tools. Other advantage of OclInEcore is allowing to attach OCL expressions in the same file in which the metamodel is written. Ecore metamodels can be integrated with formal specification languages, based on the algebraic formalism. In the context of our research we define the NEREUS language that is a formal notation closed to MOF metamodels that allows meta-designers who must manipulate metamodels to understand their formal specification. The semantic of MOF metamodels (that is specified in OCL) can be enriched and refined by integrating it with NEREUS. This integration facilitates proofs and test of models and model transformations via the formal specification of metamodels (Favre, 2009; Favre and Duarte, 2016).

The C++ Metamodel

The C++ metamodel conforms to ECORE and is partially shown in Figure 2. The root metaclass is *Program* that represents a C++ program, which owns source files, instances of *TranslationUnit*. A translation unit contains declarations such as block declaration, function definitions, template declarations, among others. A *SimpleDeclaration*, instance of *Block-Declaration*, has a *DeclSpecifierSeq* that is a sequence of *DeclSpecifiers* which refers to a declaration specifiers and a type specifier. In addition, a simple declaration has an *InitDeclaratorList* containing a variable declaration list that is a list of specifiers and the name of a variable and its corresponding initialization. A *FunctionDefinition* has a *Declarator* containing the function identifier and the parameter list. *Function* and *CtorOrDestFunction*, instances of *FunctionDefinition*, have a body that contains compound statements such as declarations, iterations, and selections. In addition, a *Function* has a *DeclSpecifierSeq* that is a sequence of *DeclSpecifiers* such as function specifiers and a type specifier. *TypeSpecifier* subclasses are *SimpleTypeSpecifier*, *ClassSpecifier* and *EnumSpecifier* among others. A *ClassSpecifier* has a *ClassHead* containing the class key (class or struct) and a *MemberSpecification* that contains *MemberDeclarations* such as variables, function declarations, function definitions, constructors, destructor and template members. The full C/C++ metamodel may be found at (Duthey and Spina, 2016).

The Haxe Metamodel

The HAXE metamodel conforms to Ecore metamodel. It is partially shown in Figure 3. The main metaclasses of the HAXE metamodel are those that allow specifying an application using HAXE as language.

One of the main metaclasses of the metamodel is *HAXEModel*, that serves as element container used to describe an application and store additional information on it, for example, some options of compilation and different metaclasses for modeling such as modules, classes and packages. *HAXEModel* owns *HAXEModule* and *HAXEPathReferentiable*.

Starting from the relations *HaxeModules*, *referenced* and *elements*, the class *HAXEModel* allows storing different information. Relation *HaxeModules* allows accessing the different HAXE modules used in the project. Through relation *elements*, it is possible to access the different elements of the package tree. Relation *referenced* provides access to elements, which are referenced in the project but are not defined completely. In the case of relations and referenced elements, the type used is *HAXEPathReferentiable*, which is the parent type of metaclasses such as *HAXEType* and *HAXEPackage*. The HAXE language includes different kind of types such as class (the types class and interface), function, abstract type, enumeration, and anonymous structures. A full description of the Haxe metamodel may be found at (Diaz Bilotto, 2015; Duthey and Spina, 2016).

Figure 2. The C/C++ Metamodel

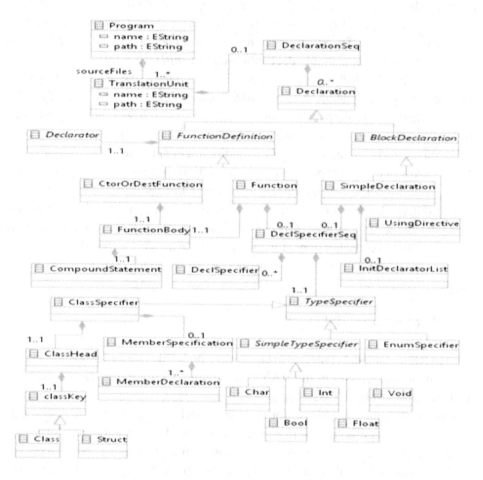

From C/C++ to Mobile Platforms

Figure 4 depicts a framework realization. The initial transformation T2M obtains a code model that conforms to the C/C++ metamodel. This transformation was based on the generation of a parsing tree with the ANTLR tool through the C ++ grammar. Also a discoverer of a C ++ model that conforms to the C ++ metamodel was built. It is a Java program whose input is the syntax tree and its output an ISM, the C++ model of the code.

M2M transformations were defined in ATL, the most mature transformation language in the context of MDE. ATL is a model transformation language and toolkit developed on top of the Eclipse platform. It provides ways to produce a set of target models from a set of source models. The ATL Integrated Development Environment (IDE) provides a number of standard development tools (such as syntax highlighting and debugger) that aims to facilitate the development of ATL transformations. ATL is a hybrid language that provides a mix of declarative and imperative constructs.

Figure 3. The Haxe Metamodel

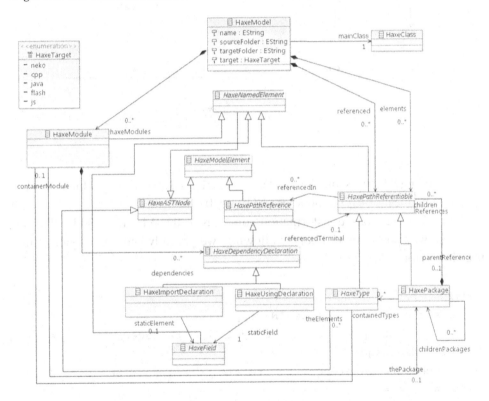

A model-to-model transformation from C++ to Haxe, called *C/C++ 2 Haxe*, was defined in ATL. It takes as input the model obtained in the reverse engineering phase and release a Haxe model. The transformation specifies families of transformations that produce Haxe models (target) from C++ models (source). Both source and target models must conform to the C++ metamodel and Haxe metamodel respectively.

Figure 4. From C/C++ to Mobile PLatforms

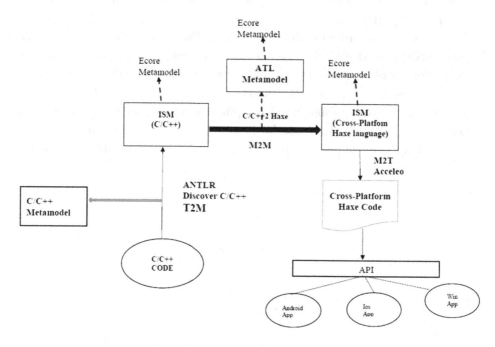

ATL mainly focuses on the model-to-model transformations, which can be specified by means of ATL modules (ATL, 2020).

The *C/C++ 2 Haxe* transformation conforms to the ATL metamodel that, in the same way conforms to Ecore. Following, we partially show the style of this transformation.

```
module CPP2Haxe ;
c r e a t e OUT: Haxe from IN: cpp;
helper context cpp ! CppPackage def: get_packages (): Sequence
(cpp ! CppPackage) =
self . childrenReferences -> iterate (elem ;acc: Sequence (cpp
! CppPackage)=
Sequence {} | if(elem. ocl IsTypeOf (cpp ! CppPackage)) then
acc->append (elem)->
union (elem . get_packages ()) else acc->union (Sequence {})
endif) ;
helper context cpp ! CppModel def: get_allpackages (): Sequence
(cpp ! CppPackage) =
self. elements->iterate (elem ; acc: Sequence (cpp !
```

```
CppPackage)= Sequence {} |
if (elem.ocl IsTypeOf (cpp! CppPackage)) then acc->append
(elem)->
union (elem. get_packages ()) else acc->union (Sequence {})
endif) ;
….
rule model {
from s: cpp!CppModel
to t: Haxe!HaxeModel (name <- s.name, sourceFolder <- s.
sourceFolder, targetFolder <-
s. targetFolder, referenced <- s. orphanTypes -> select(x |
x.usages InTypeAcces s->
notEmpty () and x.oclIsKindOf (cpp!CppType) and (not x
.oclIsTypeOf (cpp! CppClass))) ->
collect (x | thisModule.Type (x)) ->asSet (), elements <- s .
get_allpackages(),HaxeModules <- s. get_classfiles(), mainClass
<- s. mainClass)}
```

All models obtained in this chain of transformations are saved in the interchange format XMI, an OMG standard that combines XML, MOF and UML for integrating tools, repositories, and applications in distributed heterogeneous environments (XMI, 2015).

Finally, from a model Haxe, it is possible to generate a source code in Haxe by using an M2T transformation defined in Acceleo which is a code generation system based on MDE standards. More precisely, it is the oficial implementation of MOFM2T, a standard of OMG, for performing model-to-text transformations (Acceleo, 2020). Acceleo contains a code generation modules editor with syntax highlighting, completion, real time error detection and incremental code generation. It allows code generation from any kind of metamodel compatible with EMF like UML and Ecore.

Haxe allows writing mobile applications that target all major mobile platforms in a straightforward way. The generated code is syntactically correct, although, it does not compile on other platforms without doing changes due to the code refers to proprietary technologies of C++. To run on mobile environments, these technologies can be replaced with OpenFL and HAXEUI that is an open source, multi-platform application centric user interface framework designed for HAXE and OpenFL (OpenFl, 2020).

From Java to Mobile Platforms

Figure 5 depicts a framework realization that allows migrating Java to Haxe. It is based on Java and Haxe metamodels and a bridge between them specified as an ATL transformations. The Java metamodel is based on the Eclipse JDT Java model and covers the full abstract syntax ranging from package declarations and classes to method bodies, expressions and statements. A detailed description of the Java metamodel may be found at (Eclipse, 2020).

Figure 5. From Java to Mobile Platforms

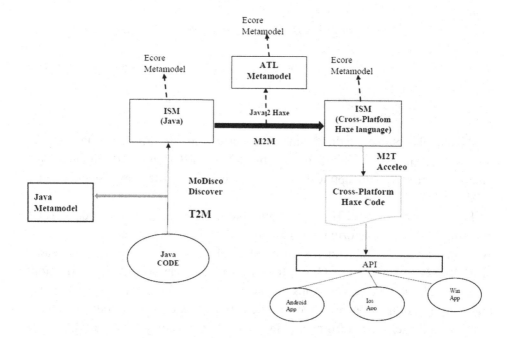

The initial transformation T2M obtain a code model that conforms to a Java metamodel. Model extraction is performed automatically by the component Java Model Discovery of the Modisco framework (Bruneliere et al, 2014; MoDisco, 2020).

The platform-to-platform bridge is defined as an ATL transformation between the source metamodel Java and the target metamodel Haxe. The main transformations are *java2haxe, javaHaxeRefactoring* and *haxeImports*. The *java2haxe* transformation is central and transforms syntactic elements between the Java metamodel and the Haxe metamodel. The *javaHaxeRefactoring* transformation reorganizes and modifies the syntactic elements in such a way to adapt own behavior of the Java language. The *haxeImports* performs changes in the imports of the own packages of the Java framework, which require a specific treatment. In this transformation, import clauses are added for items belonging to the package *java.lang* which are recognized implicitly by the framework as dependencies in Java but need to be explicit in HaXe classes. A detail description of the ATL transformations may be found at (Diaz Bilotto, 2015).The forward engineering from a model Haxe is based on M2T transformations defined in Acceleo in the way described at previous section.

Reverse Engineering Java Code to UML Models

Reverse Engineering is the process of analyzing available software artifacts such as requirements, design, architectures, code or byte code, with the objective of extracting information and providing high-level views on the underlying system (Favre, 2010).

The reverse engineering process begins with two crucial steps *model discovery* and *static analysis* that provide as a result a refined model (Figure 6). This Java model is the input to the *model transformation* step. Next, we describe them.

Figure 6. Reverse engineering: From Java to PIM

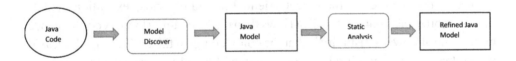

In the Model Discovery step, the source code of the program is represented through a model of the Java language, which is a representation of the input program. This is a very important step, since it allows obtaining the implementation of the program in terms of a model compatible with an Ecore metamodel.

The resulting model is an equivalent representation of the original program by an abstract syntax tree, and therefore, any reverse engineering task to be performed on the system can be performed, with the same result, using this model as a valid input representation (ASTM, 2011). This step requires to have a metamodel that describes the grammar of the source language. In our case the Java metamodel used is provided by the MoDisco tool. This metamodel is based on the Eclipse JDT Java model, and covers the full abstract syntax tree of a Java program, ranging from package declarations and classes to method bodies, expressions and statements.

Model extraction is performed automatically by the component Java Model Discovery of the MoDisco framework. The resulting model is called *initial model* since it has a direct correspondence with the elements of the original system. In the context of MoDisco this phase of the reverse engineering process is called *Model Discovery*. The idea is to represent the original system using a set of models without loss of information. The proposed reverse engineering process involves applying traditional static analysis techniques on the Java model obtained in the previous step.

The concepts and algorithms of data flow analysis described in (Tonella and Potrich, 2005) are adapted for reverse engineering object-oriented code. Data flow analysis infers information about the behavior of a program by only analyzing the text of the source code.

The basic representation of this static analysis is the Object Flow Graph (OFG) that allows tracing information of object interactions from the object creation, through its assignments to variables, attributes or their use in messages (method invocations). OFG is defined as a direct graph that represents all data flows linking objects in a program.

The static analysis is data flow sensitive, but control flow insensitive. This means that programs with different control flows and the same data flows are associated with the same analysis results. The choice of this program representation is motivated by the computational complexity of the involved algorithms. On the one hand, control flow sensitive analysis is computationally intractable and on the other hand, it is aligned to the "nature" of the object-oriented programs whose execution models impose more constraints on the data flows than on the control flows. A consequence of the control flow insensitivity is that the construction of the OFG can be described with reference to a simplified, abstract version of the object-oriented languages in which instructions related to flow control are ignored. On this OFG different types of propagation are performed. They allow obtaining information used to generate the various UML diagrams in the next step. The information resulting from this analysis is stored in the original model, either in the form of modifications to existing elements or as additional elements incorporated into the model.

Next, we describe the Model Transformation step. The "refined" Java model obtained in the previous step conforms to the input of the third and final step in the process of reverse engineering called *Model Transformation*. They are defined as model-to-model (M2M) transformations and specified in ATL.

We describe, as an example, the extraction of a representation of the interactions that occur among objects in an object-oriented system. Starting from a Java Project a Java code model (an abstract syntax tree that conforms to an Ecore metamodel) is obtained. This step is performed automatically by using the component Java Model Discovery of MoDisco.

The static recovery of the interactions among objects is done, on the one hand, inferring from the code the objects created by the program that are accessible through program variables. On the other hand, each call to a method is solved in terms of the possible source and target objects involved in the message interchange.

This information can be obtained by means of the propagation through the OFG of the objects generated at each point of the program that represents the creation of a new instance. The result of this stage will provide for each node of the OFG the set of objects to which the node can be linked at some point.

Following, we exemplify the ATL transformation called *Java2SequenceDiagram* transformation. It allows recovering a sequence diagram for each selected Java method. Different ATL rules specify the mappings that allow to generate elements of the sequence diagram from the input Java model. As an example we show a rule included in this transformation that express that for each interaction in a Java program represented by *MethodDeclaration*, an Interaction in UML is created.

```
rule javaInputMethodDeclaration2UMLInteraction {
from
javamethod: java!MethodDeclaration (javamethod.proxy = false
and thisModule.isInputMethod(javamethod))
using {
sourceLifeline: UML!Lifeline =
thisModule.getInitialLifeline(javamethod);
callerStack: Sequence(java!AbstractMethodDeclaration) =
Sequence{javamethod};
sourceMethodActivation: UML!ActionExecutionSpecification =
thisModule.createActionExecutionSpecification(sourceLifeline,ja
vamethod.name);
}
to
umlinteraction: UML!Interaction (name <- javamethod.name)
do {
thisModule.model.packagedElement <- thisModule.model.
packagedElement ->
including(umlinteraction);
thisModule.addExecutionEventToModel(sourceMethodActivation.
start.event);
thisModule.addExecutionEventToModel(sourceMethodActivation.
finish.event);
umlinteraction.lifeline <- umlinteraction.lifeline
->including(sourceLifeline);
```

```
umlinteraction.fragment <- umlinteraction.fragment -> including
(sourceMethodActivation);
umlinteraction.fragment <- umlinteraction.fragment -> including
(sourceMethodActivation.start);
thisModule.translateStatements(umlinteraction,umlinteraction,
sourceLifeline,javamethod.body.statements, callerStack);
umlinteraction.fragment <- umlinteraction.fragment ->
including(sourceMethodActivation.finish);
}
}
```

A plugin tool integrated to Eclipse that provides support for reverse engineering UML diagrams from Java code was developed (class diagram, sequence diagrams and use case diagrams). It was implemented in Java using the infrastructure provided by EMF and PDE (Plug-in Development Environment). Besides, it uses other framework and technologies such as MoDisco and ATL. The full description may be found at (Galitiello and Rolandi, 2015).

ADM MODERNIZATION

This section describes a process to migrate legacy code to different mobile platforms based on ADM standards and cross-platform development. The migration process follows model-driven development principles. For each transformation, source and target metamodels are specified. A source metamodel defines the family of source models to which transformations can be applied. A target metamodel characterizes the generated models. Different kind of transformations such as T2M, M2M, and M2T are distinguished in the steps of reverse engineering, refactoring/restructuring, and forward engineering. Figure 7 summarizes the proposed process.

Figure 7. The ADM migration process

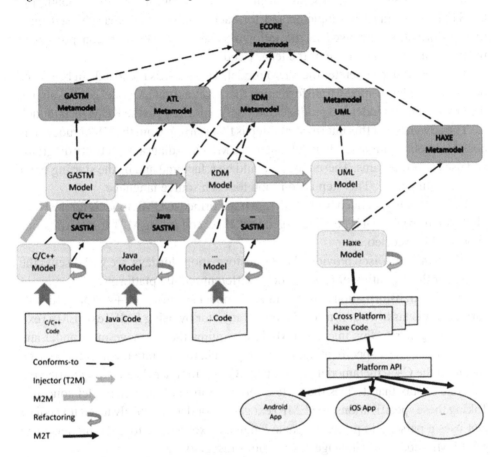

The first step is the reverse engineering of source code to obtain the abstract syntax tree of the code and consists of two stages:

- Generating the first model of the code by using a model injector. This model conforms to the source code metamodel, such as C++ and Java. The obtained model could be refactored to reorganize and modify the syntactic elements and to improve the design. The refactoring is implemented as a model-to-model transformation whose source and target models are instances of source code metamodel.
- Generating the abstract syntax tree model, instance of the GASTM metamodel, from the model obtained in the previous stage by an ATL model-to-model transformation.

In this first step of the process, an injector and a transformation to obtain the GASTM model must be implemented for each language, whereas the sequence of transformations involved in the followings steps of the migration process is independent of the language of the legacy code.

The second step generates the KDM model. This process is carried out by means of an ATL model-to-model transformation that takes as input a model conforming to the GASTM metamodel and produces a model conforming to the KDM metamodel.

The advantage of this intermediate step is that starting from the KDM model it is possible to obtain high-level models such as UML class diagrams, activity diagrams and use cases diagrams. These models could be refactored and be the starting point for generating code. This step is common for each source language.

UML models generated from KDM are transformed to UML models for the Haxe platform from which it is possible to generate Haxe code using M2T transformations expressed in Acceleo.

Given that MoDisco provides T2M transformations for Java, we will discuss the stages for the migration of C ++ code to different mobile platforms.

The first transformation extracts an AST model specific to C++ from code. To carry out this task, we constructed a model injector by using EMFText (EMFText, 2019). To generate this injector, EMFText requires the language metamodel and the concrete syntax specification. In our approach, to generate the injector we first specified the C++ metamodel based on the C++ grammar. Then, we specified the concrete syntax that defines the textual representation of all metamodel concepts. Taking these specifications, the EMFText generator derives an advanced text editor that uses a parser and printer to parse language expressions to EMF models or to print EMF models to languages expressions respectively.

The second transformation takes as input the model obtained in the previous step and release a generic AST model conforming to the GASTM metamodel. This transformation specifies the way to produce GASTM projects (target) from C++ programs (source). The previous transformations are dependent on the legacy code language, that is, the model injector and the transformation to obtain the generic AST model are dependent on C++. In contrast to the previous stage, the sequence of transformations from GASTM models to Haxe models is independent of the language.

UML models generated from KDM are transformed to UML models for the Haxe platform from which it is possible to generate Haxe code using M2T transformations expressed in Acceleo. Haxe allows writing mobile applications that target all major mobile platforms as it was already expressed.

DISCUSSION

We believe that an MDE approach provides benefits with respect to ad-hoc migration. One of the benefits of applying MDE techniques is to increase productivity in software development due to the automation that is introduced in the generation of artifacts. Besides, to use MDE in migration projects is more cost-effective when the same process must be repeated frequently as the case of migrations to different platforms.

Besides, a migration process must be independent of the source and target technologies. In our approach, the intermediate models act as decoupling elements between source and target technologies. The independence is achieved with injectors and M2M and M2T transformations. Besides, in a transformation sequence, models could be an extension point to incorporate new stages.

Another advantage is that the migration process is based on MOF-like metamodeling that is a powerful approach for interoperability. It outperforms XML due to its expressive power and, the existence of powerful model transformation languages to implement the transformations required at the different stages of the migration process. MOF-like metamodeling also includes the possibility to attach OCL restrictions to complete the model specification. In addition, MOF-like metamodels allow a clear separation of abstract and concrete syntax and thus, associate different notations for a model.

The two approaches involve preliminary activities that require time and cost, for instance the developer need to define metamodels and transformations if they do not exist. It is assumed that using a brute-force redevelopment, developers do not need training to write metamodels and model transformations. However, model transformations allow developers to concentrate on conceptual aspects of the relations between models and then to delegate most of the migration process to the transformation rules, whereas in the brute-force redevelopment, developers need to migrate by hand the legacy systems, making over and over again the same task. The validation of both process showed that it is possible to migrate Java or C / C ++ software to mobile platforms semi-automatically. In particular it is possible to migrate the logic of software applications and run them on mobile platforms without having to completely rewrite them.

In the context of our proposal, Haxe allows using the same code to deploy an application on multiple mobile platforms. The migration of object-oriented software to mobile platforms is achieved through the definition of a metamodel for Haxe and a single M2M transformation, delegating the integration with different mobile platforms to Haxe, that is, the evolution of existing platforms or the integration of new mobile platforms is considered a goal of Haxe.

The following limitations of our approach were observed. The set of metamodels and discovers that can be used is limited. In our project it was necessary to define metamodels for the C / C ++ and Haxe languages and, a model discoverer for C/C ++ either expressed as a model that conforms to GASTM or MOF depending of the specific modernization approach. In addition, although Eclipse provides its modeling framework, the tools are not yet mature, especially for the transformation phase and forward engineering, limited by scalability problems.

Regarding the comparative analysis of the two approaches, we can say that the lightweight and ADM modernization exploit the benefits of integrating MDE with Cross-Platform development. The difference between them lies in the level of abstraction of the model transformations and in the degree to which they are aligned to the ADM standard. The nature of the applications will make one or the other approach more advantageous. If the goal is to analyze legacy code to extract information and provide high-level models of the underlying software system, the ADM-based approach could be chosen. On the other hand, if the objective is to migrate a program to be able to use it in the development of mobile applications, a transformation at the level of implementation models and through a lightweight process could be more convenient. For example, suppose that given the shortage of free graphic design tools for mobile devices, a programmer needs to adapt them, for example, if GIMP (GNU Image Manipulation Program) should be adapted to different mobile platforms, the lightweight process was more convenient for this code-to-code migration. Furthermore, this approach opens the door to those communities that adhere to the MDE principles and at the same time consider that it is valuable to use other quality tools proven in other communities that do not conform to ADM standards. For example, the language engineering community produced quality tools to be used in reverse engineering. An example is ANTLR (Parr, 2013) that developers prefer to use over model-driven tools like XText (XText, 2020).

CONCLUSION AND FUTURE WORK

This chapter describes a modernization framework that allows migrating software to new technologies such as IoT in which smartphones are its great facilitators. An integration of the MDE principles with the multiplatform language called Haxe is described. Two approaches are analyzed. One of them is a lightweight process that integrates MDA with traditional static and dynamic analysis techniques. The other approach is based on a modernization under ADM standards such as KDM and ASTM. To exemplify the analysis, a specific case study scenario for the migration of C/C++ or Java software to different mobile platforms through the integration of MDE with Haxe is described. The proposal is validated in the open source platform Eclipse, notably the projects built around EMF metamodeling framework.

Regarding the definition of metamodels, the major contribution had to do with the specification of Ecore metamodels of the C / C++ and Haxe languages. They are an important contribution to both the Eclipse community and the MDE community since there were no complete metamodels of these languages.

With regard to the lightweight approach a semiautomatic tool that takes as its starting point a C++ project and produces one written in Haxe, in addition to the generated intermediate files, was developed to prove model transformations. The tool is semi-automatic because it requires additional actions on the Haxe code to make it fully functional. The tool has been used in the migration of games such as Tetris and medium-scale software applications.

With regard to the ADM approach, we remark the following considerations. The different stages were validated in medium-scale developments. However, each stage requires more research and experimentation to show the real impact on larger scale developments. Besides, it remains to analyze the generation of Haxe code from UML models more deeply. Considering that from KDM it is possible to generate UML models at the PIM level and that currently, CASE MDA / UML tools do not support multiplatform languages it is necessary to move from the stage of validation of transformations through prototypes to a real integration with existing CASE tools, either commercial or free.

REFERENCES

Acceleo. (2020). *Obeo. Acceleo Generator*. Retrieved March 28, 2020 from http://www.eclipse.org/Acceleo/

Acerbis, R., Bongio, A., Brambilla, M., & Butti, S. (2015). *Model-Driven Development Based on OMG's IFML with WebRatio Web and Mobile Platform. In Engineering the Web in the Big Data Era* (Vol. 9114). Lecture Notes in Computer Science. Springer-Verlag.

ADM. (2020). *Architecture-driven modernization task force*. Retrieved March 28, 2020 from http://www.adm.org

Améndola, F., & Favre, L. (2013). Adapting CRM Systems for Mobile Platforms: An MDA Perspective. *International Journal of Computer & Information Science*, *14*(1), 31–40. doi:10.1109/SNPD.2013.25

ASTM. (2011). *Abstract Syntax Tree Metamodel*, version 1.0, OMG Document Number: formal/2011-01-05. Retrieved March 28, 2020 from https://www.omg.org/spec/ASTM

ATL. (2020). *Atlas Transformation Language Documentation*. Retrieved March 28, 2020 from http://www.eclipse.org/atl/documentation/

Brambilla, M., Cabot, J., & Wimmer, M. (2017). Model-Driven Software Enginneering in Practice. Morgan & Claypool Publishers.

Bruneliere, N., Cabot, J., Dupé, G., & Madiot, F. (2014). MoDisco: A Model-driven Reverse Engineering Framework. *Information and Software Technology, 56*(8), 1012–1032. doi:10.1016/j.infsof.2014.04.007

Bucchiarone, A., & Cabot, J. (2020). Grand Challenges in model-driven engineering: An analysis of the state of the research. *Software & Systems Modeling*, (January), 1–12.

Cannasse, N. (2014). *Haxe. Too good to be True?* GameDuell Tech Talk. Retrieved March 28, 2020 from http://www.techtalk-berlin.de/news/read/nicolas-cannasse-introducing-Haxe/

Ciccozzi, F., Crnkovic, I., Di Ruscio, D., Malavolta, I., Pelliccione, P., & Spalazzese, R. (2017, January-February). Model-Driven Engineering for Mission-Critical IoT Systems. *IEEE Software, 34*(1), 46–53. doi:10.1109/MS.2017.1

Dasnois, B. (2011). *Haxe 2 Beginner's Guide*. Packt Publishing.

Dehlinger, J., & Dixon, J. (2011). Mobile application software engineering: Challenges and research directions. In *Proceedings of the Workshop on Mobile Software Engineering* (pp. 29-32). Berlin: Springer-Verlag.

Diaz Bilotto, P. (2015). *Software development for mobile applications through an integration of MDA and Haxe* (Undergraduate Thesis). Computer Science Department, Universidad Nacional del Centro de la Provincia de Buenos Aires, Argentina.

Diaz Bilotto, P., & Favre, L. (2016). Migrating JAVA to Mobile Platforms through HAXE: An MDD Approach. In A. M. Cruz & S. Paiva (Eds.), *Modern Software Engineering Methodologies for Mobile and Cloud Environments* (pp. 240–268). IGI Global. doi:10.4018/978-1-4666-9916-8.ch013

Duthey, M., & Spina, C. (2016). *Migrating C/C++ to mobile platforms through MDD* (Undergraduate Thesis). Computer Science Department, Universidad Nacional del Centro de la Provincia de Buenos Aires, Argentina.

Eclipse. (2020). *Eclipse-The Eclipse Foundation open source community*. http://eclipse.org/

Ejarque, J., Micsik, A., & Badia, R. (2015). Towards Automatic Application Migration to Clouds. *Proceedings IEEE 8th Int. Conf. on Cloud Computing*, 25-32.

EMF. (2020). *Eclipse Modeling Framework (EMF)*. Retrieved March 28, 2020 from http://www.eclipse.org/modeling/emf/

EMFText. (2020). *EMFText Document*. Retrieved March 28, 2020 from www.emftext.org

Favre, L. (2009). A Formal Foundation for Metamodeling. In *Proceedings of 14th Ada-Europe International Conference. Lecture Notes in Computer Science* (Vol 5570, pp.177-191). Berlin: Springer-Verlag. 10.1007/978-3-642-01924-1_13

Favre, L. (2010). *Model-driven Architecture for Reverse Engineering Technologies: Strategic Directions and System Evolution*. IGI Global. doi:10.4018/978-1-61520-649-0

Favre, L. (2018). A Framework for Modernizing Non-Mobile Software: A Model-Driven Engineering Approach. In *Protocols and Applications for the Industrial Internet of Things* (pp. 192–224). IGI Global. doi:10.4018/978-1-5225-3805-9.ch007

Favre, L., & Duarte, D. (2016). Formal MOF Metamodeling and Tool Support. In *Proceedings of the 4th International Conference on Model-Driven Engineering and Software Development. MODELSWARD 2016*. (pp. 99-110). Roma, Italy: SCITEPRESS (Science and Technology Publications).

Galitiello, E., & Rolandi, B. (2015). *Reverse engineering of Object-Oriented Code. System engineering* (Thesis). Computer Science Department. Universidad Nacional del Centro de la Provincia de Buenos Aires, Argentina.

González García, C., & Espada, J. (2015). MUSPEL: Generation of Applications to Interconnect Heterogeneous Objects Using Model-Driven Engineering. In V. G. Díaz, J. M. C. Lovelle, & B. C. P. García-Bustelo (Eds.), *Handbook of Research on Innovations in Systems and Software Engineering* (pp. 365–385). IGI Global. doi:10.4018/978-1-4666-6359-6.ch015

González García, C., Zhao, L., & García-Díaz, V. (2019, April). A User-Oriented Language for Specifying Interconnections between Heterogeneous Objects in the Internet of Things. *IEEE Internet of Things Journal*, *6*(2), 3806–3819. doi:10.1109/JIOT.2019.2891545

Haxe. (2020). *The Haxe Language*. Retrieved March 28, 2020 from https://haxe.org/

Islam, N., & Want, R. (2014). Smarthphones: Past, present and future. *IEEE Pervasive Computing*, *13*(4), 82–92. doi:10.1109/MPRV.2014.74

Joshi, P., Nivangune, A., Kumar, R., Kumar, S., Ramesh, R., Pani, S., & Chesum, A. (2015). Understanding the Challenges in Mobile Computation Offloading to Cloud through Experimentation. *2nd ACM Int. Conf. on Mobile Software Engineering and Systems*, 158-159. 10.1109/MobileSoft.2015.43

KDM. (2016). *Knowledge Discovery Meta-Model* (KDM), OMG Document Number: formal/2016-09-01. Retrieved April, 25, 2017 from https://www.omg.org/spec/KDM/1.4

Kramer, D., Clark, T., & Oussena, S. (2010). MobDSL: A domain specific language for multiple mobile platform deployment. *Proceedings of IEEE Int. Conf. on Networked Embedded Systems for Enterprise Applications*, 1-7. 10.1109/NESEA.2010.5678062

Martinez, L., Pereira, C., & Favre, L. (2017). Migrating C/C++ Software to Mobile Platforms in the ADM Context. *International Journal of Interactive Multimedia and Artificial Intelligence*, 4(3), 34–44. doi:10.9781/ijimai.2017.436

MDA. (2020). *The Model-Driven Architecture*. Retrieved March 28, 2020 from www.omg.org/mda/

Miranda, J., Makitalo, N., Garcia-Alonso, J., Berrocal, J., Mikkonen, T., Canal, C., & Murillo, J. (2015). From the Internet of Things to the Internet of People. *IEEE Internet Computing*, 19(2), 40–47. doi:10.1109/MIC.2015.24

MoDisco. (2020). *Model Discovery*. Retrieved March 28, 2020 from https://eclipse.org/MoDisco/

MOF. (2016). *Meta Object Facility (MOF) Core Specification*, Version 2.5, OMG Document Number: formal/2016-11-01. Retrieved March 28, 2020 from https://www.omg.org/spec/MOF/2.5.1/

OCL. (2014). *OMG Object constraint language* (OCL), version 2.4. OMG Document Number: formal/2014-02-03. Retrieved March 28, 2020 from https://www.omg.org/spec/OCL/2.4

OPEN FL. (2020). *OPEN FL 4.7*. Retrieved March 28, 2020 from https://www.openfl.org/

Parr, T. (2013). *The Definitive ANTLR 4 Reference* (2nd ed.). Pragmatic Bookshelf.

Pérez Castillo, R., García Rodriguez, I., Gómez Cornejo, R., Fernández Ropero, M., & Piattini, M. (2013). ANDRIU. A Technique for Migrating Graphical User Interfaces to Android. In *Proceedings of The 25th International Conference on Software Engineering and Knowledge Engineering*. Boston: Knowledge Systems Institute.

Ploennigs, J., Cohn, J., & Stanford-Clark, A. (2018, Sept.). The Future of IoT. IEEE Internet of Things Magazine, 28-33.

QVT. (2016). *QVT: MOF 2.0 query, view, transformation: Version 1.3.* OMG Document Number: formal/2016-06-03 Retrieved March 28, 2020 https://www. omg.org/spec/QVT/1.3

Raibulet, C., Arcelli Fontana, F., & Zanoni, M. (2017). Model-Driven Reverse Engineering Approaches: A Systematic Literature Review. *IEEE Access: Practical Innovations, Open Solutions, 5*, 14516–14542. doi:10.1109/ACCESS.2017.2733518

Sánchez Cuadrado, J., Cánovas, J., & García Molina, J. (2014). Applying model-driven engineering in small software enterprises. *Science of Computer Programming, 89*, 176–198. doi:10.1016/j.scico.2013.04.007

Stankovic, J. (2014). Research Directions for the Internet of Things. *IEEE Internet of Things Journal, 1*(1), 1, 3–9. doi:10.1109/JIOT.2014.2312291

Steinberg, D., Budinsky, F., Paternostro, M., & Merks, E. (2009). *EMF: Eclipse Modeling Framework* (2nd ed.). Addison-Wesley.

Thramboulidis, K., Bochalis, P., & Bouloumpasis, J. (2017). A Framework for MDE of IoT-based Manufacturing Cyber-Physical System. In *Proceedings of the Seventh International Conference on the Internet of Things*. ACM. 10.1145/3131542.3131554

Tonella, P., & Potrich, A. (2005). *Reverse engineering of Object-Oriented Code. Monographs in Computer Science.* Springer-Verlag.

Umuhoza, E., & Brambilla, M. (2016). Model-driven Development Approaches for Mobile Applications: A Survey. In *Proceedings of Mobile Web and Intelligent Information Systems - 13th International Conference, MobiWIS 2016* (pp. 93-107). Berlin: Springer.

XMI. (2015). *XML Metadata Interchange (XMI) Specification*, OMG Document Number: formal/2015-06-07. Retrieved March 28, 2020 from https://www.omg. org/spec/XMI/2.5.1

XText. (2020) *XText Documentation*. Retrieved March 28, from https//www.eclipse. org/Xtext

Zanella, A., Bui, N., Castellani, A., Vangelista, L., & Zorzi, M. (2014). Internet of Things for Smart Cities. *IEEE Internet of Things Journal, 1*(1), 22–32.

KEY TERMS AND DEFINITIONS

ADM (Architecture Driven Modernization): The process of understanding and evolving existing software assets of an existing system in the context of MDA.

ATL (Atlas Transformation Language): A model transformation language and toolkit developed on top of the Eclipse platform that provides ways to produce target models from source models.

HaXe: An open-source toolkit based on a modern, high level, strictly typed programming language, a cross-compiler, a complete cross-platform standard library and ways to access each platform's native capabilities.

KDM (Knowledge Discovery Metamodel): The core metamodel of ADM, a language-independent metamodel for representing assets of software legacy.

Metamodeling: The process of generating a "model of models"; the essence of model-driven development approaches.

Model Transformation: A mechanism for automatically creating target models based on information contained in existing source models.

Model-Driven Architecture (MDA): An initiative of the OMG for the development of software systems based on the separation of business and application logic from underlying platform technologies.

Model-Driven Engineering: Software engineering discipline that emphasizes the use of models and model transformations to raise the abstraction level and the degree of automation in software development.

Chapter 3
From Digital to Smart Tourism:
Main Challenges and Opportunities

Silvia Fernandes
iD https://orcid.org/0000-0002-1699-5415
FE, Cinturs, University of Algarve, Portugal

ABSTRACT

In the information age, activities and business models have become different. Factors such as new technologies and social media influence consumer behavior due to the variety of choices/channels. Companies are making a difference in consumers' minds by connecting with them active and creatively. Also, customers contribute with ideas and experiences, not only for products and services, but also for platforms and brands. Cyber-physical apps together with mobile media tend to revolutionize business models across multiple industries. This is important for tourism due to a contribution to link some still weakly linked activities across tourism sub-sectors in Portugal. The present work reflects on how Portugal is in terms of internet of things adoption (IoT) and digital transformation facing the challenges of sustainable and smart cities. It also explores which impacts this transformation can have through its platforms and processes in tourism and future services.

1. INTRODUCTION

Modern technologies introduce what has been called the 'smart' factory or smart platform, in which cyber-physical systems monitor the physical processes of the platform and make decentralized decisions. These systems include IoT (Internet of Things) and communications, either between machines or machine-human interactions, in real time via wireless web. This set allows a considerable number of

DOI: 10.4018/978-1-7998-6463-9.ch003

platforms or infra-structures, involving new processes. As this entails a significant speed of technological change, these issues should be increasingly addressed by enterprises and services. And an issue to introduce and develop is geolocation and related location-based services (Palos-Sanchez et al., 2018). Destinations have the possibility to present offers to customers based on location using geolocation technology, creating new opportunities for destination marketing organizations.

Tourism and travel brands tend to become "experience platforms" in order to develop travel experiences that enable travelers to grasp and participate in the activities, culture and heritage of the local communities they are visiting. This will also be an opportunity to build sustainable learning from these experiences to the tourism sector. These trends mean a considerable amount of data involved, so big data can be useful to track visitor uses and flows, identify crowded areas, evaluate industry performance/volatility, and refine tourism strategies (Peeters et al., 2018). Moreover, the usability of information can also include data-driven decision making as well as monitoring and measuring success. These data need to meet criteria such as accuracy, relevance, reliability, timeliness, accessibility, and coherence. Also, in discussing the appliance of those technologies in tourism business, the socio-demographic issues have to be considered such as age, income, country of residence, etc. as the impact of quality/price varies accordingly (Pinto & Castro, 2019).

A major challenge, but at the same time opportunity, is the level of integration that IoT can create in order to link some still weakly linked activities across tourism sub-sectors such as: accommodation; food and beverage; transports (road, air, water, etc.); equipment rental; travel agencies; other reservation services; cultural activities; sports and recreational services; retail trade of country-characteristic goods; and other country-specific tourism activities. But despite the strong influence of technology in future tourism, and the existence of some initiatives such as the Virtual Tourism Observatory, there is still a lack of data to help destinations understand future tourism patterns, motivations and expectations (Jafari, 2019). OECD suggests that a monitoring system is needed to anticipate changes in both environment and supply/demand trends in world tourism, provide public and private sector stakeholders with better visibility, and give tourism professionals a decision-making tool to improve the management of their activities (OECD, 2018).

Two research questions (Q1 & Q2) can emerge from these considerations, which are:

Q1: How is Portugal in terms of Internet of Things adoption (IoT) and digital transformation?; and

Q2: Which impacts can this 'fourth' industry have, through its platforms and processes, in tourism and related services?

In order to discuss it, the next section explores the propensity of Portugal to digital transformations toward IoT and its potentials for tourism offers and services.

2. DIGITAL ECONOMY TODAY

Denmark, Finland, Sweden and the Netherlands have the most advanced digital economies in the EU followed by Luxembourg, Belgium, the UK and Ireland. Romania, Bulgaria, Greece and Italy have the lowest scores on the DESI - Digital Economy and Society Index (figure 1). In 2016, all Member States improved on this index. Slovakia and Slovenia progressed the most (more than 0.04 as opposed to an EU average of 0.028). On the other hand, there was low increase in Portugal, Latvia and Germany (below 0.02). Portugal ranks 15th in DESI 2017. It improved its score in all DESI dimensions with the exception of Digital Public Services. Greatest progress took place in fixed and mobile broadband take-up (connectivity) as well as in the corporate use of digital technologies. Portugal's greatest challenge lies in raising the digital skills levels of its population. Despite an uptick in the share of internet users making video calls online and using social networks, there is still reluctance to engage in online transactions through online shopping and e-Banking (European Commission, 2017).

Figure 1. Digital Economy and Society Index
Source: DESI 2017

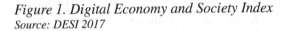

The Digital Single Market for Europe is a major priority of the European Commission. This strategy is built on three pillars: (1) better access for consumers and businesses to digital goods and services across Europe; (2) creating the right conditions and a level playing field for digital networks and innovative services to flourish; (3) maximizing the growth potential of the digital economy. Online platforms play an increasingly central role in social and economic life and are an important part of a thriving internet-enabled economy.

The wider EU policy interest is to spot business opportunities for launching services based on the internet and key enabling technologies such as social media, cloud computing, IoT, 3D printing, etc. Websites offering dynamic features to visitors and participation in social media are an important part of the digital technologies that businesses use to increase their online presence, improve marketing opportunities, and interact with partners, customers and other stakeholders.

2.1 Digital Transformation

In the information Age (from the 90s), factors such as globalization and new technologies have highly influenced consumer behavior. Kotler, Kartajaya and Setiawan (2015) explain that consumers are now better informed and consumer preferences are becoming more diverse. Now consumers can create communities by sharing knowledge and ideas. Alarcão and Silva (2013) report consumers have increased their access to information, starting to define the value of a product/ service. Hence, the organizations started to have as goal, not only sales volume, but also customer satisfaction and loyalty. According to Gomes and Kury (2013) this stage is 2.0 or 'push' because, though customers choose what they want, they are still a passive target of marketing. Today, we are in the age/stage 3.0 referred by those authors as 'pull' (or customer led). In this era, the consumer defines the rules through his desires/needs. Here it is necessary to convince the client of the company's positive convictions and good values/ideas. This important trend can be dealt by enterprises through the dynamic and varied way of building service models that the referred platforms allow.

With the development of IT, especially the Internet, communication has become bidirectional and now multidirectional. The websites appeared and the issuer got specialized, changing the message and guiding the client. In the age 3.0, communities make a difference. Communication becomes multidirectional in which any person can give an opinion and advertise (positive or negatively) any brand. This is important, because the digital issue is settled and its potential can be an important tool to nurture IoT and fourth industry's projects. Customers want to give ideas and participate, not only in products/services, but also in business value. Increasingly, interactions with them are what will make the product/service differential. This can build experiences with them and reinvigorate the ways of doing and presenting things. Taking advantage of this potential, the companies can rethink their websites and systems in order to accommodate it.

That is why research on this area endorses the importance of co-creation via customer participation. Social media platforms and company websites have encouraged the creation of user-generated content in this era of 'consumer sovereignty' (Yadav, Kamboj and Rahman, 2016). This is important for touristic activities and services which are designed based on user-generated content and experience. Today's consumer has become an active participant in the co-creation activities of companies, whether it is product or service development or their promotion. This case is evidence of a paradigm shift in power from companies to consumers. It also elucidates the role of digital/ social media in front-end innovation.

2.2 How is Portugal in the Digital Issue?

This section follows the first research question proposed - Q1: How is Portugal in terms of Internet of Things adoption (IoT) and digital transformation?. Before, it is useful to assess how the country is regarding the capture and mining of data from sources such as CRM, social networks and data analytics for digital purposes (figure 2).

Figure 2. Enterprises using software solutions for digital purposes
Source: Eurostat (2017)

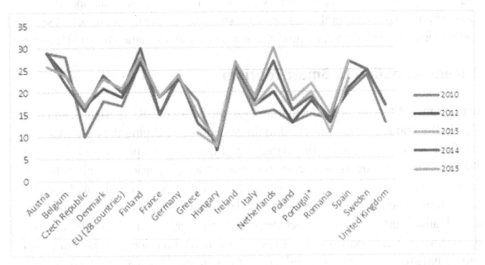

We can observe that in Portugal, from 2010 until 2015, the capture and mining of data through those tools has increased. However comparing it with Netherlands, Finland, Ireland and Germany, we see that much more can be done. According to data from the National Institute of Statistics (INE) in Portugal, 70% of companies have online presence, but more with a simple webpage than with a revolutionary digital platform. In this context, "companies are looking for more experts in this area", said Sofia Montalvo, head of Digital Marketing and e-Commerce at Michael Page (Freire, 2017). Michael Page points out that in 2017 there was an increase of 8% in the recruitment of professionals in digital marketing and of 12% in e-commerce, and that the growth in the coming years will be even greater.

In terms of technical aspects, professionals familiar with web technologies (26%), knowledge about new digital media (23%), domain of Html languages (20%) and email marketing (12%) are valued. In the case of soft skills in the digital area, analytical thinking (57%), high communication capacity (52%), creativity (52%), teamwork (50%), proactivity and passion (48%), trained critical opinion (44%), and previous experience in digital initiatives (26%) are valued. At the training level, companies especially value higher education in the areas of economics and management (36%), digital marketing (35%) and communication science (28%).

In Portugal, companies in most varied areas will need more digital skills. Professionals of the digital age are also global as new forms of work (remote, BYOD - bring your own device, co-working) are collaborative processes on a global scale, involving diverse cultures (Afonso, 2017). The processes are changing, what means a change in the business model too. IoT and cyber-physical systems are gaining space augmenting customization, scalability and real-time response. Imagine what this integration can do in several areas. As tourism is one of the most important sectors for the Portuguese economy, we further discuss this transformation for smart tourism.

3 Transformation to Smart Tourism

In tourism, IoT has the potential to transform the entire travel experience, and many hospitality companies are investing in this technology keeping the customer at the forefront. One of its areas is the marketing of destinations, products and services. Selling tourism products and services online is not only price-conscious but also an inspiration for travelers in the world. Search processes, mobile and location-based tools reach the potential traveler today within seconds. Another area is the organization's infrastructure, which determines the readiness to respond to customer requirements. Since more travelers expect personalized services, tourism businesses should have tools that can store and monitor information that meet customers' needs (Prajapati, 2014).

For instance, mobile keys were already introduced by some hoteliers. Guests no longer need to wait in line at the front desk; through a mobile app they are notified when their room is ready. Once at the room, guests simply wave their phone in front of the lock to open the door. Mobile keys increase guest satisfaction and the likelihood of a customer booking a room through the hotel's app. Each guest can then be monitored by room identity what allows hotels to collect data about their preferences in order to offer them a more customized experience during their next stay (Lubetkin, 2016). IoT also makes it possible to perform preventive maintenance remotely. Malfunctioning equipment can be detected and analyzed, long before it becomes a major issue. IoT is the infrastructure that connects physical and real objects to the internet. It has immense potential in the tourism industry. Table 1 resumes some examples:

Table 1. Internet of Things (IoT) as an enabler for tourism

Tourist tracking system	to coordinate transport as per the number of tourists
Personalization	suggestions based on tourist preferences (resulting in higher spends)
Less of the beaten path	explore more of what one likes
Deterring crime	by cameras and video analytics
Real time updates	about nearby points of interest, accommodation, eating options, weather, currency rates, etc.
Augmented reality	such as overlaying icons to explain precisely what a tourist is looking for
Targeted information	broadcast of useful information to smartphones through beacons

Source: Adapted from KSTDC (2017)

These technologies create a smart tourism setting, which supplies consumers with more relevant information, better decision support, greater mobility, and enjoyable experiences (Gretzel, 2011; Sigala and Chalkiti, 2014). These smart systems can include a wide range of technologies such as: decision support systems and the more recent context-aware systems, autonomous agents searching and mining web sources, ambient intelligence and augmented realities (Lamsfus, Wang, Alzua-Sorzabal and Xiang, 2015). In smart tourism, technology is seen as an infrastructure rather than individual information systems. It encompasses a variety of smart technologies that integrate hardware, software, apps and sensors in order to provide real-time awareness of the real world. It also provides advanced analytics to help people make more intelligent decisions about alternatives, as well as actions that optimize processes (Washburn, Sindhu, Balaouras, Dines, Hayes and Nelson, 2010).

Main impacts of this cutting-edge technology are: 1) provide tools to respond more accurately to the context around users, and 2) enable customers to become co-creators or co-innovators. Regarding the first, for example the SoCoMo (Social Context Mobile) conceptual model (Buhalis and Foerste, 2015) is a new framework that enables marketers to increase value for all stakeholders through mobile marketing. Regarding the second, customers now have enterprise-grade hardware in their pockets and their voice is amplified across the globe by social channels accessible by everyone. Customers provide insight into hidden problems, market opportunities, organic promotion, and innovation at scale. Companies cannot ignore the 'innovators' in their customer communities.

This means a significant shift involving changes to business models, organizational structure, information systems and culture (Menzies, 2016). Building a relationship with those innovative customers is critical for the co-creation process to fully grow. Once this relationship is built, they can be used as early product testers and promoters. Customers become regarded as co-producers of a service (and value co-creators), not just as simple instruments. When firms are capable of offering digital platforms for customers to participate in value creation, customer participation defines stronger path-dependent behavior connecting them with the firms. For example, tourists' involvement in the process of co-creating their trip increases their satisfaction, so they can remember the whole tourist experience (Shaw, Bailey and Williams, 2011). Another 'smart' application can be on the increasing engagement of tourists with the residents within community's activities of the destination.

The shift referred has to deal with the second research question of this work - Q2: Which impacts can this 'fourth' industry have, through its platforms and processes, in tourism and related services?

This change involves shifting from traditional enterprise architecture (EA) to digital architecture which addresses networked community capabilities (interacting with users and other stakeholders), globalization (borderless enterprise), product/ service innovation (open and virtual innovation), collaboration (employees in decision-making, mobile work), flexibility (to choose the technologies, infrastructure and applications). EA results should integrate with business planning and focus on business model architecture defining business outcome metrics. Also, EA program definition should not span for years, it should deliver business value in months or weeks.

Besides integration, mobile and cyber-physical interaction, another challenge to cope with is the context-awareness. In current systems, a wide variety of sensors are also used to acquire contextual information. Examples of sensors used are GPS (for location, speed), light and vision (to detect objects, activities), microphones (for data about noise, talking), gyroscopes (for movement, orientation), magnetic sensors (for compass to determine orientation), touch sensing (to detect user interaction), temperature sensors (to assess environments), etc. (Schmidt, 2013). Other sensors serve to detect the physiological context of the user, such as galvanic skin response. All these types of sensors available can be used to feed the enterprise systems or users with context information.

3.1 Industry 4 in Tourism

Despite industry is heavily sprayed in Portugal, it should follow emerging technological trends for greater innovation and for serving the growth of services. A relevant trend to consider is the widespread use of mobile cyber-physical platforms due to their ubiquity (concept of being everywhere at the same time). These attributes have to do with the critical role that time and place have in today's communications. Facing the increasing geographical scope and time-sensitiveness of services, their development is making the difference. One potential of these systems is the controlled execution of activities by creating processes that will resolve many problems related to the on-time delivery in the place requested. Ubiquitous systems provide mechanisms for selection and alignment of processes that meet the aspects of a context and accurately reflect its constant changes. This also leads to better and more adequate responses. This pervasive nature, related with the capacity of different integrated devices functioning together, has changed the way of developing products and processes.

Figure 3 shows a general case of a cyber-physical system which, from tourist's feedback in real time using the related mobile app, can collect relevant information about his/her integrated options. Then, a data analysis of the associated cloud database can quickly delineate either promotional or effective answers/actions. Also, based on the resulting indicators, several issues such as services required or claimed can be invoked. Other devices such as cameras, sensors, geolocation equipment, etc. (including real objects) can be involved.

Figure 3. A cyber-physical system prototype
Source: own elaboration

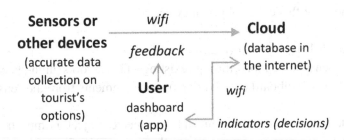

This has changed travel consumer behavior as always-connected travelers now use their mobile devices to find information and services, as well as make additional bookings during their trips (Euromonitor International, 2015). The shift of focus from 'time before trip' to 'time during trip' means, for travel companies, a change to their business models (incorporating mobile travel assistance).

Travel players will be increasingly able to suggest travelers the best things to do for them in the location they are visiting on the basis of their personal preferences, their exact location, and time of the day. Also, customers can change their choices quickly and give their feedback in real time from inter-related machines and objects. The use of travel mobile apps enhances the tourist-tourist relationship and, in turn, increases social capital (Kim and Kim, 2017). Several other apps can be used (imagined), connected for different purposes.

Smart apps and objects need a central system to create the interconnection between them. According to this goal the use of a specific system, as a IoT platform, is relevant (González García et al., 2017). The next cases are real examples of the considerable potential it can have.

3.1.1 The Case of Air Quality Management

Choosing the adequate IoT technologies and services can breathe new life into towns including the peripheries (Jara et al., 2015). This trend is related with the 'smart cities' that emerged as a significant transformation of cities to help in achieving sustainable development and smart growth. The main mission of a smart city is to optimize city functions and lead economic growth as well as improve quality of life for its residents using smart technology and data analysis (Khateeb, 2018).

Real-time communication enables to share value and increase social capital. Figure 4 shows a case of a cyber-physical system named AirQ, developed by SmartSense in Croatia. From tourists and residents' feedback in real time, using the related mobile app, the system can collect relevant information about air quality. Then, a data analysis of the associated cloud database can quickly delineate either preventive or corrective actions. Based on the resulting indicators, several issues can be managed.

Components of this cyber-physical system:

– sensors: for IoT deployment (firmware, software)
– coverage: open new locations, through existing LTE networks (high-speed wireless)
– real-time data: dashboard (quick relay of measurements from the sensors)

Data collection from the sensors and other connected objects is important to ensure that up-to-date information is available to the users of the SmartSense dashboard. Automatic decisions and actions can be triggered, depending on the data received. SmartSense have partnered with Deutsche Telekom, among other companies. They developed a NB-IoT prototyping program (GSMA, 2016a): NB-IoT (Narrowband IoT) is a low power wide area network radio technology standard to enable a wide range of cellular devices and services. It focuses specifically on indoor coverage, low cost, long battery life, and high connection density.

Figure 4. Cyber-physical system AirQ
Source: own elaboration

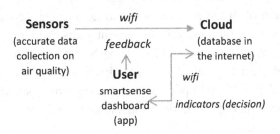

Cyber-physical system (AirQ, Croatia)
Prototyping

The AirQ sensor, with the right power and coverage, can be positioned in locations previously inaccessible. New sensors can be developed as a result, meaning that additional areas such as indoors can be monitored. These can monitor the full range of pollutants and sensors deployed to collect additional information such as weather conditions, which affect the air quality. This means that data collected is more accurate and complete. Customer experience is improved, and the costs of maintenance and installation are reduced. In result, a number of new use cases and business opportunities can arise with the data obtained from this system. The data will not only contribute to generate direct revenue for exceeding air quality levels, but also indirect results when automatic actions can be triggered. For example, traffic management systems can be controlled to ease pollution for a better user experience.

3.1.2 The Case of Crowd Management

Several other cases and projects can be developed, with impacts in tourism business. For example, mobile operators are now particularly well placed to provide tools that can be used for crowd management. Smart objects can be used and connected to cope with this issue (González García et al., 2017). A smart object allows enhancing the interaction with people and objects. These can be connected products, assets or things embedded with processors, sensors, software and connectivity that allow data to be exchanged.

City planners and service providers are realizing that urban challenges can be overcome by using smart connected services (SC, 2019). This is being felt across multiple sectors. Mobile operators are now particularly well placed to provide tools that can be used for crowd management, an increasing challenge in today's world. Tracking the location of mobile phones and analyzing data collected by mobile-enabled Internet of Things (IoT) sensors provides an accurate way to monitor and manage crowds of people across all sorts of gatherings.

With the growth of urban populations, and new threats, crowd control has a greater importance for cities and towns in recent years. New solutions to an ever-more urgent problem are being sought (figure 5). Smart crowd monitoring, defined as the use of intelligent technologies and tactics in controlling large crowds, has been discussed (SC, 2019). An important feature it captures is situational awareness, which relies on the ability to see, understand and analyze the world around us in the context of what we are doing.

Figure 5. Techno-social framework for crowd management
Source: Martella et al. (2017)

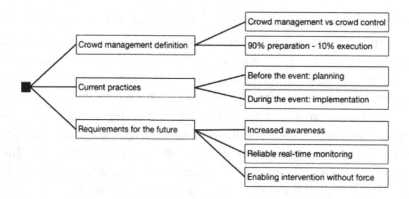

However, some issues about these cases must be safeguarded, especially citizen privacy and security and governments' coordination with national authorities and private sectors. Other issue is that effective use of large amounts of data smart cities involve demands extensive wireless coverage and fast transfer speed (to be enhanced by 5G coverage).

Developing and maintaining smart cities require high investments, whose effectiveness depends on the collaboration of private and public resources on local, state and national levels (Finextra, 2019). Reluctance of government agencies and private organizations in sharing data or resources can avoid meaningful collaboration and affect smart city development.

4. CONCLUSION

In Portugal, the companies (mostly small and medium-sized) invest little in R&D (research and development) due to their limited financial and organizational capacity. Private customers are important sources, what means that Portuguese firms use customers' information and relations for innovation purposes. These results are in line with the fact that Portuguese firms (SME) increasingly focus on services. Customers' data allow expand the knowledge base within their applied research and then materialize knowledge into goods/services (Sánchez-González and Herrera, 2014). A major challenge is keeping the same patterns when interacting with more customers and stakeholders. Specially when putting machines in interaction with each other and then with users, what is producing the systems of fourth industry.

This overwhelming potential requires more flexible process architectures in companies. The main goal is to manage knowledge and adherence to new business models supported by mobile, cloud, big-data or IoT systems. User interface design and mobile connectivity are showing that boundaries between the enterprise and its surroundings are softening. Thus, greater flexibility is essential to get more differentiating outcomes (Nolle, 2016). Recent discussions about bridging the physical and digital (around smart tourism, smart cities, etc.) have touched these aspects (European Commission, 2016).

This will require investment in human capital development and in research linked to digitalization for developing digitally-enabled services and systems. In tourism, this is important due to new sustainability challenges, such as the pressure on resources and local communities, economic uncertainty, and the influence of climate and other changes (Necstour, 2019). These new technologies, as analyzed through the cases presented, will help destinations in predicting service demand and manage slow or over-tourism. However, security and privacy, data scalability, complexity and governance still have strong driving power and so are key challenges to be addressed in sustainable cities' projects (Finextra, 2019). IoT adoption and implementation should therefore focus on breaking down complexity in manageable parts, supported by a governance structure. Smart cities can share a common smart city platform, what is relevant for small cities and towns. The cloud-based nature of IoT is appropriate for smart cities by sharing a platform based on open data. Small cities can then form a common urban ecosystem. In this way, solutions are networked and controlled via the central cloud platform. Thus, the size of a city is not an obstacle on the way to becoming smart.

ACKNOWLEDGMENT

This research was funded by National Funds provided by FCT- Foundation for Science and Technology through project UIDB/04020/2020.

REFERENCES

Afonso, C. (2017). *Competências de marketing digital: O que procura o mercado?* http://carolina-afonso.net/competencias-de-marketing-digital-o-que-procura-o-mercado-human-resources/

Alarcão, M., & Silva, S. (2013). *3.0: A evolução do paradigma do marketing.* https://www.hipersuper.pt/2013/12/18/3-0-a-evolucao-do-paradigma-do-marketing-por-susana-costa-e-silva-catolica-porto/

Buhalis, D., & Foerste, M. (2015). SoCoMo marketing for travel and tourism: Empowering co-creation of value. *Journal of Destination Marketing & Management, 4*(3), 151–161. doi:10.1016/j.jdmm.2015.04.001

El Khateeb, S. (2018). IoT architecture a gateway for smart cities in Arab world. *15th Learning and Technology Conference (L&T),* 153–160. 10.1109/LT.2018.8368500

Euromonitor International. (2015). *From the online to the mobile travel era.* http://www.euromonitor.com/from-the-online-to-the-mobile-travel-era/report

European Commission. (2016). *Smart regions conference.* https://ec.europa.eu/regional_policy/en/conferences/smart-regions/

European Commission. (2017). *The digital economy and society index (DESI).* https://ec.europa.eu/digital-single-market/en/desi

Finextra. (2019). *What is the role of IoT in Smart Cities?* https://www.finextra.com/blogposting/17931/what-is-the-role-of-iot-in-smart-cities

Freire, M. (2017). *Especialistas em digital marketing e data analytics são das profissões mais procuradas pelas empresas.* https://www.bit.pt/especialistas-em-digital-marketing-e-data-analytics-sao-as-profissoes-que-as-empresas-mais-procuram/?inf_by=59cba655671db80f3d8b46cb

Gomes, M., & Kury, G. (2013). *A evolução do marketing para o marketing 3.0: O marketing de causa.* XV Congresso de Ciências da Comunicação na Região Nordeste. Intercom - Sociedade Brasileira de Estudos Interdisciplinares da Comunicação, Mossoró, Brasil.

González García, C., Meana-Llorián, D., Pelayo G-Bustelo, C., & Cueva-Lovelle, J. M. (2017). A review about Smart Objects, Sensors, and Actuators. *International Journal of Interactive Multimedia and Artificial Intelligence, 4*(3), 7–10. doi:10.9781/ijimai.2017.431

Gretzel, U. (2011). Intelligent systems in tourism: A social science perspective. *Annals of Tourism Research, 38*(3), 757–779. doi:10.1016/j.annals.2011.04.014

GSMA. (2016a). *AirQ Internet of Things Case Study*. https://www.gsma.com/iot/airq-internet-things-case-study/

GSMA. (2016b). *Smart Cities Guide: Crowd Management*. https://www.gsma.com/iot/gsma-smart-cities-guide-crowd-management/

Jafari, J. (2019). Closing gaps in tourism intelligence for creative destination development. Creatour Conference, UAlg, Faro.

Jara, A. J., Sun, Y., Song, H., Bie, R., Genooud, D., & Bocchi, Y. (2015). Internet of Things for Cultural Heritage of Smart Cities and Smart Regions. *IEEE 29th International Conference on Advanced Information Networking and Applications Workshops*, 668-675. 10.1109/WAINA.2015.169

Kim, D., & Kim, S. (2017). The role of mobile technology in tourism: Patents, articles, news, and mobile tour app reviews. *Sustainability, 9*(11), 1–45. doi:10.3390u9112082

Kotler, P., Kartajaya, H., & Setiawan, I. (2015). *Marketing 3.0 - Do produto e do consumidor até ao espírito humano*. Actual Editora.

Lamsfus, C., Wang, D., Alzua-Sorzabal, A., & Xiang, Z. (2015). Going mobile: Defining context for on-the-go travelers. *Journal of Travel Research, 54*(6), 691–701. doi:10.1177/0047287514538839

Lubetkin, M. (2016). *Tourism and the internet of things- IoT*. https://medium.com/3baysover-tourism-networking/tourism-and-the-internet-of-things-iot-e41b125e7ddd#.3prmu1rb8

Martella, C., Li, J., Conrado, C., & Vermeeren, A. (2017). On current crowd management practices and the need for increased situation awareness, prediction, and intervention. *Safety Science, 91*, 381–393. doi:10.1016/j.ssci.2016.09.006

Menzies, A. (2016). *Co-creation for successful customer engagement*. https://www.summa.com/blog/successful-customer-engagement-with-co-creation

Necstour. (2019). *Roadmap 2019-2021: The 5 "S" of the tourism of tomorrow.* http://www.necstour.eu/system/files/NECSTouR%20Roadmap%202019-2021%20 -Tourism%20of%20Tomorrow

Nolle, T. (2016). *Enterprise architecture model helps to maximize mobile empowerment.* http://searchsoa.techtarget.com/tip/Enterprise-architecture-model- helps-to-maximize-mobile-empowerment?utm_medium=EM&asrc=EM_ NLN_65809390&utm_campaign=20161007_Enterprise%20architecture%20 holds%20the%20secret%20to%20mobile_fchurchville&utm_ source=NLN&track=NL-1806&ad=910397&src=910397

OECD. (2018). *OECD tourism trends and policies.* OECD Publishing. doi:10.1787/ tour-2018-

Palos-Sanchez, P., Saura, J., Reyes-Menendez, A., & Esquivel, I. (2018). Users acceptance of location-based marketing apps in tourism sector: An exploratory analysis. *Journal of Spatial and Organizational Dynamics, 6*(3), 258–270.

Peeters, P., Gössling, S., Klijs, J., Milano, C., Novelli, M., Dijkmans, C., Eijgelaar, E., Hartman, S., Heslinga, J., Isaac, R., Mitas, O., Moretti, S., Nawijn, J., Papp, B., & Postma, A. (2018). *Research for TRAN Committee - Overtourism: impact and possible policy responses.* Policy Department for Structural and Cohesion Policies. https://www.europarl.europa.eu/RegData/etudes/STUD/2018/629184/ IPOL_STU(2018)629184_EN.pdf

Pinto, I., & Castro, C. (2019). Online travel agencies: Factors influencing tourist purchase decision. *Tourism & Management Studies, 15*(2), 7–20. doi:10.18089/ tms.2019.150201

Prajapati, V. (2014). *Mobile technology advancements speed up the growth of tourism worldwide.* https://www.techprevue.com/mobile-technology-advancements-speed- up-the-growth-of-tourism/

Sánchez-González, G., & Herrera, L. (2014). Effects of customer cooperation on knowledge generation activities and innovation results of firms. *Business Research Quarterly, 17*(4), 292–302. doi:10.1016/j.brq.2013.11.002

SC. (2019). *The GSMA smart cities guide: Crowd management.* https://www. thesmartcityjournal.com/en/news/1301-gsma-smart-cities-guide-crowd- management

Schmidt. (2013). *Context-aware computing*. https://www.interaction-design.org/literature/book/the-encyclopedia-of-human-computer-interaction-2nd-ed/context-aware-computing-context-awareness-context-aware-user-interfaces-and-implicit-interaction

Shaw, G., Bailey, A., & Williams, A. (2011). Aspects of service-dominant logic and its implications for tourism management: Examples from the hotel industry. *Tourism Management, 32*(2), 207–214. doi:10.1016/j.tourman.2010.05.020

Sigala, M., & Chalkiti, K. (2014). Investigating the exploitation of web 2.0 for knowledge management in the Greek tourism industry: An utilisation–importance analysis. *Computers in Human Behavior, 30*, 800–812. doi:10.1016/j.chb.2013.05.032

Washburn, D., Sindhu, U., Balaouras, S., Dines, R. A., Hayes, N., & Nelson, L. (2010). *Helping CIOs understand 'smart city' initiatives*. http://www.uwforum.org/upload/board/forrester_help_cios_smart_city.pdf

Yadav, M., Kamboj, S., & Rahman, Z. (2016). Customer co-creation through social media: The case of 'Crash the Pepsi IPL 2015'. *Journal of Direct, Data and Digital Marketing Practice, 17*(4), 259–271. doi:10.1057/dddmp.2016.4

Chapter 4
An Extensive Survey of Privacy in the Internet of Things

Jayashree K.
Rajalakshmi Engineering College, India

Babu R.
Rajalakshmi Engineering College, India

ABSTRACT

The internet of things comprises billions of devices, people, and services and entitles each to connect through sensor devices. These sensor devices influence the real world by administering critical network infrastructure and sometimes may collect sensitive private information about individuals. Managing this data authentication of who can access the device data and under what circumstances it can be found and used by others is one of the major threats for consumers and businesses. So, the internet of things services deliver new privacy challenges in our day-to-day lives. Though information systems discipline addressed research in privacy to a great extent, there still prevails no robust approach for the inspection of privacy breaches in the internet of things services. This chapter provides a detailed view on the privacy concerns in various aspects and scrutinizes the challenges to be addressed to ensure that the internet of things becomes true in near future.

1. INTRODUCTION

The Internet of Things (IoT) is an interconnected network that consists of infinite number of resources like sensors and devices that are connected and it provides the value-added-services through the communications infrastructure. The IoT provides

DOI: 10.4018/978-1-7998-6463-9.ch004

facility in such a way that it connects people and things whenever required from anyplace, with any device, by anyone at any time, through any network or service (Perera et al., 2013). The World of the IoT comprises an enormous variation of devices like smart phones, personal computers, PDAs, laptops, tablets, and other hand-held embedded devices (Razzaq et al., 2017). Radio Frequency Identification (RFID) technology allows microchips for communicating the identification information of the user through wireless communication. RFID readers are attached with RFID tags that help the users in recognizing, tracing and monitoring any objects easily. This is achieved with the help of RFID tags that are attached to RFID readers (Jia et al., 2012). Wireless Sensor Networks (WSNs), is another technology for IoT that uses several intelligent sensors that are linked together, which helps in sensing and for monitoring (Xu et al., 2014). In the recent advancement of RFID, with web technologies and the low-cost wireless sensors, the IoT has become a major field in connecting the various resources or objects with the internet and communicating as an interface between the machine-to-machine and machine-to-human in the real world. In addition, various technologies, methods, techniques and devices namely barcodes, smart phones, social networks, and cloud computing are combined along with the IoT to form a huge network for supporting the IoT applications.(Wang et al., 2014, Li et al., 2013).

The IoT is used in various real-time applications and one of the major application is in monitoring the patients in hospitals and old age homes (Harini et al., 2017). Though it is more fascinating with the powerful and promising applications, lot of issues will arise. Five key IoT issue areas are considered to discuss, some of the most important problems and queries concerned to the technologies and methodologies. The challenges or issues include security and privacy; interoperability and standards, legal, regulatory and rights, as well as emerging economies and its development. Out of these challenges the most important is making users to follow the privacy rules that are framed inorder to protect privacy. (Wu & Shao, 2011, Gessner et al., 2012, Oleshchuk 2009)

The users communicate or transfer information's through internet or through wireless means, all the actions behavior and management of data in certain real time applications are traced, which becomes a major concern in terms of privacy policy. In several real time applications the data are exchanged between several resources like sensors or other devices and with users even without consideration of owners. Emergent of new technologies may increase this problem. Usage of new technologies alone do not pose the major problem but the way how the users, organizations and government use the application also plays a major role (Solove, 2006).

The remainder of this article is organized as follows: Section 2 presents the characteristic of the IoT, Section 3 reviews privacy concerns. This is followed by a thorough analysis of the IoT privacy challenges in Section 4. In Section 5, Certain privacy questions has been discussed and we present the recommended solutions for the challenges in privacy in section 6. Privacy enhancing Technologies has been presented in Section 7 and section 8 gives the conclusion.

2. CHARACTERISTICS OF THE IOT

The essential characteristics of the IoT objects and the IoT applications (Lee & Kim, 2010).

Computerization: Computerization otherwise called as digitalization or automation plays a very major role in all the IoT devices used in any real time application. The steps followed in automation includes automatic data collection, monitoring, processing, decision making and combining different IoT devices has to be reinforced in any IoT framework.

Heterogeneity (Patel & Patel, 2016): Depending upon the varied hardware platforms and networks, devices have heterogeneous nature in the IoT. These have the ability to interact with the other devices as well as service platforms with the help of various networks.

Dynamicity: Dynamic changes keep taking place in the state of the devices. Based on the environment the IoT applications should be able to readily identify and adapt to the devices used. Thus, it is very critical for the unified IoT architecture as there are across different environment and the applications in the dynamic management and integration of the objects.

Penetration: Penetration are invoked by the word intelligence, which includes the intelligence into the devices and enable them to work efficiently. Context awareness and physical intermediation condition for operating the data are the two major features that has to be considered in intelligent system.

Enormous scale (Wangi et al., 2008): Even though large number of devices are connected with each other through internet, the total number of devices used will be very huge, which has to be managed and has to communicate with each other. Managing the data produced and interpreting them for the application purposes is highly critical. This is related to the semantics of data and efficiency in handling data.

Safety: It is important to take into account safety measures in the IoT. Being both the makers and beneficiaries of the IoT, it is necessary to design for safety. This comprises the security of our personal data as well as the security of our physical well-being. Creation of a security model that is scalable, is required in order to secure the endpoints, the networks and also to move data across all of these.

Connectivity (Sarkar et al., 2014): Network availability and compatibility is enabled by connectivity. Accessibility means to get on a network while compatibility offers the common facility to use as well as produce data.

Inter-connectivity: The global information and communication infrastructure can be interconnected anywhere with concern to the IoT

3. PRIVACY

Privacy policy includes four standard features like body, communications, territory and information transfer which was actually framed by Privacy International. Privacy related to body mainly focuses on physical protection of users in terms of exterior damage. Privacy related to communication deals with reinforcing of the data that is transferred between the organizations, in which the data includes email and telephone calls. Privacy related to territory involves the limitations on physical surroundings like houses, workplace, and malls or any other public spaces. Privacy related to information includes personal data like medical examination results and credit card information's that is gathered and processed by an organization (Stefanick, 2011). According to (Ziegeldorf et al., 2014) seizures description of privacy should be in such a way that the users should be allowed to self-determinate the information to evaluate their own risks in privacy and also identify the way to overcome the issues in-order to maintain their privacy rules and has to be assured that it is cannot be manipulated beyond their direct control space.

3.1. Privacy of End-Users

The intruders or hackers will be interested in confidential data which are the data that are collected or transferred between the IoT devices. Location privacy is about guaranteeing that the privacy of the physical location of the user is preserved. Specifically, about the location privacy (Ziegeldorf et al., 2014), additional data like sensed data as well as meta data that are related to it are also supposed to be confidential (Christin et al., 2011), meta-data information's like location fixes, time stamps gathered by Global Positioning System (GPS), wireless networks, or Near Field Communication tags are taken into consideration when comes to privacy. Hence, customers should not confess the data gathered by any of the IoT devices to any third parties. Outsourcing information onto virtual environment or cloud will further increase the concern for privacy. There is recognized loss of control over data when it is outsourced to the virtual environment is the major interest of the end-users.

3.2 Privacy of Service Providers

Like end-user's privacy concerns, researchers equally give importance on privacy topic relevant for service providers. Privacy for services providers faces serious undesired challenges that range from complete non-acceptance of their service to extremely costly lawsuits (Pearson, 2009). When the functionality of services are outsourced to virtual space or cloud it becomes specifically important (Henze et al., 2013).

3.3 Privacy in Device

Various devices are used for collection of information in several real time applications. One notable example is applications used in medical field. Medical applications use numerous numbers of devices for serving patients in terms of providing personalized drugs, as well as health care applications are being used widely by people, which depends on continual fine-grained data collection from the devices, in which the human body plays a vital role for collection of data. The data obtained from users are actually gathered from the devices and are stored in cloud infrastructure or is transferred to other devices like mobile phones which sends the information to other people. The data obtained contains all the information including metadata like location, time and surroundings which is helpful in collecting personal behavior of the individuals. Since the data are transferred from one entity to other, all the individuals who use the application should follow certain privacy rules as well as follow certain mechanism and use tools depending on the type of application, to safeguard their data (Bertino, 2016).

Integrity plays a role in terms of privacy which means that a device is free from malware in the scope of devices and this property has also been called 'admissibility' (Schneier, 2006). In Trusted Platform Computing and in high sensitive, it has an issue called as the ensuring admissibility. The Communication part is handled by the authenticity of a device and they are seen as connection end point. Access should not be provided to any of third party users on the devices in-order to attain the integrity of the device. This is normally guaranteed when device integrity comes into use in-terms of privacy. Device integrity and reliability are dependable on the devices available, and connecting the device is dependable on the communication available. The illegal utilization or operation of hardware and software in these devices are disclosed in the private data (Borgohain et al., 2015).

3.4. Privacy During Communication

Privacy in communication can be achieved by encryption. Encrypting thee data will help to achieve confidentiality when the data is being transmitted (Kumar & Patel, 2014). Depending on the situation encryption adds data to packets which gives way to track the data, which may be exploited for linking packets to identify the traffic flow. To overcome this approach named Secure Communication Protocol can be used (Giannikos et al., 2013). At the time of communication data can be replaced or encrypted, to avoid the intruders know about the device or users identity, which in turn will reduce vulnerability. Most common example is Temporary Mobile Subscriber Identity [TMSI] (Polonetsky & Wolf, 2012). In TMSI devices communicate with one another only if there is a need for it, to lessen the privacy leaks occurs during communication. In certain applications like in 3GPP machine used for communication detaches the ideal devices from the network, in order to prevent unwanted collection of location information.

3.5 Privacy in Storage

Privacy is a critical factor when it comes to storage. The data and the file, safety measures are signed up by the consumers and they trust their businesses. The data is essentially utilized for actuation and smart monitoring and must be stored safely and the important automatic decision making, and the sense of the data collected by the methods like Artificial Intelligence or Novel fusion. The real identity of the consumer should not be disclosed, and the user's sensitive data must be secured adequately by the storage mechanisms.

3.6 Privacy in Processing

Privacy in processing the data for providing high level quality services to the users is based on privacy on devices and privacy on communication. It is also based on proper designing and implementation of algorithms which are needed for processing of data. Processing is often followed by the actions of actuator, but in certain cases there are several changes for the actuator to get inconsistent and incorrect outputs.

The authenticity of the processing the data is based on two major characteristics, one is authenticity of device and the other is authenticity of the communication which by itself is not sensitive in processing the data (Ivor et al., 2014). Hence the level of confidentiality in processing the data is mainly based on integrity of the devices, whereas in disturbed processing, it depends on the levels of integrity of communication.

3.7 Privacy in Localization and Tracking

Communication integrity includes two integrity features like localization and tracking (Mayer, 2009). In addition to its integrity applies even on reference signals such as GSM or GPS cell, used in localization need to be confirmed. Concealment in localization deals with hiding the identity of an individual to the intruders or attackers and without the explicit agreement or knowledge, the localization and tracking is not possible.

3.8 Privacy in Profiling

The possibility of comprising information summary about consumer to infer significance by inter relating with other profiles and data are the things that are denoted by profiling. Based on customer interests and demographics the profiling procedures are commonly used for the in-house development. In addition to it, collecting and distributing the user profiles to or information to others is commonly recognized as a privacy breach (Menn, 2012).

3.9 Privacy at Work

It equally provides challenges by surpassing the current employment law, control over our daily lives and a convenient future are the things that are assured by the IoT. The Employer's deficit clear knowledge on how to manage privacy concerns with the IoT. The efficiency to locate employees does not end when an employee goes on a break or for lunch or heads to home for the day, because of the advancement in the IoT. Even after the work place, the employers are conscious about the data collection. The necessity to precisely document privacy policies of encircling devices that are locatable or constantly record data are all must be considered by the employees (Camenisch et al, 2005).

3.10 Privacy in the Cloud Computing Layer

The things such as the ubiquitous, on-demand network access to share computing resources that can be provisioned with minimal management effort or service provider interaction (Behl & Behl, 2012) are present in them are referred as the cloud computing. Cloud providers have to maintain and control the privacy at operating system, data storage and applications hosted on the Virtual Machines in the Infrastructure-as-a-Service layer. Even from the cloud provider the private information must be hidden.

4. PRIVACY CHALLENGES IN THE IoT

The flawless amount of data that the IoT devices can yield is overwhelming. Businesses or hackers can accurately make use of a connected device to significantly assault a person's home. The risk comprises the gathering of intimate personal data, such as financial account numbers, health information, and geo location and risks already faced by conventional internet and e-commerce. These problems could put a predicament on customer's interest to buy connected devices, which in turn would forbid the IoT from accomplishing its true potential. Gupta et al., (2020) have discussed open research challenges for improving security and privacy in smart farming ecosystem. Research Challenges include Access Control, Trust and Privacy Perspective, Data Perspective, Network Perspective and Compliance and Supply Chain Perspective. Neeraj & Singh (2014) has discussed about two major issues in the area of user's privacy like how to protect user's personal information as well as how to have control over user's location and movement. To maintain privacy there is a need to improve the techniques, mechanism and also frame new privacy rules, standards that could support new tools and methods to identify and manage users and devices used in the application.

4.1 User Consent Acquisition

The most specific aim of the IoT is to rend sufficient amount of permissions from the people who are both users and non-users of the IoT. These non-users may be the people who are influenced by the services rendered in the IoT. In the early web design method, the permission acquiring technique was done by writing the policies terms and conditions in long text formats. At present the techniques used are not very effective because they do not provide full information to the user in acquiring consent. It needs to be very effective and efficient in providing detailed information to the user's consent acquisition decision.

4.2 Context Based Privacy

The IoT antedates an upgraded relevance of the awareness of context (Mehra, 2012) advanced desires to aid or help the instrumentation and combination of different services like for example, envisioned by the doing it Yourself (DiY), socio cultural practice, manageability, scalability and usability.

4.3 Control Customization

The IoT must provide services to the people who own the data where these owners can move the data to and fro and switch from one service provider to another. Existing services does not provide this flexibility, as it has certain limitations. The new service must enable the user to select both the hardware and software components (Brush, 2013). The user must also be able to select the appropriate business person from whom the software has been rented to create a highly efficient environment.

4.4 Promise and Reality

The major goal of the IoT is to render sufficient amount of functionalities to the user. The user data is collected and processed by the providers to gain knowledge. The service providers must seek permission from the user to approve them for collecting data.

4.5 Data Correlation and Information Retrieval

The IoT gives out data in dissimilar settings. Compilation of this data might aggravate innovative categories of security mechanisms that confess the implementation of more intricate security policies (Zaslavsky et al., 2012). Production of more intricate and expressive user profiles is possible through the ability to access this enormous collection of data. At present, there is no much clarity in the security mechanisms found while collecting variety of data from users and devices, the data collected will be influenced by their privacy rules or by any methods or algorithms that may simplify or reduce the drawbacks.

4.6 Anonymity Technology

Media Access Control (MAC) addresses are used in network communication by means of an interface (Sundmaeker, 2010). Merging many devices MAC addresses will create different finger prints and unique profile where a logical reasoning can also be used to infer knowledge. But, the problem is that the location of the user can be tracked.

4.7 Physical Availability of Devices

The IoT standard indicates the connection of various microscopic sensor and/or actuator devices that have to be placed in the environment which means, that the devices or resources will be available readily in the environment that would be used in a number of ways by malicious users, who will tamper the reliability and integrity of an IoT system (Radomirovic, 2010). Tampering is very difficult to discover as well as verify if they are working fine, due to the huge number of devices and also their reduced capabilities. This hazard is linked to the trouble in understanding whether the device executes in the right context, if it was liable to firmware replacement, mimicked and so on.

4.8 Data Eaves Dropping and Data Confidentiality

Health records of patients are not exposed to everyone and these records are meant to be highly personal and these are either noticeable or given only to the personnel who is responsible of to take care of the patients. It is necessary to keep all the records highly secure, so that they don't get lost while being transmitted over a wireless link. In this fashion, burglary of data that is private, without the consent of the owner, is sure to cause harm to the physically challenged by intruding in their privacy.

4.9 Conflicting Market Interest

The ability of the IoT to collect and inter relate data from different sources, is the most useful feature of it when it comes to business. This helps in improving the competitive market of producers. The principal focus is to recognize and relate diverse data sets so that it will be able to improvise the way to advertise the product through advertisements to the customers in-order to satisfy their needs or requirements in a better way. Due to correlation the current methodologies create a tension, leading to low positioning of the technologies that enable privacy (Radomirovic et al., 2012, Cave et al., 2011).

4.10 Increase the Power Imbalance Between Consumers and Companies

The in-discreetness of smart devices and the way the sensitive data are collected stored or transferred, The IoT has the capability to intensify the disproportion of power between the customers and the organizations with which they run business. Basically in e-commerce scenarios the business to consumer relationship is commonly one-sided. In most cases the companies possess the authority to modify the contracts at their own interest. These "take it or leave it" provision means the consumers are comparatively dis-empowered and do not have meaningful choice. The IoT can also advance the equivalent power of companies through the provision of additional information about customers. Through the proficient utilization of this information, the powerful companies tend to take important decisions (Schneier, 2012). This encourages the companies to use their power over users by violating privacy and security of user's personal data and information by reporting. Instead of instigating or encouraging behavioral change, reporting has the tendency to be status-based, which is, placing the consumers on to significant categories, making it difficult for them to escape (Potoczny-Jones, 2015).

Ramirez (2014) has described about certain challenges related to privacy and data protection related to the IoT. The challenges includes lack of control and information asymmetry, quality of user´s consent, conclusions derived from data and repurposing of original processing and intrusive identification of behavior patterns and profiling.

5. PRIVACY QUESTIONS

Scott has described certain privacy questions (Rose et al., 2015)

5.1 Fairness in Data Collection and Use

Based on how the data is collected certain questions like what are the ways that has to be followed to establish market space relationship between data collectors and data sources in terms of the IoT. Personal data given by the user while using the application is worthy and has a value in both personal and in commercial space, which will be valued in a different way by data collectors and data sources, either separately or by aggregating based on their interests that may be different. In such case, the question is how one can reveal those unique interests, so that it can lead to fair and stable rules for sources as well as the collectors relating to access, control, transparency, and protection?

5.2 Transparency, Expression, and Enforcement of Privacy Preferences

In the context of the IoT, how can the privacy practices and policies be made available readily as well as made understandable? Is there any other alternatives for existing notice and consent privacy policy that will discuss the various aspects on the IoT? The next question is which model will be an effective one to state, apply and to impose ones privacy and multiparty preferences. Is it possible to construct such a multiparty model, and if so, what would it look like? How will it be applied to explicit situations that include privacy preference of individual, how will the privacy settings to commercial services be handled, is there any market for subcontracting so that the users options are put into effect. Is there any privacy servers that would manipulate and apply user's preferences among various devices in an array, as well as eliminate the need for one-to-one communication?

5.3 Wide-Ranging Privacy Expectations

Based on the background of the users, norms and needs of the users will be different among different groups, states, country or nation. Most of the IoT set-ups include distribution of devices and collecting of data with global space that goes beyond social and cultural boundary or margins. The question is what is the use of this for the advancement of a traditionally used model for privacy protection in the IoT? How can we identify and honor the privacy expectations of users and various laws through adaption of the IoT devices and systems?

5.4 Privacy by Design

How can the manufacturers of the IoT devices be motivated to give importance on principles framed on privacy design. What is the way to substitute the addition to consumer privacy contemplation's in every stage of development and operation of product? What are the ways to combine functionality and privacy necessities? By principle, manufacturers need to assume that products and practices that respect privacy, build long-term customer trust, gratification, as well as brand loyalty. Compared to the challenging needs for achieving simplicity in design and speed to market, is that an adequate compelling motivation? Is it necessary to design devices with default settings constructed to suite the highly conventional data collection mode?

5.5 Identification

How the data gathered by the IoT should be protected, when it doesn't appear personal at the time of collection, but turns out to be personal data.

6. PRIVACY SOLUTIONS

Privacy is a serious concern and vendors must respect their customers enough to understand that privacy is a legitimate human need. There are few issues which has to be taken into consideration to enforce privacy policies which include Informed Consent, Control over Privacy Settings, Vendor Regulation, Access to User Data and Opt-Out, Ongoing Reputation Access, and User Identification and Authentication. Several approaches have been proposed to deal with the privacy concerns of both end users and that of service providers (Wang et al., 2016).

6.1 Information Manipulation by Cryptography

Among the various privacy preserving schemes proposed so far by the researchers, cryptography is still the prominent and widely used technique for preserving privacy. In real time, various types of sensors will not be able to provide adequate security protocols due to shortage of sufficient capacity for storage and resources for computation. So, cryptography might be used to ensure privacy of information (Feng & Fu, 2010).

6.2 Flexible Privacy Control Interface

A user-friendly design that consolidates personal data relationships and context to end-users must be framed. Understanding these associations will lead to meaningful approval, and setting up user privacy policies. These policies will serve as input to the authentication systems (Aleisa & Renaud 2017).

6.3 Context Awareness

Users of smart devices like smart phones, smart televisions, health monitors, and wearable fitness devices are given awareness before they use the device, that their personal data will be collected. In such a way that individual applications are focused as a solution for privacy intimacy.

6.4 Access Control

An alternate to encryption and awareness about privacy to users is access control. It makes users to have control over their own data which they give while using the application.

6.5 Data Minimization

The concept of data minimization is to gather personal information to something that is immediately connected has to be limited by the service providers of the IoT. Also, they are supposed to retain the data only until it is required to fulfil the services provided by the technology.

In (Evans & Eyers, 2011) a managing privacy on the IoT through data tagging has been described. Techniques followed in information flow control process can be used to integrate data which represent network events with various properties related to Privacy, hence tagging the data helps the system to protect privacy of individuals and give purpose to the flow of data. In (Cao et al., 2011) the authors have discussed about a cluster based scheme which is known as CASTLE a Continuously Anonymizing Streaming data Through Adaptive Clustering. This clustering scheme guarantees anonymity, freshness of data and delay constraints on streams of data which in turn enhances privacy preserving mechanisms like k-anonymity. As k-anonymity is intended to be used only on static data sets and will not be supported for continuous, refrained and temporary data set. In (Yang & Fang 2011), there are two categories of traditional privacy mechanisms one is discretionary access, where minimal privacy risks are considered to prevent the exposure and duplication of sensitive data. The other mechanism is limited access which restricts the security access, which in-turn strives to avoid malicious illegal attacks. In (Wang & Wen, 2011) authors have discussed about risk in privacy that occurs when the domain name which is static is assigned to a specific IoT node. The researchers have proposed a Domain Name System (DNS), which improves the privacy protection mechanism on smart devices, which provides authentication process to find the original user, which helps to prevent illegal access of smart devices. This scheme is suitable when DNS and Domain Name System Security Extensions protocols are used. Peng et al., (2014) have discussed about two authentication protocols which change the keys mutually, for systems like RFID and for WSN. This protocol reduces the risks of replay, replication and denial of service, spoofing and tag tracking by assimilating the random number generator found in the tag and the reader, then implementation is done through one way hash function. The various requirements to maintain privacy in data in discussed in (Sicari et al., 2014), which describes a layered architectural model for the IoT as to maintain both quality, security and privacy level of data.

Preserving User Privacy in the IoT Domain.

Since the IoT collect, manipulate, communicate and store huge amount of data from various devices, there is a need for privacy prevention. (Celdran et al., 2014) has discussed about context awareness policy framework to preserve user privacy in the IoT. Researcher (Huang et al., 2012) has discussed a user interactive privacy preserved access control methodology and also has designed a content awareness privacy policy k-anonymity and filter. By this mechanism and design user can have control over their personal data that is collected while using the application.

Device Manufacturers (Perera et al., 2014):

Privacy preserving techniques have to be introduced into their devices by the device manufacturers. Precisely, at the firmware level the certain characteristics like storage security, deletion of data, and have to be implemented by the manufactures.

IoT Cloud Services and Platform Providers:

Cloud based services are provided in IoT to provide advanced analysis on data support for local software platforms. Users should be able to delete and move the data form one provider to another only by using common set of interfaces and data formats.

Third Party Application Developers:

Application developers are responsible for authenticating the applications for ensuring that it does not contain any malware. They should permit the users to change the agreement, withdraw and also grant the agreement as well as user has to be given privilege to know what data are collected through the IoT devices.

In-order to maintain privacy in the IoT, metadata should also be considered. Commonly used mechanism like encryption will not be an efficient way to preserve privacy, as the metadata can be processed in different locations in case of data aggregation and this has led to the development of various privacy-preservation mechanisms focusing on data aggregation, namely: (i) privacy preservation based on anonymity, (ii) privacy preservation based on encryption and (iii) privacy preservation based on perturbation. Mainly, in anonymity based privacy preservation, number of correlated anonymity techniques like k-anonymity, L-diversity, T-closeness can be utilized while aggregating the data so that privacy related to identifying the information can be preserved. Apart from this, anonymous communication systems could be affected by the traffic analysis techniques. In privacy preservation based on encryption, various mechanisms were used while aggregation of data. The mechanisms include homomorphic encryption, commitment mechanism, secret sharing and zero-knowledge proofing, these mechanisms are used during data aggregation to make sure that the data is not visible to the intruders or attackers. Drawback of using traditional encryption technique is that it helps only to protect the secrecy while transmitting the data but it will not be useful to protect or preserve the privacy policy. To overcome this new mechanisms on preservation which depends upon perturbation, perturbation, data customization, data sharing, random noise injection can be utilized while aggregating data, which will rearrange the raw data, as the result helps in ensuring preservation of privacy but still, the utilization of data might hamper the implementation of this methodology in the IoT. Privacy preserving schemes that based on perturbation are highly popular in the IoT. The reason is, because it performs extraordinarily while process the raw data directly. Mostly all the perturbation-based privacy preservation mechanisms gives out great performance by bringing down the utility of the data (Lin et al., 2016).

7. PRIVACY ENHANCING TECHNOLOGIES

The major concern in open world of the IoT is the privacy of the user data and on every cost it should be protected (Rehman et al., 2016). There are few technologies to enhance the privacy of user personal data such as

7.1 Transport Layer Security

Transport Layer Security (TLS) improves confidentiality and integrity of information in the IoT. But the drawback is each and every device used in the IoT application must need a new TLS connection, which searches for information that will halt its search by adding additional layers, as the result it will create overhead in the system.

7.2. Encryption

Most of the devices used in the IoT applications are operated by battery to follow the rules, in such cases encryption is done for data integrity, whenever the data is transported.

7.3 Virtual Private Network

Virtual Private Network (VPN) is a network which is used by a small group of companies, using which the system can be accessed anywhere. The companies involved it can only access the system and there should be bond between them to make the personal data secure and also to maintain data integrity.

7.4 Onion Routing

Onion routing helps in encrypting and merging internet traffic from several sources. It works in such a way that, it encloses the data by adding various layers of encryption.

To resolve the issues that might arise in the IoT application in nearby future, privacy policies for each and every domain can be defined in specific (Stankovic et al., 2014). Eventually, the IoT models should be designed in a way that, when users send the request for accessing the data and policies, the request has to be automatically compared with the existing privacy policy and decision has to be taken whether to grant or deny the request given by the user. New technology or algorithm has to be formulated to express privacy policy, because certain requirements that are listed below cannot be easily supported by present privacy techniques and algorithms:

The various characteristics based on the environment or surroundings like space, time, environmental, physical sensing and noisy data are needed to be expressed. Mostly all the requirements have to be analysed and collected in the real time. The question is, Will collecting the information in real time gather data and policies in a way that it supports privacy. Will that be done on individual application or on utility infrastructure or on some new approach?

Key features like the number of data owners, request domains, number of outside users and their rights are need to be represented when domain interact.

- Representing the number of times the sensitive data is requested by the users can be done grouping the queries in terms of average, minimum and maximum request. This can be done by anonymizing aggregation functions.
- There is a need to examine privacy set on requesting to set parameters in the system, in addition to traditional privacy policies.
- Dynamic changes has to be made on policies.

- The recommendations common to all stakeholders are:
- Privacy has to be applied by default and also by design principles.
- At any time, the user has to be permitted to control their own data, hence rights has to be offered to the used so that they have the right to either refuse or request the consent, and it has to be made user friendly.
- Even the resources and applications has to be designed in such a way that it informs users and non-user data subjects.

8. CONCLUSION

The IoT has raised attention in numerous fields, both from the industrial sector and from researchers and public stakeholders (Moreno et al., 2014). The IoT offers various advantages to the users, and gives chance to change the way of interaction between the users and the technology. Since application of the IoT are distributed in different fields ranging from health care, smart cities, automation in commerce to monitoring the surrounding, it is necessary to describe and define better privacy solutions. By doing so the sensitive data that is collected can be handled properly. Hence for all the IoT applications users requires a proper ways to protect their own personal information, which depends on their location, behavior, habits and their interaction with the other people, in other words proper methods has to be established to protect all the information of their personal life. Privacy is the major concern in the IoT applications.

Privacy rights are essential to assure user confidence and trust on devices that are connected with one another. User specificity and data streams furnished by the IoT devices will invite more of the IoT users to use the application but issues like potential harms and privacy make people think twice before using the IoT. Finally, the two-core idea that is most suitable for a privacy-aware IoTs is: First, privacy is an enduring challenge and it must be dealt with necessary mechanism or precaution has to be taken. Another idea is productive results needs combined action in-order to give technical solutions, which has to be supported by most suitable framework. This chapter has provided an extensive survey regarding privacy challenges and its solution in the IoT.

REFERENCES

Aleisa, N., & Renaud, K. (2017). Privacy of the Internet of Things: A Systematic Literature Review. *Proceedings of the 50th Hawaii International Conference on System Sciences*. 10.24251/HICSS.2017.717

Behl, A., & Behl, K. (2012). An Analysis of Cloud Computing Security Issues. *Information and Communication Technologies (WICT), 2012 World Congress on,* 109-114. 10.1109/WICT.2012.6409059

Bertino, E. (2016). Data Security and Privacy in the IoT. *Proc. 19th International Conference on Extending Database Technology (EDBT).*

Borgohain, T., Kumar, U., & Sanyal, S. (2015). Survey of Security and Privacy Issues of Internet of Things. *Int. J. Advanced Networking and Applications, 6*(4), 2372–2378.

Brush, A. B. (2013). Lab of Things: A Platform for Conducting Studies with Connected Devices in Multiple Homes. *Proc. 2013 ACM Conf. Pervasive and Ubiquitous Computing,* 35–38. 10.1145/2494091.2502068

Camenisch, J., Shelat, A., Sommer, D., Hubner, F., Hansen, M., Krasemann, H., Lacoste, G., Leenes, R., & Tseng, J. (2005). Privacy and identity management for everyone. In *Proceedings of the 2005 workshop on Digital identity management, DIM '05.* ACM. 10.1145/1102486.1102491

Cao, J. (2011). CASTLE: Continuously anonymizing data streams. *IEEE Transactions on Dependable and Secure Computing, 8*(3), 337–352. doi:10.1109/TDSC.2009.47

Cave, J. (2011). *Does It Help or Hinder? Promotion of Innovation on the Internet and Citizens' Right to Privacy. Economic and Scientific Policy report.* European Parliament.

Celdran, A. H. (2014). A semantic aware policy framework for developing privacy-preserving and context-aware smart applications. *IEEE Systems Journal.*

Christin, D., & Reinhardt, A. (2011). A survey on privacy in 1245 mobile participatory sensing applications. *Journal of Systems and Software, 84*(11), 1928–1946. doi:10.1016/j.jss.2011.06.073

Evans, D., & Eyers, D. (2012). Efficient data tagging for managing privacy in the internet of things. Conf. on Internet of Things, iThings 2012 and Conf. on Cyber, Physical and Social Computing, CPSCom 2012, 244–248. doi:10.1109/GreenCom.2012.45

Feng, H., & Fu, W. (2010). Study of recent development about privacy and security of the internet of things. *Web Information Systems and Mining (WISM), 2010 International Conference on,* 2, 91–95. 10.1109/WISM.2010.179

Gessner, D. (2012). Trustworthy Infrastructure Services for a Secure and Privacy-Respecting Internet of Things. *International Conference on Trust, Security and Privacy in Computing and Communications*, 998-1003.

Giannikos, M. (2013). Towards secure and context-aware information lookup for the Internet of Things. *Computing, Networking and Communications (ICNC). Proceedings of the IEEE*, 632–636.

Gupta, M., & Abdelsalam, M. (2020). *Security and Privacy in Smart Farming: Challenges and Opportunities* (Vol. 8). IEEE Access.

Harini, S., Jothika, K. & Jayashree, K. (2017). A Survey on Privacy and Security in Internet of Things. *International Journal of Innovations in Engineering and Technology, 8*(1).

Henze, M. (2013). *The Cloud Needs Cross-Layer Data Handling Annotations. In 2013 IEEE Security and Privacy Workshops (SPW)*. IEEE.

Huang, X., Fu, R., Chen, B., Zhang, T., & Roscoe, A. (2012). User interactive internet of things privacy preserved access control. *7th International Conference for Internet Technology and Secured Transactions, ICITST 2012*, 597–602.

Ivor, D. (2014). Reference Architectures For Privacy Preservation In Cloud-Based Iot Applications. *International Journal of Services Computing, 2*, 65–78.

Jia, X., Feng, O., Fan, T., & Lei, Q. (2012). RFID technology and its applications in internet of things (IoT). *Proc. 2nd IEEE Int. Conf. Consum. Electron. Commun. Netw. (CECNet)*, 1282–1285. 10.1109/CECNet.2012.6201508

Kumar, J. S., & Patel, D. R. (2014). A Survey on Internet of Things: Security and Privacy Issues. *International Journal of Computers and Applications, 90*(11), 20–25. doi:10.5120/15764-4454

Lee, G. M., & Kim, J. Y. (2010). The internet of things: A problem statement. *Information and Communication Technology Convergence (ICTC), 2010 International Conference on*, 517–518. 10.1109/ICTC.2010.5674788

Li, Q., Wang, Z. Y., Li, W. H., Li, J., Wang, C., & Du, R. (2013). Applications integration in a hybrid cloud computing environment: Modelling and platform. *Enterprise Information Systems, 7*(3), 237–271. doi:10.1080/17517575.2012.677479

Li, S., Xu, L., Wang, X., & Wang, J. (2012). Integration of hybrid wireless networks in cloud services oriented enterprise information systems. *Enterprise Information Systems, 6*(2), 165–187. doi:10.1080/17517575.2011.654266

Lin, J., Yuy, W., Zhangz, N., Yang, X., Zhangx, H., & Zhao, W. (2016). *A Survey on Internet of Things: Architecture, Enabling Technologies, Security and Privacy, and Applications*. Academic Press.

Mayer, C. P. (2009). *Security and Privacy Challenges in the Internet of Things*. Workshops on Scientific Conf. Communication in Distributed Systems.

Mehra, P. (2012). Context-Aware Computing: Beyond Search and Location-Based Services. *IEEE Internet Computing, 16*(2), 12–16. doi:10.1109/MIC.2012.31

Menn, J. (2012). *Social networks scan for sexual predators, with uneven results*. Reuters. http://reut.rs/Nnejb7

Neeraj & Singh, A. (2016). Internet of Things and Trust Management in IOT – Review. *International Research Journal of Engineering and Technology, 3*(6).

Oleshchuk, V. (2009). Internet of Things and Privacy Preserving Technologies. *International Conference on Wireless Communication, Vehicular Technology, Information Theory and Aerospace & Electronic Systems Technology*, 336-340. 10.1109/WIRELESSVITAE.2009.5172470

Patel, K. K., & Patel, S. M. (2016). Internet of Things-IOT: Definition, Characteristics, Architecture, Enabling Technologies, Application & Future Challenges. *International Journal of Engineering Science and Computing, 6*(5).

Pearson, S. (2009). Taking Account of Privacy when Designing Cloud Computing Services. *2009 ICSE Workshop on Software Engineering Challenges of Cloud Computing*, 44–52. 10.1109/CLOUD.2009.5071532

Peng, L.B. Ru-Chuan, W.B. Xiao-Yu, S., & Long, C. (2014). Privacy protection based on key-changed mutual authentication protocol in internet of things. *Commun. Comput. Inf. Sci., 418*, 345–355.

Perera, C., Liu, C.H., Jayawardena, S., & Chen, M. (2014). A Survey on Internet of Things From Industrial Market Perspective. *IEEE Access, 2*.

Perera, C., Zaslavsky, A., Christen, P., & Georgakopoulos, D. (2013). Context Aware Computing for The Internet of Things: A Survey. Communications Surveys Tutorials, IEEE, 16(1), 414-454.

Polonetsky, J., & Wolf, C. (2012). *Spring Privacy Series: Mobile Device Tracking*. Retrieved from https://fpf.org/wp-content/uploads/Comments-of-the-Future-of-Privacy-Forum-on-Mobile-Device-Tracking.pdf

Potoczny-JonesI. (2015). www.networkcomputing.com/internet-things/iot-security-privacy-reducing vulnerabilities /807681850

Radomirovic, S. (2010). Towards a Model for Security and Privacy in the Internet of Things. *1st International Workshop on the Security of the Internet of Things*, 1-6.

Ramirez, E. (2014). *Privacy and security in the internet of things: Challenge or Opportunity*. Academic Press.

Razzaq, M. A., Habib, M. Q. S., & Ullah, G. S. (2017). Security Issues in the Internet of Things (IoT): A Comprehensive Study. *International Journal of Advanced Computer Science and Applications*, 8(6), 383–388.

Rehman, A. (2016). Security and Privacy Issues in IoT. *International Journal of Communication Networks and Information Security*, 8(3), 147–157.

Rose, K., Eldridge, S., & Chapin, L. (2015). *The Internet of Things: An Overview Understanding the Issues and Challenges of a More Connected World*. The Internet Society (ISOC).

Santa Moreno, M. V., Zamora, J., & Skarmeta, A.F. (2014). A Holistic IoT-based Management Platform for Smart Environments. *IEEE International Conference on Communications (ICC)*, 3823-3828.

Sarkar, C., Nambi, A.U., Prasad, S. N., Rahim, A., Neisse, R., & Baldini, G. (2014). A Scalable Distributed Architecture for IoT. IEEE Internet of Things Journal.

Schindler, H. R. (2012). *Europe's policy options for a dynamic and trustworthy development of the Internet of Things*. RAND Europe.

Schneier, B. (2012). When It Comes to Security, We're Back to Feudalism. *Wired*. https://www.wired.com/opinion/2012/11/feudal-security/

Schneier, E. (2006). *Updating the Traditional Security Model*. https://www.schneier. com/blog/ archives/ 2006/08/updating the tr.html

Sicari, S. (2014). A security-and quality-aware system architecture for internet of things. *Information Systems Frontiers*, 1–13.

Silva, B. N. (2017). Internet of Things: A Comprehensive Review of Enabling Technologies, Architecture, and Challenges. *IETE Technical Review*, 1–16.

Solove, D. J. (2006). A Taxonomy of Privacy. *University of Pennsylvania Law Review*, *154*(3), 477. doi:10.2307/40041279

Stankovic, J. A. (2014). Research directions for the Internet of Things. *IEEE Internet of Things Journal, 1*(1), 3–9. doi:10.1109/JIOT.2014.2312291

Stefanick, L. (2011). *Controlling Knowledge: Freedom of Information and Privacy Protection in a Networked World*. DOAB Directory of Open Access Books. AU Press.

Sundmaeker, H. (2010). *Vision and Challenges for Realizing the Internet of Things*. Cluster of European Research Projects on the Internet of Things.

Suryawanshi, S. R. (2016). A Study on Privacy and Security concerns in Internet of Things. *International Journal of Innovative Research in Computer and Communication Engineering, 4*(9).

Wang, F. (2016). Recent Advances in the Internet of Things: Multiple Perspectives. *IETE Technical Review*, 1–11.

Wang, L., Da-Xu, L., Bi, Z., & Xu, Y. (2014). Data cleaning for RFID and WSN integration. *Ind. Inform. IEEE Trans, 10*(1), 408–418. doi:10.1109/TII.2013.2250510

Wang, Y., & Wen, Q. (2011). A privacy enhanced dns scheme for the internet of things. *IET International Conference on Communication Technology and Application*, 699–702.

Wangi, N. I. C., Prasad, R. V., Jacobsson, M., & Niemegeers, I. (2008 Address autoconfiguration in wireless ad hoc networks: Protocols and techniques. *Wireless Communications, IEEE, 15*(1), 70–80. doi:10.1109/MWC.2008.4454707

Wu, L., & Shao, P. (2011). Research on the Protection Algorithm and Model of Personal Privacy Information in Internet of Thing. *International Conference on E-Business and E-Government*, 1-4.

Xu, L., He, S., & Li, S. (2014). Internet of Things in Industries: A Survey. *IEEE Transactions on Industrial Informatics, 10*(4), 2233–2243. doi:10.1109/TII.2014.2300753

Yang, J., & Fang, B. (2011). Security model and key technologies for the internet of things. *Journal of China Universities of Posts and Telecommunications, 8*(2), 109–112. doi:10.1016/S1005-8885(10)60159-8

Zaslavsky, A., Perera, C., & Georgakopoulos, D. (2012). Sensing as a Service and Big Data. *Proc. Int'l Conf. Advances in Cloud Computing*, 21–29.

Ziegeldorf, H., Morchon, O. G., & Wehrle, K. (2014). Privacy in the Internet of Things: Threats and challenges. *Security and Communication Networks, 7*(12), 2728–2742. doi:10.1002ec.795

Ziegeldorf, J. H., Viol, N., Henze, M., & Wehrle, K. (2014). Privacy preserving Indoor Localization. *7th ACM Conference on Security and Privacy in Wireless and Mobile Networks*, 1–2.

Chapter 5
Reliable Medchain Management System

Ambika N.

https://orcid.org/0000-0003-4452-5514

*Department of computer Applications, Sivananda Sarma Memorial RV College,
Bangalore, India*

ABSTRACT

The internet of things, popularly known as IoT, is intelligent sensors working together to accomplish a task. These devices are used in innumerable applications, and they are aiming to minimize human efforts. These unsupervised devices require some amount of security. Hence, the previous systems use blockchains to enhance security. The hashing system used in this technology preserves the security and confidentiality among the stakeholders. Medchain is a system that communicates between the personnel and insurance dealings securely. To enhance reliability of the previous work, the proposal is proposed. The methodology used in the contribution enhances the reliability by 2.89% compared to the previous proposal.

1. INTRODUCTION

Internet-of-things (Balandina, Balandin, Koucheryavy, & Mouromtsev, 2015) (Ambika N., 2019) is an assembly of multiple types of equipment of different caliber and functionality working towards a single goal. The gathering aims at communicating with each other, utilizing the common platform provided to them. The medical system (Ambika N., 2020) is one of the applications where these systems are engaged in continuously monitoring the patient. Notwithstanding customary clinical assessment, the patient's body states, including pulse, diabetes,

DOI: 10.4018/978-1-7998-6463-9.ch005

electroencephalogram, and other crucial biomedical testimony, undergo checking by applying different clinical GPS beacons. The sharing of such a tremendous measure of information among associations can encourage clinical findings, biomedical research, and approach making. The procedure happens in three stages nowadays-

- The performance calculates Information Acquisition by using various wearable sensors that provide physiological readings. Some examples include ECG, skin temperature, respiratory rate, EMG muscle movement, and walk. The sensors interface with the system through an aggregator.
- The Data Transmission parts of the framework transmit the chronicle readings of the patient from the patient's home to the server of the Healthcare Organization with guaranteed security. The tangible securing stage undergoes furnishing with a short-extend radio device. Some examples include Zigbee or low-power Bluetooth devices. It uses to move sensor information to the aggregator. Amassed information is additionally handed-off to the Organization for long haul stockpiling utilizing the Internet network. The concatenation of data uses a cell phone's WiFi or cell information association. Sensors in the information, procurement structure have the Internet of Things (IoT) (Nagaraj, 2021) - based design (Lin, Yu, Zhang, Yang, Zhang, & Zhao, 2017).
- Cloud Processing has three segments: stockpiling, examination, and representation. The framework is intended for long haul stockpiling of patient's biomedical data for helping wellbeing experts with symptomatic data. The scrutiny utilizes the sensor information alongside e-Health records that are turning out to be predominant. It can help with analyses for various wellbeing conditions and ailments.

The previous contribution is the communication between the hospital and the insurance companies. Medchain (Shen, Guo, & Yang, 2019) is developed on a decentralized system, which associates all medicinal services, suppliers, including emergency clinics, clinical focuses, centers, and social insurance corporate. The Medchain arrangement contains two kinds of hubs. Super companions comprise of the servers from enormous social insurance distributor, (like national emergency clinics) which are progressively fit in figuring and giving the principle foundation of information sharing. The edge hubs are the servers from minor suppliers (network centre) which store the patient information. The assets of a super-peer partition into three modules contain blockchain administration, catalog administration, and human services database (HDB). The blockchain server keeps up an aggregated amass (Atlam & Wills, 2019). The proposal aims to provide better reliability and security to the previous system. The suggestion creates a hash code for the hospital where the infected undergoes treatment. The insurance company derives the cipher that usage made for verification.

The proposal provides 2.89% more reliability compared to (Shen, Guo, & Yang, 2019). The work is divided into eight sections. Literature survey follows the introduction in section 2. The notations used in the study are jolted in section 3. The contribution is explained in section 4. Section 5 provides the analysis of the work. Future work is narrated in section 6. The work is concluded in section 7.

2. LITERATURE SURVEY

Blockchain (Sankar, Sindhu, & Sethumadhavan, 2017) has aided healthcare in many ways. Various authors have suggested their usage in their contributions. A summary of the same details this section. The contribution (Liang, Zhao, Shetty, Liu, & Li, 2017) is creative client-driven wellbeing information-sharing arrangement by using a decentralized blockchain to enhance security. The system improves the personality of the board utilizes the participation of administration upheld by the square chain. A versatile application sends to gather wellbeing information from individual wearable gadgets, manual info, and clinical gadgets. It synchronizes information to the cloud with data throughout the medical services. To safeguard the uprightness of wellbeing information and to preserve proof of honesty, the cloud database is secured using the blockchain arrangement. Additionally, for versatile set up tree-based information preparing and grouping technique to deal with enormous informer indexes of individual wellbeing information is utilized.

(Al Omar, Rahman, Basu, & Kiyomoto, 2017), is a patient-driven medical services information system. The board framework uses the blockchain methodology to enhance security. Pseudonymity guarantees by utilizing cryptographic capacities. The information sender is the patient, who will send her wellbeing information to the framework. The information collector will demand the information in the wake of confirming itself and getting to the frame. The Enrollment Unit will involve in the authentication. Utilizing a few accreditations enlisted processes happen. Both the gatherings of the framework will cooperate with a Private accessible unit (PAU) after verification. It ties with an enrolment unit (PAU will send their information to the frame). It is the delegate unit through which the component of one level could communicate with the other. Blockchain will hold the data of the clients. Every exchange will restore an identifier. This exchange identifier will assist the clients in accessing the data further. A public-key encryption procedure adopted scrambles private information.

If other patients show up to the emergency clinic for treatment, the patient should initially enlist with the registration counter (RC) before heading off to the specialist

(Ramani, Kumar, Bracken, Liyanage, & Ylianttila, 2018). . Since it is a one-time registration, they have to give their subtleties utilizing their cell phone. Next, the RC sends the subtitles, marked by the patient and by the RC. The specialist can refresh/ include information into the BC, with the endorsement of the patient. Hence, the specialist initially encodes the data with a typical key. Next, the patient checks the legitimacy of the encryption and positive if it plays out its mark on the scrambled worth. At last, the specialist favors the same of the patient and transmits the data to the BC. The BC checks the information and stores information on the positive affirmation.

The work (Gordon & Catalini, 2018) provides Step by step instructions to blockchain innovation. The five components contain advanced access rules, information total, information liquidity, understanding personality, and content-consistent nature. The principal method improves tolerant driven interoperability using the administration of computerized regulation. It empowers shared components for the management during confirmation and approval rules. A subsequent way innovation could cultivate tolerant driven interoperability is through information accessibility. As patients move to take more responsibility for wellbeing information, one of their first errands will assemble the entirety of their clinical data. The third significant way could improve interoperability in the patient setting. A fourth way may encourage the progress to quiet, determined interoperability around persistent personality.

(Mamoshina, et al., 2018), has given an outline of the cutting edge of the fabricated reasoning and blockchain advances. The working includes creative arrangements that quicken the biomedical exploration and empower patients with new apparatuses to control and benefit from their information with the motivating forces to experience steady well being. The authors have acquainted new ideas with access to the individual records, including the mix, time-and relationship-estimation of the information. They present a guide for a block chain-empowered decentralized for individual wellbeing information biological system. It empowers novel methodologies for sedate disclosure, biomarker advancement, and deterrent social insurance. A protected and straightforward dispersed for individual information commercial center uses blockchain technology, and profound learning advances might have the option to determine the difficulties looked by the controllers and return the authority over close to home information contains clinical records back to the people.

MedRec (Ekblaw, Azaria, Halamka, & Lippman, 2016) suggestion oversees validation, secrecy, responsibility, and information sharing—critical contemplations. It gives patients an exhaustive, unchanging log and simple access to their clinical data across distributors and treatment destinations. The system furnishes them with complete information. MedRec empowers the development of data, financial matters, providing enormous information to enable scientists while drawing in patients and suppliers in the decision to discharge metadata. It utilizes public-key cryptography to enhance security to the system.

A remote observed by a specialist is available to different clinical devices (Griggs, Ossipova, Kohlios, Baccarini, Howson, & Hayajneh, 2018). The main gadget receives crude information. This device is commonly a cell phone or tablet. When complete, the organized data is sent to the pertinent keen agreement for full examination alongside altered edge esteems. The bargain will assess the information and issue cautions to the patient and social insurance supplier. The estimations themselves will be sent to an assigned Electronic Health Records (EHR) stockpiling database, while another exchange adds to the chain. The framework will incorporate EHR APIs and send information straightforwardly to the EHR. All treatment orders from the agreement and human services supplier recordings as it completes the blockchain exchange.

BlocHIE (Jiang, Cao, Wu, Yang, Ma, & He., 2018) is a Blockchain-based stage for social insurance data trade. The creators considered various prerequisites for sharing medicinal services information. It utilizes two approximately coupled blockchains to deals with different human services information. It joins off-chain stockpiling and on-bind check to fulfill the prerequisites of security and verification. It provides reasonableness based pricing calculations to improve framework throughput. Bloch imagines for putting away and sharing medical services information from clinical establishments and people. There are predominantly three parts in BlocHIE. The principal segment is the Blockchain arrangement. It is answerable for putting away and sharing the gathered medicinal services information. The clinical organizations go about as the subsequent part. The third segment comprises of a considerable number of people who are happy to store and offer their day by day medicinal services information.

Modelchain (Kuo & Ohno-Machado, 2018) manages blockchain innovation for the security of machines working with AI capabilities. It adds to display boundary estimation without uncovering any patient wellbeing data. They have coordinated private protecting on the web AI with a private blockchain arrangement, apply exchange metadata to scatter fractional models, and decide the request for the internet learning process. Use the metadata in the exchanges to spread the partial models and the metadata to coordinate protection saving on the web AI with a private-saving system. It comprises of four methods - initializes, updates, evaluate, and transfer. They have incorporated the hash of the model to spare extra rooms.

(Dwivedi, Srivastava, Dhar, & Singh, 2019), contributed a novel model of appropriate for IoT gadgets (Li, 2017) (Sánchez-Arias, García, & G-Bustelo, 2017). The model depends on the dispersed nature of the system. Exchanges in the blockchain are communicated freely on the arrangement and contain extra data about both the sender and beneficiary. A ring impression permits an endorser to sign a message namelessly. This mark blends with different gatherings. The twofold encryption of information utilizing lightweight encryption calculations adds better security to the system. The data uses symmetric key encryption to encrypt and later scrambles the symmetric key using the public key. It trades cryptographic keys over the unrestricted channel using Diffie–Hellman key generation methodology (Ambika.N, 2020).

Medchain (Shen, Guo, & Yang, 2019) developed on a decentralized system associates all medicinal services, suppliers, including emergency clinics, clinical focuses, centers, and social insurance corporate. The Medchain arrangement contains two kinds of hubs. Super companions comprise of the servers from enormous social insurance distributor, (like national emergency clinics) are progressively fit in figuring and giving the principle foundation of information sharing. The edge hubs are the servers from minor suppliers (network center) which store the patient information. The assets of a super-peer partition into three modules contain blockchain administration, catalog administration, and human services database (HDB). The blockchain server keeps up an aggregated amass (Atlam & Wills, 2019) for checking information trustworthiness and reviewing exercises. The index server keeps up the stock of client social insurance information, maps them to the authentic area, and oversees meetings for information sharing. The servers of both kinds on every single super-peer structure consist of two sub-systems. HDB stores the genuine medicinal services, information of patients.

Healthcare Data Gateways (Yue, Wang, Jin, Li, & Jiang, 2016) follows the "transfer information once, inquiry it ordinarily" model. Information is changeless once transferred. In this way, rather than arranging information into tables, the creators have proposed to utilize one basic diagram to show a wide range of data and free the clients from the mapping issue. Every patient has one such mapping table that accepts the patient's data as a table name. The patient recognition happens using a blueprint. The strategy is known as the Indicator Centric Schema model. In one kind of indexing, information recording is dependent on Indicator utilizing Hash-file. The pointer is additionally filed on time using a B+ tree list. The index is a list as well as a registry to arrange the information. Information recovery analyzes the hash file, B+ tree file, and data on the leaf hub.

Parallel medicinal services provide help in parallel hypothesis execution. The medicative services framework (Wang, et al., 2018) is the clinical scene for specialists and patients. The physical, social insurance process comprises making illness analysis, deciding a treatment plan, and making treatment plans. There will be fake specialists and fake patients. At first, the AHS will make analyses dependent on the patient's side effects, as indicated by clinical information from clinical distributions and specialists' clinical investigations. Afterward, the counterfeit framework will assess a wide range of helpful routines in uncovering the best arrangement against the patient's ailment. The fake frame will screen the patients for the treatment adequacy through virtual–genuine collaboration between the AHS and the physical human services framework along with treatment results.

DASH (DApp for Smart Health) (Zhang, White, Schmidt, & Lenz, 2017) gives an electronic entryway to patients to access and update their clinical records as remedy demands. The application permits Suppliers to survey understanding information and satisfy remedy demands in light of consents given by patients. The system is actualized on an Ethereum test blockchain, with SMART (Substitutable Medical Apps, Reusable Technology) on FHIR (Fast Healthcare Interoperability Resources) construction as the standard information group to put away patient information. Using the smart agreement support in Ethereum, the patient registers with the contract store. This maps between remarkable patient identifiers and their related Patient Account contract addresses. Every Patient Account contract likewise contains a rundown of wellbeing suppliers that are allowed to the patient's clinical accounts.

The EHR-sharing framework (Tanwar, Parekh, & Evans, 2020) engineering is blockchain-based. Members register through the customer application or the SDK, mentioning an enrolment declaration employing a Membership Service Provider (MSP) to the endorsement authority. At that point, the testament authority gives the private key with another ID to select the member. All exchanges circulated over the hyper-ledger texture square chain arrangement. Patients can include records utilizing the customer application that conjures the chain code. In the wake of submitting the exchange into the blockchain arrange, the refreshed ones disperse over the system.

The design (Mikula & Jacobsen, 2018) comprises of a customer application, an application server, database, and a confirmation and approval server. The framework verifies and approves clients by approving exchanges in the blockchain arrange. In a basic situation, the App speaks with the Application server, which verifies clients by accreditations put away in the DB. After the client validates effectively, it performs the ideal activity. Some examples include recovering or refreshing the information in the database. The Application server delegates work to the Approval server to confirm the validness of the client and to approve access to the DB. The Approval server goes about as a middle person between the Application server and blockchain organize. It validates and agrees with the client by questioning the blockchain arrange.

HaBits (Gupta, Tanwar, Tyagi, Kumar, Obaidat, & Sadoun, 2019) are a protected human services executive framework which disposes of reliance between middle people to build up the trust among specialists and the social insurance associations. The dispersed idea of the blockchain takes out the need for staggered conformation and lessens the social insurance administration conveyance cost. It is an open-source permissioned blockchain stage with various jobs characterized by SC. It is a measured and adaptable compositional component. It develops control of the instrument, which makes it reasonable for the secure telesurgery framework. It comprises of specialists who effectively take an interest in the telesurgery methodology and the human framework interface (HSI) for order passing. A specialist can direct or control the careful robot at slave sites by going orders through HSI. It additionally has a specialist hyper-record texture or consortium blockchain. Every specialist has the privilege to get to his/her blockchain, which contains data. It comprises of a robot called teleoperator, which executes the orders of a specialist. It sets the corresponding way between the ace and the slave space of the telesurgery framework to share requests, information, and brilliant agreements.

Malignant growth is a genuine ailment that may require a durable treatment and a lifetime observing of a patient. The blockchain innovation makes a model of an oncology-explicit clinical information sharing framework (Dubovitskaya, Xu, Ryu, Schumacher, & Wang, 2017). The system comprises of the Membership administration, Databases for putting away medicinal services & information, agreement procedure, and APIs for various client jobs. The primary use of the Membership administration is to enroll clients with different work. To check this, the National Practitioner Data Bank has made use of it. The participation administration is likewise facilitating an affirmation authority engaged with the age for marking and an encryption key pair for each client. The patient produces a symmetric encryption key used to scramble/unscramble the information relating to the patient. This key creates pseudonyms that solitary approved clients could check whether the record stores any data about the patient.

The contribution (Sun, Zhang, Wang, Gao, & Liu, 1-9) is a decentralized quality based signature method for human services blockchain that gives proficient protection save check of the genuineness of EHR information and endorser character. The plan has two striking highlights. It can viably check the qualities of the underwriter without uncovering the endorser, and the decentralized characteristic based marking property makes it reasonable for the disseminated blockchain framework.

Social insurance exchanges related to a partner arranges into a chain of human services exchange squares (Witchey, 2019). The chain is an account of an individual's medicinal services way through life. The exchange communicated to at least one approval gadget. The device builds up the legitimacy by producing another square employing proof - of - work standard. It tends to annex to the partner social insurance blockchain.

3. NOTATIONS USED IN THE STUDY

Table 1.

Notations used in the study	Description
H_i	Hash code generated by the hospital
L_i	Location of the hospital
S_{id}	Specialist (doctor) identity
IC_i	Hash code derived by the insurance company
T_i	Time of updating the data
A_i	Amount claimed
Ack_i	Amount dispatched details
$Data_i$	Data dispatched
L_{ic}	Location details of the insurance company
E_{id}	Insurance company employee identification

4. PROPOSED WORK

Reliability is a property of the system that brings in trust among the stakeholders. The internet is an enormous web connecting devices of different capacities. The system provides a foundation for various instruments to communicate in the language. Medchain is the system a subsystem in this web system that brings in trust among many communicating devices using the blockchain methodology. The system communicates with the insurance companies using the technology.

Step 1: The authentication is maintained using the hash key. Equation (1) represents the same.

$$H_i \rightarrow hash\left(L_i, T_i, S_{id}, A_i\right). \tag{1}$$

In equation (1), the hospital is using L_i (location of the hospital obtained by the GPS), S_{id} (doctor identity), and A_i (amount claimed).

Step 2: The generated amount claimed details of the patient are attached with the hash key and dispatched to the insurance company. In equation (2), the patient details $Data_i$ and hash key H_i generated by the hospital are concatenated and sent to the insurance company IC_i.

$$H_i \| Data_i \rightarrow IC_i. \tag{2}$$

Step 3: Similarly the insurance company transmits its generated hash key and the amount dispatch details. The hash key H_{ic} is generated using the location details of the insurance company L_{ic}, employee identity details E_{id} and time T_i. The same is represented in equation (3).

$$H_{ic} \rightarrow hash(L_{ic}, E_{id}, T_i). \tag{3}$$

Step 4: The hash key H_{ic} is generated by the insurance company IC_i and is concatenated with the amount dispatch details Ack_i. The same is represented in the equation (4).

$$IC_i \rightarrow H_{ic} \| Ack_i. \tag{4}$$

5. ANALYSIS OF THE WORK

The previous contribution is the communication between the hospital and the insurance companies. Medchain (Shen, Guo, & Yang, 2019) is developed on a decentralized system, which associates all medicinal services, suppliers, including emergency clinics, clinical focuses, centers, and social insurance corporate. The Medchain arrangement contains two kinds of hubs. Super companions comprise of the servers from enormous social insurance distributor, (like national emergency clinics) which are progressively fit in figuring and giving the principle foundation of information sharing. The edge hubs are the servers from minor suppliers (network centre) which store the patient information. The assets of a super-peer partition into three modules contain blockchain administration, catalog administration, and human services database (HDB). The blockchain server keeps up an aggregated amass (Atlam & Wills, 2019). The proposal aims to provide better reliability and security to the previous system. The suggestion creates a hash code for the hospital where the infected undergoes treatment. The insurance company derives the cipher that usage made for verification.

The proposal brings better reliability to the system. The work simulates using NS2. The parameters used in the study are in table 2. The proposal uses location details, personnel identification to increase the reliability of the network. Figure 1 represents the comparison of both the work. The work provides 2.89% more trust than (Shen, Guo, & Yang, 2019). Table 2 jolts the parameters used in the study. Table 3 lists the steps in hashing algorithm.

Table 2. Parameters used in the study

Parameters used in the study	Description
Area under surveillance	200m * 200m
No of devices considered (1 hospital + 1 insurance company)	2
Length of time duration	16 bits
Length of the social security number of personnel/executive	32 bits
Maximum Length of data(amount claimed details)	256bits
Length of the location information	16 bits
Length of amount claimed	20 bits
Simulation time	60 ms

Figure 1. Comparison of previous work with the proposal w.r.t reliability

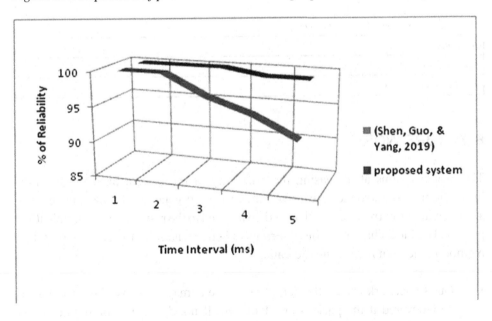

Table 3. Algorithm for Hashing

Step 1: Convert the values into binary bits(binary_bits).
Step 2: Assign Total_bits = binary_bits
Step 3: Shift the position of the bits
Step 3.1: For i=1 to length (total_bits) do
If total_bits[i]%5 ==0 then
Total_bits[i]<<2
Break
Step 4: Rearrange the total_bits
Step 4.1: For i=1 to length (total_bits) do
If total_bits[i]%3==1 then
Temp=Total_bits[i]
Total_bits[i]=total_bits[i+2]
Total_bits[i+2]= Temp
Step 5: Reduce the bits
Step 5.1: Divide the total_bits into two halves
Step 5.2: For i=1 to length (total_bits)/2 do
For j= [length (total_bits)/2]+1 to length (total_bits) do
Total_bits[i]=Total_bits[i] XOR Total_bits[j]
If length (Total_bits)>10
Goto Step 5.1
Hash_code=Total_bits

6. FUTURE WORK

The proposal aims at increasing the reliability of the system by using location information and personnel/executive information to generate the hash code. It is affixed with the corresponding data and dispatched to the respective communicating parties. The blockchain technology brings in better reliability to the system. Better methodologies can regenerate the data.

- Due to network issues, the data sent can be damaged or lost. The data has to be recovered if the packets are damaged. If not done, the communicated is again requested. It leads to energy consumption. The data recovery minimizes the energy consumption of the network.

7. CONCLUSION

IoT is an assembly of smart sensors communicating to accomplish the task assigned to them. Blockchain is the backbone providing ample security to these unsupervised devices. IoT with blockchain methodology has eased human life. These unsupervised devices have created a lot of changes in technology. The system together has aided many applications to better heights. Medchain is a system that aids in secure communication between the hospital and the insurance company. The work increases the reliability of the previous contribution. The suggestion uses blockchain methodology where the location of both the communicating parties and identification of the executives/personnel undergoes hashing to increase reliability to the previous contribution. The proposal increases reliability by 2.89% compared to the former endeavor.

REFERENCES

Al Omar, A., Rahman, M. S., Basu, A., & Kiyomoto, S. (2017). Medibchain: A blockchain based privacy preserving platform for healthcare data. In *International conference on security, privacy and anonymity in computation, communication and storage* (pp. 534-543). Guangzhou, China: Springer. 10.1007/978-3-319-72395-2_49

Ambika, N. (2019). Energy-Perceptive Authentication in Virtual Private Networks Using GPS Data. In *Security, Privacy and Trust in the IoT Environment* (pp. 25–38). Springer. doi:10.1007/978-3-030-18075-1_2

Ambika, N. (2020). Methodical IoT-Based Information System in Healthcare. In c. Chakraborthy (Ed.), Smart Medical Data Sensing and IoT Systems Design in Healthcare (pp. 155-177). Bangalore, India: IGI Global.

Ambika, N. (2020). Diffie-Hellman Algorithm Pedestal to Authenticate Nodes in Wireless Sensor Network. In B. K. Bhargava, M. Paprzycki, N. C. Kaushal, P. K. Singh, & W. C. Hong (Eds.), *Handbook of Wireless Sensor Networks: Issues and Challenges in Current Scenario's* (Vol. 1132, pp. 348–363). Springer Nature. doi:10.1007/978-3-030-40305-8_17

Atlam, H. F., & Wills, G. B. (2019). Technical aspects of blockchain and IoT. In Role of Blockchain Technology in IoT Applications (Vol. 115). doi:10.1016/bs.adcom.2018.10.006

Balandina, E., Balandin, S., Koucheryavy, Y., & Mouromtsev, D. (2015). IoT use cases in healthcare and tourism. *IEEE 17th Conference on Business Informatics, 2*, 37-44.

Dubovitskaya, A., Xu, Z., Ryu, S., Schumacher, M., & Wang, F. (2017). *Secure and trustable electronic medical records sharing using blockchain. In AMIA annual symposium proceedings*. American Medical Informatics Association.

Dwivedi, A. D., Srivastava, G., Dhar, S., & Singh, R. (2019). A decentralized privacy-preserving healthcare blockchain for IoT. *Sensors (Basel), 19*(2), 326. doi:10.339019020326 PMID:30650612

Ekblaw, A., Azaria, A., Halamka, J. D., & Lippman, A. (2016). A Case Study for Blockchain in Healthcare:"MedRec" prototype for electronic health records and medical research data. *OBD 2016: The 2nd International Conference on Open and Big Data, 13*, 1-13.

Gordon, W. J., & Catalini, C. (2018). Blockchain technology for healthcare: Facilitating the transition to patient-driven interoperability. *Computational and Structural Biotechnology Journal, 16*, 224–230. doi:10.1016/j.csbj.2018.06.003 PMID:30069284

Griggs, K. N., Ossipova, O., Kohlios, C. P., Baccarini, A. N., Howson, E. A., & Hayajneh, T. (2018). Healthcare blockchain system using smart contracts for secure automated remote patient monitoring. *Journal of Medical Systems, 42*(7), 1–7. doi:10.100710916-018-0982-x PMID:29876661

Gupta, R., Tanwar, S., Tyagi, S., Kumar, N., Obaidat, M. S., & Sadoun, B. (2019). HaBiTs: Blockchain-based telesurgery framework for healthcare 4.0. In *International Conference on Computer, Information and Telecommunication Systems (CITS)* (pp. 1-5). Beijing, China: IEEE. 10.1109/CITS.2019.8862127

Jiang, S., Cao, J., Wu, H., Yang, Y., Ma, M., & He, J. (2018). *Blochie: a blockchain-based platform for healthcare information exchange. In International Conference on Smart Computing (SMARTCOMP)*. IEEE.

Kuo, T. T., & Ohno-Machado, L. (2018). Modelchain: Decentralized privacy-preserving healthcare predictive modeling framework on private blockchain networks. *Cryptography and Security*, 1-13.

Li, S. (2017). Security Requirements in IoT Architecture. In S. Li & L. D. Xu (Eds.), *Securing the internet of things* (pp. 97–108). Syngress. doi:10.1016/B978-0-12-804458-2.00005-6

Liang, X., Zhao, J., Shetty, S., Liu, J., & Li, D. (2017). Integrating blockchain for data sharing and collaboration in mobile healthcare applications. In *IEEE 28th annual international symposium on personal, indoor, and mobile radio communications (PIMRC)* (pp. 1-5). Montreal, Canada: IEEE.

Lin, J., Yu, W., Zhang, N., Yang, X., Zhang, H., & Zhao, W. (2017). A survey on internet of things: Architecture, enabling technologies, security and privacy, and applications. *Internet of Things Journal, 4*(5), 1125–1142. doi:10.1109/JIOT.2017.2683200

Mamoshina, P., Ojomoko, L., Yanovich, Y., Ostrovski, A., Botezatu, A., Prikhodko, P., Izumchenko, E., Aliper, A., Romantsov, K., Zhebrak, A., Ogu, I. O., & Zhavoronkov, A. (2018). Converging blockchain and next-generation artificial intelligence technologies to decentralize and accelerate biomedical research and healthcare. *Oncotarget, 9*(5), 5665–5690. doi:10.18632/oncotarget.22345 PMID:29464026

Mikula, T., & Jacobsen, R. H. (2018). Identity and access management with blockchain in electronic healthcare records. In *21st Euromicro conference on digital system design (DSD)* (pp. 699-706). Prague, Czech Republic: IEEE. 10.1109/DSD.2018.00008

Nagaraj, A. (2021). *Introduction to Sensors in IoT and Cloud Computing Applications.* Bentham Science Publishers.

Ramani, V., Kumar, T., Bracken, A., Liyanage, M., & Ylianttila, M. (2018). Secure and efficient data accessibility in blockchain based healthcare systems. In *IEEE Global Communications Conference (GLOBECOM)* (pp. 206-212). Abu Dhabi, UAE: IEEE. 10.1109/GLOCOM.2018.8647221

Sánchez-Arias, G., & García, C. G. (2017). Midgar: Study of communications security among Smart Objects using a platform of heterogeneous devices for the Internet of Things. *Future Generation Computer Systems, 74,* 444–466. doi:10.1016/j.future.2017.01.033

Sankar, L. S., Sindhu, M., & Sethumadhavan, M. (2017). Survey of consensus protocols on blockchain applications. In *4th International Conference on Advanced Computing and Communication Systems (ICACCS)* (pp. 1-5). Coimbatore, India: IEEE. 10.1109/ICACCS.2017.8014672

Shen, B., Guo, J., & Yang, Y. (2019). MedChain: Efficient healthcare data sharing via blockchain. *Applied Sciences (Basel, Switzerland), 9*(6), 1207. doi:10.3390/app9061207

Sun, Y., Zhang, R., Wang, X., Gao, K., & Liu, L. (1-9). A decentralizing attribute-based signature for healthcare blockchain. In *International conference on computer communication and networks (ICCCN)* (p. 2018). Hangzhou, China: IEEE. 10.1109/ICCCN.2018.8487349

Tanwar, S., Parekh, K., & Evans, R. (2020). Blockchain-based electronic healthcare record system for healthcare 4.0 applications. *Journal of Information Security and Applications, 50*, 1–13. doi:10.1016/j.jisa.2019.102407

Wang, S., Wang, J., Wang, X., Qiu, T., Yuan, Y., Ouyang, L., Guo, Y., & Wang, F.-Y. (2018). Blockchain-powered parallel healthcare systems based on the ACP approach. *IEEE Transactions on Computational Social Systems, 5*(4), 942–950. doi:10.1109/TCSS.2018.2865526

Witchey, N. J. (2019). *Patent No. 10,340,038.* Washington, DC: U.S.

Yue, X., Wang, H., Jin, D., Li, M., & Jiang, W. (2016). Healthcare data gateways: Found healthcare intelligence on blockchain with novel privacy risk control. *Journal of Medical Systems, 40*(10), 1–8. doi:10.100710916-016-0574-6 PMID:27565509

Zhang, P., White, J., Schmidt, D. C., & Lenz, G. (2017). Applying software patterns to address interoperability in blockchain-based healthcare apps. *24th Pattern Languages of Programming conference*, 1-17.

Chapter 6
Security for IoT:
Challenges, Attacks, and Prevention

Anjum Nazir Qureshi Sheikh
Kalinga University, India

Asha Ambhaikar
Kalinga University, India

Sunil Kumar
Kalinga University, India

ABSTRACT

The internet of things is a versatile technology that helps to connect devices with other devices or humans in any part of the world at any time. Some of the researchers claim that the number of IoT devices around the world will surpass the total population on the earth after a few years. The technology has made life easier, but these comforts are backed up with a lot of security threats. Wireless medium for communication, large amount of data, and device constraints of the IoT devices are some of the factors that increase their vulnerability to security threats. This chapter provides information about the attacks at different layers of IoT architecture. It also mentions the benefits of technologies like blockchain and machine learning that can help to solve the security issues of IoT.

1. INTRODUCTION

Internet of Things (IoT) has become one of the emerging technologies which are set to revolutionize the lifestyle of people by enabling digital connectivity everywhere. Decades ago we connected computers using the internet but now all the devices,

DOI: 10.4018/978-1-7998-6463-9.ch006

animals, and human beings can be connected wirelessly through this technology. IoT is a platform where every device will be connected, controlled through the internet, collect store data, and communicate data. It enables the exchange of information either from device to device or among a human and device. Many researchers have been working to upgrade the technology to increase its acceptability among the users. The reports Statista research department has predicted a major boost in the number of IoT connected devices which reveals that there will be 75.44 billion IoT devices worldwide in 2025 which is approximately a fivefold increase as compared to the year 2015 which had 15.4 billion connected devices. Applicability scenario of IoT has evolved rapidly in the last decade due to which it is being deployed in different domains like smart home, smart cities, smart transportation, health care, agriculture, etc. Internet of Things instills connectivity and intelligence in the devices thereby enhancing power, precision, and availability of the existing devices. The primary objective of this chapter is to discuss the security and privacy issues faced by the IoT platforms. The popularity of IoT among the users had to lead to an increase in the number of IoT devices, applications as well as the data that is being sent or received on the network. The chapter will be arranged as follows:

There is a need to minimize the security risks on IoT platforms to make it widely acceptable so that more and more people adopt it to make their life easier. But there are few issues mainly the device constraints and the lack of encryption methods which are increasing the vulnerability of IoT. In section 2 authors will list out some of the factors that need attention to mitigate the effects of security attacks on the IoT devices and also on the communication paths. Ensuring the security of IoT needs to consider devices as well as the communication platforms that are being utilized for implementing a particular application. The essential security methods have to utilize after having an overview of applications, networks as well as the devices. A secure IoT environment is difficult to achieve if all these factors are not recognized appropriately.

Section 3 will discuss the various attacks that are faced while ensuring security for the Internet of Things. This section will give brief information about the five-layer architecture of IoT that includes the perception layer, network, processing, application, and business layer. All the five layers are susceptible to different types of attacks and therefore in this section will shed light on the attacks each layer of the five-layer architecture is subjected to.

The security risks are increased proportionately with the number of IoT devices and their users. Some of the security threats can be avoided if the IoT end-users know how to keep their devices secure. Section 4 sheds light on the simple measures to be adopted by the IoT consumers to keep your data secure on the IoT devices, networks, clouds, and applications.

Efforts are being made to use techniques like Blockchain and machine learning to minimize security risks on these systems. In section 5 authors will discuss benefits of using the above-mentioned techniques for facing the challenges of security. This section will be followed by future scopes for the security techniques and conclusion.

Figure 1. Number of Connected IoT Devices (source: Statista 2020)

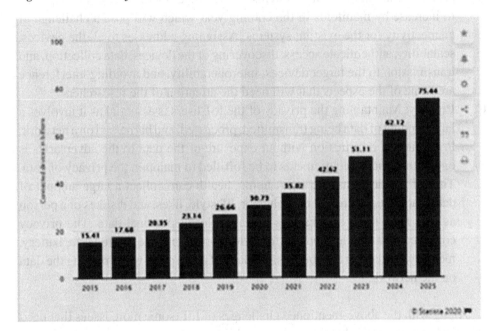

2. BACKGROUND

As numerous organizations are trying to integrate IoT for deriving additional benefits they are coming across numerous challenges. Some of the challenges faced by IoT that require more attention are:

A. **Security:** One of the fundamental problems that need to be addressed is the security of IoT devices. As the technology connects and controls the devices through the internet and as most of the applications support wireless connectivity, security concerns creep in automatically. With the significant increase in the number of IoT users, the risks of security threats will increase. Though there are a lot of algorithms or protocols available to protect the internet networks from breaching it is not possible to use those algorithms directly. The security architectures for the internet have been designed for human communication whereas the IoT networks are a combination of things, services, and networks due to which security of IoT must have additional features than the traditional networks.

B.   **Connectivity:** The Internet of Things has created a network that enables people and devices to be connected anywhere with anyone at any time. Server –client model or centralized approach is being extensively used for connectivity of servers, work stations, and systems. The number of IoT devices is expected to increase by manifolds in the coming year which will pose a challenge of connectivity for the existing systems. Assigning addresses to all the devices, scalability, authenticate access, discovering of the devices, data collection, and transmission to the target devices, interoperability, and avoiding interference are some of the aspects that will need the attention of the researchers.

C.   **Privacy:** Maintaining the privacy of the IoT users is essential as it involves a large amount of data being transmitted, processed, and harnessed on a network. Protection of information without exposure of the data to the adversaries is one of the crucial requirements to be fulfilled to maintain the privacy of data. The IoT applications like smart home, health care collect a large amount of data that can easily reveal the behavior, lifestyle, likes, and dislikes of a person as data from these applications contain a lot of personal data. The privacy complications are elevated due to device constraints like limited size, battery, memory processing capabilities, and lack of encryption while passing the data on the network.

Along with the above-mentioned challenges of IoT, some more issues that need attention are regarding hardware, compatibility, and government regulations or policies.

A report on IoT attacks by SonicWall released in 2019 provides a detailed comparison of IoT attacks in the years 2017 and 2018. The study indicates that the percentage of IoT attacks in 2018 has increased by 217.5% as compared to the year 2017. The number of attacks in 2017 was reported to be 10.3 million which steeply increased to 32.8 in 2018. Another study by the researchers of SonicWall in 2020 disclosed that there was a moderate increase of 5.7% attacks as compared to 2018 which were a total 34.3 million attacks. One of the primary reasons behind the increase in the number of attacks was that the manufacturers were unable to apply security methods to protect devices from the invaders. Besides this weak password, insecure networks, and lack of safe updates process are some common IoT weakness that helps the attackers to initiate attacks comfortably. Outdated software serves to be a prominent factor to increase the vulnerability of attacks on most of the devices that are used for applications like smart homes and healthcare. But with the flooding of fresh IoT devices every day it has become essential to come up with strategies for blocking these attacks rather than expecting attacks due to the shortcomings of the present IoT system.

Figure 2. IoT Attacks Comparison (Source: SonicWall Cyber Threat Report 2019)

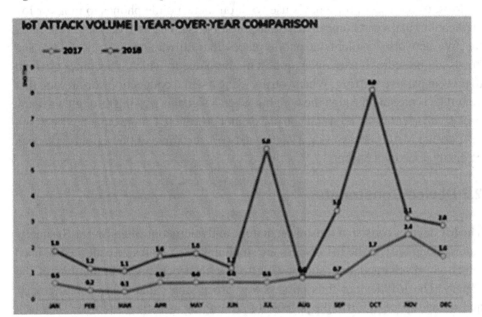

3. FACTORS THAT MAKE IOT VULNERABLE TO SECURITY

Though IoT is being recognized as a versatile technology but overcoming its security concerns has become one of the primary issues to increase trustworthiness among the people. The security attacks on IoT can be minimized by taking care of the devices as well as the connectivity mediums that are being deployed for the various applications. In this section, we discuss some of the factors that increase vulnerability. The security issues of IoT can be classified depending upon devices, applications, connectivity, and storage/processing techniques.

2.1 Wireless Connectivity

The connectivity technologies used for IoT applications are mostly implemented through a wireless medium. According to Sadlier and Sabri (2017), wireless technologies can be classified into short-range networks and wide area networks. Bluetooth, Local Area Network (PAN), Personal Area Network (PAN), Zigbee,

Near Field Communication (NFC) are used for localized connectivity while cellular networks and Low Power Wide Area (LWPA) networks are used to connect devices over large areas. The wireless connectivity technologies have enabled ubiquitous coverage for the IoT applications but the wireless medium comes with a disadvantage that they can be hacked very easily.

Most of the users now a day's use wi-fi on their mobile phones to monitor IoT applications like smart homes, smart transportation, etc. The wi-fi networks especially the free networks available at public places like railway stations, hospitals, and hotels are insecure. It uses open air as a medium due to which it becomes difficult to prevent passive sniffing. When you are using a wired connection you are sure that your data is passing through the wire but when a signal is passing through wi-fi any hacker can access your data and you just cannot prevent it. Compromising Bluetooth or spoofing MAC addresses on a Zigbee network are some of the activities that can be easily done by a hacker.

2.2 Device Constraints

The IoT devices consist of sensors, actuators, and microcontrollers and are basically battery operated. As the IoT devices are small in sizes, small size batteries are used which get discharged very soon owing to the electrochemical limitations of the battery. The IoT devices thus possess low processing capabilities, low memory, and storage space to fulfill the purpose of prolonging its battery lifetime. They lack significant processing and storage capacities to implement encryptions as well as the decryption algorithms. The process of encrypt- decrypt - re-crypt requires space for transmission and storage of information which is beyond the capacity of IoT devices. It is therefore challenging for the IoT device manufacturers and software developers to design security algorithms within a footprint of 64 kb to 640 kb.

2.3 Big Data

The smart devices or the IoT nodes collect sensitive information and are also able to process it for further use. Since these IoT devices are being controlled by the internet they are susceptible to security or cyber threats just like any other internet-enabled device. The explosion in the number of IoT devices being connected to the network has raised concerns for the data that is being transmitted or received through these networks. This large amount of data is quite difficult to manage with perspectives of data collection and networking. At such a high volume of data channelizing efforts to keep data secure has to be maintained as one of the primary objectives because along with the large information being transmitted a lot of personal data is going into these systems. Business enterprises for example may use IoT enabled printers, doorbells, security cameras, etc. In case these types of equipment are hacked by a cybercriminal the attacker can quickly observe the functioning of the enterprise. If this data gets leaked, hacked, or gets into the wrong hands it can lead to disastrous results.

2.4 Cloud Computing

Cloud computing is a technology that is being widely used to overcome the limitations of the storage and processing capabilities of IoT devices. Botta et. al. (2016) describes Cloud Computing as mature technology with virtually unlimited capacities in terms of storage and processing power. The growing rate of IoT users and data on the network requires more storage space for collecting and sharing valuable information needed by its users. Cloud computing has proved beneficial in handling large storage needs of the customers which can be further increased on users' demand. As more and more organizations are moving towards the cloud, security risks are about to increase not due to cloud insecurity but due to a lack of security awareness among the employees. Cloud computing according to Donno et. al. (2019) has provided benefits like flexibility, economic savings, and support of new services but security issues associated with it are hindering its widespread adoption. IoT users and organizations keep on updating their data on clouds. Most of the users do not have strong passwords while many of them do not regularly update their passwords. The tech companies manufacture IoT products but fail to pay attention to the probable security risks. Most of the IoT devices fail to receive enough updates due to insufficient knowledge of security risks among the users. All these factors maximize the data security and privacy risks associated with the furnishing of continuous data over the cloud. The attackers are more interested in data due to which security attacks that cause data breaching and data loss are being considered to be the biggest security risks of cloud computing.

3. SECURITY ISSUES FOR FIVE LAYERED ARCHITECTURE OF IOT

The extensive research on IoT led to the development of different types of architecture to foster a better understanding of the technology and to promote more research opportunities in this area. The basic three layered or three-tiered architecture proposed by Duan et.al (2011) consisted of a perception layer, a network layer, and an application layer. ITU-T (2012) mentions an IoT reference model with a four-layered architecture which includes management service layers in addition to the previous architecture. According to Rayes. A and Salem. S (2019)addition of one more layer to the existing structure provided benefits of solving problems on the interoperability of IoT devices, help vendors to develop joint solutions, facilitate the process of troubleshooting, design, and component development. Khan R. et.al (2012) proposed a five-layered architecture that includes an additional business layer. The five different layers have different functions or objectives due to which they are subjected to different kinds of attacks.

Figure 3. Five Layered Architecture of IoT

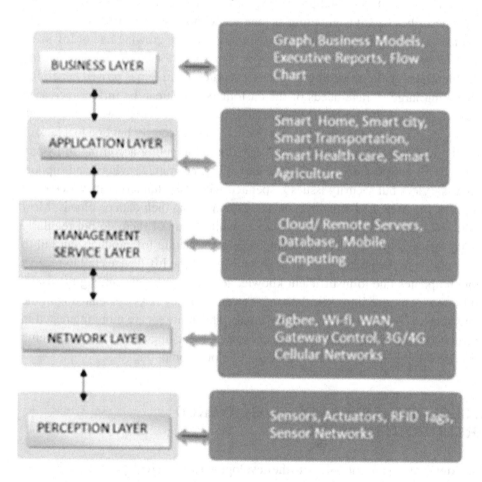

This section covers a brief description of the five layers and the common security threats at these layers.

i.   **Perception Layer:** This layer sometimes referred to as a device or sensing layer mainly consists of sensors, devices actuators, and controllers. A sensor collects data from the surrounding environment by using a physical interface that is converted into an electrical signal so that it can be used by a computing device or can be interpreted to determine. There are numerous varieties of sensors available that can be deployed to attain the desired objectives. Some commonly used sensors are temperature sensors, humidity sensors, moisture sensors, pressure sensors, image sensors, and noise sensors. With the advancements in technology sensors with increased accuracy and decreased size as well as cost are readily available today. Another important content of the perception layer is the actuator that takes an electrical input to convert it into a physical quantity. The devices at this level may include smartphones, tablets, and single-board computers.

The attackers are interested in knowing the information being collected by the sensors for which they may replace it with fake devices. Wurn (2016) considers that gaining physical access to a remote IoT device is easier for an intruder as most of the devices available today lack basic security mechanisms. It happens because providing continuous protection and regular monitoring for a lightweight, low-cost device is not economically viable.

(Hany and Gary,2019; Deogiriakar and Vidhate 2017) has mentioned that some of the security threats at the perception layer are node capture, RF interference on RFID, node jamming, malicious code injection, physical damage, social engineering, sleep deprivation attack, and malicious code injection.

- **Node Capture/Tampering:** In this type of attack the intruder can have access to sensitive data, leak it with the help of important keys like encryption or cryptographic keys and also alter the data being transmitted from the sender to the receiver nodes. It is sometimes considered to be one of the hazardous attacks as the attacker can physically damage the node and also make either partial change in its hardware or alter the entire node. Two problems encountered after these types of attacks are DoS attack against availability by which a captured node can generate random queries on behalf of the attacker and attack against integrity through which the captured node transfers incorrect data to the authentic users.
- **RF interference on RFID:** Radio frequency identification (RFID) provides a great potential to the IoT applications but has a limitation that it is insecure due to its susceptibility to electromagnetic interference. The attackers use noise or electromagnetic interference from other RF devices to corrupt transmission.

- **Node Jamming:** Jamming is commonly called as a Dedicated Denial of Service (DDoS) in the field of cybersecurity. It is a destructive security attack in the WSNs based IoT as it jams the traffic in the network by blocking the channel. This attack causes a quick discharge of batteries for the target devices by disrupting data transmissions and allowing repeated retransmissions. It introduces noise in the carrier which reduces the signal to noise ratio considerably due to which the channels are unable to receive correct data. Jamming can be done permanently that will hamper all the communications in the region or can be done temporarily at regular intervals.

- **Fake node Injection:** The attacker controls data flow on the communicating path by injecting malicious nodes. A malicious node can stop all the data transmissions by dropping the entire packet that has to be forwarded to other nodes. These nodes avoid their detection at occasions by dropping a few packets on the communication path while allowing the remaining packets to the destination. It may at times receive data packets from the source nodes and forward it to other malicious nodes.

- **Malicious Code Injection:** In this type of attack the hacker introduces malicious code into the node or device's memory for achieving full control over the IoT system. Efficient code authentication techniques should be developed to overcome these attacks.

- **Sleep Deprivation:** The protocols or the algorithms developed for communication through the IoT nodes are developed by taking into account the limited available power of the battery-operated devices. Some of the algorithms keep the unused or idol nodes in sleeping mode to elongate the battery lifetime. Through sleep deprivation attacks the intruders keep on running the nodes continuously so that the batteries get discharged soon which results in shut down of the IoT system.

- **Social Engineering:** Most of the IoT users are ignorant about the security techniques required for the safety of their data and devices. This characteristic of the users is utilized by the attacker to sniff sensitive data from the devices without the knowledge of the users. The attacker can sniff data from the sender, manipulate it, and forward it to the receiver due to which the receiver may act according to the manipulated instructions received by it.

- **Physical Damage:** The attacker can destroy the nodes or the physical components by using electrical surge or physical force. The attacker has to reach the place where the IoT devices or nodes are located for accomplishing this type of attack. Physical damage can cause direct damage to the IoT system as for some of the topologies unavailability of a node can disrupt the whole communication path.

ii.   **Network Layer:** The function of the network layer or transport layer is to transmit the data collected from the perception layer to the upper layers of the IoT architecture. The upper layer can be an application layer in the case of three-layered architecture and management service/ processing layers for the four and five-layered architecture. The data can be transferred through the internet, cellular networks, or any other reliable wireless sensor networks.

An IoT system is a combination of several adjoining networks that connect for exchanging information. The network layer uses routing algorithms for data communication over the network. A network layer is divided into two sub-layers known as routing and encapsulation layer. The routing layer delivers data packets from source to destination while the encapsulation layer forms the packets. Along with the transmission of data this layer is expected to provide reliability, avoid congestion, and ensure that all the data packets reach their assigned destinations within the designated time limits. This layer can be more appealing for the intruder as all the devices get connected to the network for either transferring or receiving data. At the network layer, the two protocols that are widely used for data transfer among connected devices are RPL and 6LoWPAN. According to Mayzaud et.al (2015), some of the routing attacks on IoT are flooding, routing table overload, increased rank, decreased rank, eavesdropping, sinkhole, wormhole, and black hole attack.

- **Sinkhole Attack:** It is considered to be the most destructive routing attacks as it compromises the authenticity and integrity of the information being transferred by the devices. The attacker attracts data traffic with a motive to prevent the reception of data by the destination nodes. The compromised node is then used by the attacker to launch an attack by sending fake information to the neighboring nodes about its link quality that is used in routing metrics for choosing the best possible routes for data transmission on the network. All the data packets thus pass through the comprised nodes due to which the destination node is unable to acquire accurate and complete sensing data from the nodes.

- **Wormhole attack:** Wormhole is an internal attack that is very hard to detect because the attacker listens to the activities of the network without any interference. It uses mostly more than one malicious node and these nodes have a tunnel between them. These malicious nodes communicate with each other at a slightly different frequency as compared to other nodes. In this attack, a malicious node receives all the data packets coming towards it and also captures packets from other nodes to forward it through the tunnel for the other malicious node. It disrupts the routing path by creating nonoptimized routes which may lead to early arrival, delayed arrival, or in some cases nonarrival of the data packets at the destined nodes.

Figure 4. Wormhole Attack

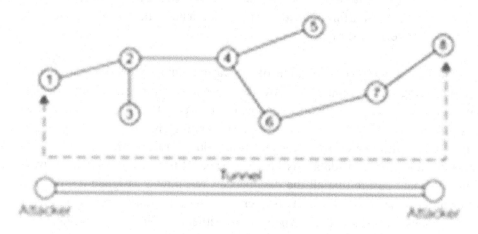

- **Blackhole Attacks:** Routing protocols use intermediate nodes for sending data packets over the network. An intruder utilizes this feature and inserts a fake node in the communication path. This fake node advertises itself to be the best possible route to attract data traffic towards it and thus a blackhole attack occurs. The fake node silently drops all the data packets coming towards it thus preventing transmission of data towards the destination nodes. It causes loss of data, exhaustion of energy resources, and increases transmission delay.
- **Flooding Attack:** Flooding or sometimes referred to as the HELLO flooding attack generates a large amount of traffic in the network which makes nodes and links unavailable for routing. A malicious node joins the network by broadcasting a HELLO message to all neighboring nodes. This node sends HELLO packets with high routing metrics or high energy due to which most of the nodes select it to be the parent node. All the messages are then transmitted through this malicious node which increases the transmission time of messages. As all the neighboring nodes select it to be parent node network traffic and delay increases considerably which in turn depletes the energy of nodes.
- **Routing Table Overload:** In this category of attack the intruder causes resource exhaustion by overloading the routing table. This attack is generally used for the proactive routing protocols as they maintain a routing table that

gets regularly updated. For routing overload, the attacker generates fake routes that cause overloading of the routing table for the targeted nodes. This overloading prevents the formation of appropriated, affects the functioning of the network, and may result in memory overflow.

- **Increased Rank:** Routing protocols for low power lossy networks (RPL) use Destination oriented directed acrylic graph (DODAG) to identify and maintain a topology over a network. Every node is assigned a rank that corresponds to its position according to the root node on the graph. This rank characteristic is used by the attackers to launch an attack by altering the ranks. An Increased rank attack is launched by using a malfunctioning node that increases its rank to a value greater than its actual value to display that it is closer to the root node. The compromised nodes select a malicious node as its preferred parent. This process creates additional routes due to which the data packets either fail to reach their destination or do not forward all the data packets.

- **Version Number Attack:** The version number is a field that is propagated unaltered down the DODAG graph which can be incremented only by the root. An attacker uses a malicious node to change the version number and forwards it to the neighbors. When the nodes receive this new version number, the formation of a new DODAG tree starts. The successive rebuilding of trees will exhaust network resources, increase traffic congestion, and cause loss of data packets.

- **Eavesdropping Attack:** An intruder can launch an eavesdropping attack on an insecure network that is being used for data transfer. It includes activities like sniffing and traffic analysis of the network. These attacks are difficult to detect as no significant change is observed in the network transmissions. An attacker performs sniffing by listening to the exchange of information on the networks. It is a very common attack for a wired as well as the wireless medium which can be done through a compromised device or by capturing of data packets. In a traffic analysis attack, the intruder tries to collect routing information to know the partial view of topology. The attacker can gather information regarding the network through this attack and then decide the type of attack that can be used to disrupt the data transfer.

Figure 5. Attacks of Five Layered Architecture of IoT

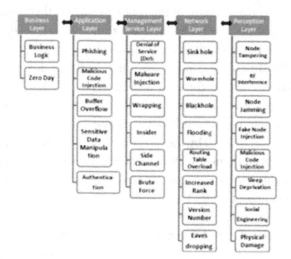

iii. **Management Service Layer:** The three-layer architecture developed in the initial days of IoT did not consider security risks and the network layer was directly transferred to the application layer. The management service layer sometimes referred to as the processing layer or middleware layer performs the task of storing, analyzing, and processing the huge amount of data coming from the network layer. This layer mainly consists of remote servers placed on the cloud. As the cloud offers a large or virtually never-ending space more and more organizations are relying on the cloud for storing their data. Cloud provides security and privacy by using effective authentication and encryption techniques. But still, the cloud is not completely safe from the attackers or the security threats. As the cloud collects data from different networks and organizations the attackers consider it to be a source of enormous data that has increased the possibilities of attacks on the cloud. Adamou (2019) and Swamy et.al (2017) have explained some of the security threats to cloud storage that can take place at the management service layer like DoS attacks, Malware Injection attack, Wrapping attack, side-channel attack, and the malicious insider.

○ **Denial of Service (DoS) attack:** In one of the works of literature by Deshmukh and Dewadkar (2015) among all the different kind of attacks on the cloud environment 14% of them are DDoS and according to a survey as the usage of cloud increases the rate of DDoS attacks will increase proportionately. An attacker overloads the target cloud with a large number of service requests due to which the cloud is unable to respond to the incoming requests from the users. This attack can reduce the performance of the cloud by damaging the virtual servers or in some cases may lead to the unavailability of resources to the users. The attackers scan the network for vulnerabilities and then use these vulnerable machines as agents to launch an attack.

○ **Malware Injection Attack:** A malware injection attack is launched on a cloud; the attacker inserts a malicious service or virtual machine in the cloud. A malicious service implementation module or virtual machine instance is created by the attacker for adding it to the cloud. These attacks are implemented by the intruders to have control of the user's information. When the attacker is successful in hacking a cloud, its user's requests are diverted towards the hacker. The malicious code execution is initiated after which the invader can manipulate or steal data and cloud services go through the problem of eavesdropping. The attacker can use a malware injection attack to perform data modifications and changes or reverse in functionality. It is considered to be a dominant attack that results in misusing service to a cloud environment.

○ **Wrapping Attack:** One of the reasons that elevate the risk of wrapping attack on clouds is that most of the cloud users get connected to services through a web browser and the problems caused by the attackers are seen during the execution of the web service request. When a user makes a request it reaches the server through the browser which leads to the generation of a SOAP message. The XML documents are signed, canonicalization is done and signature values are added at the end of the document before passing the SOAP message. The attacker launches a wrapping attack during the translation of the SOAP message as the SOAP header contains all the required information about the destination. In cloud computing, a wrapping attack is launched by using XML (eXtensible Markup Language) signature wrapping through which the attacker can change the contents of the XML document that is being exchanged. XML signature is generally used for securing user's credentials from unauthorized access but it is not able to provide complete security to positions in the document. The attacker duplicates the SOAP message and transfers it to the server which in turn fails to check the integrity of the message owing to the duplication of the signature value. When a server fails to detect the duplication an attacker interferes with the working of the cloud by running malicious code.

○ **Insider attack:** This kind of threat is initiated by a person who is a current or former employee of a cloud service provider, who has access to the organization's data, system, and functionality. The attacker in this case commonly called as malicious insider misuses his position to fulfill some offensive intentions that adversely affect the confidentiality, integrity, and availability of the company's information system. A malicious insider can attempt his attack in a shorter period as compared to an external attacker as he has complete knowledge regarding the system policies and functionality of the organization. Moreover, a company exercises most of its efforts for protection from external attackers without sensing security threats from the insiders. Some of the factors responsible for insider attacks are poor authentication, lack of techniques to observe user behavior, and deficiency of methods to protect devices. The attackers can steal data, share it with unauthorized parties, and inject malware/ viruses in the system that can severely affect a company's performance.

- ○ **Side Channel Attack:** This attack is considered to be a threat to data security over the cloud. Highly sensitive data, encryption, or decryption keys are some of the targets of side-channel attacks. It creates a hidden channel by using hardware and software techniques that are utilized to obtain information and the information acquired through these hidden channels is called side-channel information. An attack that is initiated using the side-channel information is called a side-channel attack. This type of attack can be either passive or active. For active attacks, the attackers modify the contents of the target thereby forcing it to carry out some abnormal tasks. On the other hand, in a passive attack, the intruder keeps on examining the activities of the target to obtain information but does not make any changes.

- ○ **Brute Force Attack:** Brute force attacks are used by cheap cloud providers to target users, organizations, and other cloud service providers. It is generally a trial and error method used for decoding data. Some of the common targets of this attack are passwords, encryption keys, and API keys. To implement a brute force attack the intruder does not use any intellectual strategy but keeps on trying different combinations of characters and evaluates the response until he is successful. This attack is easy to perform but the time required to complete it can be very long in some cases as the attackers have to check through all possible combinations of characters till the task is completed.

iv. **Application Layer:** An application layer consists of several applications like smart home, smart city, smart health care, smart agriculture, a smart grid that uses IoT. These applications are regulated by the information obtained from the management service layer. It provides a virtual service layer to ensure data transport, security, and service discovery and device management without being dependent on technologies utilized for connectivity at the lower layers. The application layer furnishes the data received from the devices and performance of the actuators. This layer provides services and at the same time defines a set of protocols to interact directly with the users. Virtual reality, augmented reality, human-computer interface, and multimedia applications are some of the technologies used for connecting intelligent IoT applications with its users. The application layer is intended to be used by the people and therefore is considered to be a wide attack surface by the malicious users. Some of the security attacks on the application layer as mentioned by Molugu et.al. (2018) and Chen et.al (2018) are phishing attacks, malicious code injection, butter overflow, sensitive data manipulation, and authentication.

- **Phishing Attack:** One of the security risks associated with IoT is a phishing attack which is sometimes referred to as a social engineering attack as it targets human beings through devices rather than sending attacks on devices. The attacker gets involved in communication with the victim to gather some confidential data like user identity or passwords, which may become the source for bigger attacks. Another method used for a phishing attack is when an attacker persuades the victim for acting like that would support attacks like clicking on a link or going to a website. Phishing emails are the most common source of this attack.

- **Malicious Code Injection:** This attack destroys the IoT system's function by adding, removing, or modifying software by introducing malicious codes. Some of the different purposes the attackers try to fulfill through these attacks are to have unauthorized access to data, propagate worms, and to acquire system control. These attacks can cause the system to lose control by which the privacy of the user is lost and in some cases may lead to a complete shutdown.

- **Buffer Overflow Attack:** Ina buffer overflow attack, the attacker tries to exploit the program vulnerabilities by using software coding to place extra data in the buffer which is more than its storage capability. This causes an overflow of the excess data, which may get leaked to other buffers thereby corrupting or overwriting the data in those buffers. The extra data induced by the attacker consists of some specific instructions for the accomplishment of tasks like corrupting files, modifying data, and accessing some private information

- **Sensitive Data Manipulation:** This attack violates user privacy as the attacker gets illicit access to sensitive or confidential data to manipulate it. An attacker tries to analyze the defects in the permission model and obtain illicit access to data. An application is then controlled by the attacker who makes the applications operate in a way that is different from their tasks they have been originally assigned to do. For example, a smart device and smart App exchange a lot of sensitive data by using events. Lack of sufficient protection of events can cause leakage of the event. If the user input lacks sufficient protection, these attacks may cause a violation of the privacy of users and harm the users seriously.

○ **Authentication/ Authorization:** Authentication is a process used in IoT to identify its users, devices, and applications to limit unauthorized access by the adversaries. Authentication thus helps the users in having secure communication, avoid data leakage, and develop new services. But most of the authentication mechanisms are not perfect due to which they fail to provide firm security to the applications. Many of the IoT applications like the smart home, smart transportation, health care are being managed by mobile phones. The attackers introduce some malicious apps and tempt users to download it. The attackers are then able to remotely control these devices containing malicious apps and also gain access to their usernames, passwords and also launch attacks in varying degrees. Lack of two-factor authentication, weak passwords that are easy to be guessed, and no limit to failed attempts that allows the attackers to attempt access to a device number of times without getting blocked are some of the factors that increase the vulnerability of authentication attacks.

V. **Business Layer:** The business layer being at the top level of the five-layered IoT architecture symbolizes the purpose of an IoT application and at the same time plays a significant role in regulating the overall working of the IoT system. It is closely associated with the real-world in terms of handling the user's information. Some common security problems as mentioned by Burhan et.al (2018) are business logic attacks and zero-day attacks.

○ **Business Logic Attack:** A business logic attack takes advantage of the loopholes in the programming which has been adopted to control data exchange among the users and application's supporting database. The attackers download the application to know about its weaknesses and then program bots called business logic bots (BLB) to launch attacks. Some of the business logic flaws are poor validation process for password recovery and inappropriate coding techniques used by the programmer in case of encryption as well as for input validation. These attacks are imperceptible as they arrive as regular requests and contain legitimate values. Attackers use business logic attacks to steal information, removing business-related crucial information, and perform server-based or application-level attacks.

    ◦   **Zero-Day Attack:** Zero-day attack is one more type of attack on the business layer that tries to take advantage of infirmity in the security algorithms which remain unattended by the vendors or developers owing to lack of awareness among them. It is called a zero-day attack because it occurs before the software developer comes to know about the problem. These attacks are launched by inserting malware or spyware to steal information from the companies without the knowledge of the software developers. The intruders target a software system with a malware which integrates with the existing system to prevent it from executing its normal operations. They send malware in the systems in the form of website links and as the user clicks the link the malicious software begins to download on the system. These attacks can prove to be very harmful if not detected at the proper time because it may lead to the failure of the entire network.

4. INTERNET OF THINGS SECURITY SOLUTIONS

The various attacks on the IoT system that occur at different levels of architecture raise an alarming situation for the users thereby making it essential for everyone to know the remedies or solutions to deal with these types of attacks. Most of the attacks that are being implemented by the invaders are happening due to the vulnerabilities with the device or networks or clouds or at the application level. Inadequate information among the users related to the security solutions and lack of concern among the manufacturers or the vendors has increased the vulnerabilities of IoT. Security mechanisms should be devised for devices, networks, storage, and also the applications.

4.1 Solutions at Device Layer

The IoT devices should be smart enough to handle processes like encryption, authentication, time stamps, firewalls, and connection loss. Most of the IoT devices are microprocessor-based which hinders their ability to handle the intricacies involved in being connected through the internet. The IoT devices generally used can communicate with the cloud through Ethernet or Wi-Fi but due to their incapability to handle data and low storage space, all data has to be stored in the cloud which increases the risks of data breaching. Therefore we should opt for devices that can process data locally. An advantage of using such kind of devices will be that the forwarding of sensitive data to the cloud can be avoided.

The attackers keep on discovering new vulnerabilities in the existing system. At the same time, device manufacturers and service providers devote time to develop innovative methods to handle security risks. The users should keep on regularly updating their operating systems firmware, and application software. Along with these, the users should be careful about their passwords. Unique and strong passwords should be used and the same passwords for a long time or different applications should be avoided. Similarly, passwords that can be easily guessed should be avoided.

The users should read the privacy policies before downloading any applications and avoid the ones that appear to be harmful. Before the selection of devices try to know if the data on your devices is being collected by a third party and in that case, the manufacturers should be ready to inform about the protection policies envisaged regarding data breaches.

4.2 Solutions at Network Layer

According to Hameed et.al (2019), the network topology or the designs should be tolerant of any kind of malicious attack coming towards it. Early detection of unwanted intrusions is another desirable feature that can prevent major damage and the effect of attacks can be mitigated before it spreads across the network. The protocols must be able to recover quickly from network failures caused due to security threats as disruption of networks for a long time may prove to be disastrous in case of applications like disaster management. Hence algorithms or protocols or techniques used at the communication layer should be able to detect as well as recover from the threats.

Transfer of encrypted data over the networks is preferred so that even if it is intercepted, it will be of no use to the people who do not possess the appropriate encryption key to unlock the code. The process of data transfer between device and cloud or the remote server should be initiated by the devices. A bidirectional connection with the cloud can be allowed in specific circumstances to facilitate remote control of the devices. But it is preferred to avoid any incoming connections towards a device or connection from the internet to the device. Many of the field devices do not have to reconfigure, testing, or monitoring software that are applicable to cloud service. If incoming connections are allowed, individuals or network or field devices outside the communication network can enter to utilize its resources which can increase the security risks of a network.

It is essential to handle information exchange, either a transmitted message from a device or a received message with equal attention. A suitable security policy should be used for handling messages and techniques like double encryption, filtering, queuing should be used according to the purpose of communication. For example, if some confidential data is to be sent to the desired location, all the messages carrying client information can be double encrypted. Careful handling of the messages is a powerful tool to avoid inappropriate access at the communication or network layer.

Node location privacy algorithms have been discussed in some research works. Guangjie et.al (2019) has discussed the source location privacy algorithm that protects the privacy of source location from the adversaries. Similarly, Liu et.al (2017) has discussed the sink location privacy algorithm and Babu and Balasubadra (2018) have discussed an algorithm that preserves the location of the source as well as sink nodes. All these algorithms use different techniques to inject false packets or false nodes in the path between source and destination. The presence of false packets confuses the adversaries and they are unable to detect the exact location of the source and destination nodes and therefore fail to capture data on the networks.

a. Solutions on the Management Service layer

Connection to the cloud by the users or by the devices should be based on an authentication system. Research by Chouhan and Singh (2016) signifies the importance of a one-time password for authentication as the one-time passwords are immune to the man in the middle of eavesdropping attacks. Accessing the clouds can be done by using two-step authentications where a password and then a one-time password can be used to assure secure access to the cloud. Passwords can be used as an authentication mechanism for humans but to enhance the security environment for the cloud digital certificate can be used. An asymmetric, encryption-based system is used by the digital certificate to encrypt the communication path from device to cloud to verify data exchange. Cryptographic identification is another advantage that a digital certificate provides over the traditional access methods done with user identification and passwords. Some of the issues that need to be addressed are suitable time slots for loading data on the cloud, level of encryption required by data elements, and the kind of firewalls that are being used for the cloud.

In some of the authentication methods, the attacker can easily present themselves as legitimate users by knowing passwords. To overcome this problem Cirani et.al (2013) have suggested an open authorization method to determine the validity of the requesting user. The open authorization (OAuth) protocol uses four roles: Resources owner that grants access to an end-user, Resource server than maintains user-related information, a client or the third party that desires to achieve user's data, and authorization servers that accomplishes the task of authentication by issuing access tokens. OAuth process starts with the client sending an authorization request to the resources owner. Approval of the resource owner gets confirmed when the client receives an authorization grant. The client forwards this authorization grant to the Authorized server which in turn issues an access token only if the grant request if found valid. The access token is presented by the client to the resource server that provides the requested resources to the client after validation of the token. OAuth is thus an effective method to grant secure permission to the requesting users and also to restrict the access of a third party.

Figure 6. Open Authorization Protocol for IoT

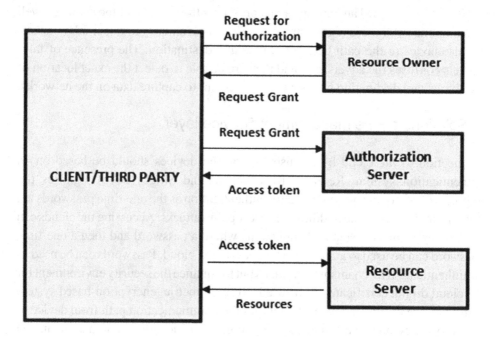

b. Solutions at Application Layer

Application layer security threats need to be handled cautiously as any amendments in the application level by the hackers can be dangerous for the users. If we consider a medical application a hacker can vary the limit of medicine dosage that can prove to be fatal and may deteriorate the health condition of the patient. To protect the application layer from the intruders it is essential to check if the maintenance activities make the applications susceptible to some new threats. Authenticated software should be used and it should be updated regularly. Access or privilege levels assigned to the users should be of optimum limits to avoid any undesirable changes by the users. A fundamental prerequisite for an application is that it should be able to control its associated devices through remote or far locations. The ability of remote control can facilitate sending commands to devices during its whole lifecycle, detecting problems that may arise during functioning, updating software, and include some new functions.

To aid the proper handling of devices without granting more privilege to the users and to encourage safe communication Gyory and Chuah (2017) have suggested IoTOne solutions. It is a technology that examines security weaknesses before publishing IoT Apps. IoTOne is a user-friendly platform that supports devices from different vendors thus providing its customer an opportunity to select a product that will correspond to their necessities at lower deployment costs. This platform allows all the devices to run the internet and supports third-party applications. IoTOne handles the risks associated with third-party integration by imposing restrictions on them to avoid any unreliable methodologies that may harm the system. The third-party developers have to submit their backend programs to IoTOne system for verification of any insecure parameters. A third-party app will be available in the IoTOne app store only if it is verified that the code provided by the third party has correct commands, uses safe programming techniques, and confirms that the endpoints have not allotted more privileges to the apps. All these restrictions on third-party apps reduce the risks of attacks on the IoT applications.

5. TECHNOLOGIES FOR SECURITY OF IOT

Machine learning and Blockchain are some of the emerging technologies that help to deal with security issues in IoT.

5.1 Machine learning (ML)

ML is an application of Artificial Intelligence that aims to turn our machines into intelligent gadgets without being programmed or without any human interference. The programmers do not need to worry about algorithms while working with ML. An appropriate dataset and the expected outputs are supplied to a computer which is then converted into a meaningful program for the users. It is like asking a computer to learn an algorithm according to the input and anticipated outputs. Four types of learning generally used are Supervised/Inductive Learning in which the training data includes expected outputs, Unsupervised Learning that does not include desired outputs in training data, Semi-supervised learning where the training data involves some of the expected outcomes, and Reinforcement learning which is utilized for making robots. ML can be used in IoT to provide intelligent services.

Machine learning can efficiently process large amounts of data generated by the IoT networks and at the same time enable IoT systems to make intelligent systems. ML is therefore envisaged to be a promising technique for better utilization of data. Some of the characteristics that make ML more flexible for IoT include its support for self-organizing operations, optimization of overall system performance by processing analytical data received from devices/users, and its distributed nature which eliminates the requirement of centralized information exchange for users and devices. Research by Hussain et. al (2019) shows that ML can be used for solving security issues like Authentication and access control, detection of attacks and to decrease its effects, DoS as well as DDoS attacks, intrusion detection, and analysis of malicious code that are injected by the invaders.

5.2 BlockChain

Blockchain consists of a group of blocks that are linked through cryptography. It is composed of a distributed digital ledger that cannot be altered and is shared by all the participants in the Blockchain network. A block consists of a cryptographic hash, a list of validated transactions, and a pointer to the cryptographic hash of the previous block. It uses a decentralized approach in which a node can verify if a participant is the real owner of the asset. Decentralized architecture, trustless peer to peer transactions, immutable transactions, the record of transactions, and consensus mechanism are the key characteristics that have made Blockchain a favorable technology for solving security or privacy issues.

Blockchain is another potential solution that can prove to be fruitful in handling the existing security aspects of IoT. It can help in the favorable processing of numerous transactions, tracking and managing the billions of connected smart IoT devices. In a centralized model used by IoT, several security threats are observed because devices are identified and connected through cloud services and need the internet to communicate even if they are located close to each other. Integration of Blockchain with IoT can improve the overall security of the IoT environment by (i) using powerful data encryptions that are difficult to be hacked (ii) decentralized approach which will reduce the risks of single-point failures in which the attackers target a single point through spoofing or DDoS attacks to disrupt network functioning (iii) mitigation of Man in the Middle attacks by using cryptographic signatures as it will be difficult to interrupt any communication (iv) ability to track the node status that will help in preventing data tampering by locking access for the IoT devices and shutting down the compromised devices.

6. FUTURE DIRECTIONS

The voluminous data being exchanged over the IoT platforms is a principal factor that draws the attention of the invaders. A lot of private data is exchanged through the communication networks there is a need to embrace innovative solutions to secure the data of the users. The storage facilities should be upgraded as there is no facility available to maintain the safety of the stored data. Authentication facilities are available but passwords are not sufficient to keep our data secure due to a large number of devices. Passwords can be guessed or obtained by victimizing the users so new systems ought to be developed that will use unique identification systems like fingerprint or iris scanning. IoT devices are away from the users and they have to access remotely due to which connectivity in IoT depends on wireless communication techniques for information transfer. There is a need to ensure more security at the network layer. The source and sink node location privacy algorithms provide security but the energy consumption increases due to the presence of false packets in the route which in turn reduces the network lifetime. As our IoT devices are battery-powered there is a need to develop algorithms that can balance the energy requirements of the network in the presence of security algorithms.

7. CONCLUSION

Attainment of security goals for the IoT system seems to be a herculean task due to many challenges like a large amount of data, heterogeneous environment, device constraints like low storage capacity and power, varying network topology, and lack of safe storage facility for data. This chapter has discussed security attacks at the five-layer architecture of IoT. Some of the common attacks observed at all the layers are Denial of Service (DoS), Eavesdropping attacks, and malicious code injection attack. The security requirements at all the levels are different and therefore techniques to deal with them are also different. It is not possible to achieve a safe IoT system by implementing security algorithms at any one of the layers. Machine learning and Blockchain are two technologies that can help to ensure security for the IoT system. Security algorithms should be updated regularly to keep IoT systems for a long time because as the developers bring up with new security solutions the attackers may try to find new vulnerabilities in the system. So whatever technology or protocol or algorithm is used it should be able to minimize security risks to satisfy the demands of users. Security is an important parameter to maintain trust among the consumers and at the same time increase the usability of the versatile technology.

REFERENCES

Ari, A.A., Ngangmo, O.K., Titouna, C., Thiare, O., Mohamadou, A., & Gueroui, A.M. (2019). Enabling privacy and security in Cloud of Things: Architecture, applications, security & privacy challenges. *Applied Computing and Informatics.*

Babu, S. S., & Balasaubadra, K. (2018). Chronic Privacy Protection from Source to Sink in Sensor Network Routing. *International Journal of Applied Engineering Research, 13*(5), 2798-2808.

Botta, A., Donato, W. D., Persico, V., & Pescape, A. (2016). Integration of Cloud computing and Internet of Things: A survey. In *Future Generation Computer Systems.* Elsevier.

Burhan, M., Rehman, R. A., Khan, B., & Kim, B. S. (2018). IoT Elements, Layered Architectures, and SecurityIssues: A Comprehensive Survey. *Mdpi Sensors.*

Chen, K., Zhang, S., Li, Z., Zhang, Y., Deng, Q., Ray, S., & Jin, Y. (2018). Internet-of-Things Security and Vulnerabilities: Taxonomy, Challenges, and Practice. *Journal of Hardware and Systems Security, 2,* 97–110.

Chouhan, P., & Singh, R. (2016). Security Attacks on Cloud Computing With Possible Solution. *International Journal of Advanced Research in Computer Science and Software Engineering, 6*(1).

Cirani, S., Ferrari, G., & Veltri, L. (2013). Enforcing security mechanisms in the IP-based Internet of things: An algorithmic overview. *Algorithms,* 197–226.

Deogirikar, J., & Vidhate, A. S. (2017). Security Attacks in IoT: A Survey. *International Conference on I-SMAC (IoT in Social, Mobile, Analytics, and Cloud, 32-37.*

Donno, M. D., Giaretta, A., Dragoni, N., Bucchiarone, A., & Mazzara, M. (2019). *Cyber-Storms Come from Clouds: Security of Cloud Computing in the IoT Era.* Future Internet.

Duan, R., Chen, X., & Xing, T. (2011). A QoS Architecture for IoT. *IEEE International Conferences on Internet of Things, and Cyber, Physical and Social Computing.*

Gyory, M., & Chuah, M. (2017). IoT One: Integrated Platform for Heterogeneous IoT Devices. *International Conference on Computing, Networking, and Communications (ICNC): Workshop.*

Hameed, S., Khan, F.I., & Hameed, B. (2019). Understanding Security Requirements and Challenges in The Internet of Things (IoT): A Review. *Hindawi, Journal of Computer Networks and Communication.*

Hany, F. A., & Gary, B. W. (2019). *IoT security, Privacy, Safety, and Ethics*. Springer Nature Switzerland.

He, Y., Han, G., Wang, H., Ansere, J. A., & Zhang, W. (2019). A Sector Based Random Routing Scheme for Protecting the Source Location Privacy in WSNs for the Internet of Things. *Elsevier Future Generation Computer Systems*.

Hussain, F., Hussain, R., Hassan, S. A., & Hossain, E. (2019). *Machine Learning in IoT Security: Current Solutions and Future Challenges*. Arxiv: 1904.05735v1 [cs.CR].

Khan, R., Khan, S. N., Zaheer, R., & Khan, S. (2012). Future Internet: The Internet of Things Architecture, Possible Applications, and Key Challenges. *10th International Conference on Frontiers of Information Technology (FIT): Proceedings*.

Liu, A., Liu, X., Tang, Z., Yang, L. T., & Shao, Z. (2017). Preserving Smart Sink-Location Privacy with Delay Guaranteed Routing Scheme for WSNs. *ACM Transactions on Embedded Computing Systems*, 16(3), 68.

Mayzaud, A., Badonnel, R., Chrisment, I. (2016) A Taxonomy of Attacks in RPL-based Internet of Things. *International Journal of Network Security, 18*(3), 459-473.

Molugu, S. V., Bindu, S. M., Aishwarya, B., Dhanush, B. N., & Manjunath, R. K. (2018). Security and Privacy Challenges in Internet of Things. *Proceedings of the 2nd International Conference on Trends in Electronics and Informatics*.

Rayes, A., & Salem, S. (2019). *Internet of Things from Hype to Reality: The Road to digitization*. Springer.

Sadier, G., & Sabri, F. (2017). *Nanosatellite Communications: A Market Study for IoT/M2M applications*. London Economics, Market Sizing, and Requirements Report.

Sharma, R., Pandey, N., & Khatri, S. K. (2017). Analysis of IoT Security at Network Layer. *Proceedings of 6th International Conference on Reliability, Infocom Technologies and Optimization (ICRITO) (Trends and Future Directions)*, 585-590.

Wurm, J., Jin, Y., Liu, Y., Hu, S., Heffner, K., Rahman, F., & Tehranipoor, M. (2016). *Introduction to cyber-physical system security: A cross-layer perspective*. *IEEE Transactions on Multi-Scale Computing Systems*.

Chapter 7
Guidelines for the Specification of IoT Requirements:
A Smart Cars Case

Asmaa Achtaich
CRI, Université Paris 1 Panthéon Sorbonne, France & Siweb, Université Mohammed 5, Morocco

Mines de Rabat, Morocco & Siweb, Université Mohammed 5, Morocco

Camille Salinesi
CRI, Université Paris 1 Panthéon Sorbonne, France

Raul Mazo
Lab-STICC, ENSTA Bretagne, France & GIDITIC, Universidad EAFIT, Colombia

Nissrine Souissi
Ecole Nationale Supérieure des

Ounsa Roudies
Siweb, Université Mohammed 5, Morocco

ABSTRACT

In the last five years, we witnessed the shift from the vision of the internet of things (IoT) to an actual reality. It is currently shifting again from specific and single applications to larger and more generic ones, which serves the needs of thousands of users across borders and platforms. To avoid losing the personification of applications, on account of genericity, new approaches and languages that use generic knowledge as a steppingstone while taking into consideration users and context's specific and evolutive needs are on the rise. This chapter aims to provide a framework to support the creation of such approaches (DSPL4IoT). It is later on used to assess notable IoT specification approaches and extract conclusion of the trends and persistent challenges and directions. An approach for the specification of natural language (NL) requirements for IoT systems is also provided to assist domain and application engineers with the formulations of such requirements.

DOI: 10.4018/978-1-7998-6463-9.ch007

1 INTRODUCTION

The Internet of Things (IoT) is here to stay. In 2020, a swapping 99% of companies maintained or increased their budget for IoT (Gartner, 2020). And as the world recovers from a pandemic that froze life as we know it (Covid-19) (World Health Organization, 2020), companies that have succeeded digitalizing their business are the most likely to survive the aftermath. While for some businesses this translates to moving their assets to the cloud, for others like manufacturing, health or agriculture, digitalizing the business is much more complicated. It requires much more advanced devices and technologies, mainly, IoT related. This means that sensors, actuators, smartphones, computers, vehicles, buildings and even people and animal should evolve into "things" (ITU, 2012). That simply -but not so simply- means that they should all eventually possess the ability to remotely communicate, collaborate, have an impact on the environment they serve and, in advanced scenarios, be artificially intelligent.

This new reality emphasizes the need for IoT dedicated standards, best practices and Frameworks. While a plethora of existing works covers various IoT related issues, from its enabling technology like middleware (Ngu et al, 2017), dedicated operating systems or lightweight communication protocols (Baccelli et al., 2018), to storing and processing the big amount of generated data (Chang et al., 2020) (Mohammadi et al., 2018), there's been less focus on requirement specification for this category of systems. After all, requirements are the core of any software system as they convey the expectations of its users. Therefore, a "good" IoT system highly depends on the accuracy, exhaustiveness and quality of the expressed and specified requirements. Conceiving approaches that rise to the expectations of IoT developers and users ought to follow clear guidelines that respect the requirement engineering process and that are drawn from theory and practice in the field of the IoT. This chapter unfolds and organizes these guidelines in the form of an IoT reference framework (DSPL4IoT). The chapter also presents and implementation of the Framework in the form of a semi-formal language for the specification of requirements for IoT development. The language, presented in Natural Language, and delineated by an EBNF grammar (Feynman & Objectives, 2016), can be used by IoT engineers as a blueprint for the definition of their specification. It presents a) an exhaustive view of requirement types that should be considered, at one point or the other, b) interactions with various elements of the environment, including the execution and running context, other devices, people, etc, and finally c) considers the technical, business and contextual evolutions of the IoT field.

The chapter is organized as follows. First it introduces DSPL4IoT along with a definition of its dimensions. Then, in section 3, the chapter defines the fundamentals of requirement specification. Section 4 presents a motivational example. Section

5 introduces the NL specification template, and section 6 maps other existing languages with the proposed Framework, in order to identify current trends in IoT development as well as future directions. Section 7 exposes related similar works before concluding the chapter in section 8.

2 IOT DESIGN FRAMEWORK

In order to design comprehensive IoT solutions that guarantee the characteristics discussed in the previous section, three essential aspect should be taken into account:

- **Reusability:** in a specific domain, IoT applications tend to share similar functionalities and qualities, as a result of related requirements. Therefore, existing knowledge shall not be designed for single use. It should rather be stored, organized and capitalized upon for the creation of different IoT applications, for different users and usages.
- **Personalization:** IoT applications shall represent the exact needs and expectations of their users. While reusability helps develop new solutions, faster, and with lowers costs and resources, IoT solutions are very specific to their client's needs, in terms of the choice of devices, the choice of components, and the execution environment.
- **Evolution:** The internet of things connects smart devices, in a "dumb" environment. The first should adapt to the latter to maintain the required functionality and performance, and at times, to adjust it. In addition to that, the environment is also uncertain. This often leads to change in requirements after the execution of IoT software. Besides the evolution of requirements, the composition of IoT solutions is also unstable, new devices can be added, while others can get broken or disconnected. In a like manner, embedded software changes too. All these adjustments shall be thought-out and managed.

The two first qualities are at the heart of software product line engineering. It's a paradigm that manages variability by considering a *domain* layer, where reusable knowledge is organized in variability models, and an *application* layer, where single products are derived, in conformity with final client's requirements. Evolution is partially tackled in dynamic software product line engineering, which restates the (re)configuration capabilities at runtime. This additional layer, commonly referred to as *adaptation* layer, helps build self-adaptive software product lines.

Moreover, requirements only exist in a context (Pohl, 2010), therefore, at each engineering level, the dependencies between requirements and the context in which they are valid should clearly be stated, and separated from the larger environment that can be relevant for the system, but which does not have a direct impact on it, at a time being.

2.1 Three Engineering Processes

Building IoT software that provides for all three characteristics follows the guidelines of the three respective engineering processes, namely domain, application and adaptation engineering, as previously stated by Mazo et al. (Mazo, 2018). The three engineering processes are illustrated in Figure 1.

- **Domain engineering** is a development phase for reuse. It is a systematic approach to identify the similarities and differences between protentional applications in a domain, particularly in terms of requirements, architectures and components that can be reused across the IoT product line (Pohl et al., 2005). This phase in the IoT development process is realized by a domain expert, who's likely to have a comprehensive knowledge of it. It offers a description of all the artifacts and their dependencies, provides the means for their effective use and proposes an approach for their implementation. Connectivity for example is a prominent concern for the IoT, as IoT application depend entirely on the internet (Hinai & Singh, 2018) (Lin et al., 2017) (Sánchez-Arias et al., 2017). Communication protocol can therefore be designed as a variable which ought to be implemented as a Wi-Fi, Zigbee, RFID or Bluetooth, etc.
- **Application engineering** is a development phase through reuse (Pohl et al., 2005). It's a process where the reusable artefacts, defined during the study of the domain, are exploited for the construction of compliant products. Thus, and based on the needs of end users, the selection and assembly of the artefacts is carried out at this level, by an application engineer. The result of this activity is an executable IoT application, an architecture, a test unit, etc. During this phase, the application user can decide to alternate between the Wi-fi or RFID protocols to connect his devices, according to a pre-set logic.
- **Adaptation engineering** maintains activities of application engineering after the IoT solutions is executed. It manages the behavior of the derived product, i the face of changing requirements, environments and internal alterations (Danny Weyns, 2017). As a reaction to an internet interruption for example and in order to ensure service durability, the communication protocol can dynamically switch to RFID technology instead if a Wi-Fi based communication.

2.2 Three Requirement Engineering Aspects

Three addition dimensions should be considered in IoT design. The system, the (relevant) context, the (generic) environment, as illustrated in Figure 1.

- **The system** is a collection of components, organized to perform a function (INCOSE, 2018). It's everything that "is" the IoT application, including devices, the communication protocols, but also the components and their current configuration. As adaptations occur, the devices involved in the IoT application along with the configuration of active components may change, therefore changing the system too. It is therefore a dynamic dimension.
- **The context** is every information that can be used to characterize the situation of an entity. Therefore, everything that surrounds IoT applications, and which has a direct impact on it, is part of the context (Sezer et al., 2018). Users that interact with the IoT application's interfaces, the weather, the state of batteries or the statistics about device' usage is considered part of the context. The elements of a context are not static. They are relevant in specific configurations but can become inconsequential in other. This means that the context is a dynamic dimension too, as its elements alternate between contextual and environmental. Moreover, the composition of the IoT application itself evolves as adaptations take place. Therefore, the context and system dimension are partially blended as well.
- **The environment** is a dimension that is not affected, nor does it affect the system. It contains information relating to the domain of the IoT application, along with some other correlated domains which has the potential to be of value.

Figure 1 presents the IoT design framework which shows the different concern levels that should be specified, for a proper realization of IoT. The vertical dimensions guarantee reusability, personalization and evolution, and the horizontal dimensions represent the IoT system, along with its dependencies to its context and environment.

3 REQUIREMENTS SPECIFICATION FUNDAMENTALS

Requirements are the heart of any software (Chakraborty et al., 2012), including IoT systems. A proper understanding of their engineering process is fundamental to a proper design, and ultimatly, to a better user experience. Before diving into a classification of requirements (in section 4) and mapping formal requirement specification approaches for IoT to the proposed framework (in section 6), it is important to grasp the fundamental concepts of requirement engineering development, from elicitation, specification, to verification and validation (Pohl, 2016).

While the focus of this chapter remains of the aspects of specification, the other activities are discussed to provide the reader with a holistic view of the requirement engineering process, for the development of IoT solutions.

Figure 1. IoT design Framework

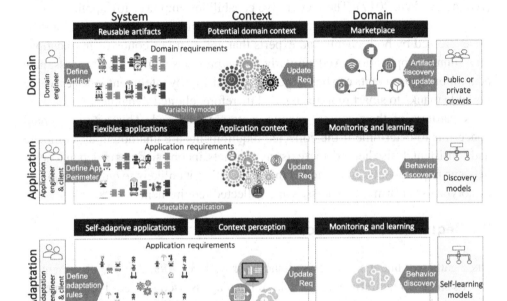

3.1 Requirement Elicitation

Gathering requirements is a decisive phase in a requirement engineering development approach (Lahboube et al., 2014). While it may appear evident, however, deciding what to build is sometimes the hardest part about software development (Bowen & Hinchey, 1999). Building software for the internet of things is specifically challenging, due to the fact that requirements are constantly gathered, even after the IoT application is running (Antonino et al., 2018). First, at the domain level, requirement elicitation is the responsibility of domain engineers who define what the IoT application can do by eliciting reusable requirements. Also, with new devices, new protocols and new services lunched to the market with a speed that's never been witnessed before (Atzori et al., 2017), come new requirements that shall dynamically be discovered. As illustrated previously in the framework in figure 1, a marketplace has the potential to collect the new requirements, formally through specialized crowdsourcing platforms (Salinesi et al., 2018), or informally through public marketplaces. Then, at the application level, requirements are gathered from the users of the final application. Through questioning, observation, or by the means of other elicitation techniques (Khan et al., 2014). Yet again, contrary to conventional software, IoT benefits from the powerful services that come with real time context-awareness, cloud data supplied by thousands of connected devices, and the latest artificial intelligence algorithms (Hwang & Chen, 2017). These cognitive capabilities empower IoT applications to anticipate completely new user needs. Finally, at the adaptation level, requirements are expressed by both clients and experts that are aware of context's implications on a running application. And similarly, to the previous engineering process, new adaptation requirements can be learned, progressively, by intelligent services, made possible thanks to smart monitoring, and therefore, elicited dynamically.

Regardless of their source, requirements are analyzed. This activity's main concern is to determine if the collected requirements are unambiguous, complete and consistent. It also helps detect existing conflicts, inconsistencies or dependencies between requirements. At the end of this phase, it's not unlikely to build a simplistic prototype to confirm the expressed and collected requirements.

3.2 Requirement Specification

Once gathered, understood, revised and improved, requirements are documented. At this stage, a requirement specification language is used to record requirements, in a formal, semi-formal or even informal fashion.

According to the proposed Framework, at the domain level, domain experts provide a full map of all possible capabilities, qualities, components at different levels of abstractions, and the relationships and dependencies that govern these entities. They can also identify context elements that potentially affect the behavior of the IoT application. Furthermore, as new requirements arise to accompany a technological or business evolution in the IoT domains, the specification can be performed by the use of external resources and services (i.e. Marketplace APIs) automatically (self-adaptive model). Then, at the application/adaptation level, the project manager/expert who accompanies the client at the elicitation phase drafts the specification document, taking into account the causes and consequences of each derivation/adaptation. Once more, as new requirements are learned on the go (i.e. New usage patterns, new execution environment, etc), the corresponding specification should automatically be formulated too.

Requirement specification is very critical to the overall process. As a matter of fact, it's a binding contact between whoever the IoT solution is conceived for, and whoever is building it. Any mistakes or even imperfections at this level may have exponential repercussions as the project evolves, which often comes at a high cost or loss for both parties (Knauss et al., 2009).

Consequently, a variety of rigorous requirement specification languages exist. Some of them are formal, other are unformal, and some are in between, and are therefore semi-formal (also called hybrid or structured).

- **Formal** specification languages are specification documents, who's syntax and semantics are expressed and defined formally, using logic, algebra or standard mathematics (Spivey, 1989)(Jones, 1995). Formal languages are usually automatically processed and can preserve traceability throughout the complete engineering process. Formality remains however difficult to attain and use, especially when untrained software engineers are the ones usually responsible to draft the specifications document, without much tool support either.
- **Informal** specification languages mainly refer to the use of human language to document the specifications of a software system. Natural languages (NL) can either be unrestricted and without any defined format, which leaves room to ambiguity, personal interpretation, bias, and other quality defects. They are widely adopted nevertheless, thanks to their instinctive and universal format
- **Semi-formal** specification languages rely on predefined graphical or textural notations that constrain the expression and form of specification documents. Although they may lack formality in the definition of their syntax or semantics, but they specify requirements in a structured form, regulated by clear guidelines, and supported by tools. UML (OMG, 2017) and KAOS (Lamsweerde, 2009) are some of the most notable semi-formal specification languages. Some NL specification languages also belong to this category of languages due to the fact that they have been improved by complementary concepts that enhance their uniformity, like templates (Robertson & Robertson, 2012), ontologies (Körner & Brumm, 2009), or metamodels (Videira & Da Silva, 2005).

3.3 Requirement Validation

Verification and validation are the final steps of requirement devolvement. During this stage, the specifications document is assessed, to verify its correctness, completeness and consistency with regards to the expressed needs of final users, before moving to the software system development phase (Boehm, 1984). A variety of validation techniques can be employed (Maalem & Zarour, 2016). For instance, when the specification language is formal, this stage is often automatically achieved, as most formal approaches generate prototypes (Yang et al., 2019). In the case of semi-formal languages, traceability between user goals and the specifications is model-based (Iqbal et al., 2020). Natural language specifications usually involve both clients and the requirements development team.

4 MOTIVATIONAL EXAMPLE: THE CHAMELEON SMART CAR

Chameleon is a hand-picked smart car manufacturer on the rise. What differentiates it from the competition is the diversity of its catalogue, assembled from years of experience in the automotive, electronics and digital fields. The power of Chameleon smart cars goes beyond car related applications, like smart tracking, smart parking, smart traffic, or smart braking. It also includes services from other areas such as smart health, smart surveillance, or smart supply chain. It can be destined for a variety of clients; like a logistics company, a special needs centre, a housing complex or even the city. Therefore, confronted with such a diversity and genericity, decisions regarding the quality and quantity of devices, components or services embedded in the car for a specific application, is tedious. Furthermore, even after building the car, requirements are prone to change, and sometimes, evolution. This change is a result of the varying and uncertain circumstances in which cars run. In addition to changing requirements as projects progress, the chameleon car faces challenges related to the consistent evolution of the embedded devices and their software on the one hand, and the dynamic physical composition of the smart car on the other. Both cases require runtime adaptation. This section describes the case in further details and presents an application scenario.

The domain of the Chameleon solutions englobes all knowledge that has been collected in the domain of smart cars. Starting from the mechanical parts and their components (i.e: engine, wheels, brakes, etc), going through the embedded smart devices and their potential configurations (i.e: Cameras, speed or proximity sensors, etc), all the way to possible smart applications (i.e: Face recognition, smart braking, photo analysis, etc) or technologies (communication technologies, routing protocols, etc). Requirements that articulate this knowledge are connected to contextual information that might be relevant for the final user. Some cities for example may prohibit self-driving cars during rush hours, while others don't. Time and location are therefore potentially relevant contextual elements. Moreover, information about domains other than smart cars, like smart health, may not appear relevant for all applications, but can if the car is destined for elderly clients. New devices, which have proven more practical, and more accurate for the measurements of cardiovascular endurance, should be presented to domain engineers in order to be considered as an alternative or replacement for old versions of the same device, insuring thus state-of-the-art smart products.

These three dimensions of the Framework can be respectively implemented through domain variability, context, and crowdsourcing models that enable public contribution.

Figure 2. The Chameleon cars domain

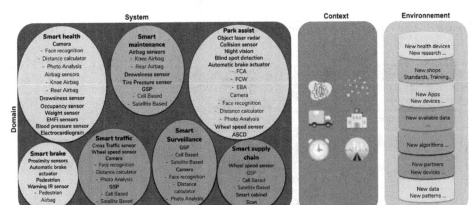

Figure 2 illustrates the first layer of the framework; the domain. The chameleon domain can embed a multitude of functionalities, like smart health smart maintenance, park assist, smart brake, smart supply chain, smart surveillance and smart traffic. Each of which can be implemented in a variable manner as well. The context illustrated in the figure includes time and place, nearest hospital and logistics, city public data, etc. The environment of the smart car is a marketplace that contributes to each of the functionalities of the system dimension with new devices, new requirements, new research, new patterns, etc.

With every client, new requirements come to light. Some of which are derived from the domain knowledge, and some are specific to the new clients.

Both cars derived for a retirement home and a logistics company may want to use path calculation algorithms, along with the sensors and cloud information required for that purpose. several algorithm options are selected. Each activated depending on the state of certain devices and the availability of specific data. The first application focuses on smart health devices and applications to monitor vital signs. At specific times during the day, other services such as smart brake and parking are also enabled to anticipate elderly drivers' slow reflexes and reduced sight. The second application requires smart traffic and surveillance devices, together with data analysis application, without much regard to the other possible options.

New requirements should also be considered, as each client operates according to its own specific agenda. For instance, the Chameleon domain requirements to manage connectivity include Wi-fi, RFID and 4G communication protocols. However, as the logistics company operates using a ZigBee built-in platform, related requirements are added accordingly.

Figure 3. The case of the Village Retirement Home fleet of cars

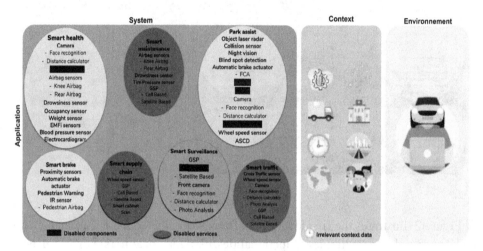

As illustrated in Figure 3 for the case of the Village Retirement Home (VRH), the smart maintenance, smart supply chain and smart traffic are not selected. Amongst the remaining functions, irrelevant devices and component for this client are disabled as well. Thus, creating a fleet of cars that answer, without access, the needs of the client, while maintaining a certain level of autonomy for reconfiguration at runtime.

As a matter of fact, the chameleon car is set to operate in dynamic circumstances, where the context is constantly changing, the running software often updated and the composition of the car itself is likely to be altered. For instance, the smart cars can be part of a national safety program that helps track wanted profiles. Embedded cameras are empowered with face recognition applications, connected to the police information system. This is called, smart surveillance. When traveling in different countries, these applications are prohibited, as they are conceived a breach of privacy. There are therefore disabled as a response to change in the context. More flexible requirements are also expressed to deal with the uncertainties of the context, like the state or battery level of sensors or the availability of certain services like road information.

Figure 4. An adaptation for the Village Retirement Home cars

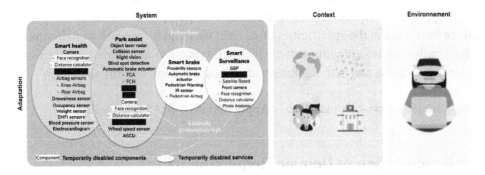

Figure 4 shows simple adaptations of the smart car, as a result of decrease in charge, and specific time in the day. In the first event, optional functionality like smart surveillance, along with optional components like face recognition or weight sensors, are disabled to maintain the operability of other mandatory services. The second event illustrates the smart brake functionality case, which is only enabled at night-time, when the eyesight of elderly people decreases.

5 HOW TO SPECIFY NL REQUIREMENTS FOR IOT SYSTEMS

In order to develop a representative typology of requirements for the specification of IoT systems, a first draft of the classification is drawn from the chameleon cars case. A modified systematic search in the current state of the art is then carried out in order to complete the list with new types of requirements.

Table 1. Description of the EBNF grammar

Symbol	Description
<non-terminal>	Syntax variables that define the requirement Natural Language
« terminal »	Character strings that appear in the Natural Language
+	(Non) Terminals which can be instantiated in one or more occurrences
?	Optional (Non)terminals
		An OR relation between two (Non)terminals

The typology of requirements presented below follows the rules of an EBNF grammar. The syntax used is summarized in Table 1.

The resulting requirements fall under three main categories. First, high level requirements that ensure reusability, they describe the main capabilities and qualities of a category of systems, along with various possible compositions of single systems. Then, application requirements, which describe the properties of the running system, taking into account the specificities of its final user and its execution environment. And finally, runtime requirements, which are typical to autonomous systems, as context-awareness and self-adaptation are innate properties of IoT systems.

<Requirement>::= <DomainRq>|<ApplicationRq>|<AdaptationRq>

5.1 Specification of Domain Requirements

Domain requirements are characteristic of a particular market segment, they describe the basic functions that any system belonging to that domain is likely to have (Pohl et al., 2005). These functions can be qualitative or quantitative, and thus are specified by means of functional or non-functional requirements. In addition to that, variability requirements are introduced to describe the possible relationships between "things", which are categorized as hierarchical, group, dependency or numeric (Mazo et al., 2012; Salinesi et al., 2011). The first three refer to the possible compositions of the IoT product, and the last one describes parametric elements that can be configured at runtime.

<DomainRq>

::= <FunctionalRq>|<NfunctionalRq>|<VariablityRq>

<FunctionalRq> ::= The <thing> (shall|could|Might) (Insure|maintain) <Task>

<NFunctionalRq> ::= The <thing> (shall|could|Might) be <Quality>

<VariabilityRq> ::= <HierchicalRq>|<GroupRq>|<DependencyRq>|<Numeric Rq>

<HierchicalRq> ::= The <thing> (shall|could|Might) be composed with (<thing> ("AND" <thing>)+)

<GroupRq> ::= The <thing> (shall|could|Might) be composed of at least <min> AND at most (<max>|*) (instances of <thing>|(among (<thing> ("AND" <thing>)+))

<DependencyRq> ::= The <thing> shall (combine|dissociate) <thing> ("AND" <thing>)+)

<NumericRq> ::= The <thing> (shall|could|Might) be valuated within (<domain>|<enumeration>)

The grammar presented above describes a semi-formal NL approach that can be followed to specify the elicited high-level reusable requirements for IoT applications. The non-terminal <thing> used in the grammar refers to any element that composes the IoT application. This is derived from the very definition of the term in the IoT glossary (ITU, 2012). A sample of domain requirements for the chameleon car manufacturer, specified using this grammar, is presented in the following table.

Table 2. Sample of domain requirement for the Chameleon cars

ID	Req Type	Requirements
Rq_6	**FunctionalRq**	*The cars could insure automatic brake*
Rq_19	**NfunctionalRq**	*The cars could be efficient in terms of electric consumption*
Rq_45	**HierchicalRq**	*The bumper may include pedestrian airbags*
Rq_66	**HierchicalRq**	*The seat shall include drowsiness sensors*
Rq_84	**NumericRq**	*The cars shall include at least three front and two back proximity sensors*
Rq_398	**GroupRq**	*The gateway could mutate between three means of communication*
Rq_576	**DependencyRq**	*The cars shall combine every airbag, with at least two active seat sensors, and a control unit.*

5.2 Specification of Application Requirements

Application requirements are designed in collaboration with the clients. They include functionalities and qualities retained, represented by means of functional and non-functional requirements. (Abbas et al., 2010; D'Ippolito et al., 2014; Muñoz-Fernández et al., 2018; Yang et al., 2013). These requirements can be operationalized in various manners, in accordance with other user requirements, like preference, cost, optimization or autonomy (Soares et al., 2017). Preferability requirements describe explicit choices. Cost requirement describe the budgetary constraints assigned to the product in question. Proportionality requirements specify the rules that define logical relationships between various elements. Optimization requirements define an optimum on the level of required performance or on specific values of the application And finally, autonomy requirements represent flexibility, which offers adaptation alternatives for dynamic contexts at runtime (Vassev, 2015) .

Table 3. A sample from application requirement for the of the Village Retirement Home case

ID	Req Type	Requirements
VRH_Rq4	FunctionalRq	*The cars shall insure smart health monitoring.*
VRH_Rq66	NfunctionalRq	*The cars shall be energy efficient.*
VRH_Rq34 VRH_Rq166	PreferenceRq	*The bumper shall include pedestrian airbags.* *The cars shall not have front recording cameras*
VRH_Rq89	CostRq	*The cars shall cost at most 15000$*
VRH_Rq104	OptimizationRq	*The cars shall maximize the number of proximity sensors*
VRH_Rq153	ProportionalityRq	*The cars shall respectively select 2, 4 and 5 airbags together with 2, 5 and 7 seats*
VRH_Rq193	AutonomyRq	*The cars could include smart assist services.* *The gateway could mutate between various means of emergency communications*

<ApplicationRq>

::= <FunctionalRq>|<NFunctionalRq>|<PrefereabilityRq>|<CostRq>| <Optimi zationRq>|<ProportionalityRq>|<AutonomyRq>

<FunctionalRq> ::= The <thing> shall (Insure|maintain) (<Task>|<AppParam>)

<NFunctionalRq> ::= The <thing> shall be (<Quality>|<AppParam>)

<PrefereabilityRq> ::= The <thing> shall (Not)? include (<thing>|<AppParam>) (with the value <Operator><Value>)?

<CostRq> :== The <thing> shall cost (at most|at least) <Price>

<OptimizationRq> ::= The <thing> shall (maximize|minimize) the (<Quality>|number of <thing>)

<ProportionalityRq> ::= The <thing> shall repsectively select (<Param> ("AND" <Param>)+) <thing> together with (<Param > ("AND" <Param>)+) <thing>

<AutonomyRq> ::= <VariabilityRq>

<AppParam> ::= <NewTast>|<NewQuality>|<NewThing>

The grammar above defines rules for a natural language specification of application requirements. A sample of such requirements, as expressed in the retiring home case, is presented in Table 3.

5.3 Specification of Adaptation Requirements

Adaptation requirements describe the behaviour of IoT applications in dynamic contexts. They describe the necessary reconfigurations to maintain required levels of satisfaction. Contextual requirements define circumstances under which requirements shall be satisfied. Temporal requirements determine the time, order or frequency with which requirements must be satisfied. Optimization requirements maintain their role of maximization or minimization of parameter values or cardinalities (Uthariaraj & Florence, 2011). Relaxable requirements refer to those that are necessary in particular contexts, but which may prove to be less essential in other ones (Whittle et al., 2010). Awareness requirements are sensitivity requirements that constrain the degrees of success or failure in implementing other adaptation requirements (Souza et al., 2013). And finally, resilience requirements also called evolution requirements, determine the requirements which specify the response to be given in the event of failure to implement other adaptation requirements (Souza et al., 2012).

<AdaptationRq>

::= <ContextualRq>|<TemporalRq>|<OptimizationRq>|<RelaxableRq>|

<AwarenessRq>|<ResilienceRq>

<ContextualRq> ::= When <Event> if <condition>, <Requirement>

<TemporalRq> ::= (At <Time> | (Before|After) (<Time>|reinforcing that <Requirement>)|Between <Time> and <Time> |as soon as (<Time>|<Requirement> is realized)), <Requirement>

\<OptimizationRq\> ::= When \<Event\> if \<condition\>, the \<thing\> shall (maximize|minimize) the (\<Quality\>|number of \<thing\>)

\<RelaxableRq\> ::= \<OptimizationRq\>, (eventually|until) \<Requirement\>

\<AwarenessRq\> ::= \<AggregationRq\>|\<MetaRq\>|\<DeltaRq\>

\<AggregationRq\> ::= \<Requirement\> should (succeed|fail) \<Percentage\> ((More|less) than \<Requirement\>)?

\<MetaRq\> ::= \<Requirement\> should be satisfied within \<TimeDuration\>

\<DeltaRq\> ::= \<Requirement\> success rate should not (decrese|increase) (\<TimeDuration\> \<Frequency\>)

\<ResilienceRq\> ::= When \<Event\> if \<condition\>, \<Requirement\> shall be (ignored|modified (into \<Requirement\>)?)

The grammar described above introduces for each requirement type, a semi-formal approach for the specification of adaptation requirements. A sample from the specification document of the village retiring home case is presented Table 4.

Table 4. A sample from adaptation requirements for the of the Village Retirement Home case

ID	Req Type	Requirements
VRH_Rq566	ContextualRq	*When a seat detector detects a new passenger, the cars shall be able to communicate with the occupant's health monitor wearable.*
VRH_Rq587	TemporalRq	*After 6 am, the cars shall enable all devices that contribute to smart brakes.*
VRH_Rq645	OptimizationRq	*When electricity consumption is higher than 60%, the cars shall optimize the use of slave sensors*
VRH_Rq699	RelaxableRq	*The cars shall use the least possible sensors, eventually, all sensor's battery levels shall stay superior than 40%.*
VRH_Rq702	AwarenessRq	*The car shall be able to reach the closest ambulance in the case of a crash, within 10 seconds*
VRH_Rq725	ResilienceRq	*When the health emergency state is active, if VRH_Rq645 is not satisfied, the cars shall use another meant of emergency communication*

Reusable domain requirements of IoT solutions on the one hand, and application and adaptation requirements on the other, reveal the need to specify an extremely diverse set of configuration requirements. Although this typology is based on the standard typology of requirements (IEEE, 2009)(Lin et al. 1996), they differ from the latter as they are not always binding. In reality, they are only verifiable in specific contexts. The specification of these requirements, which can be described as "dynamic", is a steppingstone for the realization of highly reconfigurable IoT solutions, which meet different needs, while ensuring the natural evolution of this category of systems.

6 OUTLOOK ON NEXT GENERATION IOT DESIGN

For the last decade, a multitude of approaches have been proposed in order to specify and design applications in the challenging but promising field of the Internet of things. This section presents and overview of these approaches. Furthermore, to understand the scope of these contributions along with the other aspects that need further investigation, each of the selected approaches is mapped to the framework.

- **Approach 1**: SysADL (Leite et al., 2017) is an architecture-based approach for building IoT applications. According to the approach, all elements of the IoT application are defined before they are used in the system architecture. Along with the structural definition, data, components, actions, connections and executables are all defined as part of the system's environment. Both are defined in block definition diagrams. Data that flows in and out of each element is also specified using the concept of ports. Instances of systems correspond in SysADL to configurations. They describe how components are connected, thus, how actual instances of the IoT application can be configured. Internal block diagrams are used to describe possible configurations of components, connected using ports that send their respective values. All of the above is defined as part of a *structural viewpoint*, which correspond to the *domain system and context* dimensions of the proposed Framework. This next view, called *behaviour viewpoint*, describes how the IoT elements contribute to the fulfilment of high-level requirements described in this previous viewpoint. This shows different application scenarios using an activity diagram and correspond to the *application system and context* dimensions or the proposed framework. Several other SysML based approaches like SysML4IoT are used for the specification of IoT solutions (Costa et al., 2016). The mapping of these approaches with the IoT design Framework is presented in figure 6.
- **Approach 2:** Authors in (Hussein et al., 2019) extended the previously discussed notation, SysML4IoT, with self-adaptation capabilities, using a publish/subscribe adaptation paradigm to model environment information

and their relationship with the system. This is preformed using a system management component which model adaptation triggers and runtime configurations using the concept of states. This model matches with the *system and application adaptation* dimensions of the proposed Framework as illustrated in figure 6.

- **Approach 3** : State Constraint Transition is a language for the formal specification of IoT systems (Achtaich et al., 2019). SCT is a variant of finite state machines (FSM) whose power of expression is extended by means of the concept of constraints. This modelling language provides an answer to the problems linked to the specification of dynamic requirements by introducing the concept of configuration states, in which requirements are translated into constraints. First, all IoT elements, together with the anticipated domain context are defined in the form of variables. A *domain variability model* specifies the dependencies and relationships between these elements, in the form of constraints. A *configuration model* specifies application requirement as an instance of the domain variability model. Contextual elements that arise with each specific application are defined within the application's corresponding state. A *reconfiguration model* specifies adaptation requirements, by the means of configuration states embedded with constraints which formally specify dynamic requirements. A *perception model* informs the generated constraint program with real time contextual data or parameters, which potentially leads to a reconfiguration of the IoT solution. The models described above are a projection of *domain, application and adaptation* requirements, regarding both the *system and its context.* A projection of these models on the framework described above are presented in figure 6.

- **Approach 4**: The approach proposed by Karakostas (Karakostas, 2016) is based on the author's observation that it is difficult to predict with certainty when and if events will occur in an IoT application. Thus, his proposal implements a *bayesian model* that predicts relevant events and consequences. Through an air flight case study, the authors predict if a connecting flight will be departing late, by calculating the probability of the incoming/arriving flights doing departing or arriving late. This model is an implementation of the *application environment* dimension and is presented in figure 6. Similar implementations are found in the literature, like the works of Basu et al. (Basu et al., 2018) who tackle the problem using cognitive bio-inspired models.

- **Approach 5**: This contribution by authors Lunardi et al. (Lunardi et al., 2018) is based on the Model Centred Architecture (MCA) paradigm, where a system is a compound of various models and model handlers. Specifically, authors define *M1* to specify all system and data components. This coincides with *system and context* dimensions of the *domain engineering process* in the proposed framework. Concrete functions and processes are later on specified at an M0 level, which is an instance of M1 models. M0 corresponds to the *application level*, and both system and context dimensions are specified using this approach. Furthermore, the authors propose an extension to a semantic core model, using probabilistic ontology, in order to predict human actions. This engine injects new knowledge as new behavioural patterns are predicted. This model refers to the *environmental dimension of the application engineering process*. The mapping of this approach with the Framewok is illustrated in figure 6.

- **Approach 6:** Google Nest[1] is one of the most commercially successful cases of IoT. It's a smart home solution that sets up, monitors and manages home appliances like thermostats, cameras and locks. While the design process and methods are not displayed to the public, we can deduct from the actual solution that Google Nest solution follows generic and adaptable specifications, which we labelled *domain*. While this solution offers a range of possible configurations (*applications*), the derived applications are not flexible in terms of requirements, and solutions are only personalized within the boundaries of the supported devices and configurations. Devices and related applications are available on the Google Store, which is a marketplace that is often updated with the latest supported technology. This corresponds to the *environment dimension* of the framework. The various dimension implemented by this technology are displayed in figure 6.

- **Approach 7:** Comma[2] is a self-driving car software. It's an IoT solutions that can operate with any car that supports automatic acceleration, brake and parking. The design of Comma is one of the most fitting to the proposed Framework. On the one hand, it offers a generic solution that fits to different car application. It can work with a Honda as well as it does with a Toyota, therefore supporting the *domain system and context* dimensions. The software is opensource and available for the public. It is therefore crowdsourced, which makes for the *environment* dimension of the *domain*. Comma collects application requirements through a user interface in order to present a solution that is tailored to each specific case scenario. This coincides with the *application system and context*, presented in the Framework. As the car runs, adaptation scenarios are successfully specified and implemented. Moreover, comma is a self-learning software. Its design specifies basic functionality and learns on the ground and as the car drives itself, in order to improve its functionality, and provide most fitting actions and reactions. This corresponds to the *adaptation engineering* process in totality. Figure 6 illustrates the projection of the comma specification process on the Framework (Yellow).

Figure 5. IoT design trends

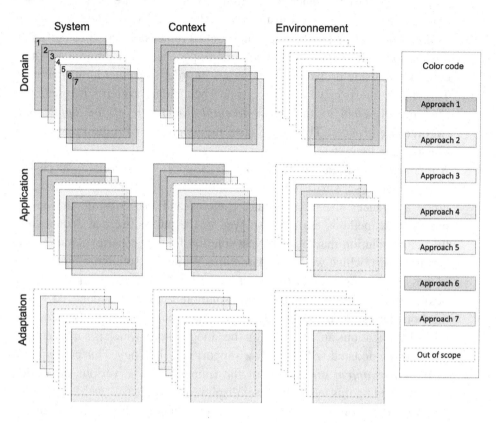

The approaches presented above are selected from different IoT applications, including smart homes, smart cars and smart cities. They also represent examples evoked both from academic research and from the industry. This clearly outlines the current trends in IoT development, but also pinpoints the aspects that are just as important for building comprehensive technologies for the future, that require more attention from academia and from the smart industry.

6.1 IoT and SoS

A great number of IoT solutions are specified, partially or completely, using the SysML notation and principles. This is clearly displayed in figure 5, as most approaches focus on domain and application requirement specification. This is not a coincidence. As a matter of fact, ever since IoT became a hot topic in research, a lot of authors debated the need for new terminology to something that had already existed and matured in the literature, under the name System of Systems (SoS) (de C Henshaw, 2016; Mahya & Tahayori, 2016; Nikolopoulos et al. 2019). While there are definitely new capabilities and specification challenges brought by the smart nature of devices used in IoT applications, broadening the scope of SoS could be an approach to embracing such progress instead of rethinking and reinventing a whole new paradigm.

6.2 IoT and Autonomy

Specifying ad-hoc IoT applications for a static usage, without considering the dynamic context and use cases, can be considered unrealistic. This approach may even lead to error-prone and contradictory results a consequence of uncertainty. Self-adaptation, both to context and to requirements, is a rising interest in IoT development. The main goal of research in this area is to introduce new languages, patterns and algorithms that not only handle uncertainty, but also discover and implement autonomously new requirements and usage scenarios at runtime.

6.3 IoT and AI

The focus around IoT for the last decade have revolved around three major topics. First, standardizing the architecture in order to define and classify the main components and interfaces depending on their features and purposes. Then, reinforcing the security of IoT software, devices and the networks they're connected to in order to protect the user's data and infrastructure. And finally, building light software and communication protocols to cope with IoT constrained storage, processing and bandwidth resources. This coming decade will evidently revolve around the 3 Ds. Data, Discovery and Decision. Data is most relevant enabler for the future of IoT. As the amount of collected information grows, and the quality and precision of data analytics algorithms evolve, new requirements, devices and services can seamlessly be discovered, and decisions regarding their implementation can be determined.

6.4 IoT and Globalization

IoT is bigger than us. It's bigger than one company. It's even bigger than one country. If the ethical and political implications of this acclamation are put aside, to reach its full potential, IoT ought to belong to everyone and device ought to be connected with everything across the globe. If one cannot drive his connected car across countries, seamlessly and without constraints and complications, smart self-driving car solutions cannot compete with current cars. If smart health is not globalized, including patient records and monitoring, a sick person could never comfortably travel abroad without having to worry about consequences. In other words, IoT should be for all, and all should be at its service.

7 CONCLUSION

The first ever application of the Internet of Things was created in 1990. Ever since, and for the last three decades, new applications, devices, standards, and approaches expanded the reach and significance of the internet of things paradigm. While several authors have proposed frameworks and blueprints to structure the growing knowledge and complexity, the main efforts remained on connectivity, security and data. This chapter is positioned as a reference IoT design Framework to assist the requirement specification process. The main idea of the framework is to assist IoT engineers in specifying reusable, client-tailored, self-adaptive, dynamic and cognitive IoT applications. The chapter illustrates these capabilities using the case of a smart car company that designs specific fleets of self-adaptive smart cars from a reusable and expandable set of functionalities. Furthermore, an approach for the specification of natural language requirements for IoT systems was elaborated. It describes on the one hand a typology for the requirements that engineers often deal with while specifying this category of systems. On the other hand, it provides a template for a proper formulation of requirements at the specification phase, in order to increase precision and avoid ambiguity. The smart car case is used to provide explicit examples for the specification of the various requirement types. Furthermore, in order to assess the IoT specification current state, seven approaches from the literature and the industry were briefly discussed and mapped to the proposed framework. This process emphasized the current trends in IoT requirement specification, which mostly revolve around reusability and adaptation. It also revealed emerging areas of interest, especially in terms of self-learning and artificial intelligence capabilities.

REFERENCES

Abbas, N., Andersson, J., & Löwe, W. (2010). Autonomic Software Product Lines (ASPL). *ACM International Conference Proceeding Series*, 324–331.

Achtaich, A., Roudies, O., Souissi, N., Salinesi, C., & Mazo, R. (2019). Evaluation of the State-Constraint Transition Modeling Language: A Goal Question Metric Approach. *Software Product Line Conference Proceedings* - Volume B.

Al Hinai, S., & Singh, A. V. (2018). Internet of things: Architecture, security challenges and solutions. In *2017 International Conference on Infocom Technologies and Unmanned Systems: Trends and Future Directions, ICTUS 2017* (Vol. 2018– January, pp. 1–4). Institute of Electrical and Electronics Engineers Inc.

Antonino, P. O., Morgenstern, A., Kallweit, B., Becker, M., & Kuhn, T. (2018). Straightforward Specification of Adaptation-Architecture-Significant Requirements of IoT-enabled Cyber-Physical Systems. In *Proceedings - 2018 IEEE 15th International Conference on Software Architecture Companion, ICSA-C 2018,* 19–26. IEEE. 10.1109/ICSA-C.2018.00012

Atzori, L., Iera, A., & Morabito, G. (2017). Understanding the Internet of Things: Definition, potentials, and societal role of a fast evolving paradigm. *Ad Hoc Networks, 56,* 122–140. doi:10.1016/j.adhoc.2016.12.004

Baccelli, E., Gundogan, C., Hahm, O., Kietzmann, P., Lenders, M. S., Petersen, H., Schleiser, K., Schmidt, T. C., & Wahlisch, M. (2018). RIOT: An Open Source Operating System for Low-End Embedded Devices in the IoT. *IEEE Internet of Things Journal, 5*(6), 4428–4440. doi:10.1109/JIOT.2018.2815038

Basu, S., Karuppiah, M., Selvakumar, K., Li, K. C., Islam, S. K. H., Hassan, M. M., & Bhuiyan, M. Z. A. (2018). An intelligent/cognitive model of task scheduling for IoT applications in cloud computing environment. *Future Generation Computer Systems, 88*(June), 254–261. doi:10.1016/j.future.2018.05.056

Boehm, B. W. (1984). Verifying and Validating Software Requirements and Design Specifications. *IEEE Software, 1*(1), 75–88. doi:10.1109/MS.1984.233702

Bowen, J. P., & Hinchey, M. G. (1999). *High-Integrity System Specification and Design. High-Integrity System Specification and Design.* Springer London. doi:10.1007/978-1-4471-3431-2

Chakraborty, A., Kanti Baowaly, M., Arefin, A., & Newaz Bahar, A. (2012). The Role of Requirement Engineering in Software Development Life Cycle. *Journal of Emerging Trends in Computing and Information Sciences, 3*(5), 723–729.

Chang, V., Sharma, S., & Li, C. S. (2020). Smart cities in the 21st century. *Technological Forecasting and Social Change, 153.*

Costa, B., Pires, P. F., & Delicato, F. C. (2016). Modeling IoT Applications with SysML4IoT. *Proceedings - 42nd Euromicro Conference on Software Engineering and Advanced Applications, SEAA 2016,* 157–164. 10.1109/SEAA.2016.19

D'Ippolito, N., Braberman, V., Kramer, J., Magee, J., Sykes, D., & Uchitel, S. (2014). Hope for the Best, Prepare for the Worst: Multi-tier Control for Adaptive Systems. *Proceedings of the 36th International Conference on Software Engineering.* 10.1145/2568225.2568264 de C Henshaw, M. J. (2016). Systems Of Systems, Cyber-Physical Systems, The Internet-Of-Things...Whatever Next? *Insight (American Society of Ophthalmic Registered Nurses)*, *19*(3), 51–54.

Feynman, R., & Objectives, C. (2016). *EBNF A Notation to Describe Syntax*. Academic Press.

Gartner. (2020). *IoT Adoption Trends*. Retrieved June 23, 2020, from https://www.gartner.com/en/innovation-strategy/trends/iot-adoption-trends

Hussein, M., Li, S., & Radermacher, A. (2019). Model-driven development of adaptive IoT systems. *CEUR Workshop Proceedings*, 17–23.

Hwang, K., & Chen, M. (2017). *Big-Data Analytics for Cloud, IoT and Cognitive Computing*. John Wiley & Sons.

IEEE. (2009). *830-1998 - IEEE Recommended Practice for Software Requirements Specifications*. Retrieved March 1, 2020, from https://standards.ieee.org/standard/830-1998.html

INCOSE. (2018). Systems Engineering Handbook. *Insight, 1*(2), 20–20. Retrieved February 9, 2020, from http://doi.wiley.com/10.1002/inst.19981220

International Telecommunication Union — ITU-T Y.2060. (2012). *Overview of the Internet of things. Next Generation Networks — Frameworks and functional architecture models*.

Iqbal, D., Abbas, A., Ali, M., Khan, M. U. S., & Nawaz, R. (2020). Requirement Validation for Embedded Systems in Automotive Industry through Modeling. *IEEE Access: Practical Innovations, Open Solutions*, *8*, 8697–8719. doi:10.1109/ACCESS.2019.2963774

Jones, C. B. (1995). *Systematic software development using VDM*. Prentice Hall International.

Karakostas, B. (2016). Event Prediction in an IoT Environment Using Naïve Bayesian Models. *Procedia Computer Science, 83*(Ant), 11–17. doi:10.1016/j.procs.2016.04.093

Khan, S., Dulloo Aruna, B., & Verma, M. (2014). Systematic Review of Requirement Elicitation Techniques. *International Journal of Information and Computation Technology, 4*(2), 133–138. Retrieved February 12, 2020, from http://www.irphouse.com/ijict.htm

Knauss, E., Boustani, C. E. I., & Flohr, T. (2009). Investigating the impact of software requirements specification quality on project success. In *International Conference on Product-Focused Software Process Improvement* (Vol. 32, pp. 28–42). Springer Verlag. 10.1007/978-3-642-02152-7_4

Körner, S. J., & Brumm, T. (2009). Natural language specification improvement with ontologies. *International Journal of Semantic Computing, 3*(4), 445–470. doi:10.1142/S1793351X09000872

Lahboube, F., Haidrar, S., Roudies, O., Souissi, N., & Adil, A. (2014). Systems of Systems Paradigm in a Hospital Environment: Benefits for Requirements Elicitation Process. *International Review on Computers and Software, 9*(10), 1798–1806.

Leite, J., Batista, T., & Oquendo, F. (2017). Architecting IoT applications with SysADL. *2017 IEEE International Conference on Software Architecture Workshops, ICSAW 2017: Side Track Proceedings*, 92–99. 10.1109/ICSAW.2017.57

Lin, J., Yu, W., Zhang, N., Yang, X., Zhang, H., & Zhao, W. (2017). A Survey on Internet of Things: Architecture, Enabling Technologies, Security and Privacy, and Applications. *IEEE Internet of Things Journal, 4*(5), 1125–1142. doi:10.1109/JIOT.2017.2683200

Lunardi, G. M., Al Machot, F., Shekhovtsov, V. A., Maran, V., Machado, G. M., Machado, A., & Mayr, H. C. (2018). IoT-based human action prediction and support. *Internet of Things, 3–4*, 52–68. doi:10.1016/j.iot.2018.09.007

Maalem, S., & Zarour, N. (2016). Challenge of validation in requirements engineering. *Journal of Innovation in Digital Ecosystems, 3*(1), 15–21. doi:10.1016/j.jides.2016.05.001

Mahya, P., & Tahayori, H. (2016). IoT is SoS. *Int'l Conf. Internet Computing and Internet of Things*, 38–42.

Mazo, R. (2018). Software Product Lines, from Reuse to Self Adaptive Systems. Université Paris 1 Panthéon - Sorbonne.

Mazo, R., Salinesi, C., Djebbi, O., Diaz, D., & Lora-Michiels, A. (2012). Constraints: the Heart of Domain and Application Engineering in the Product Lines Engineering Strategy. *International Journal of Information System Modeling and Design, 3*(2).

Mohammadi, M., Al-Fuqaha, A., Sorour, S., & Guizani, M. (2018, October 1). Deep learning for IoT big data and streaming analytics: A survey. In *IEEE Communications Surveys and Tutorials*. Institute of Electrical and Electronics Engineers Inc.

Muñoz-Fernández, J. C., Mazo, R., Salinesi, C., & Tamura, G. (2018). 10 Challenges for the specification of self-adaptive software. *Proceedings - International Conference on Research Challenges in Information Science,* 1–12.

Ngu, A. H., Gutierrez, M., Metsis, V., Nepal, S., & Sheng, Q. Z. (2017). IoT Middleware: A Survey on Issues and Enabling Technologies. *IEEE Internet of Things Journal, 4*(1), 1–20.

Nikolopoulos, B., Dimopoulos, A. C., Nikolaidou, M., Dimitrakopoulos, G., & Anagnostopoulos, D. (2019). *A System of Systems Architecture for the Internet of Things exploiting Autonomous Components.* Int. J. System of Systems Engineering.

OMG. (2017). *Unified Modeling Language Specification.* Retrieved February 12, 2020, from https://www.omg.org/spec/UML/About-UML/

Pohl, K. (2010). *Requirements engineering: fundamentals, principles, and techniques.* Springer Publishing Company, Incorporated. doi:10.1007/978-3-642-12578-2

Pohl, K. (2016). Requirements Engineering Fundamentals (2nd ed.). Rocky Nook.

Pohl, K., Böckle, G., & van der Linden, F. J. (2005). *Software Product Line Engineering. Foundations, Principles, and Techniques. Uwplatt.Edu* (Vol. 49). Academic Press.

Robertson, S., & Robertson, J. (2012). *Mastering the Requirements Process: Getting Requirements Right.* Addison-Wesley.

Salinesi, C., Kusumah, I., & Rohleder, C. (2018). New Approach for Supporting Future Collaborative Business in Automotive Industry. In *2018 IEEE International Conference on Engineering, Technology and Innovation, ICE/ITMC 2018 - Proceedings.* Institute of Electrical and Electronics Engineers Inc. 10.1109/ICE.2018.8436382

Salinesi, C., Mazo, R., Djebbi, O., Diaz, D., & Lora-Michiels, A. (2011). Constraints: The core of product line engineering. In *Fifth International Conference On Research Challenges In Information Science* (pp. 1–10). IEEE. 10.1109/RCIS.2011.6006825

Sánchez-Arias, G., González García, C., & Pelayo G-Bustelo, B. C. (2017). Midgar: Study of communications security among Smart Objects using a platform of heterogeneous devices for the Internet of Things. *Future Generation Computer Systems, 74,* 444–466. doi:10.1016/j.future.2017.01.033

Sezer, O. B., Dogdu, E., & Ozbayoglu, A. M. (2018). Context-Aware Computing, Learning, and Big Data in Internet of Things: A Survey. *IEEE Internet of Things Journal, 5*(1), 1–27. doi:10.1109/JIOT.2017.2773600

Soares, M., Jéssyka, V., Guedes, G., Silva, C., & Castro, J. (2017). Core Ontology to Aid the Goal Oriented Specification for Self-Adaptive Systems. *Advances in Intelligent Systems and Computing, 571*, V–VI.

Souza, V. E. S., Lapouchnian, A., & Mylopoulos, J. (2012). (Requirement) evolution requirements for adaptive systems. *ICSE Workshop on Software Engineering for Adaptive and Self-Managing Systems*, 155–164.

Souza, V. E. S., Lapouchnian, A., Robinson, W. N., & Mylopoulos, J. (2013). Awareness requirements. Lecture Notes in Computer Science, 7475, 133–161.

Spivey, J. M. (1989). *The Z notation: a reference manual | Guide books*. Prentice-Hall, Inc.

Uthariaraj, V. R., & Florence, P. M. (2011). *QoS With Reliability And Scalability In Adaptive Service-Based Systems*. Academic Press.

Van Lamsweerde, A. (2009). Requirements Engineering: From System Goals to UML Models to Software Specifications. *Change.*

Vassev, E. (2015). Requirements Engineering for Self-Adaptive Systems with ARE and KnowLang. *EAI Endorsed Transactions on Self-Adaptive Systems, 1*(1), e6. doi:10.4108as.1.1.e6

Videira, C., & Da Silva, A. R. (2005). Patterns and metamodel for a natural-language-based requirements specification language. *CAiSE, 05*, 189–194.

Weyns. (2017). Software Engineering of Self-Adaptive Systems: An Organised Tour and Future Challenges. Handbook of Software Engineering, 1–41.

Whittle, J., Sawyer, P., Bencomo, N., Cheng, B. H. C., & Bruel, J. M. (2010). RELAX: A language to address uncertainty in self-adaptive systems requirement. *Requirements Engineering, 15*(2), 177–196. doi:10.100700766-010-0101-0

World Health Organization. (2020). *Coronavirus disease 2019 (COVID-19) Situation Report-72 highlights*. Author.

Yang, Q. L., Lv, J., Tao, X. P., Ma, X. X., Xing, J. C., & Song, W. (2013). Fuzzy self-adaptation of mission-critical software under uncertainty. *Journal of Computer Science and Technology, 28*(1), 165–187. doi:10.100711390-013-1321-9

Yang, Y., Li, X., Ke, W., & Liu, Z. (2019). Automated Prototype Generation From Formal Requirements Model. *IEEE Transactions on Reliability*, 1–25. doi:10.1109/TR.2019.2934348

ENDNOTES

1   https://nest.com/
2   https://comma.ai/

Chapter 8

A Reliable IDS System Using Blockchain for SDN-Enabled IIoT Systems

Ambika N.

(iD) https://orcid.org/0000-0003-4452-5514

Department of Computer Applications, Sivananda Sarma Memorial RV College, Bangalore,, India

ABSTRACT

The internet of things is the technology that aims to provide a common platform to the devices of varying capabilities to communicate. Industrial internet of things (IIoT) systems can perform better using these devices in combination with SDN network and blockchain technology. The suggestion uses random space learning (RSL) comprising three stages. The random subspace learning strategy is a troupe learning procedure called attributes bagging. It improves forecast and order errands as it utilizes group development of base classifiers rather than a solitary classifier, and it takes arbitrary subsets of properties rather than the whole arrangement of attributes. The system uses the blockchain methodology to secure the system. SDN networks aim to better the transmission of data in industrial IoT devices. Misrouting and forged attacks are some of the common attacks in these systems. The proposal provides better reliability than the previous contribution by 2.7%.

1. INTRODUCTION

The Internet of Things (IoT) (Khan & Salah, 2018) (Ambika, 2020) becomes the fundamental wellspring of changing over things into shrewd, including keen homes,

DOI: 10.4018/978-1-7998-6463-9.ch008

brilliant urban communities, savvy enterprises, and so forth. IoT can interface billions of things simultaneously, which looks to create data sharing necessities that improve our lives. The blockchain idea attempts to interlink the associations or exchanges of information in the groups. The group characterizes as the information structure which incorporates numerous budgetary interchanges.

Blockchain (Banerjee, et.al., 2018) members are any individual or foundation that acknowledges convention strings and creates them. The coordinators of these systems and those answerable for programming upkeep don't share the blockchain. Blockchain members are any individual or foundation that acknowledges convention strings and creates them. The coordinators of these systems and those liable for programming upkeep don't share the blockchain. The designated to a gathering of people or elements that can get to information as it were. They can peruse target information and compose as it were. In this manner, an authorized Blockchain is a focal element. For example, a bank that can control the privileges of people and recognize them to take an interest during the time spent in composing information. The Blockchain guarantees higher degrees of security. Web of Things (IoT) (Ambika, 2019) becomes a crucial wellspring of changing over things into brilliant, including intelligent homes, keen urban communities, savvy ventures, and so on.

Software-Defined Network (SDN)(Cherian & Chatterjee, 2018) encourages arranges administrators to program and deal with the system. SDN motivates the IoT system to be overseen powerfully in an asset compelled organize. It gives chances to improve security in IoT (Nagaraj, 2021) systems on SDN (Sahay, et.al. 2019) to forestall, identify, and respond to dangers. The principal usefulness of SDN is to decouple the information planes and control planes in a system. Dynamic in SDN finishes by the control plane, and information sent is taken care of by switches. They come with the customary framework and elevated level calculations used for dynamic operations requiring modern control. SDN requires less administration.

The SDN establishes three significant layers: foundation, controller, and application layers, as the interfaces between progressive layers. The framework layer involves organizing gadgets that perform bundle sending. The ðrst key attribute of SDN is the division of the sending and control planes in systems gadgets. The sending plane actualizes sending usefulness, including the rationale and tables for picking how to manage approaching parcels, in light of qualities, for example, MAC and IP address. The vital activities performed by the sending plane can be portrayed by how it dispatches showing up parcels. It might advance, drop, devour, or duplicate an approaching packet. It might likewise change the bundle in some way before making further moves. For essential sending, the gadget decides the right yield port by playing out a query in the location table in the equipment switch or switch. A parcel drops due to speciðc ðltering. The rationale and calculations programs the sending plane dwells in the control plane. A large number of these conventions and calculations require worldwide information on the system. The control plane decides how the sending tables and rationale in the information plane ought to be customized or conðgured. Since in a conventional procedure, every gadget has its control plane, the essential undertaking of that control plane is to run directing or exchanging conventions with the goal that all the dispersed sending tables on the gadgets all through the system remain synchronized. In SDN, the control plane is gotten off of the exchanging device and onto an incorporated controller.

Expanding on the possibility of division of sending and control planes, the following attribute of SDN is the simpliðcation of system gadgets, which are then constrained by a brought together framework that runs the executives and control programming. Rather than a large number of lines of entangled control plane programming running on the gadget, permitting the instrument to carry on self-sufficiently, that product is expelled from the device and put in a unified controller. This product-based controller may then deal with the system dependent on more elevated level strategies. The controller gives unrefined directions to the simpliðed gadgets when proper to permit them to settle on quick choices about how to manage approaching bundles. The incorporated programming based controller in SDN gives an open interface on the controller to take into consideration computerized control of the system. The controller offers a northbound API, permitting programming applications to be connected to the controller, and subsequently permitting that product to give the calculations and conventions that can run the system efðciently. These applications can rapidly and powerfully organize changes as the need emerges. The northbound API of the controller gives a deliberation of the system gadgets and topology. There are three credential beneðts that the application engineer ought to get from the northbound API. It changes over to a language structure that is increasingly recognizable to designers. It gives a reflection of the system topology and system layer authorizing the application software engineer to manage the system overall as opposed to singular hubs, and deliberation of the system conventions themselves, concealing the application designer from the subtleties of OpenFlow or BGP.

The proposed system brings better reliability to adding endorsement hash value to the dispatched messages. The message is verified by the server and forwarded by suffixing the endorsement hash value to the data. The evaluated received message brings in reliability to the system by 2.7% than the previous contribution. The received data by the firewall undergo verification against the trail values and aggregated values.

The literature survey follows the introduction in section 2. Assumptions made in the study are in segment 3. The segment four explains the previous architecture. Portion five explains the proposed architecture. Section 6 contains an analysis of the proposed work. Section 7 concludes with a brief explanation of the proposed study.

2. LITERATURE SURVEY

Various contributions are present to authenticate the system in SDN networks. The proposal (Derhab, et al., 2019) focuses on the security of directions in mechanical IoT against fashioned methods and misrouting. The creators propose a security design coordinating with the Blockchain and the Software-characterized arrange (SDN) innovations. The proposed security engineering is an interruption identification framework, RSL-KNN. It joins the Random Subspace Learning (RSL) and K-Nearest Neighbor (KNN) to protect against the produced directions. It focusses on the modern control procedure and a Blockchain-based Integrity Checking System (BICS) (Li, et.al., 2017), which can forestall the misrouting assault, which alters the OpenFlow rules of the SDN-empowered mechanical IoT frameworks. A Blockchain-based Integrity Checking System (BICS), which can guard against the misrouting assault by recognizing in a short timeframe, any messing with the OpenFlow governs and forestalling the execution of the standards.

The proposed arrangement plans to remember the versatility of the particular IoT framework. It is an interruption identification and avoidance instrument by executing an insightful security engineering utilizing Random neural systems (RNNs) (Saeed, et.al., 2016). In the RNN, a sign goes as a driving force between the neurons. On the off chance that the getting signal has a positive potential, it speaks to excite. If the capability of the info signal is negative, it communicates to a hindrance to the accepting neuron. The wise interruption identification arrangements depend on producing a forecast model using the removed element dataset. It confirms the usefulness of the proposed interruption location component. The substantial element dataset is developed by profiling the intelligent controller application, speaking to the framework conduct under ordinary conditions. During the preparation stage, legitimate scopes of the yields produced by the base station handset are recorded, which decides the invalid cases.

(Khan & Herrmann, 2017)makes it conceivable to single out maliciously carrying on units in preparing and vitality inviting way. They utilize a trust the board component that permits gadgets to oversee notoriety data about their neighbors. This system makes it conceivable to single out perniciously carrying on units in handling and vitality in a gracious way. They utilize a trust the board component that permits gadgets to oversee notoriety data about their neighbors. Trust points sent to the outskirt switch total them to notoriety esteems. If terrible notoriety esteem shows a hub as a potential one, the fringe switch expels it from the system and tells the administrator. It calculates Forwarding Check, Ranking Check, and Version Number Check. The hubs likewise forward their trust esteems to the outskirt switch or a group head that totals them to the notoriety esteems in the system or a bunch. Three calculations recommended are Neighbor Based Trust Dissemination

(NBTD), Clustered Neighbor Based Trust Dissemination (CNTD), and Tree-Based Trust Dissemination (TTD).

(Fu, et.al 2017) is automata-based IDS of IoT arranges additionally comprise of four significant segments: Event Monitor, Event Database, Event Analyzer, and Response Unit. The authority needs to record the transmitting information into advanced documents and send the records to the IDS Occasion Analyzer. The system occasion portrays as the conceptual activity streams, and such system activities depict with advances of the proposed GluedIOLTS model. Three databases executed are Standard Protocol Library, Abnormal Action Library, and Normal Action Libraries are required. The IDS Event Analyzer contains three essential models: Network Structure Learning Model, Action Flows Abstraction Model, and Intrusion Detection Model. The gathered parcel information ought to be sent to this model first to cause the IDS framework to get a general perspective on the system topologies. The IoT gadgets recognize with the unique ID. It dissects the gathered data of the information bundles, for example, the source IP, goal IP, port number, timestamp, and convention type, the system can recognize the IoT gadgets from the others. The gathered continuous parcels from IoT likewise should be sent to the Action Flows Abstraction Model. Through this model, the bundles designate as indicated by the gadget having a place, meeting ID, timestamps, and convention types perceived through the guides of the Network Structure Learning Model and the Standard Protocol Library.

The work (Hamza, et.al. 2018) creates and actualizes a framework. It interprets MUD strategies to stream decisions, proactively designed into organizing switches. It is as responsively embedded dependent on run-time ties of DNS. The framework involves a handle, whose stream table rules are overseen powerfully by the SDN controller, a parcel investigation motor, and a mark based IDS.

(Lopez-Martin, et.al. 1967) depends on a contingent variational auto-encoder with a particular design that coordinates the interruption names inside the decoder layers. ID-CVAE is a solo strategy prepared in a managed way to utilize the class marks during preparation.

It (Alshahrani, et.al. 2019) is a lightweight verification system that uses dynamic personalities and impermanent keys for IoT hubs in intelligent homes. Three principle members engage with the convention: IoT hub (N), controller hub (CRN), and manufacturer fog node (MFR). A neighborhood IoT arrange is an interconnection of the IoT hubs N (obliged gadgets), and controller hubs CRN. The MFR is a competent processing gadget like a server and can live inside or outside the neighborhood IoT organize. These dynamic personalities and keys are developed from a blend of fixed and variable segments and advancing time-subordinate subdivision. The proposed verification conspire into three stages: the registration stage, enrollment stage, and the confirmation and key trade stage. IoT hub connects with the controller hub CRN for secure unknown shared verification and meeting credential trade.

The work (Singh, et.al. 2019) is a productive lightweight-secure verification convention for human-focused IIoT. The suggestion accepts an enrollment place that essentially produces open and mystery data for a hub when it at first joins the system. After enrollment, the enlistment place isn't required any longer, and propelled forms like shared verification, secure credential trade, and correspondences are autonomously done by hubs included. Secure authentication and encryption is lower calculation and correspondence cost for human-focused IIoT dependent on Guillou-Quisquater's Protocol. It decreases the exponential calculation and augmentation overheads in the verification process. Secure key sharing through the confirmation procedure is dependent on the Diffie-Hellman solution understanding calculation. Device personality approval uses Elliptic Curve computerized signature open key recuperation calculation.

The proposal (Kandi, et.al. 2019) is a profoundly versatile Multi-Group Key Management convention for IoT. It guarantees the forward and in reverse mystery productively recoups from conspiracy assaults, ensures the protected conjunction of a few administrations in a solitary system, and parities the heaps between its heterogeneous gadgets as indicated by their capacities. It has two layers. The upper layer deals with various gatherings and allots hubs to them, as indicated by the administrations to which they buy-in. Then again, the lower layer circulates the devices of each assembly into coherent subgroups to diminish the convention overheads on them. The system isolates into a few gatherings. It will end up with a few further divided subgroups. Each assembly is related to an ID that is exceptional inside the system. It contains then the hubs taking an interest in a given blend of administrations. At the point when a device joins the system, it is doled out to a gathering as indicated by the mix of administrations to which it buys in. Then again, if a present part buys in or withdraws from administrations, it moves from a gathering to another as indicated by its new blend of administrations.

Overhead traffic can make an IDS drop numerous parcels without appropriate assessment, corrupting the security level of its whole conveyed organize. In such a situation, traffic-based trust calculation would become incapable as a result of the loss of bundles. Whitelisted parcels (Meng, 2018) can go straightforwardly to the objective system. Stream-based strategy characterizes parcels into streams and afterward applies an examining procedure to the whole stream as opposed to specific bundles. The blacklist based filtration is On the off chance that the source IP address of approaching bundles coordinates a thing in the process. The relating parcels can be blocked or dealt with regarding predefined security rules. The packet-based strategy utilizes irregularity in the inspecting procedure to forestall synchronization with any instance examples in the rush hour traffic.

(Surendar & Umamakeswari, 2016)a novel exertion at building up an Intrusion Detection and Response System (InDReS) which depends on a requirement based particular model identifies sinkhole assault. Every hub chooses itself as a pioneer hub depending on a probabilistic methodology and communicates its accessibility to all the sensor hubs present in the gathering. It receives the signal quality, which is legitimately relative to the Probability of a sensor node. It decides the pioneer hub and separation between the devices. The pioneer hubs do the collection of the bundles got from all the instruments present in their gathering. The number of parcels missed at the directing layer of 6LoWPAN tallies to decide how adequately the system handles the bundles. The proof worth determines dependent on the likelihood of beta dispersion capacity. The detection system hypothesis applies to every hub. If it is not similar to the edge esteem, the device considers as noxious. The positioning calculation insists that it is a detested hub.

It is (Alexopoulos, et.al. 2020) Communitarian IDS. The crude ready information produced by the screens is put away as exchanges in a blockchain, repeated among the taking a hub of the system. The suspicious devices run an accord convention to ensure the legitimacy of the interchanges before including them in a square. The members are responsible for their activities, as the last is straightforward to the system. The correspondence overhead can be overseen. For example, by putting away hashes of the ready information in the blockchain rather than the crude data. The partaking hubs in the block arrange are either screen units, investigation units, or perform the two undertakings all the while, which is the broadest case. Correspondence between the hubs happens in two sensible layers, in particular the Alert Exchange layer and the Consensus layer. In the Alert Exchange layer, the executed CIDS plays out the ready information scattering process. A Consensus layer is a subset of companions that runs an accord convention and concede to which exchanges. The hubs ought to approach these particular cautions, can take an interest in a different synergistic system, and make various blocks.

(Golomb, et.al. 2018) a lightweight system that uses the blockchain idea to perform disseminated and community-oriented peculiarity identification for gadgets with constrained assets. CIoTA utilizes blockchain to gradually refresh a believed oddity recognition model through self-validation and agreement among IoT gadgets. The framework intends to identify vindictive acts and assemble data about what's going on, and occasionally share an assortment with different specialists. Since a specialist is in the hostile areas, the operator may get bogus talk that brings commotion into the gossipy tidbits passed on to various operators. Each IoT gadget has an operator that keeps up a neighborhood model that uses to distinguish malicious practices in a specific application. A specialist records new Intel by the refreshing nearby models with perceptions of the application's conduct. A specialist shares its Intel nearby operator, like gossip, by adding nearby operators to the chain's incomplete square and afterward sending the chain to neighboring operators in the system. Different specialists will possibly acknowledge this halfway square on the off chance that it is longer than their fractional square, and on the off chance that they can validate the sheltered. A specialist gets the latest knowledge from its kindred operators by supplanting neighborhood specialist with the consolidated model contained inside the freshest shut square.

(Li, et.al. 2019) a nonexclusive system of community-oriented blockchain signature-based IDSs, which can steadily manufacture and update a confided in the signature database in a synergistic IoT condition. In CBSigIDS, every id hub (or blockchain hub) in the consortium blockchain can screen the system traffic, distinguish assaults, and occasionally share a lot of marks (rules) with others. This arrangement is marked by a private key from a hub, to comprehend the wellspring of the accord. Different devices acknowledge these guidelines by checking them against their nearby database.

The authors (Pajouh, et.al., 2016) have exhibited a novel model for interruption identification dependent on two-layer measurement decrease and two-level arrangement module, intended to distinguish noxious exercises, for example, User to Root (U2R) and Remote to Local (R2L) assaults. The proposed model is utilizing segment investigation and direct separate examination of measurement decrease module to spate the high dimensional dataset to a lower one with lesser highlights. They apply a two-level characterization module using Naïve Bayes and Certainty Factor rendition of K-Nearest Neighbor to recognize guilty practices. The proposed model, intended for oddity based interruption location in IoT spine systems, utilizes two-layer measurement decrease and two-level order identification procedures to identify "hard-to-recognize" interruptions, for example, U2R and R2L assaults. Straight Discriminant Analysis (LDA) and Principal Component Analysis to address the high dimensionality issue utilization in the organization. A subset of all chosen highlights is dependent on their viability in the higher arrangement and a subset of new highlights by consolidating existing highlights. Cross-Validation (CV) assesses ideal principals with the least mistakes.

The creator has proposed an interruption discovery and moderation structure, called IoT-IDM (Nobakht, et.al., 2016), to give system-level security to intelligent gadgets sent in home situations. IoT-IDM screens the system exercises of proposed devices inside the home and examines whether there is any suspicious or vindictive movement. When an interruption is recognized, it hinders the gate-device in getting to the injured individual gadget on the fly. The measured plan of IoT-IDM gives its clients the adaptability to utilize AI strategies for discovery dependent on learned mark examples of known assaults. IoT-IDM bridles the appearance of SDN innovation, which offers organize permeability and gives adaptability to arrange, oversee and make sure about the system remotely and the development of AI methods in the discovery of system inconsistency designs. Five key modules used are Device Manager, Sensor Element, Feature Extractor, Detection, and Mitigation.

(Hodo, et al., 2016) centers around the arrangement of typical and dangerous designs of the IoT Network. The multi-layer perception (MLP) is design with three layers of feed-forward Neural Network. The Artificial Neural network (ANN) is utilized as disconnected IDS to assemble and examine data from different pieces of the IoT organize and distinguish a DoS assault on the system. The neurons of the ANN shape complex theories. Assessing the speculations is finished by setting the information hubs in a criticism procedure, and the occasion streams are spread through the system to the yield where it is named ordinary or traded off. At this stage, the inclination plummets push the blunder in the yield hub back through the system by a back-propagation procedure to assess the mistake in the concealed devices. The tendency of the expense – function is determined. Neural system framework experiences preparing to become familiar with the example made in the framework.

The interruption identification design (Sforzin, et.al., 2016) is a little, convenient gadget, pre-bundled with an IDS. The devices move to anyplace in the smart home. It could utilize to ensure intelligent objects. The city organizations could convey it in avenues, squares, college grounds, arenas, or in other swarmed regions, to screen the system traffic of the encompassing territory. It is successfully a compact, on-request, IDS that informs the clients, or the overseers of the system, at whatever point it recognizes a progressing assault or suspicious system exercises. Every gadget will gather assaults' insights locally, and afterward send them to a remote server running a Security Information and Event Management (SIEM) programming, from which organize overseers can perform upkeep or crisis activities.

The intelligent home and the encompassing scene are observed with conduct demonstrating an interruption discovery framework called Behavioral Modeling Intrusion Detection system. (BMIDS) (Arrington, et.al., 2016). The BMIDS utilizes invulnerability roused calculations to recognize whether standards of conduct separated to match the show the deviation from the ideal behavior. The reenactment screens scale all-important movement to check the development of similar conducts models. The BMIDS shows how the catch of IoT sensor information movement linked as a lot of occasion arrangements alongside the reproduced world state gives the parts to build up a numerical portrayal for conduct character. Making conduct models through inescapable framework observes before, and nearby digital-physical framework experimentation with the BMIDS reproduction is cost-proficient, effectively undeniable, and advances self-ruling checking for an autonomic checking system. Additionally, execution estimations can be scaled all the more precisely during the subjective and quantitative examination, delivers the ideal conduct model as portrayed by the predetermined scripted or non-scripted conduct.

The appropriated and lightweight IDS is dependent on an Artificial Immune System (AIS) (Hosseinpour, et.al., 2016). The IDS disseminates in a three-layered IoT structure consisting of the cloud, mist, and edge layers. Because of this engineering, distributed computing obliges the IDS fundamental motor of two sub-motors called a grouping/clustering motor and a training motor. The clustering motor, utilizing solo grouping techniques, separates the essential system traffic into self (typical) and non-self (interruption) bundles as the web-based preparing informational index for our AIS based IDS. The training motor trains a lot of finders dependent on the taking in information acquired from the grouping motor by utilizing a pessimistic choice calculation. These indicators are called essential identifiers. The vital locators after the preparation stage, are put away in a finder archive database at the cloud. It disseminates to the gadgets at the edge of the system. They go about as sensors for IDS that screen the conduct of the edge gadgets. An inconsistency will start a procedure for examining the oddity by delivering a keen information cell.

In SDN, the Data plane comprises switches that are dumb. Each handle is simple equipment with a little capacity to be customized. The rest will be the Control plane. In SDN, controllers are not quite the same as usual systems and OpenFlow switches (Bianco, et.al., 2010). All OpenFlow switches constraints by SDN controller/controllers. The cleverness from controllers moves to the SDN controller. SDN controller can deal with the system, for example, directing information parcels by programming orders. SDN controller (Gheisari, et.al., 2018) isolates it's leveled out IoT gadgets into two classes finishes through grouping techniques. The controller sends a protection class mark of every device to it. The controller sends the encryption strategy IoT gadget should utilize. The IoT gadget applies the relating encryption strategy as its protection conservation technique.

The creators propose a job-based security controller engineering called Rol-Sec(Kalkan & Zeadally, 2017) for the SDN-IoT condition. Each SDN-IoT passage (SDN-IoT GW) speaks with different entryways without considering its own space. It additionally improves organization data transfer capacity of the correspondence connects between the portals and the controllers because the correspondence traffic disseminates. The messages identified with cryptographic activities don't meddle with the progression of control traffic. The interruption controller screens the traffic and deals with the standards for each stream. It can likewise recognize and moderate interruptions that expect to make the framework inaccessible. The solution administrator can be an archive for both symmetric and public keys. The vital dissemination of shared keys is taken care of by this module. This module goes about as a confided in an outsider for both symmetric and public solutions. The controller gives vital administration to the framework. It resembles a catalog that has symmetric keys and shared credential sets. It likewise handles every cryptographic activity requires during administration. The crypto controller offers the accompanying cryptographic types of assistance: uprightness, secrecy, security, confirmation, and personality the board.

STewARD (Boussard, et.al., 2019) permits clients to effortlessly demand from their intelligent home system controller the production of remote programming characterized arrange cuts, to which they allot a necessary trust level utilizing preliminary hazard appraisal. It empowers the arrange controllers to settle on nearby choices in light of worldwide information. By accepting reports on the trust score of gadgets they oversee, controllers can rapidly react to devices. The clients mark gatherings of gadgets utilizing the scale. The component recovers the class of a recently associated device.

Edge computing Architecture (ECA) engineering (Gheisari, et al., 2019) that depends on philosophy for security safeguarding in the IoT-based savvy city condition. ECA has two fundamental subclasses- ontology and nature. It has three security protecting levels. Three focuses on protection safeguarding including security clamor, conceivable deniability, and honest populace. Each IoT gadget sends its ID to the server in the edge cloud. At the point when the protection rules lifetime equivalents to zero, the proprietor of the IoT gadget ought to be changed. At that point, the edge server picks the following appropriate security rule to be applied. We utilize the proprietor of the device to befuddle aggressors more. Something else, the server diminishes one from its protection rule lifetime. The IoT gadget sends its prepared information to the edge cloud as well as to the remote cloud for additional examination. Cloud is a framework that underpins the IoT foundation to accomplish better execution.

IoT botnet discovery and detachment approach (Chaabouni, et.al. 2019) comprise of various smart home systems. These Smart Home systems are associated with employing an Internet association. It utilizes an entrance switch and different IoT gadgets. The methodology is sent inside the entrance switch and comprises the two principle segments checking and detachment. The work has four stages. In the primary phase, the method recognizes the subnet address of the nearby system and outputs for associated IoT gadgets. In the subsequent one, mechanized segregation is performed by composing firewall rules to the entrance switches inside UCI (Unified Configuration Interface) firewall. In the third stage, the Common Vulnerability Enumeration (CVE) online-administration is questioned in standard time interims (default is hourly) to recognize conceivably defenseless administrations and IoT gadgets. These inquiries sift by MAC address prefixes of the found nearby IoT gadgets. The determined port quantities of the past stage are self-improving checking approach in the last phase.

The suggested a lightweight instrument (Maloney, et.al. 2019) to perform security and other gadgets the board refreshes utilizing a golang-based operator. The light-weight specialist is 1.4MB in size and communicates with an IoT gadget's working framework without meddling with other gadget forms. The operator adequately conveys exceptionally focused on updates to an IoT gadget's working framework that doesn't require a framework restart to produce results. It diminishes the danger of bricking a device or meddling with continually running procedures on gadgets expected to work day in and day out. The employed limit administration level shared for digital-physical gadgets are like a vitality conveyance framework. The operator is fit for giving simultaneous procedure execution, not securing intelligent urban areas in an assigned biological system of devices.

The suggested model uses Principal Component Analysis (PCA) (Zhao, et.al 2017) to decrease measurements of the dataset from countless highlights to a modest number. The softmax relapse and k-closest neighbor calculations are applied to build up a classifier. The model comprises of a measurement decrease part and a classifier. PCA is an element extraction instrument, communicates to a subset of new highlights made by anticipating existing highlights to anew measurements. K-closest neighbor calculation uses a classifier without pre-preparing progress.

The engineering (Salman, et.al. 2019) comprises of four segments: highlights extractor, IoT gadget recognizable proof, traffic-type ID, and interruption discovery. The highlights, to be specific, parcel size, timestamp, bearing, and transport convention, are extricated for each system stream. A system stream dictates by the five-tuple- source IP address, source port number, goal IP address, goal port number, and transport convention. The highlights extractor keeps a refreshed rundown of the dynamic streams. When a parcel shows up at the highlights extractor segment, and on the off chance, it has a place with a functioning stream. If there is no dynamic stream for this bundle, another stream inclusion, and the parcel highlights recording. After getting 16 chunks of a similar stream, the stream highlights sent to the classifier. The IoT gadget distinguishing proof part is liable for arranging the devices dependent on their system traffic stream measurable highlights. The traffic-type recognizes proof part targets grouping the produced traffic dependent on the sort. On the off chance, there is confusion between the normal traffic-type from a specific gadget and the generated traffic. The interruption recognition segment has the job of profiling typical gadget conduct and can distinguish strange movement.

(Salman, et.al. 2018) is designed to recognize the gadget type and the traffic type dependent on the created traffic, utilizing AI. When it cultivates, a portal can choose to confine access from/to specific gadgets introducing a few vulnerabilities or identifying some traffic variations from the norm. The work comprises pushing the insight into the system edge. These hubs are mindful extricating stream related highlights, figure measurable stream-based highlights, and send the highlights vectors to a focal controller. The controller, executing a traffic classifier, a traffic screen, and a security orchestrator, is answerable for gadget and traffic types order, traffic variations from the norm recognition, and security rules design. The system is a little edge system where various sorts of IoT gadgets are associated. Each IoT sub-domain associates with an intelligent programming-based edge. The edge hubs of an IoT area constrains by a controller executing diverse system capacities. The traffic investigation module comprises of three segments: the classifier, the traffic screen, and the security orchestrator. At the point when a parcel shows up at the system edge, the edge hub records the appearance time, the size, the vehicle convention, and the heading (forward or in reverse) of this bundle. The stream characterizes by the arrangement of parcels having the same source port number, source IP, destination port number, destination IP, and transport convention. The edge hub spares a rundown of dynamic streams.

SVELTE (Raza, et.al. 2013) has three fundamental incorporated modules. The principle module, called 6LoWPAN Mapper (6Mapper), assembles data about the RPL organize and reproduces the system in the e6LoWPAN fringe switch (6BR). The subsequent module is the interruption discovery segment that examines the mapped information and identifies an interruption. The third module, a conveyed smaller than usual firewall, is intended to offload hubs by separating undesirable traffic before it enters the asset obliged arrange. The incorporated modules have two comparing light-weight modules in each obliged device. The principal module gives mapping data to the 6BR so it can perform interruption location. The subsequent module works with the firewall. Each compelled hub additionally has a third module to deal with start to finish bundle loss packets.

3. ASSUMPTIONS MADE IN THE WORK

- The server will have all the details of the registered devices.
- The devices send the samples by endorsing the generated hash value.
- The hash value is generated using the device id and the location details. The transmitted message by the devices is verified by the server.
- The adversary is capable of launching forged attacks. These are Assaults that issue produced orders to insightful electronic gadgets, which trigger the execution of undesired activities, for example, power outage.
- The adversary is into redirecting the packets received. Assaults forestall the right directing of orders and other data between the server and the various gadgets. The assault accomplishes by adjusting the stream rules.

4. PREVIOUS WORK ARCHITECTURE

(Derhab, et al., 2019) the architecture consists of a private cloud, IP network, SDN controller, and virtual handle. The cloud has all the parts that offer an incorporated control for ICS as virtual machines. The SDN controller is an application that oversees stream control by utilizing conventions that advice changes where to send information parcels. The OpenFlow convention is a southbound interface between the controller and the sending components, for example, switches. The northbound interface thinks about the correspondence between the controller and the applications.

SD-WAN design decreases the system cost by offering zero-contact organization, i.e., there is no compelling reason to arrange the system gadget by connecting it. The private cloud has all the segments having an incorporated control for ICS as virtual machines, for example, SCADA server, DCS server, and SDN controller. SDN controller is an application that oversees stream control by utilizing conventions. For example, OpenFlow advises changes where to send information parcels. The OpenFlow convention is a southbound interface between the controller and the sending components. The northbound interface thinks about the correspondence between the controller and the applications. Virtual Switch is an application that interconnects numerous virtual machines of the equivalent or various hypervisors. It additionally interconnects these virtual machines with other physical switches.

In the first stage (preparation stage), the authors haphazardly select S characteristic from a lot of F characteristic with the end goal that S £ F. The chosen attribute is taken care of to an AI calculation to create a classifier. This activity is rehashed B times, and at each time S, the characteristic is picked aimlessly with substitution to produce an alternate classifier.

In the second stage (testing stage), the yields from every unmistakable student are consolidated by a larger part casting a ballot to acquire the last forecast or characterization result.

The IDS (Ambika & Raju, 2014) is utilizing Random Subspace learning (RSL). The Random Subspace Learning (RSL) strategy is a troupe learning method. It attributes stowing or characteristics sacking. It improves expectation and arrangement undertakings as it utilizes gathering development of base classifiers rather than a solitary classifier, and it takes arbitrary subsets of attributes rather than the whole arrangement of characteristics.

Blockchain-based uprightness checking framework expects to distinguish any infusion of false stream leads in the vSwitches is adopted. The Random Subspace Learning (RSL) strategy is a troupe learning procedure called attributes bagging. It improves forecast and order errands as it utilizes group development of base classifiers rather than a solitary classifier, and it takes arbitrary subsets of properties rather than the whole arrangement of the attribute. The irregular subspace learning process comprises two stages preparing and testing. In the preparation stage, we arbitrarily select a subset. The chosen highlights are taken care of to an AI calculation to produce a classifier. This activity is rehashed B times, and sub-assembly highlights are picked indiscriminately with substitution to create an alternate classifier. In the testing stage, the yields from every unmistakable student are consolidated by the part casting a ballot to get the last expectation or grouping result.

The blockchain has two hubs- an SDN controller and a firewall. The SDN controller makes squares and offers it to the firewall through the blockchain. The principal device has all the authorizations while the firewall can peruse and get. SDN controller hashes the stream rules and places them in a square circulating to different hubs of the blockchain. At the point when the stream rules arrive at the vSwitch hub, the last update its stream table and spare the principles in the log document. The Firewall gathers the vSwitch logs and gets to the BlockChain to acquire the stream rules sent by the controller. On the off chance that the firewall finds that the two standards, from vSwitch and blockchain, are not comparative, it tells the Administrator to take the countermeasures to fix this bungling.

5. PROPOSED ARCHITECTURE

The suggested RSL architecture follows the same architecture as considered (Derhab, et al., 2019). The proposal is an improvement of the previous contribution. The architecture contains a private cloud, IP network, SDN controller, and virtual switch. The cloud has all the parts that offer an incorporated control for ICS as virtual machines. The SDN controller is an application that oversees stream control by utilizing conventions that advice changes where to send information parcels. The OpenFlow convention is a southbound interface between the controller and the sending components, for example, switches. The northbound interface thinks about the correspondence between the controller and the applications. The proposal used RSL methodology. The method has a trial phase where the subset creation in attack free environment. They provide a set of safe readings. The threat is identified using safe readings. Hence the method provides better reliability than (Derhab, et al., 2019). The procedure has three stages –

5.1. Trial Phase

The devices installed in the environment uses The Random subspace model. Random list R_i is created using attack free environment. This set is treated initial values. The safe readings are made a subset R_s. The treat readings are made as another set R_t.

$$R_s = \{r_{i1}, r_{i2}, \ldots \ldots r_{ik}\} \text{ -------------------} \tag{1}$$

$$R_t = \{r_{i(k+1)}, r_{i(k+2)}, \ldots \ldots r_{in}\} \text{ ------------------} \tag{2}$$

In the notation (1) the values $r_{i1}, r_{i2}, \ldots \ldots r_{ik}$ belong to the safe set R_s. In the notation (2) $r_{i(k+1)}, r_{i(k+2)}, \ldots \ldots r_{in}$ belong to the treat value set R_t.

$$\text{-------------------------} \tag{3}$$

In the notation (3), R_i is the combination of safe values R_s and treat values R_t.

$$I_i \circledR S_i : R_i = \{r_{i1}, r_{i2}, \ldots \ldots r_{in}\} \| E_i \text{ -------------------} \tag{4}$$

$$S_i \circledR F_i : R_i = \{r_{i1}, r_{i2}, \ldots \ldots r_{in}\} \| E_s \text{ -------------------} \tag{5}$$

In notation (4) the list of values generated during the trial session is dispatched by the device I_i to the server S_i suffixing the endorsement of the device E_i. The endorsements sent by the devices are detached after validation. In notation (5) the list of values generated is communicated by the server S_i to the firewall F_i.

5.2 Training Phase

Another random list is generated by collecting the values from the IoT devices. Let R_j be the set of values collected.

$$I_i \circledR S_i : R_j = \{r_{j1}, r_{j2}, \ldots \ldots r_{jn}\} \text{ -------------------} \tag{6}$$

Notation (6) represents the list of values generated during the training phase dispatched by the device I_i to the server S_i.

5.3 Testing Phase

The trail values are saved in the server S_i and the firewall F_i. Once the server receives the values during the training phase, it provides a mapping to the values (values of testing phase is mapped to the values in the trail phase). The received message is also made a comparison to other values send by various devices to detect the genuine of the message. The blockchain methodology is adopted similar to (Derhab, et al., 2019).

6. ANALYSIS OF THE WORK

6.1 Reliability

The proposed work uses the endorsement keys verified by the server and the firewall that adds more reliability to the system compared to (Derhab, et al., 2019) by 2.7%. Figure 1 represents the same. The proposed work undergoes three phases namely the trial phase, training phase, and testing phase. The verification is done at server as well as by the firewall. The genuine values are opted by making a comparison to the trail session values and the aggregated values from various devices.

Figure 1. Comparison of the proposed work with (Derhab, et al., 2019)

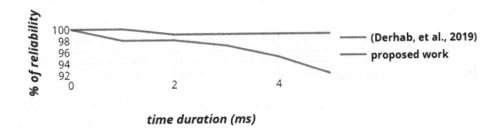

7. CONCLUSION

SDN encourages the IoT system to be overseen powerfully in an asset compelled organize. It gives chances to improve security in IoT systems. The applications can be made on SDN to forestall, identify, and respond to dangers. The Industrial IoT system requires safety to bring in reliability to the system. The proposal has better reliability in adding endorsement hash value to the dispatched messages. The message is verified by the server and forwarded by suffixing the endorsement hash value to the data. The received message evaluates to bring in reliability to the system by 2.7% than the previous contribution. The received data by the firewall undergoes verification against the trail values and aggregated values.

REFERENCES

Alexopoulos, N., Vasilomanolakis, E., Roux, S. L., Rowe, S., & Mühlhäuser, M. (2020). TRIDEnT: towards a decentralized threat indicator marketplace. In *35th Annual ACM Symposium on Applied Computing* (pp. 332–341). Brno Czech Republic: ACM. 10.1145/3341105.3374020

Alshahrani, M., Traore, I., & Woungang, I. (2019). Design and Implementation of a Lightweight Authentication Framework for the Internet of Things (IoT). In *Sixth International Conference on Internet of Things: Systems, Management and Security (IOTSMS)* (pp. 185-194). Granada, Spain: IEEE. 10.1109/IOTSMS48152.2019.8939190

Ambika, N. (2019). Energy-Perceptive Authentication in Virtual Private Networks Using GPS Data. In Security, Privacy and Trust in the IoT Environment (pp. 25-38). Springer.

Ambika, N. (2020). Encryption of Data in Cloud-Based Industrial IoT Devices. In S. Pal & V. G. Díaz (Eds.), *IoT: Security and Privacy Paradigm* (pp. 111–129). CRC Press, Taylor & Francis Group.

Arrington, B., Barnett, L., Rufus, R., & Esterline, A. (2016). Behavioral modeling intrusion detection system (bmids) using internet of things (iot) behavior-based anomaly detection via immunity-inspired algorithms. In *25th International Conference on Computer Communication and Networks (ICCCN)* (pp. 1-6). Waikoloa, HI: IEEE. 10.1109/ICCCN.2016.7568495

Banerjee, M., Lee, J., & Choo, K. K. (2018). A blockchain future for internet of things security: A position paper. *Digital Communications and Networks*, 4(3), 149–160. doi:10.1016/j.dcan.2017.10.006

Bianco, A., Birke, R., Giraudo, L., & Palacin, M. (2010). Openflow switching: Data plane performance. In *International Conference on Communications* (pp. 1-5). Cape Town, South Africa: IEEE.

Boussard, M., Papillon, S., Peloso, P., Signorini, M., & Waisbard, E. (2019). STewARD: SDN and blockchain-based Trust evaluation for Automated Risk management on IoT Devices. In *INFOCOM 2019-IEEE Conference on Computer Communications Workshops (INFOCOM WKSHPS)* (pp. 841-846). Paris, France: IEEE.

Chaabouni, N., Mosbah, M., Zemmari, A., Sauvignac, C., & Faruki, P. (2019). Network intrusion detection for IoT security based on learning techniques. *IEEE Communications Surveys and Tutorials*, *21*(3), 2671–2701. doi:10.1109/COMST.2019.2896380

Cherian, M., & Chatterjee, M. (2018). Survey of security threats in iot and emerging countermeasures. In *International Symposium on Security in Computing and Communication* (pp. 591-604). Bangalore: Springer.

Derhab, A., Guerroumi, M., Gumaei, A., Maglaras, L., Ferrag, M. A., Mukherjee, M., & Khan, F. A. (2019). Blockchain and Random Subspace Learning-Based IDS for SDN-Enabled Industrial IoT Security. *Sensors (Basel)*, *19*(3119), 3119. doi:10.339019143119 PMID:31311136

Fu, Y., Yan, Z., Cao, J., Koné, O., & Cao, X. (2017). An automata based intrusion detection method for internet of things. *Mobile Information Systems*, 1-14.

Gheisari, M., Pham, Q. V., Alazab, M., Zhang, X., Fernández-Campusano, C., & Srivastava, G. (2019). ECA: An Edge Computing Architecture for Privacy-Preserving in IoT-Based Smart City. *IEEE Access: Practical Innovations, Open Solutions*, *7*, 155779–155786. doi:10.1109/ACCESS.2019.2937177

Gheisari, M., Wang, G., Chen, S., & Ghorbani, H. (2018). IoT-SDNPP: A Method for Privacy-Preserving in Smart City with Software Defined Networking. In *International Conference on Algorithms and Architectures for Parallel Processing* (pp. 303-312). Guangzhou, China: Springer. 10.1007/978-3-030-05063-4_24

Golomb, T., Mirsky, Y., & Elovici, Y. (2018). Ciota: Collaborative iot anomaly detection via blockchain. In *Workshop on Decentralized IoT Security and Standards (DISS) of the Network and Distributed Systems Security Symposium (NDSS)* (pp. 1-6). San Diego, CA: NDSS.

Hamza, A., Gharakheili, H. H., & Sivaraman, V. (2018). Combining MUD policies with SDN for IoT intrusion detection. In *Proceedings of the 2018 Workshop on IoT Security and Privacy* (pp. 1-7). ACM. 10.1145/3229565.3229571

Hodo, E., Bellekens, X., Hamilton, A., Dubouilh, P. L., Iorkyase, E., Tachtatzis, C., & Atkinson, R. (2016). Threat analysis of IoT networks using artificial neural network intrusion detection system. In *International Symposium on Networks, Computers and Communications (ISNCC)* (pp. 1-6). IEEE. 10.1109/ISNCC.2016.7746067

Hosseinpour, F., Vahdani Amoli, P., Plosila, J., Hämäläinen, T., & Tenhunen, H. (2016). An intrusion detection system for fog computing and IoT based logistic systems using a smart data approach. *International Journal of Digital Content Technology and its Applications, 10*, 34-48.

Kalkan, K., & Zeadally, S. (2017). Securing internet of things with software defined networking. *IEEE Communications Magazine, 56*(9), 186–192. doi:10.1109/MCOM.2017.1700714

Kandi, M. A., Lakhlef, H., Bouabdallah, A., & Challal, Y. (2019). An Efficient Multi-Group Key Management Protocol for Heterogeneous IoT Devices. In *Wireless Communications and Networking Conference (WCNC)* (pp. 1-6). Marrakesh, Morocco: IEEE. 10.1109/WCNC.2019.8885613

Khan, M. A., & Salah, K. (2018). IoT security: Review, blockchain solutions, and open challenges. *Future Generation Computer Systems, 82*, 395–411. doi:10.1016/j.future.2017.11.022

Khan, Z. A., & Herrmann, P. (2017). A trust based distributed intrusion detection mechanism for internet of things. In *IEEE 31st International Conference on Advanced Information Networking and Applications (AINA)* (pp. 1169-1176). Taipei, Taiwan: IEEE.

Li, W., Tug, S., Meng, W., & Wang, Y. (2019). Designing collaborative blockchained signature-based intrusion detection in IoT environments. *Future Generation Computer Systems, 96*, 481–489. doi:10.1016/j.future.2019.02.064

Liu, B., Yu, X. L., Chen, S., Xu, X., & Zhu, L. (2017). Blockchain based data integrity service framework for IoT data. In *IEEE International Conference on Web Services (ICWS)* (pp. 468-475). IEEE. 10.1109/ICWS.2017.54

Lopez-Martin, M., Carro, B., Sanchez-Esguevillas, A., & Lloret, J. (1967). Conditional variational autoencoder for prediction and feature recovery applied to intrusion detection in iot. *Sensors (Basel), 17*(9), 2017. PMID:28846608

Maloney, M., Reilly, E., Siegel, M., & Falco, G. (2019). *Cyber Physical IoT Device Management Using a Lightweight Agent. In IEEE Green Computing and Communications (GreenCom).* IEEE.

Meng, W. (2018). Intrusion detection in the era of IoT: Building trust via traffic filtering and sampling. *Computer, 51*(7), 36–43. doi:10.1109/MC.2018.3011034

Nagaraj, A. (2021). *Introduction to Sensors in IoT and Cloud Computing Applications.* Bentham Science Publishers.

Nobakht, M., Sivaraman, V., & Boreli, R. (2016). A host-based intrusion detection and mitigation framework for smart home IoT using OpenFlow. In *11th International conference on availability, reliability and security (ARES)* (pp. 147-156). Salzburg, Austria: IEEE. 10.1109/ARES.2016.64

Pajouh, H. H., Javidan, R., Khayami, R., Ali, D., & Choo, K. K. (2016). A two-layer dimension reduction and two-tier classification model for anomaly-based intrusion detection in IoT backbone networks. *IEEE Transactions on Emerging Topics in Computing.*

Raza, S., Wallgren, L., & Voigt, T. (2013). Real-time intrusion detection in the Internet of Things. *Ad Hoc Networks, 11*(8), 2661–2674. doi:10.1016/j.adhoc.2013.04.014

Saeed, A., Ahmadinia, A., Javed, A., & Larijani, H. (2016). Intelligent intrusion detection in low-power IoTs. *ACM Transactions on Internet Technology, 16*(4), 1–25. doi:10.1145/2990499

Sahay, R., Meng, W., & Jensen, C. D. (2019). The application of Software Defined Networking on securing computer networks: A survey. *Journal of Network and Computer Applications, 131*, 89–108. doi:10.1016/j.jnca.2019.01.019

Salman, O., Chaddad, L., Elhajj, I. H., Chehab, A., & Kayssi, A. (2018). Pushing intelligence to the network edge. In *Fifth International Conference on Software Defined Systems (SDS)* (pp. 87-92). Barcelona, Spain: IEEE. 10.1109/SDS.2018.8370427

Salman, O., Elhajj, I. H., Chehab, A., & Kayssi, A. (2019). A machine learning based framework for IoT device identification and abnormal traffic detection. *Transactions on Emerging Telecommunications Technologies*, 3743. doi:10.1002/ett.3743

Sforzin, A., Mármol, F. G., Conti, M., & Bohli, J. M. (2016). RPiDS: Raspberry Pi IDS—A fruitful intrusion detection system for IoT. In *Intl IEEE Conferences on Ubiquitous Intelligence & Computing, Advanced and Trusted Computing, Scalable Computing and Communications, Cloud and Big Data Computing, Internet of People, and Smart World Congress (UIC/ATC/ScalCom/CBDCom/IoP/SmartWorld)* (pp. 440-448). IEEE.

Singh, J., Gimekar, A., & Venkatesan, S. (2019). An efficient lightweight authentication scheme for human-centered industrial Internet of Things. *International Journal of Communication Systems*, 4189. doi:10.1002/dac.4189

Surendar, M., & Umamakeswari, A. (2016). InDReS: An Intrusion Detection and response system for Internet of Things with 6LoWPAN. In *International Conference on Wireless Communications, Signal Processing and Networking (WiSPNET)* (pp. 1903-1908). Chennai, India: IEEE. 10.1109/WiSPNET.2016.7566473

Zhao, S., Li, W., Zia, T., & Zomaya, A. Y. (2017). A dimension reduction model and classifier for anomaly-based intrusion detection in internet of things. In *IEEE 15th Intl Conf on Dependable, Autonomic and Secure Computing* (pp. 836-843). IEEE.

Chapter 9

Design of an IoT–Based Quantity Controlled Pesticide Sprayer Using Plant Identification

Jerin Geo Jacob
Mount Zion College of Engineering,
India

Siji A. Thomas
Mount Zion College of Engineering,
India

Bivin Biju
Mount Zion College of Engineering,

India

Richard John
Mount Zion College of Engineering,
India

Abhilash P. R.
Mount Zion College of Engineering,
India

ABSTRACT

This chapter discusses the design of a quantitative controlled pesticide sprayer and the development of an efficient algorithm for plant identification. The whole system is controlled using the raspberry pi and convolutional neural networks (CNN) algorithm for training the proposed model. Once the algorithm identifies the plant by processing the image, it is captured by using a pi camera, and it determines the pesticide and its dosage. The sensors will collect the information related to the plant condition such as humidity and surrounding temperature, which is simultaneously sent to the farmers/agriculture officers through the internet of things (IoT), for the purpose of live analysis, and they are stored using cloud services, making the system suitable for remote farming. The proposed algorithm is trained mainly for three types of plant leaves, which include tomato, brinjal, and chilly. The CNN algorithm scores accuracy of 97.2% with sensitivity and specificity of 0.94 and 0.95,

DOI: 10.4018/978-1-7998-6463-9.ch009

respectively. The robot is intended to encourage the agriculturists for next-level farming to facilitate their work.

INTRODUCTION

Aimed at increasing the crop yield, many pesticides are available in the market, but its prolonged exposure causes serious health impairments such as immune malfunction, neurological impairments, dermal problems, cancer and vision related issues to humans. Some highly dangerous chemicals such as endosulfan can cause serious genetic problems also. In 2017, 40 farmer deaths were reported in Maharashtra due to the inhalation of chemical pesticides. Similar deaths were also reported in Tamil Nadu and many parts of the country. Another negative impact includes skin related irritation to farmers and contamination of nearby water bodies. Nowadays, pesticides are sprayed without analyzing the dosage required for a particular crop and it is the core reason behind most of the harmful effects on people. The algorithm described in this work identifies the pesticide type and it predicts the dosage to be sprayed by the robot, thus preventing the over-dosing issues, thereby avoiding its intensive effects. The developed model can also sense the present condition of plant such as humidity, surrounding temperature, hence making the system, a next level farming.

Along with the advancement in the modern technology, this work incorporates IoT, a very promising and innovative technology which can be considered as an ideal solution in agricultural domains since continuous controlling as well as manual monitoring is not required. The whole applications of IoT in agricultural domain are controlled by using different IoT based devices which helps the farmers/ agricultural officers to collect relevant data from the field. In the proposed method, telegram cloud services have also been used that helps authorized person to make better decision, thus improving the production chain which makes the system more advanced.

BACKGROUND

Logeswari *et al.* (2015) designed a robotic system to sense surrounding temperature, humidity and air quality of remote agricultural fields. The system uses Global System for Mobile Communication (GSM) and it communicates with the cloud through Raspberry Pi, thereby helping the data to be used in future to create awareness about the environmental changes. The work of Gowrishankar *et al.* (2018) aim at designing multipurpose autonomous agricultural robotic vehicle which can be controlled through IoT for seeding and spraying of pesticides which in turn helps to reduce the human intervention, ensuring high yield and efficient utilization of resources. The authors also developed an android mobile application to control the robot and uses Wi-Fi module for communication.

Hemalatha *et al.* (2018) proposed a multitasking Farm-Bot to integrate agriculture process in single robotic system by incorporating cloud services. The bot can perform live streaming of crops, sprinkling of pesticides, seed sowing and automatic irrigation. In addition, this venture attempted to monitor parameters associated with plants and crops such as moisture level, humidity, temperature etc through sensors and can upload the same to a cloud database. The authors of Kavitha et *al.* (2018) proposed a fully automated system from sowing of seeds to fertilizing using the concept of IoT. The system maintains its ability to be extremely precise and done with similar technology that has been around for decades in printers, manufacturing equipment, and more recently 3D printers and CNC milling machines. The webpage designed, along with the help of HTML will control the module. The work of Rahul D S *et al.* (2018) discusses the development of an IoT based solar powered agribot that automates irrigation task and enables remote farm monitoring. While executing the task of irrigation, it moves along a pre-determined path of a given farm, and senses soil moisture content and temperature at regular points. At each sensing point, data acquired from multiple sensors is processed to decide the necessity of irrigation and accordingly the irrigation task is done. The authors developed their system using an Arduino microcontroller and the system acts as an IoT device, transmitting the data collected from multiple sensors to a remote server using Wi-Fi link. At the remote server, the raw data is processed using signal processing operations such as filtering, compression a control the module with the help of HTML and prediction. Senthil *et al.* (2020) explains the design of a cost effective automated irrigation system with the use of IoT. It is important to measure different parameters such as soil moisture sensor, temperature sensor etc to calculate the quantity of water required for plants. All the sensors were interfaced into the Raspberry Pi to control the opening/ closing of irrigation valve. The soil moisture sensor is used for the measurement of soil wetness and pH sensor for measuring the pH value. The system developed by Senthil *et al.* also identifies leaf diseases if any; by analysing the colour change occurred in the captured image. Balaji *et al.* (2018) proposed a multipurpose agricultural robot which can be used for digging the soil, leveller to close the mud and also to spray water. The vehicle is controlled by relay switch through IR sensor input and the whole system works with battery and solar power. PIC 16F877A Microcontroller is used in this agribot. The authors of G. Hu (2012) and E. Guizzo (2011) made a study on cloud computing technology with robotics especially for agricultural applications].The incorporation of Artificial Intelligence in Internet of Things is well explained by García *et al* (2018), discusses many examples regarding the applications of AI in IoT domain with four main sub-fields which include Machine Learning, Computer Vision, Fuzzy Logic and Natural Language

Processing. The work done by the authors in A. Kapoor et *al* (2016) explains about the use of Internet of Things in agricultural domain. The various image processing applications in agricultural domain is discussed by the authors in Latha *et al* (2014) in which the authors mainly focused on methods to reduce the usage of herbicides in plants. Bo *et al* (2011) made a study on cloud computing in IoT for agriculture and forestry applications.

As discussed in the above section, the combination of IoT and Image Processing algorithms can enhance the production gain in agricultural domain by reducing the crop failures. The IoT paradigm helps us to reduce the time spent for data collection because collecting the tedious readings in the conventional manner is costlier. Presently, there is no efficient state-of-the art classification algorithm for identification of plant and to decide the type of pesticide and its required dosage. Hence, the novelty of the proposed work includes the classification of crops into Tomato, Brinjal or Chilly by the identification of plant leaf. Furthermore, it identifies the pesticide type and its required quantity to be sprayed, also analyses the surrounding temperature and humidity. In the proposed work, CNN is used for the classification purpose as it is a widely used classifier for high level applications. Thus, the proposed system reduces the human intervention and overcomes the current issues related to overdosing and ensures high yield.

METHODOLOGY

The design model of a remotely controlled fully autonomous robotic system is discussed in this section. The selection of pesticides and its quantity is the core objective of the work. The whole system can be briefly described into three sub-sections: firstly, the application of digital image processing for the identification of crop by extracting the features, secondly; spraying of pesticides based on the predetermined quantity and finally data transferring through IoT.

Crop Identification Using CNN Algorithm

The Pi- Camera captures the video and is separated into frames to get the leaf image. The plant leaf image is then directly given to the CNN algorithm after the rescaling process. The CNN is a class of deep learning and, it requires fewer parameters to set up the processing model and it works very effectively for image processing operations. The challenging facts of manual feature extraction steps can be completely avoided since the raw image can be processed directly and its classification accuracy is very high with relatively lower classification time.

Figure 1. Feature Extraction Using CNN Algorithm

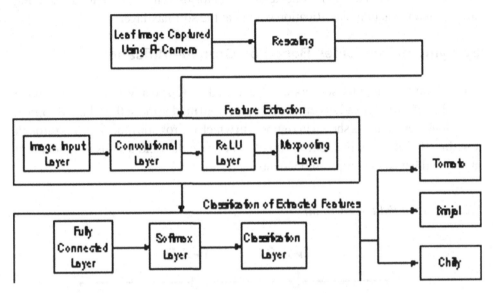

Here the crop leaf images trained were of size 256* 256. The patterns of raw image are learnt deeply by different layers in CNN model. The feature learning is performed by Convolutional layer, ReLU layer and Maxpooling layer; these layers can also be repeated over many times if required. The pixel value of the image is depicted by the image input layer of CNN. Most of the core operations are done by the Convolutional layer, usually known as the "core building block" in which a sliding window performs the convolution operation. The spatial informations about the image are preserved during the extraction of features. A filter size of '3' is selected for performing the convolution, as the filter size increases, more the features can be extracted. Theoretically, the total number of features can be calculated using equation 1.

$$W^T.x + b \tag{1}$$

Where, x is the small part of the image, W the weight, b the bias parameter.

The next layer is called the Rectified Linear Unit (ReLU) satisfying the concept of max (0, x), where x represents the pixel value, performs the conversion of all negative pixel values to zero followed by a Maxpooling layer. This layer down samples the input image or in other words the size gets shrinked, reducing the computational complexities. After feature extraction the network then moves to the fully connected layer, softmax layer and finally the classification layer correctly classifies the extracted features for predicting the results. In fully connected layer, the filtered and shrinked image is concatenated and forms a single list, called flattening process and the actual classification occurs at the softmax layer.

Spraying of Pesticides Based on Crop Identification

All the components and sensors are connected to Raspberry Pi and is the main controller of the proposed system. For the proposed model, the authors have designed a line follower circuit as shown in figure 2, in which the robotic model moves through it within 10 fields and the nodes present in between the field's stops the robot as it moves and hence the crop can be identified.

Figure 2. Line Follower Circuit

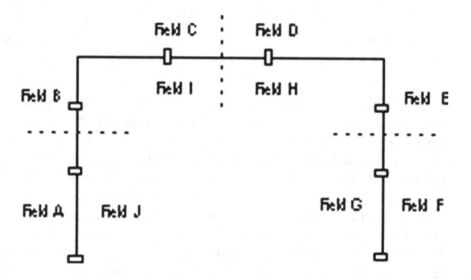

Once the crop identification is done, the pesticide selection is made and its dosage is defined. In the proposed work, the authors considered for two different pesticides for three varieties of crops. It continues until it reaches its end position and then it starts from the initial position itself for checking the crops at the other side. IR array is used to find the robotic path and if it tends to divert away from line, it sends the signal to the Raspberry Pi and correction of path is being made by sending the instructions back to the motor through motor driver IC. The motor is controlled using L293D which can simultaneously control two motors; and it can drive the motors in both directions. In this manner, the identification of plant helps to spray the pesticides with right quantity to drastically reduce the negative impacts on human bodies as well as to the nearby water bodies. The block diagram of the proposed model is as shown in figure 3.

Figure 3. Block Diagram of the proposed Method

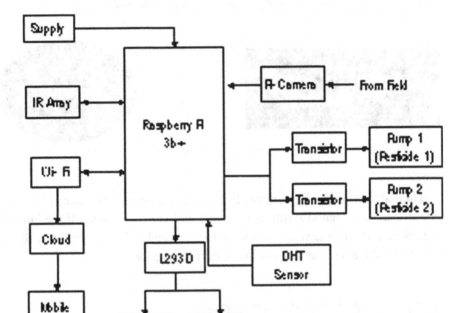

Transferring of Collected Information via Internet of Things

The applications of IoT has been achieved a great level of success. This paradigm reduces the human intervention in the physical world, which in turn enhances the production chain. In this section, the incorporation of IoT with Image processing has been discussed which makes the system suitable for precision farming. Furthermore, the Bot is also capable of providing suggestions related to the plant condition such as humidity and surrounding temperature using a DHT sensor. The temperature and humidity are the main parameters responsible for the drastic condition of a plant. The informations collected from the field is simultaneously sent to the farmers/ agriculture officers through IoT for the purpose of live analysis and the data's are stored using telegram cloud services thereby making the system suitable for next level farming. The sensors and Camera are assembled in the Raspberry Pi board.

The whole framework of the IoT sensing devices must be ensured the safety from severe climatic conditions. A brief flow diagram of IoT application used in the proposed methodology is depicted in figure 4.

Figure 4. Flow Diagram of IoT in Proposed Methodology

The real time monitoring of agricultural field aim not only the objectives mentioned in above sections, but also improves the irrigation management. If the humidity is high, then normally the water content at the surface level of the ground will be less. This will reduce the water requirement during irrigation.

RESULT AND INTERPRETATIONS

Experimental analysis was done using MATLAB 2017b version. For performance analysis, 203 images were trained, the images were collected from different publicly available datasets as well as real time images captured using iPhone 7s plus. Figure 5 shows examples for images that the authors has trained using CNN algorithm.

Figure 5. Figures Showing the Trained Leaf Images a) Tomato b) Brinjal c) Chilly

The performance of deep learning depends on how the network architecture is created. The CNN is trained for 50 epochs since the accuracy improves for each epoch value. The below figure 6 shows the validation of algorithm with its accuracy and loss for epoch value 50. As the epoch value increases, accuracy increases and correspondingly the loss decrease. The selection of learning rate also plays an important role for improving the performance of the training algorithm.

Figure 6. Figure Showing the Validation Accuracy and Loss with Epoch Value 50

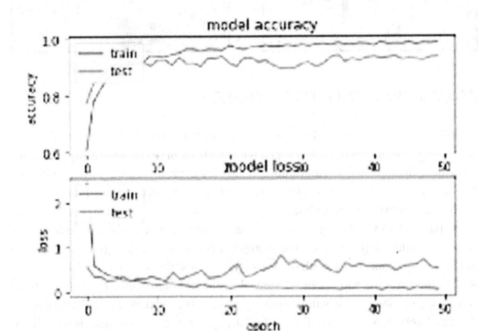

The evaluation is based on four parameters such as accuracy, sensitivity or the True Positive Rate (TPR), specificity or the True Negative Rate (TNR) and precision. Randomly 50 images were tested and it achieved accuracy, sensitivity and specificity of 97.2%, 0.94 and 0.95 respectively with precision of 97.50%. The pesticide dosage for the corresponding crop is calculated based on many parameters such as toxicity, dilution rate, its concentration etc. and is predefined in the algorithm. All the calculation related to the dosage depends on the active ingredient present in the pesticides which is responsible for the toxic effect. Therefore discussions were also made with the expert agricultural officers.

Figure 7. Different Views of the Developed Model

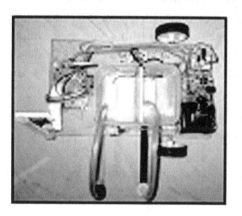 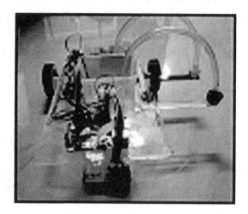

CONCLUSION AND FUTURE TRENDS

Robotics has an immense role in modern agriculture. An agribot with a pesticide controlling scheme has been developed with an efficient deep learning algorithm for plant identification, which could automatically detect the plant and spray accordingly. The developed model is very useful, reducing the risk of over dosage of chemicals that are sprayed on to the plant without properly analysing its requirement. Furthermore, it is capable of providing suggestions related to the plant condition such as humidity and surrounding temperature. The complete procedure of programming can be monitored by connecting it with the Wi-Fi module and the information can be stored in the cloud storage and it can be viewed in the mobile phone. The informations collected from the field is simultaneously send to the farmers/ agriculture officers through Internet of Things (IoT) for the purpose of live analysis and the data's are stored using telegram cloud services. CNN algorithm is trained with 50 epochs to get virtuous accuracy, sensitivity, specificity and precision. The simplicity of the algorithm makes the system suitable for next level farming.

Deep learning usually takes much time for training but it takes less time during testing. This algorithm performs much faster and better if high end systems are used. Deep learning is going to be the most rising and ruling technology in the upcoming years. As future scopes, Multistage CNN technology can be used to make the system more advanced and precise. Also, if we adopt the same methodology to a drone, then large areas of agricultural fields can be monitored to make the system more modernized.

REFERENCES

Balaji, B. S., Shivakumara, M. C., Sunil, Y. S., Yamuna, A. S., & Shruthi, M. (2018). Smart Phone Operated Multipurpose Agricultural Robot. *International Journal of Engineering Research & Technology (Ahmedabad)*, 7(5), 478–481.

Cristian García, E. (2018). A Review of Artificial Intelligence in the Internet of Things. *International Journal of Interactive Multimedia and Artificial Intelligence*, 5(4), 9–20. doi:10.9781/ijimai.2018.03.004

Gowrishankar & Venkatachalam. (2018). IoT Based Precision Agriculture using Agribot. *GRD Journals-Global Research and Development Journal for Engineering*, 3(5), 98-101.

Guizzo, E. (2011). Robots with their Heads in the Clouds. *IEEE Spectrum*, 48(3), 17–18. doi:10.1109/MSPEC.2011.5719709

Hemalatha, Dhanalakshmi, Matilda, & Bala Anand. (2018). Farmbot- A Smart Agriculture Assistor Using Internet of Things. *International Journal of Pure and Applied Mathematics, 119*(10), 557-566.

Hu, G., Tay, W., & Wen, Y. (2012). Cloud Robotics: Architecture, Challenges and Applications. *IEEE Network*, 26(3), 21–28. doi:10.1109/MNET.2012.6201212

Kapoor, S., Suchetha, & Mehra. (2016). Implementation of IoT (Internet of Things) and Image processing in Smart Agriculture. *International Conference on Computation System and Information Technology for Sustainable Solutions (CSITSS)*, 21-26.

Kumar, & Kumar Raja, & Karthik. (2020). Agriculture based on Robot Using Raspberry Pi. *International Journal of Engineering Research & Technology (Ahmedabad)*, 8(7), 1–3.

Latha, Reddy, & Kumar. (2014). Image Processing in Agriculture. *International Journal of Innovative Research in Electrical, Electronics. Instrumentation and Control Engineering*, 2(6), 1562–1565.

Logeswari, S., & Subhashini, R. (2015). Cloud Robot with Agriculture Using Raspberry Pi. *International Journal of Engineering Research & Technology (Ahmedabad)*, 3(4), 1–5.

Rahul, D. S., Sudarshan, S. K., Meghana, K., Nandan, K., & Kirthana, R. (2018). IoT based Solar Powered Agribot for Irrigation and Farm Monitoring. *2nd International Conference on Inventive Systems and Control (ICISC)*, 826- 831.

Sapre, K., Savekar, S., Sharma, R., & Chougule, M. (2018). IoT Based Agribot for Backyard Farming. *International Research Journal of Engineering and Technology*, 5(4), 1647–1651.

Yifan & Wang. (2011). The Application of Cloud Computing and the Internet of Things in Agriculture and Forestry. *International Joint Conference on Service Sciences*, 168-172.

KEY TERMS AND DEFINITIONS

Convolutional Neural Networks (CNN): It is a class of deep learning technology mainly used for accurate classification of images.

Internet of Things (IoT): Internet of things is the interconnection of computing devices embedded in any objects, enabling them to send and receive data.

Next-Level Farming: It is defined as providing over-all solutions in other words complete modernization from the start till the end of the agricultural applications.

Pesticide: The chemicals used to control or kill the pests.

Raspberry Pi: It is a credit card sized computer especially used for exploring the applications of internet of things (IoT).

Remote Farming: It is defined as monitoring and managing of farm remotely through the application of Internet, with less/ without direct human intervention.

Chapter 10
Security Aspects of the Internet of Things

Dominik Hromada
FBM, Brno University of Technology, Czech Republic

Rogério Luís de C. Costa
iD https://orcid.org/0000-0003-2306-7585
CIC, Polytechnic of Leiria, Portugal

Leonel Santos
CIIC, ESTG, Polytechnic of Leiria, Portugal

Carlos Rabadão
iD https://orcid.org/0000-0001-7332-4397
CIIC, ESTG, Polytechnic of Leiria, Portugal

ABSTRACT

The Internet of Things (IoT) comprises the interconnection of a wide range of different devices, from Smart Bluetooth speakers to humidity sensors. The great variety of devices enables applications in several contexts, including Smart Cities and Smart Industry. IoT devices collect and process a large amount of data on machines and the environment and even monitor people's activities. Due to their characteristics and architecture, IoT devices and networks are potential targets for cyberattacks. Indeed, cyberattacks can lead to malfunctions of the IoT environment and access and misuse of private data. This chapter addresses security concerns in the IoT ecosystem. It identifies common threats for each of IoT layers and presents advantages, challenges, and limitations of promising countermeasures based on new technologies and strategies, like Blockchain and Machine Learning. It also contains a more in-depth discussion on Intrusion Detection Systems (IDS) for IoT, a promising solution for cybersecurity in IoT ecosystems.

DOI: 10.4018/978-1-7998-6463-9.ch010

I. INTRODUCTION

Internet of Things (IoT) as a term was used for the first time in 1999 by Kevin Ashton, a British technology pioneer (Farooq, Waseem, Khairi, & Mazhar, 2015). He defines IoT as the system of physical objects in the world that connects to the internet via a sensor. This ecosystem is full of intelligent machines interacting with each other, with objects, environments, and infrastructures. This new technology has impacted the whole population from everyday people's lives to industry solutions, helping people to work smarter and efficiently, and giving them more control over monitored environments, objects, and infrastructures.

In several market areas, IoT became an essential part of business activities, e.g., providing real-time data about operation activities or measuring the performance of supply chain machines and logistic operations. The data collected by IoT devices can be analyzed later, and provide decision-makers with invaluable insights into their processes with the help of Business Intelligence (BI) to make business processes even more efficient, faster, environmentally friendly, and less expensive. Therefore, IoT opened new opportunities for data analysis and knowledge discovery (Gubbi, Buyya, Marusic, & Palaniswami, 2013). Main IoT applications areas include transportation and logistics, Smart Healthcare, Smart Environments, and City Information Modeling (Ullah, Ahmad, Ahmad, Ata-ur-Rehman, & Junaid, 2019).

On the other hand, the data collected are a double-edged sword. It may be a significant help, but also a threat to people's privacy and security, as their activity can be monitored everywhere and anytime (Neisse et al., 2015). Also, poorly secured devices may lead to attacks on other systems and lead to personal information leaks and misuses due to unauthorized access.

Some of the main security concerns in the context of IoT are related to basic processes (for example, identification, authentication, and access control), data integrity, data confidentiality, data privacy, and data availability (Sicari, Rizzardi, Grieco, & Coen-Porisini, 2015; Farooq et al., 2015). But the layered architecture of IoT is also subject to several attacks and threats, each of them being most common in or targeted to a specific layer (Weyrich & Ebert, 2016; Swamy, Jadhav, & Kulkarni, 2017).

Some of the *traditional* security countermeasures (e.g., the use of security protocols, authentication controls, and privacy by design) may fit in the IoT context. But the new solutions for IoT security include the use of Fog Computing, Blockchain Technology, Edge computing, and Machine Learning-based techniques (Baouya, Chehida, Bensalem, & Bozga, 2020; Ozay, Esnaola, Yarman Vural, Kulkarni, & Poor, 2016).

The use of Intrusion Detection Systems (IDS) in IoT networks is subject to some additional challenges. Deep packet inspection (DPI) and stateful packet inspection

(SPI) are computationally expensive and not adequate for the IoT network. An alternative solution in IoT ecosystems may go through an IDS based on IP flow analysis. Additional challenges related to an efficient IDS for IoT networks include aspects related to chosen incident detection methodology, the IDS implementation strategy, and IDS's intrusion detection capabilities.

In the following section, we present the main aspects related to the IoT processing cycle. Then, Section III presents the main security concerns in the IoT context. The IoT layered architecture and the most common threats of each layer are described in Section IV. Section V discusses some current countermeasures based on *nontraditional* solutions and Section V presents open issues and future directions. Finally, Section VII concludes the chapter.

II. ASPECTS OF IOT NETWORK PROCESSING CYCLE

The IoT opened several new opportunities in a wide range of applications. Figure 1 presents the main components of a processing cycle in the IoT.

A. Recognition

All the involved objects in the network must have unique identification and must be recognized accordingly. That means that two entities present in the network cannot have a similar identification representation. Hence, the two main components of successful recognition are addressing and naming. Each entity is assigned a particular address and name, where their combination is unique for it. The allocating address task uses IPv6 as the number addressing scheme of 128 bits. The naming process can use several methods, such as IP-based codes, electronic products codes (EPC), and ubiquitous codes (Al-Fuqaha, Guizani, Mohammadi, Aledhari, & Ayyash, 2015).

Figure 1. Processing cycle in IoT networks

B. Obtaining

IoT obtains and collects data from different devices via sensing utilities, such as RFID (radio-frequency indicators) tags, actuators, wearables, etc. These data are further transported via gateways and stored in areas such as cloud storage (Sehrawat & Gill, 2019).

C. Conveyance

Responsibilities of reference of information from one point to another are assigned to ensure data transportation, which is essential for the proper functioning of IoT. In other words, all the communication, including messages, conversations, files, and other data, is transmitted through this component, which uses specific protocols, such as z-wave, Zigbee and 6LoWPAN (Low power Wireless Personal Area Networks) (AlSarawi, Anbar, Alieyan, & Alzubaidi, 2017).

D. Processing

The data collected via sensors are then processed with the help of a variety of operating systems, such as Android and TinyOs, using a range of hardware platforms like Intel Galileo and Audrino (Basha & S A K, 2016).

E. Assistance

IoT applications can provide several types of assistance. The most helpful is the assistance related to identity. The next is the assistance associated with data aggregation, which can be done without any communication channel, and unifies different technologies in a single application. The following assistance deals with the aggregated information to perform task decisions and actions needed. The fourth assistance is the ability to be omnipresent that provides the services of IoT ubiquitously without the strictness of time and location (Gigli & Koo, 2011).

F. Connotation

The whole cycle ends with this component, which acts as the brain of the IoT process. All the devices can get the response as all the data and decisions are connoted here (Basha & S A K, 2016).

III. IOT SECURITY CONCERNS

The use of IoT devices has an unmediated impact on users' lives, hence high priority to the security measures must be given together with well-defined security guidelines consisting of new systems and protocols to ensure that the possible threats related to security and privacy will be limited. Specifically, the processes of authentication, integrity, data confidentiality, and data privacy are among the main elements of IoT security (Farooq et al., 2015). Other important concerns include identification, trust and access control (Sicari et al., 2015), and data availability (Atzori, Iera, & Morabito, 2010).

A. Identification

The identification process is crucial for the network to decide whether the smart device can be trusted or not. Serious threats may arise from permitting an intruder to enter the secured network (Sicari et al., 2015). Despite this fact, we must prevail a system that can detect these possible security threats but is still able to provide its device identity to other qualified devices. Therefore, devices interacting with their users must know their identity and can distinguish them too (Atzori et al., 2010).

B. Authentication

In the case of IoT, authentication is quite challenging as it usually requires appropriate authentication infrastructures and servers to be secure, such as two-factor authentication. As in IoT passive utilities are used, such as RFID tags or sensor nodes, the standard procedures commonly used in other IT sectors cannot be used, as these passive utilities cannot exchange too many messages with the authentication servers (Atzori et al., 2010), (Farooq et al., 2015), (Sicari et al., 2015).

C. Data Integrity

The data transmission can be disrupted by plenty of factors that cannot be controlled by the nodes involved. For example, data changes during transmission, server outages, or electromagnetic interference (Riahi Sfar, Natalizio, Challal, & Chtourou, 2018). Hence, data integrity is preserved with the help of common surveillance methods to protect the data transmitted from cyberattacks and to avoid external interference during the communication itself. For this purpose, methods like checksums and cyclic redundancy checks (CRC) are used to guarantee data accuracy and reliability with the help of error detection mechanisms (Sicari et al., 2015), (Atzori et al., 2010).

D. Trust

Trust is a very broad term covering many disciplines beyond security, hence it is more difficult to be established (Atzori et al., 2010). Nitti et al. (Nitti, Girau, & Atzori, 2014) conducted a study that had as main objective to explore how users accept the IoT objects around them. Interestingly, 43% of respondents say they are worried about their data, therefore are afraid to use the IoT utilities. 18% think that IoT objects used are not operational and 8% believe they are not reliable. Users are concerned with the fact that they cannot always determine when, whether, and to whom the personal information could and could not be exposed (Riahi Sfar et al., 2018). It is believed that as soon as the users gain certainty that the IoT objects are secured enough by the manufacturer and their data cannot be misused, the IoT technologies will be most likely better adopted by their users (Sicari et al., 2015).

E. Data Confidentiality

User is secured by data confidentiality which ensures that confidential information is trusted. This process is done by various mechanisms to prevent any exposure against the user's will. These security mechanisms ensure data privacy work with the help of data encryption, two stage authentication, and biometric authentication mechanisms which protect data from unauthorized access. In the case of IoT devices, these mechanisms ensure that sensor networks maintain their sensor nodes hidden from unauthorized neighboring nodes as well as their communication from unauthorized readers (Farooq et al., 2015).

F. Access Control

Access control is associated with permissions in the usage of resources that are assigned to different entities connected to the IoT network. These permissions specify whether the user is granted access and the user's authorizations to perform specified tasks. Access Control List (ACL) is used to specify a device used and the user's access level. Here the administrator of the network must be careful with access granting as a mistake can result in serious threats (Riahi Sfar et al., 2018).

G. Data Privacy

In the IoT environment, the amount of data collected and stored is rapidly increasing and users cannot be sure that this data will be used only for the purposes they gave consent to or will not be misused in the nearest future. Hence, protecting stored data has the same priority as securing its transmission. The IoT environment is full of devices, readers, sensors, and applications that might collect data on multiple levels that together can expose user's habits, their actual or most common locations, where the user lives and goes to work, does shopping, or even their diet via smart fridges. As nowadays we can evaluate many aggregated data with the help of Business Intelligence, the data leak may result from useful insight from market sectors to unwanted surveillance by the cyber attacker or even the government. As data are stored on centered cloud services and they are not anonymous and collected all the time, their privacy should be given high priority (Farooq et al., 2015; Gubbi et al., 2013; Riahi Sfar et al., 2018).

H. Data Availability

IoT gathers, analyses, and provides data to its users. Data availability ensures that the data is provided to its user when needed without necessary delays. This state is supposed to be maintained even under unfavorable conditions, such as cyberattacks, by implementing appropriate secure measurements, such as firewalls preventing denial of service attack (DoS) or its advanced version - distributed denial of service attack (DDoS). Moreover, this should be facilitated by the corresponding hardware infrastructure which is supposed to be well secured as well. In the case of data loss prevention, data should be sufficiently backed up, which helps to ensure system components replication in the case of system failure, providing reliability and availability (Atzori et al., 2010).

IV. IOT SECURITY AND LAYERS ARCHITECTURE

Internet of Things can be broadly defined in four layers. Going top-down, it begins with the *application layer,* followed by the *middleware layer* (or *data processing layer*) (Sikder, Petracca, Aksu, Jaeger, & Uluagac, 2018) and by the *network layer* (also known as *transport layer*). The *perception layer* (or *sensing layer*) is the last one. Figure 2 represents this layered architecture.

Figure 2. IoT Layers and Components (Adapted from Sikder, Petracca, Aksu, Jaeger, & Uluagac, 2018)

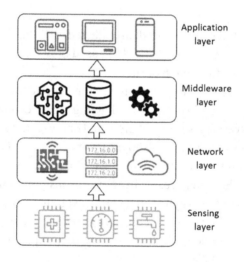

The first two layers represent the utilization of data in the application, the following two where data are captured (Weyrich & Ebert, 2016). Some authors (e.g., Antão, Pinto, Reis, & Gonçalves, 2018) refer to a *business layer* as a layer above the application layer, which is supposed to manage the whole IoT system, including applications, business models, and users' privacy. Discussing such a business layer is out of the scope of this chapter.

Each IoT layer has its objectives and characteristics and may suffer distinct types of threats. Figure 3 presents some of the most common threats of each layer. In the following, we identify the main components of each layer and the threats which may occur on the layer.

Figure 3. Common threats in IoT layers

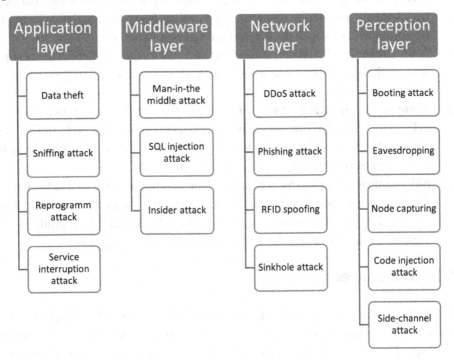

A. Perception Layer

The perception layer represents the physical layer of IoT and is responsible for data collection and its transmission. Utilities working on this layer include sensors (e.g., camera sensors, temperature sensors, chemical sensors, detection sensors, and humidity sensors), and wireless sensors networks (WSNs), global positioning systems (GPS), RFID systems, and electronic data interfaces (EDI). Hence, this layer provides most of the data collection. The attacks on utilities working on this layer are mainly aimed at the sensors. In the following, we list the most common attacks (Tukur, Thakker, & Awan, 2019).

1) **Booting attack:** Usually, all the security services are enabled when a device is in working mode. But between the booting, or startup, and working mode there is a window when the security services are not fully enabled. Hence, at this moment a device is vulnerable to possible attacks. Moreover, edge devices due to power savings are in constant sleep-wake modes. Therefore, they are more likely to be vulnerable to these attacks.

2)   **Eavesdropping:** An interloper can get in the communication stream between nodes within a closed network to listen to the data transmitted. For example, this often happens with poorly secured baby cameras, smart TVs, etc.

3)   **Node capturing:** This type of attack is executed via replacement of the original node with the intruder's one which enables him to get access to parts or, in the worst case, to the entire network.

4)   **Code injection attack:** As the software of the IoT nodes is usually updated OTA (over the air), the opportunity to inject a malicious code during this activity by the assailer might give him unauthorized access to the system, which can lead to the execution of unwanted actions.

5)   **Side-channel attacks (SCA):** A data leak can happen due to a side-channel attack which involves gaining delicate information from the processor chips by so-called electromagnetic attacks, timing attacks, radiation emitted by a computer screen to view the information before its encryption.

B. Network Layer

The main function of the network layer is data handling, which includes data preparation and transmission, message routing, publishing, and managing the messages. The data are obtained from the perception layer and then sent further to the middleware layer by divergent communication channels as GSM (Global System for Mobile), WiFi (Wireless Fidelity), and Ethernet (Weyrich & Ebert, 2016). As Weyrich et al. (Weyrich & Ebert, 2016) mentioned, the network layer transmits data between perception and middleware layers, hence plenty of attacks here can be experienced (Mao, Kawamoto, Liu, & Kato, 2019).

1)   **DDoS attack (Distributed denial of service):** Attackers using DDoS attacks try to disrupt the normal traffic functioning of a targeted server resulting in overflooding the server with unwanted requests, thus making the service unavailable for other users. The DDoS attack is like DoS (Denial of service attack), but it is used for attacking other compromised devices, such as poorly secured infected IoT. Such a group of devices is known as a botnet.

2)   **Phishing attacks:** This technique is used to gain full access to a particular IoT network with the help of the human factor. The basic principle is that the attacker sends an e-mail containing a link to some page that requires the user to enter his credentials, in most cases e-mail and password. Either for registration into a fake internet game, where the user can win a prize, or into a page that looks like a login page of a social network or online payment service website (e.g. PayPal), asking for the user's credentials. As this e-mail is sent to thousands of e-mail addresses, the attacker relies on somebody entering his

credentials. As users usually have only one password and e-mail for all their accounts, after this action the attacker can gain access to all their sensitive data, including full access to a particular IoT network.

3) **RFID spoofing and cloning:** Even though RFID tags use plenty of security measures, such as different operational frequencies and different protocols, they can still be compromised. First, they can be cloned, which is a process of duplication of the original RFID tag. Therefore, they can be used for spoofing, which means to use a cloned RFID tag to gain access somewhere. Hence, it is used in access or asset management operations.

4) **Sinkhole attack:** It is a type of routing attack where false routing details are forwarded to nodes in a network causing a huge amount of network traffic. The attack is initiated from a compromised node that has been compromised by the attacker which infiltrated into the network. Besides false routing attacks, this can be used to issue a variety of other attacks.

C. Middleware Layer

This layer provides software utilities that make the communication between IoT components possible by data filtering, analysis of data semantic, management, and discovery of the device and access control (Weyrich & Ebert, 2016). Hence, the middleware layer has two main tasks. The first one is confirming the authenticity of the user, and the second is data transfer. The main tasks of this layer (Hu, Zhang, & Wen, 2011) are listed below.

1) **Man-in-The-Middle attack:** In this type of attack, the perpetrator pretends to be the legitimate user of an IoT system being in between the communication of two users who are communicating within their network with each other. As their communication goes through the cyber attacker, he can interact with both participating sides, impersonates them both trying to gain access to the information they are trying to send to each other. Thus, the perpetrator can control and manipulate the conversation.

2) **SQL injection attack:** A very serious threat to any system may result in unauthorized access, confidential data loss or even exploiting the whole network or individual machines. An intruder inserts a particular malicious SQL statement in the vulnerable web applications, which are connected to the backend databases, resulting in their compromising.

3) **Insider attack:** During this attack, the cyber attacker appears to be an authentic member of the network. Hence, it is very difficult to identify attacks like these. The perpetrator can be a present or former member with access to the details

of the system resulting in the ability to launch different types of attacks within the network. Hence, it is very important to keep ACL up to date at any time.

D. Application Layer

The application layer is the topmost one in this architecture responsible for providing services and establishing the sets of protocols used for messages passing at the application layer. It is the interface bridge between the IoT devices and the network. For instance, the end IoT device is a computer with a browser as an application layer using protocols such as HTTP, HTTPS, DNS, SMTP, and FTP. This layer can be further divided into two sub-layers (Weyrich & Ebert, 2016):

- **Application service sub-layer:** Its main function is to span the connection between the end-user and applications; hence it is over the application layer of IoT.
- **Data management sub-layer:** Tasks performed by this sub-layer include machine-to-machine (M2M) services, Quality of Service (QoS), data process, and directory services. As this layer is in this architecture considered as the final one where the end-user has a direct connection to, plenty of threats are possible to occur.
    1) **Data theft:** The data which are collected by IoT devices with their sensors are most vulnerable while in transit. Intruders can steal the data easily and misuse them for personal use or resell it to another person if proper security protocols are not applied and followed.
    2) **Sniffing attack:** If the data packets are poorly encrypted or without encryption at all, they can be caught, and sensitive data can be extracted with the use of sniffers during its transmission.
    3) **Reprogram attacks:** If the IoT device's programming process is not secured, an intruder can remotely reprogram the IoT device easily resulting in making another infected device in his growing botnet, misusing collected data, etc.
    4) **Service interruption attack:** Due to artificially making the services of an application's network too busy to access to the legitimate users, the network becomes unavailable resulting in its significant slowdown or denial of service.

V. COUNTERMEASURES

The whole IoT ecosystem contains three major elements: users, hardware, and software. Hence, to ensure a secure environment within a network, designers and developers must focus on all of the elements involved. Focusing on the users and their behavior within the network can give the designers and developers valuable insights, and enable them to understand better the problems of the whole system, resulting in the enhancement of overall IoT security, and protecting users' privacy and minimizing their risks by educating them to be more aware of their surroundings. Furthermore, to observe how the users interact with the system can be useful to implement appropriate security countermeasures. Some of the *traditional* countermeasures include security protocols, single sign-on, access, and authentication controls, security awareness, establishing trust and privacy by design (Ogonji, Okeyo, & Wafula, 2020).

In this section, we present some new technologies, strategies, and architectures that have gained popularity over the years for being very helpful in enhancing security, including Fog Computing, Blockchain Technology, Edge computing, and Machine learning (Baouya et al., 2020; Ozay et al., 2016). We also present the main challenges related to the creation of an Intrusion Detection System (IDS) for IoT.

A. Fog Computing

Internet of Things and cloud computing are powerful technologies that can work together. IoT facilitates utilizing and incorporating smart applications and cloud computing provides needed space and functionalities that can help manage, store and process the data (Rahman et al., 2019). As IoT gathers a lot of data in real-time using all sorts of devices, services, and technologies, there is a need for storage of this gathered data for possible future analyses and processing. Hence, the cooperation between both technologies has become a beneficial solution which leads to better efficiency in organization and security of the stored data. As the technologies evolve, the attacks and threats become more sophisticated as well. Hence, it was found that cloud computing itself lacks some features. Therefore, the fog computing was introduced to aid the drawbacks of cloud computing itself and make it more efficient and secure.

The basic principle of fog computing is that the fog extends the cloud enabling it to be closer to the things which interact with IoT data. The fog can be described as an additional layer between the end nodes and the cloud. It provides additional detection, invalidation, and reporting of malicious activities. The fog works as a smaller inner cloud within the big cloud, and, thus, the fog also provides isolation from the major cloud to be infected and deals with the security incidents on its own.

Figure 4 represents how the fog can extend the cloud. Devices with computing, network connectivity, and storage, known as fog nodes, can be deployed anywhere with a network connection, such as in a vehicle, water reservoir, or traffic systems. Examples are switches, routers, embedded servers, and video surveillance cameras.

Figure 4. The Fog extends the Cloud closer to the devices producing data

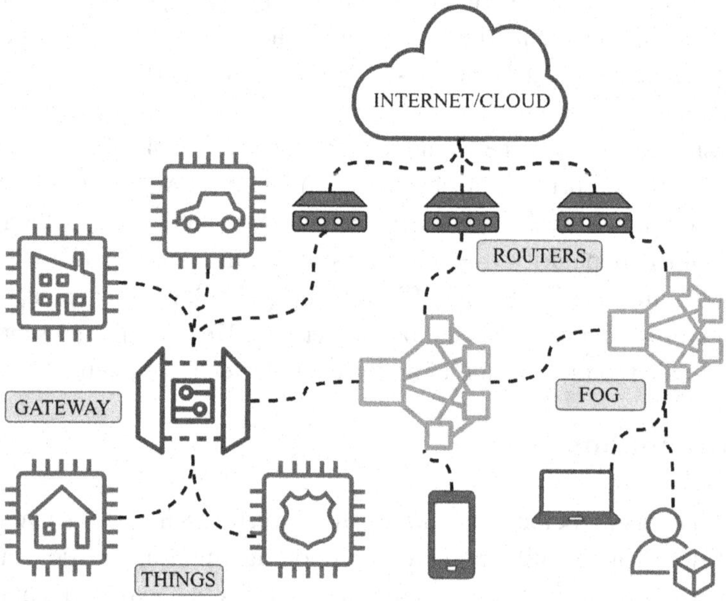

The major advantages of fog computing for IoT security are:

- Whenever the IoT system is attacked, this attack must go through the fog layer where it can be identified and mitigated. This layer acts as a middleman between the end-user and the cloud.
- As the data is stored in the fog rather than on the devices, the risk of attacks to a great extent has been reduced. Moreover, as the fog is a smaller unit than the cloud unit, it can identify these issues faster and react accordingly preventing the broader part of the network to be compromised.
- Fog computing facilitates discovering malicious activities, such as malware, by being able to red flag them when a problem appears.
- As fog computing is a relatively closed unit, the information transmitted is transported within the fog network rather than through the whole network, if

possible. Hence, the chances of eavesdropping are minimized as the network traffic is reduced (Rahman et al., 2019).

This solution also presents some challenges and limitations such as the guarantee of privacy between the fog and IoT devices, the software update capabilities of IoT devices need to handle remote security updates, and the scalability and efficiency of IoT solutions need to be designed to overcome the limitations of resource constrained IoT devices.

B. Blockchain Technology Security Solution

From a security point of view, the IoT applications and platforms lack the security feature in the decentralization of information collected as all data are stored on a centralized cloud. Hence, this issue may be solved by implementing blockchain technology into the centralized cloud system (Kshetri, 2017). Moreover, blockchain technology prevents data duplicity, sensors' data tracking, and offers safe data transfer. With the help of various cryptography techniques, continuously growing blocks containing lists of records are made forming a circulated ledger known as blockchain.

The advantages of implementing blockchain technology in IoT are:

- As blockchain is a distributed system, when a particular part of a system is attacked and its security fails, the entire system is not affected.
- Blockchain can be implemented in every layer of IoT as a suitable utility for data transport.
- Being a decentralized system with cryptographic hash functions for data encryption, it is much harder for the attacker to perform successful cyber theft as data are not centralized on one cloud.
- Based on smart contracts (as represented in Figure 5), data in blockchain can be only accessed by authorized users. Even if the node in a network is infected, the data cannot be read as they are encrypted with appropriate keys.
- IP spoofing and IP address forgery attacks are more difficult due to blockchain-based identity and access management systems as the blockchains cannot be altered. Hence, devices can't be connected to a network using a fake identity and fake signatures.

As presented in the previous list, blockchain technology can be part of IoT security solutions. However, blockchain technology in itself poses research challenges to be tackled with regards to its scalability, efficiency, arbitration/regulations, and key collision.

Figure 5. Smart contracts

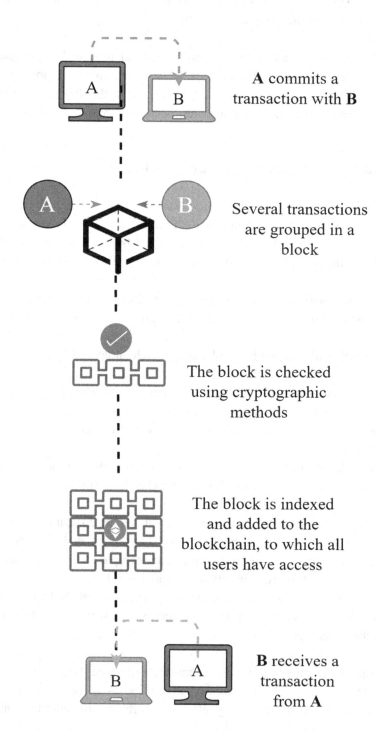

A commits a transaction with **B**

Several transactions are grouped in a block

The block is checked using cryptographic methods

The block is indexed and added to the blockchain, to which all users have access

B receives a transaction from **A**

Some examples of challenges and limitations in this field are blockchain vulnerabilities, such as the consensus mechanism depending upon the miner's hashing power can be compromised, and the private keys with limited randomness, which attackers exploit to compromise the blockchain accounts.

C. Edge Computing Security Solutions

Edge computing takes the storage of data and computation much closer to the location of use, thus saving the bandwidth of the network and improving response time (Sodhro, Pirbhulal, & de Albuquerque, 2019). It is very similar to fog computing, but the main difference is that fog computing processes data within a fog node or IoT gateway situated within LAN, whereas edge computing processes the data on the devices or sensors themselves without transferring them. Figure 6 represents the main differences between fog and edge computing.

Hence, edge computing is a fast-processing utility that has multiple positive effects of implementation in IoT applications:

- As data can be processed at the edge, only necessary data can be sent to the cloud for further processing and storage. Therefore, it leads to saving the cost of bandwidth and faster processing of basic tasks.
- Unlike in fog computing, data are stored at the local internet or within the device itself. This reduces the possibility of data theft during its transmission due to lowering the amount of data transported.
- One of the most notable advantages of edge computing is the ability to respond very quickly as the data are processed in the device or nearby. Moreover, with a combination of fog computing and edge computing, we can achieve even better results in terms of response time and security of the system, which can even save lives. For instance, consider an Ambient Assisted Living (AAL) application in which an elderly person has a smart wearable device monitoring their heart rate or other life functions. As the wearable device would be the edge, it can detect a sudden life-threatening change in the elderly person's body and send this information to the caregiver. Without the fog layer, there might be a possibility that the cloud is under DDoS attack, hence the caregiver would not receive the information and do necessary steps to save the person's life. But as the fog would be implemented as the processing middle layer, the possibility of dysfunction is lowered, hence the alert can be processed by fog itself without the cloud involvement resulting in a convenient and quicker response.

Figure 6. Data process within network

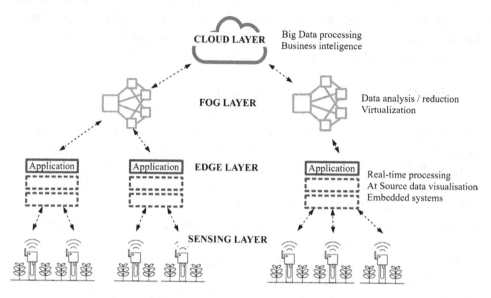

We have introduced some positive effects on using edge computing in IoT security but there are still many challenging and open research issues that include: securing the edge layer, dealing with untrusted edge layer, lightweight protocols for end device-edge communications, as well as secure operating systems and lightweight virtual machines.

D. Machine Learning Security Solutions

Machine learning (ML) is part of the Artificial Intelligence (AI) discipline and can make devices and machines infer knowledge from the data (Hussain, Hussain, Hassan, & Hossain, 2020). Some well-known applications of ML in IoT devices include Google Assistant, Amazon Alexa, or Apple Siri. As machine learning has plenty of advantages in other disciplines, some of the ones applicable for IoT are:

- Use of machine learning can enhance the security in terms of malware and DDoS attack detection and, with the use of Deep Learning (DL), it can effectively find patterns in the previously made attacks. Hence, potentially future attacks can be predicted, identified, and mitigated faster and more efficiently.
- The following point is coherent with the previous one in terms of attack detection. As machine learning algorithms can detect possible attacks, they can also mitigate false attack alerts and false error alerts by using various

techniques of machine learning, such as Support Vector Machines (SVM) (Hussain et al., 2020).

- Utilization of machine learning properties can lead to cost and energy consumption reduction, improvement of customer care, and efficiency.

ML algorithms could be used to improve the IoT security domain, although they have some limitations in the IoT environment, such as scalability, complexity, latency, compatibility, and vulnerability. Learning efficiency, response time, automatic feature selection and parameter tuning strategies are also challenging in such context.

E. Intrusion Detection Systems

Conventional intrusion detection systems use techniques based on packet capture and analysis to detect intrusions or attacks. *Deep packed inspection* (DPI) techniques scan packet headers and examine the content in the application data field, looking for any evidence of attack (Abuadlla, Kvascev, Gajin, & Jovanovic, 2014). However, the use of DPI-type IDS is impractical for high-speed connections and inspection is not possible when the contents of the packet data field are encrypted (Husak, Velan, & Vykopal, 2015). In *stateful packet inspection* (SPI) techniques, the semantics of the protocol are checked and any record outside the defined is considered an intrusion or anomaly. However, this technique is oriented towards known protocols and does not affect unknown protocols. Also, it does very little when it comes to malicious code as it does not analyze the payload of packages. Finally, both techniques are computationally expensive and can create a bottleneck in the network (Koch, 2011; Liao, Lin, Lin, & Tung, 2013).

Considering the limitations of techniques based on packet analysis, DPI, and SPI, and considering the less computational and resource requirements of the approach based on flow analysis, an alternative solution against intrusions and attacks in IoT ecosystems may be using an IDS based on IP flow analysis (Santos, Rabadão, & Gonçalves, 2019). This type of IDS has as a strong point in its favor: the lower need for computational resources to operate, as they only analyze the flow records that contain aggregated information from packet headers, reducing the amount of data that needs to be processed. In this way, they can provide an answer almost in real-time, low implementation cost, fewer privacy concerns, and that can be used with traffic consisting of packages that have their encrypted payload. A weakness of these IDS is the difficulty in detecting some attacks using only information from the packet header, so many of the known attacks are not detected. When compared to IDS based on packet detection, with the cryptographically unprotected payload, the detection of network attacks hidden in the packet payload is not as accurate as packet-based detection. However, the increasing use of end-to-end encryption in distributed applications, such as web portals, mobile applications, and e-mails, has left limited space for the application of payload-based intrusion detection systems and opens the way for the IDS based on flow analysis.

Recently, there has been a huge increase in research on IDS for IoT, especially concerning the application of ML techniques (especially deep learning) (Dutta & Granjal, 2020). However, ML-based techniques face the challenge of the low availability of realistic, high-quality datasets that contain diverse attacks for the IoT. In Dutta & Granjal (2020), the authors also identify a strong effort in the optimization of existing algorithms for implementation in IoT, and in the development of nodes with high computational performance to perform the tasks of IDS in IoT, through the adoption of fog and edge computing. Implementing an IoT IDS using edge and fog computing would allow the detection of intrusions in IoT ecosystems with less resource consumption. (Chaabouni, Mosbah, Zemmari, Sauvignac, & Faruki, 2019). However, most of the existing proposals detect a low number of attacks and focus mostly on attacks on routing and DoS and, less frequently, on attacks related to the source of the data (Dutta & Granjal, 2020).

VI. FUTURE DIRECTIONS

The use of Intrusion Detection Systems (IDS) in the context of IoT is still an open and promising issue. Despite considerable progress in the development of IDS solutions designed specifically for IoT ecosystems, existing solutions still have numerous limitations. Also, some solutions require considerable computational overhead or modification of the software of IoT devices that, in an environment of limited computational resources, turns out to be a weakness.

Regarding the detection methodology, and although there is no consensus on which of the methodologies will be the most appropriate, the solutions that use the methodology based on anomalies are the ones that consume more computational and energy resources, while the methodologies based on signatures or specifications are the ones that require fewer resources. However, anomaly-based detection is the one most often proposed in studies, in part because of its potential to detect unknown attacks. For this, it is necessary to develop, analyze and compare lighter and optimized anomaly detection algorithms, mainly based on ML (especially deep learning) for IoT networks (Dutta & Granjal, 2020).

Also, integration of detection techniques based on rules, anomalies, and specifications should be used, to avoid their weaknesses and obtain their benefits. To this end, it will be necessary to dedicate greater effort to the refinement of this integration, namely by improving the modeling of the behavior of IoT ecosystems to allow a better definition and parameterization of network parameters to detect intrusions (Cervantes, Poplade, Nogueira, & Santos, 2015; Bostani & Sheikhan, 2017; Fu, Yan, Cao, Kone, & Cao, 2017).

At the level of the IDS implementation strategy, given the computational limitations of the IoT devices and the privacy and confidentiality requirements of the information collected, the solution may include the exploration of hybrid detection solutions, using edge and fog computing (Chaabouni et al., 2019). This approach will allow decision making close to the perception layer, improving the privacy and confidentiality issues of the information collected and minimizing the need for necessary network resources between the perception layer and the cloud, making use of the computing power of the cloud, during the training phase of machine learning algorithms.

Regarding the intrusion detection capability, the existing solutions are limited concerning the diversity of attacks they detect. Most of the intrusions detected are located at the perception layer of the IoT architecture, at the DoS level, and at the network layer, at the level of routing attacks, possibly due to the use of existing generalist datasets, which do not represent the particularities of IoT systems and applications, leaving other types of intrusions, internal and external, and from other layers, without specific solutions for some IoT protocols. Although some works propose datasets more suited to the reality of IoT (e.g. (Moustafa & Slay, 2015; Sivanathan et al., 2017; Bezerra et al., 2018; Verma & Ranga, 2019)), there is a need to intensify this work, in the sense of creating public datasets that include the different IoT protocols and their threats/attacks, to be able to develop IDS solutions adapted to the diversity of threats to which the IoT ecosystems are subject.

These datasets, specifically suitable for IoT, must be public and serve as a reference for the validation of solutions proposed by the scientific community, and must be properly labeled and support a wide variety of attacks and protocols used in IoT ecosystems. In this way, it will be possible to improve the IDS validation strategy, as it will be possible to compare, in a clear, practical, and convenient way, the different IDS developed.

At the level of IoT technologies and protocols, the vast majority only cover perceptual layer protocols such as 6LoWPAN and RPL, which means support, interoperability, and expandability with other technologies and protocols, used at the network layer or application, are not addressed in the analyzed proposals.

Besides, only a few solutions refer to aspects or features related to the privacy of network traffic and the management of the communication of internal messages and IDS alerts. This is an important topic, because if the internal messages between the various components of an IDS or the intrusion alert messages are intercepted and tampered with it will result in the loss of the reliability and effectiveness of the IDS.

Finally, it should be noted that most solutions presented make use of packet capture, and respective payloads, to develop their intrusion detection processes. Intrusion detection solutions based on the analysis of IP traffic flows can be considered, reduce the use of resources, such as the processing and storage of network packets, which is especially important when using devices with limited resources at the computational level.

VII. CONCLUSION

In this chapter, the authors identified the main security aspects of the Internet of Things. and identified possible attacks, threats, and vulnerabilities of IoT.

The authors characterized the IoT in terms of its processing cycle. Then, the authors identified the processes and features that are the most common security concerns in IoT networks, namely identification, authentication, data integrity, trust, data confidentiality, access control, data privacy, and data availability. The authors described the IoT layers and architecture, and the attacks and threats that are the most common for each layer.

Then, the authors presented a set of countermeasures based on new technologies, strategies, and architectures to enhance IoT security, namely security solutions based on Fog and Edge Computing, Blockchain Technology, Machine learning, and Intrusion Detection Systems (IDS) for IoT. Each of such solutions has its advantages and application challenges, but the limitations of resource constrained IoT devices impose constraints on the scalability and efficiency of most proposed IoT cybersecurity solutions.

The IDS for IoT is the authors' main research direction in terms of countermeasures for IoT. Such IDS should use lighter and optimized anomaly detection algorithms, mainly based on machine learning. Also, integrating detection techniques based on rules, anomalies, and specifications would increase the IDS efficiency. Computational limitations of the IoT devices and privacy and confidentiality requirements of collected data lead to hybrid solutions, which use Edge and Fog computing.

Datasets specifically suitable for IoT must be created and turned public to serve as a reference for the validation of proposed solutions. Such datasets must be labeled and support a wide variety of attacks and protocols used in IoT ecosystems. Also, the use of intrusion detection solutions based on the analysis of IP traffic flows can be considered, reducing the use of resources, such as the processing and storage of network packets, which is especially important when using devices with limited resources at the computational level.

As future work, the authors intend to advance the study of IDS for IoT, mainly with the application of machine learning techniques in this context. The authors also plan to prepare data sets of the IoT context for benchmarking solutions of the literature.

ACKNOWLEDGMENT

This work was partially funded by National Funds through the FCT (Foundation for Science and Technology) in the context of the project UIDB/04524/2020.

REFERENCES

Abuadlla, Y., Kvascev, G., Gajin, S., & Jovanovic, Z. (2014). Flow-based anomaly intrusion detection system using two neural network stages. *Computer Science and Information Systems*, *11*(2), 601–622.

Al-Fuqaha, A., Guizani, M., Mohammadi, M., Aledhari, M., & Ayyash, M. (2015). Internet of Things: A survey on enabling technologies, protocols, and applications. *IEEE Communications Surveys and Tutorials*, *17*(4), 2347–2376. doi:10.1109/COMST. 2015.2444095

Al-Sarawi, S., Anbar, M., Alieyan, K., & Alzubaidi, M. (2017). Internet of Things (IoT) communication protocols: Review. In *2017 8th International Conference on Information Technology (ICIT)* (pp. 685-690). doi: 10.1109/ICITECH.2017.8079928

Antao, L., Pinto, R., Reis, J. P., & Gonçalves, G. (2018). ˜Requirements for testing and validating the industrial Internet of Things. In *2018 IEEE International Conference on Software Testing, Verification and Validation Workshops (ICSTW)* (p. 110-115). doi: 10.1109/ICSTW.2018.00036

Atzori, L., Iera, A., & Morabito, G. (2010). 10). The Internet of Things: A survey. *Computer Networks*, 2787–2805. doi:10.1016/j.comnet.2010.05.010

Baouya, A., Chehida, S., Bensalem, S., & Bozga, M. (2020). Fog computing and blockchain for massive IoT deployment. In *2020 9th Mediterranean Conference on Embedded Computing (MECO)* (p. 14). doi: 10.1109/MECO49872.2020.9134098

Basha, S., & S. A. K., J. (2016, 03). An intelligent door system using raspberry pi and amazon web services IoT. *International Journal of Engineering Trends and Technology*, *33*, 84-89. doi:10.14445/22315381/IJETT-V33P217

Bezerra, V. H., da Costa, V. G. T., Martins, R. A., Junior, S. B., Miani, R. S., & Zarpelao, B. B. (2018). Providing IoT host-based datasets for intrusion detection research. In Anais do XVIII Simpósio Brasileiro em Segurança da Informação e de Sistemas Computacionais (pp. 15–28). Academic Press.

Bostani, H., & Sheikhan, M. (2017). Hybrid of anomaly-based and specification-based IDS for Internet of Things using Unsupervised OPF based on Map-Reduce Approach. *Computer Communications*, *98*, 52–71.

Cervantes, C., Poplade, D., Nogueira, M., & Santos, A. (2015). Detection of sinkhole attacks for supporting secure routing on 6LoWPAN for Internet of Things. In *2015 IFIP/IEEE International Symposium on Integrated Network Management* (pp. 606–611). IEEE.

Chaabouni, N., Mosbah, M., Zemmari, A., Sauvignac, C., & Faruki, P. (2019). Network intrusion detection for IoT security based on learning techniques. *IEEE Communications Surveys and Tutorials*, *21*(3), 2671–2701.

Dutta, M., & Granjal, J. (2020). Towards a secure Internet of Things: A comprehensive study of second line defense mechanisms. *IEEE Access: Practical Innovations, Open Solutions*, *8*, 127272–127312.

Farooq, M., Waseem, M., Khairi, A., & Mazhar, P. (2015). 02). A critical analysis on the security concerns of Internet of Things (IoT). *International Journal of Computers and Applications*, *111*, 1–6.

Fu, Y., Yan, Z., Cao, J., Kone, O., & Cao, X. (2017). An automata-based intrusion detection method for Internet of Things. *Mobile Information Systems*, *2017*.

Gigli, M., & Koo, S. (2011). 01). Internet of Things: Services and applications categorization abstract. *Adv. Internet of Things*, *1*, 27–31. doi:10.4236/ait.2011.12004

Gubbi, J., Buyya, R., Marusic, S., & Palaniswami, M. (2013). Internet of Things (IoT): A vision, architectural elements, and future directions. *Future Generation Computer Systems*, *29*(7), 1645–1660. doi:10.1016/j.future.2013.01.010

Hu, C., Zhang, J., & Wen, Q. (2011). An identity-based personal location system with protected privacy in IoT. In *2011 4th IEEE International Conference on Broadband Network and Multimedia Technology* (pp. 192-195). doi: 10.1109/ICBNMT.2011.6155923

Husak, M., Velan, P., & Vykopal, J. (2015). Security monitoring of HTTP traffic using extended flows. In *2015 10th International Conference on Availability, Reliability and Security* (pp. 258–265). Academic Press.

Hussain, F., Hussain, R., Hassan, S. A., & Hossain, E. (2020). Machine learning in IoT security: Current solutions and future challenges. *IEEE Communications Surveys and Tutorials*, *22*(3), 16861721. doi:10.1109/COMST.2020.2986444

Koch, R. (2011). Towards next-generation intrusion detection. In *2011 3rd International Conference on Cyber Conflict* (pp. 1–18). Academic Press.

Kshetri, N. (2017). Can blockchain strengthen the Internet of Things? *IT Professional*, *19*(4), 68–72. doi:10.1109/MITP.2017.3051335

Liao, H.-J., Lin, C.-H. R., Lin, Y.-C., & Tung, K.-Y. (2013). Intrusion detection system: A comprehensive review. *Journal of Network and Computer Applications*, *36*(1), 16–24.

Mao, B., Kawamoto, Y., Liu, J., & Kato, N. (2019). Harvesting and threat aware security configuration strategy for IEEE 802.15.4 based IoT networks. *IEEE Communications Letters*, *23*(11), 2130–2134. doi:10.1109/LCOMM.2019.2932988

Moustafa, N., & Slay, J. (2015). UNSW-NB15: a comprehensive data set for network intrusion detection systems (UNSW-NB15 network data set). In 2015 Military Communications and Information Systems Conference (pp. 1–6). Academic Press.

Neisse, R., Steri, G., Baldini, G., Tragos, E., Nai Fovino, I., & Botterman, M. (2015). *Dynamic context-aware scalable and trust-based IoT security, privacy framework*. River Publishers.

Nitti, M., Girau, R., & Atzori, L. (2014). Trustworthiness management in the social Internet of Things. *IEEE Transactions on Knowledge and Data Engineering*, *26*(5), 1253–1266. doi:10.1109/TKDE.2013. 105

Ogonji, M. M., Okeyo, G., & Wafula, J. M. (2020). A survey on privacy and security of Internet of Things. *Computer Science Review*, *38*, 100312. doi:10.1016/j.cosrev.2020.100312

Ozay, M., Esnaola, I., Yarman Vural, F. T., Kulkarni, S. R., & Poor, H. V. (2016). Machine learn-ing methods for attack detection in the smart grid. *IEEE Transactions on Neural Networks and Learning Systems*, *27*(8), 1773–1786. doi:10.1109/TNNLS.2015.2404803

Rahman, M. A., Rashid, M. M., Hossain, M. S., Hassanain, E., Alhamid, M. F., & Guizani, M. (2019). Blockchain and IoT-based cognitive edge framework for sharing economy services in a smart city. *IEEE Access: Practical Innovations, Open Solutions*, *7*, 18611–18621. doi:10.1109/ ACCESS.2019.2896065

Riahi Sfar, A., Natalizio, E., Challal, Y., & Chtourou, Z. (2018). A roadmap for security challenges in the Internet of Things. *Digital Communications and Networks*, *4*(2), 118–137. doi:10.1016/j.dcan.2017.04.003

Santos, L., Rabadão, C., & Gonçalves, R. (2019). Flow monitoring system for IoT networks. In *World conference on information systems and technologies* (pp. 420–430). Academic Press.

Sehrawat, D., & Gill, N. S. (2019). Smart sensors: Analysis of different types of IoT sensors. In *2019 3rd International Conference on Trends in Electronics and Informatics* (pp. 523-528). doi: 10.1109/ICOEI.2019.8862778

Sicari, S., Rizzardi, A., Grieco, L., & Coen-Porisini, A. (2015). Security, privacy and trust in Internet of Things: The road ahead. *Computer Networks*, *76*, 146–164. doi:10.1016/j.comnet. 2014.11.008

Sikder, A. K., Petracca, G., Aksu, H., Jaeger, T., & Uluagac, S. (2018). *A survey on sensor-based threats to internet-of-things (IoT) devices and applications*. arXiv preprint arXiv:1802.02041.

Sivanathan, A., Sherratt, D., Gharakheili, H. H., Radford, A., Wijenayake, C., Vishwanath, A., & Sivaraman, V. (2017). Characterizing and classifying IoT traffic in smart cities and campuses. In *2017 IEEE Conference on Computer Communications Workshops (Infocom Wkshps)* (pp. 559–564). IEEE.

Sodhro, A. H., Pirbhulal, S., & de Albuquerque, V. H. C. (2019). Artificial intelligence-driven mechanism for edge computing-based industrial applications. *IEEE Transactions on Industrial Informatics*, *15*(7), 4235–4243. doi:10.1109/TII. 2019.2902878

Swamy, S. N., Jadhav, D., & Kulkarni, N. (2017). Security threats in the application layer in IoT applications. In *2017 International Conference on I-SMAC (IoT in social, mobile, analytics and cloud) (I-SMAC)* (p. 477-480). doi: 10.1109/I-SMAC.2017. 8058395

Tukur, Y. M., Thakker, D., & Awan, I. (2019). Ethereum blockchain-based solution to insider threats on perception layer of IoT systems. In *2019 IEEE Global Conference on Internet of Things (GCIoT)* (p. 1-6). doi: 10.1109/GCIoT47977.2019.9058395

Ullah, Z., Ahmad, S., & Ahmad, M. Ata-ur-Rehman, & Junaid, M. (2019). A preview on Internet of Things (IoT) and its applications. In *2019 2nd International Conference on Computing, Mathematics and Engineering Technologies (iCoMet)* (p. 1-6). doi: 10.1109/ICOMET.2019.8673468

Verma, A., & Ranga, V. (2019). Evaluation of network intrusion detection systems for rpl based 6LoWPAN networks in IoT. *Wireless Personal Communications*, *108*(3), 1571–1594.

Weyrich, M., & Ebert, C. (2016). Reference architectures for the Internet of Things. *IEEE Software, 33*(1), 112–116. doi:10.1109/MS.2016.20

Chapter 11
Securing the Internet of Things Applications Using Blockchain Technology in the Manufacturing Industry

Kamalendu Pal
https://orcid.org/0000-0001-7158-6481
City, University of London, UK

ABSTRACT

The manufacturing industry tends to worldwide business operations due to the economic benefits of product design and distribution operations. The design and development of a manufacturing enterprise information system (EIS) involve different types of decision making at various levels of business control. This decision making is complex and requires real-time data collection from machines, business processes, and operating environments. Enterprise information systems are used to support data acquisition, communication, and all decision-making activities. Hence, information technology (IT) infrastructure for data acquisition and sharing affects the performance of an EIS significantly. The chapter highlights the advantages and disadvantages of an integrated internet of things (IoT) and blockchain technology on EIS in the modern manufacturing industry. Also, it presents a review of security-related issues in the context of an EIS consisting of IoT-based blockchain technology. Finally, the chapter discusses the future research directions.

DOI: 10.4018/978-1-7998-6463-9.ch011

INTRODUCTION

Modern manufacturing has got a long history of evolution for several hundred years. The first industrial revolution began in the last part of the 18th century (Lukac, 2015). It symbolized production systems powered by water and steam, followed by the second industrial revolution, which started in the early part of the 20th century with the characteristics of mass labour deployment and manufacturing systems based on electrical power. The third industrial revolution began in the early part of the 1970s with automatic production or manufacturing based on electronics and computer data communication technology. The concept of Industry 4.0 was put forward for developing the German economy in 2011 (Roblek et al., 2016) (Vogel-Heuser & Hess, 2016). Industry 4.0 is characterized by cyber-physical systems (CPS) production based on heterogeneous data and knowledge integration. It is closely related to the Internet of Things (IoT), CPS, information and communication technology (ICT), enterprise information systems (EIS), and integration of EIS. This way, a new generation of CPS controls industrial manufacturing and supply chain management (SCM).

Moreover, because of changes in the economic, environmental, and business environments, the modern manufacturing industry appears to be riskier than ever before, which created a need for improving its supply chain privacy and security. These changes are for several reasons. First, the increasingly global economy produces and depends on people's free flow, goods, and information. Second, disasters have increased in number and intensity during the recent decades. Natural disasters such as earthquakes, floods, or pandemic (e.g., coronavirus) strike more often and have a more significant economic impact. Simultaneously, the number of human-made disasters such as industrial sabotage, wars, and terrorist attacks that affects manufacturing supply networks has increased (Colema, 2006). These factors have created significant challenges for manufacturers, the country, and the global economic condition. Manufacturers must also deploy continuous improvement in business processes, which improve supply chain activities execution and security enhancement.

Besides, today's manufacturing industry inclines worldwide business operations due to the socioeconomic advantage of the globalization of product design and development (Pal, 2020). For example, a typical apparel manufacturing network consists of organizations' sequence, facilities, functions, and activities to produce and develop an ultimate product or related services. The action starts with raw materials purchase from selective suppliers and products produced at one or more production facilities (Pal, 2019). Next, these products are moved to intermediate collection points (e.g., warehouse, distribution centers) to store temporarily to move to the next stage of the manufacturing network and finally deliver the products to intermediate storages or retailers or customers (Pal, 2017) (Pal, 2018).

This way, global manufacturing networks are becoming increasingly complicated due to a growing need for inter-organizational and intra-organizational connectedness that enabled by advances in modern Information technologies (e.g., RFID, Internet of Things, Blockchain, Service-Oriented Computing, Big Data Analytics) (Okorie et al., 2017) and tightly coupled business processes. Also, the manufacturing business networks use information systems to monitor operational activities in a nearly real-time situation.

The digitalization of business activities attracts attention from manufacturing network management purpose, improves communication, collaboration, and enhances trust within business partners due to real-time information sharing and better business process integration. However, the above new technologies come with different types of disruptions to operations and ultimate productivity. For example, some of the operational disruptions are malicious threats that hinder the safety of goods, services, and customers' trust to do business with the manufacturing companies.

As a potential solution to tackle the security problems, practitioners and academics have reported some attractive research with IoT and blockchain-based information systems for maintaining transparency, data integrity, privacy, and security related issues. In a manufacturing communication network context, the Internet of Things (IoT) system integrates different heterogeneous objects and sensors, which surround manufacturing operations (Pal, 2019) and facilitates the information exchange within the business stakeholders (also known as nodes in networking term). With the rapid enlargement of the data communication network scale and the intelligent evolution of hardware technologies, typical standalone IoT-based applications may no longer satisfy the advanced need for efficiency and security in the high degree of heterogeneity of hardware devices and complex data formats. Firstly, burdensome connectivity and maintenance costs brought by centralized architecture result in its low scalability. Secondly, centralized systems are more vulnerable to adversaries' targeted attacks under network expansion (Pal & Yasar, 2020).

Intuitively, a decentralized approach based on blockchain technology may solve the above problems in a typical centralized IoT-based information system. Mainly, the above justification is for three reasons. Firstly, an autonomous decentralized information system is feasible for trusted business partners to join the network, improving the business task-processing ability independently. Secondly, multiparty coordination enhances nodes' state consistency that information system crashes are avoidable due to being a single-point failure. Thirdly, nodes could synchronize the whole information system state only by coping with the blockchain ledger to minimize the computation related activities and improve storage load. Besides, blockchain-based IoT architecture for manufacturing information systems attracted researchers' attention (Pal, 2020).

Despite the potential of blockchain-based technology, severe security issues have been raised in its integration with IoT to form an architecture for manufacturing business applications. This chapter presents different types of security-related problems for information system design purpose. Below, this chapter introduces first the basic idea of digitation of manufacturing business process. Next, the chapter presents the use of blockchain technology in IoT for the manufacturing industry. Then, it discusses the future research directions that include data security and industrial data breach-related issues. Finally, the chapter presents the concluding remarks and future research directions.

DIGITATION OF MANUFACTURING BUSINESS PROCESS

Inherent within manufacturing is information creation, communication, and decision making (or action). For example, a design is created via a drawing, design software, or scanning a physical object, creating data. These data are then conveyed to machines that execute the design, bringing it forth from the digital to the physical realm. Ideally, data from the creation process (and subsequent use) is further captured, sparking ongoing cycles between the digital and physical realms. Information Technology (IT) plays an important part in capturing, storing, and processing stored data. Besides, manufacturing business networks use information systems to monitor manufacturing business network activities(Pal, 2017) (Pal, 2020). Organizational connectedness, which enabled by advances in modern technologies and tightly coupled business processes.

There is massive use of IoT devices in the manufacturing industry. However, most IoT devices are easy to attack, and industrial sabotage can be accomplished. Ideally, these IoT devices are limited in computational capability, network capacity, storage, and hence they are much more vulnerable to attacks than other endpoint devices such as smartphones, tablets, or computers. This chapter presents a survey of many security issues for IoT. The chapter reviews and categorizes popular security issues regarding the IoT layered architecture, in addition to protocols used for networking, communication, and management. It also outlines security requirements for IoT along with the existing attacks, threats, and state-of-the-art solutions. Besides, the chapter tabulates and map IoT security problems against existing solutions found in the academic literature. More importantly, the chapter discusses how blockchain technology can be a crucial enabler to solve many IoT security problems. The chapter also identifies open research problems and challenges for IoT security.

Figure 1. A diagrammatic representation of manufacturing business process

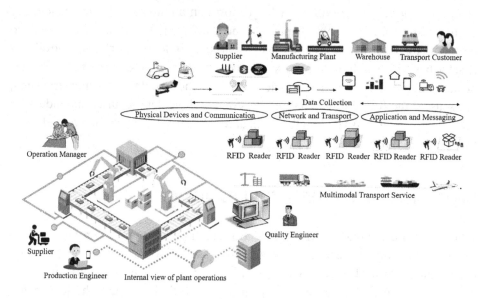

With the quickest increase of smart devices and high-speed data communication networks, IoT-based technology has gained huge popularity for automating manufacturing business processes. This popularity is mainly due to (i) low power consumption in standard IoT devices and (ii) lossy data communication networks having constrained resources. It represents a network where "things" or embedded devices having sensors are interconnected through a private or a public data communication network. The devices in IoT-based technology can be controlled remotely to perform the desired functionality. The information sharing among the devices then occurs through the network, which employs the standard communication protocols. The smart connected devices or "things" range from simple wearable accessories to large machines, each containing sensor chips. For example, the smart warehouse smart robots contain chips that support tracking and analyzing material management data. Similarly, electrical appliances, including machinery and inventory rack tracking robots, can be controlled remotely through IoT devices. The security cameras used for surveillance of a location can be monitored remotely anywhere in the world.

Apart from the industry-specific use, IoT serves the different business process automation needs as well. Different smart electromechanical types of machinery (or devices) perform various business processes functionalities (e.g., detecting transport vehicles movement within manufacturing plants, providing tracking and connectivity in industrial robots, measuring temperature and pressure in highly inhuman conditions). This way, an IoT-based system comprises "Things" (or IoT devices) that have remote sensing and actuating abilities and can exchange data with other connected devices and applications (e.g., directly, or indirectly).

The data collected through these devices may be sent locally or sent to centralized servers or cloud-based applications to perform the real-time processing, monitoring, and improvement of the entire industrial manufacturing systems. In recent years, an on-demand model of manufacturing that is leveraging IoT technologies is called Cloud-Based Manufacturing (CBM) (Rosen et al., 2015) highlighted some of the leading technical themes. CBM provides a convenient, ubiquitous computing environment, on-demand network access to a shared pool of configurable manufacturing resources that can be quickly available for indented service.

The IoT application continues to proliferate due to the evolution of hardware-related issues (e.g., bandwidth improvement using cognitive radio-based networks) to address the underutilization of the frequency spectrum. In addition, the wireless sensor network (WSN) and machine-to-machine (M2M) or cyber-physical systems (CPS) have now evolved as integral parts of the broader concept of the technical term IoT. Consequently, the security-related problems to WSN, M2M, or CPS are lurking a threat for IoT-based manufacturing applications, with the internet protocol (IP) being the central standard for connectivity. The industrial deployment architecture hence needs to be secured from attacks that may create problems for the services provided by IoT and may pose a threat to confidentiality, privacy, and integrity of data. Since the IoT technology-based applications deal with a collection of interconnected data communication networks and heterogeneous devices, it inherits the conventional security issues related to the computer networks. The constrained resources pose extra challenges to IoT security since the small devices or things containing sensors have limited power and memory. As a result, the security solutions need to be adapted to the constrained architectures.

Along with the rapid growth of IoT application and devices in the manufacturing industry, there has been an increasing number of research efforts highlighting security issues in the IoT environment. Some of these research target security issues at a specific layer, whereas other researchers aim at presenting end-to-end security for IoT applications. A research group presented an IoT applications survey and tried to categorize security issues in the application, architecture, communication, and data (Alaba et al., 2017). This proposed categorization for IoT security is different from the conventional layered architecture. The threats on IoT applications are highlighted for the hardware layer, network layer, and application layers. In another survey, a research group (Granjal et al., 2015) highlighted security related issues for the IoT application protocols. The security analyses presented by other research groups (Roman et al., 2011) (Granjal et al., 2008) (Cirani et al., 2013) discuss and compare different critical management systems and algorithmic cryptographic techniques.

Besides, other researchers (Butun et al., 2014) (Abduvaliyev et al., 2013) (Mitchell & Chen, 2014) presented a comparative evaluation of intrusion detection systems. The IoT applications in the *'fog computing environment'* were analyzed and presented by few research groups (Yi et al., 2015) (Wang et al., 2015). A systematic survey by Sicari and colleagues (Sicari et al., 2015) provided different aspects of middleware related technical issues (e.g., confidentiality, security, access control, privacy). The authors highlighted trust management, privacy-related issues, authentication, network security, data security, and intrusion detection systems. For edge-computing based applications, including mobile cloud computing, mobile edge computing and computing, identity and authentication, access control systems, network security, trust management, fault tolerance and implementation of forensics are surveyed by a group of researchers (Roman et al., 2016).

Motivated by an increasing number of vulnerabilities, a researcher (Oleshchuk, 2009) presented a survey of privacy-preserving mechanisms for specific IoT applications. The author explained in the research paper the secure multiparty computations to preserving privacy for IoT-based application users. Zhou and collaborative researchers (Zhou et al., 2017) discussed various security threats and possible solutions for cloud based IoT applications. The authors described identity and location privacy, node compromising, layer removing or adding, and critical management threats for IoT using the cloud. In another survey, Zhang and colleagues (Zhan et al., 2014) presented some crucial IoT security issues about unique identification of objects, privacy, authorization, authentication, and the requirement of lightweight cryptographic techniques, malware, and software vulnerabilities. The IoT-A project (IoT-A, 2013) described a reference architecture for IoT that compliance needs implementation for privacy, security, and trust. The used trust model provides data integrity and confidentiality while creating end-to-end data communication through an authentication technique. Besides, to eliminate improper usage of data, the privacy model needs defining access policies and methods for encrypting and decrypting data. The security-related issues are included in a three-layers corresponding to the services, communication, and application. In the same way, the Open Web Application Security Project (OWASP) (OWASP, 2016) introduced ten vulnerabilities for the IoT architecture. Notably, these vulnerabilities include insecure interfaces of entities of the IoT architecture, inappropriate security configuration, physical security, and insecure firmware/software.

IoT ARCHITECTURE AND SECURITY CHALLENGES

IoT becomes the foundation for connecting things, sensors, actuators, and other smart technologies. IoT technology gives an immediate access to information about physical objects and lends to innovative services with high efficiency and productivity. The characteristics of IoT includes: (i) the pervasive sensing of objects; (ii) the hardware and software integration; and (iii) many nodes. In developing an IoT, objects must be capable of interacting with each other, reaching autonomously to the change of manufacturing environment (e.g., temperature, pressure, humidity).

IoT Protocols and Standards

A typical IoT deployment in manufacturing industry contains heterogeneous devices with embedded sensors interconnected through a network, as shown in Figure 1. This architecture consists of three layers, such as physical devices and communication layer, network and transport layer, and application and messaging layer. Radio Frequency Identification (RFID) technology has received massive attention from the manufacturing industry's daily operations as a critical component of the Internet of Things (IoT) world. In RFID-enabled manufacturing chain automation, an EPC (Electronic Product Code) is allocated to an individual item of interest and is attached to an RFID tag for tracking and tracing purpose.

Figure 2. Common IoT standards and protocols

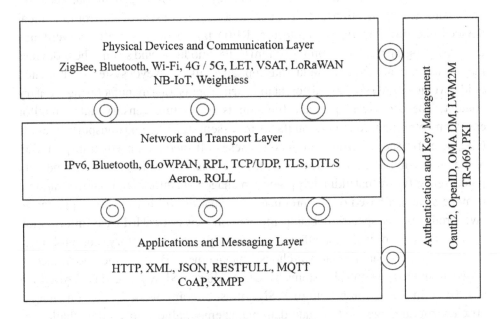

In addition, wireless sensor networks (WSNs) are used to provide computing services to enterprises. WSNs are the essential infrastructure for the implementation of IoT. Various hardware and software systems are available to WSNs: (i) Internet Protocol version 6 (IPv6) makes it possible to connect an unlimited number of devices, (ii) Wi-Fi and WiMAX provide high-speed and low-cost communication, (iii) Zigbee, Bluetooth, and RFID provide the communication in low-speed and local communication, and (iv) a mobile platform offers communications for anytime, anywhere, and anything.

Figure 2 shows a layered architecture with the standard IoT protocols used for manufacturing applications and messaging, and routing or forwarding, physical devices and those for key management and authentication. It shows the standards and protocols for the commonly used low-rate wireless personal area networks (LR-WPANs) (IEEE, 2012) and the recently evolved protocols for the low power wide area network (LPWAN) based protocols.

Again, LR-WPANs (i.e., IEEE standard 802.15.15.4) consists of two low-level layers; and they are the Physical Layer and the Medium Access Control (MAC) layer. The physical layer specification is related to communication over wireless channels having diverse frequency bands and data rate. The MAC layer specification is related to mechanisms for channels access as well as for synchronization.

A simple IoT architecture composed of devices (e.g., machinery and equipment), networks, cloud-based storage, and information system applications are shown in Figure 1. This architecture consists of four layers, such as perception, network, processing, and application layer. The perception layer consists of electromechanical devices like different types of sensors, RFID tag readers, security surveillance cameras, geographical positioning system (GPS) modules, and so on. These devices may be accompanied by other industrial appliances like conveyor systems, automated guided vehicles (AGVs), and different industrial robots for a manufacturing industry context. These devices' primary function is to capture sensory data, monitor environmental conditions and manufacturing assembly areas, and transport materials (e.g., semi-finished, finished products). These collected data needs transportation to the processing layer. The processing layer consists of dedicated servers and data processing software that ultimately produce management information, and operational managers can act based on the produced information. In this way, the application layer produces user-specific decision information. Few critical IoT based information system applications in the manufacturing industry are smart factory, smart robotics, intelligent supply chain, smart warehouse management. Besides, the importance of WSNs to industrial control systems have been discussed by researchers (Araujo et al., 2014). In the research field of WSNs, most ongoing work focuses on energy-efficient routing, aggregation, and data management algorithms; other challenges include the large-scale deployment and semantic integration of massive data (Aberer et al., 2014), and security (Gandino et al., 2014).

Security Requirements for IoT

To secure IoT-based information systems applications in manufacturing industry the following issues need to consider.

Data privacy, confidentiality, and integrity: As IoT data moves in a data communication network, an appropriate encryption algorithm is needed to ensure the confidentiality of data. Due to a diverse integration of services, devices and data communication network, the data stored on a device is vulnerable to privacy violation by compromising nodes existing in an IoT applications network. The IoT devices susceptible to attacks may cause an attacker to disturb the integrity of stored data by modifying the stored data for malicious intentions.

Authentication, authorization, and accounting: To secure communication in IoT, the authentication is required between two parties communicating with each other. For privileged access to services, the devices must be authenticated. The diversity of authentication mechanisms for IoT exists mainly due to the diverse heterogenous underlying architectures and environments that support IoT devices. These environments pose a challenge for defining standard and global protocol for authentication in IoT devices and applications.

The access control systems face many problems, such as third-party, inefficiency, and lack of privacy. These problems can be address by blockchain, the technology that received significant attention in recent years, and many potentials. Jemel and other researchers (Jemel & Serhrouchni, 2017) report a couple of centralised access control systems problems. As there is a third party with access to the data, the risk of privacy leakage exists. Also, a major party is in charge to control the access, so the risk of a single point of failure also exists. This study presents an access control mechanism with a temporal dimension to solve these problems and adapts a blockchain-based solution for verifying access permissions. The attribute-based Encryption method (Sahai & Waters, 2005) also has some problems, such as privacy leakage from the private key generator (PKG) (Hur & Noh, 2011) and a single point of failure as mentioned before. Wang and colleagues (Wang et al.,2018) introduce a framework for data sharing and access control to address this problem by implementing decentralized storage.

IoT Devices Management: In IoT, devices management relates to security solutions for the physical devices, embedded software, and residing data on the devices. Internet of Things (IoT) comprises of "Things" (or IoT devices) that have remote sensing and data collecting capabilities and can exchange data with other connected devices and applications (directly or indirectly). IoT devices can collect data and process the data either locally or send them to centralize servers or cloud-based application back-ends for processing. A recent on-demand model of manufacturing that is leveraging IoT technologies is called Cloud-Based Manufacturing (CBM).

It enables ubiquitous, convenient, on-demand network access to a shared pool of configurable manufacturing business processes information collection and use it service provision.

However, attackers seek to exfiltrate IoT devices' data using malicious codes in malware, especially on the open-source Android platform. Gu et al. (Gu et al., 2018) reported a malware identification system in a blockchain-based system named CB-MDEE composed of detecting consortium chain by test members and public chain users. The CB-MDEE system uses a soft-computing-based comparison technique and more than one marking function to minimise the false-positive rate and improve malware variants' identification ability.

Availability of Services: The attacks on IoT devices may hinder the provision of services through the conventional denial-of-service attacks. Different strategies (e.g., jamming adversaries, sinkhole attacks, replay attacks) are used for deteriorating the quality of service (QoS) to IoT manufacturing application users.

Single points of failure: A huge growth of heterogeneous networks for the IoT-based global manufacturing infrastructure may expose many *'single points of failure'* that may in turn deteriorate the services envisioned through IoT applications. Hence, it is essential to develop a tamper-proof ecosystem for a huge number of IoT devices as well as to provide alternative mechanisms for implementation of a fault tolerant IoT applications network.

Categorization of Security Issues

With the development of ubiquitous computing (e.g., IoT based applications in manufacturing, logistics, and smart grid) uses become widely used in the world (e.g., manufacturing, digital healthcare, smart city). According to statistics website Statista (TSP, 2021), the number of connected devices in industry will drastically increase in coming years. At the same time, with the huge growth of IoT application and devices, security attacks pose a more serious threat for industries. For example, remote adversaries could compromise health services implantable medical devices (3), or smart cars (4), which will create massive economic losses to the world. IoT devices are widely used in industry, military, and other critical operational areas of society. Malicious attackers can jeopardize public and national security. For example, on 21 October 2016, multiple distributed denial of service (DDoS) (5) attacks took place by Domain Name System provider Dyn, which caused the inaccessibility of several websites (e.g., GitHub, Twitter). For example, Stuxnet (6), a malicious computer worm that targeted industrial computer systems were responsible for causing a substantial problem to Iran's nuclear program. The ransomware attack, WannaCry was a worldwide cyberattack in May 2017, which targeted computer systems worldwide. A new variant of WannaCry forced Taiwan Semiconductor

Manufacturing Company (TSMC) to temporarily shut down several of its chip-fabrication factories in August 2018 (Wikipedia, 2021). The virus spread to 10,000 machines in TSMC's most advanced facilities.

Inspired by an increasing number of vulnerabilities, predatorial attacks and information leaks, IoT device manufacturers, service-oriented computing service providers, and researchers are working on designing systems to securely control the flow of information between devices, to find out new vulnerabilities, and to provide security and privacy within the context of users and the devices. For example, adversaries can exploit the envisioned design and verification limitations to compromise the system's security. The system becomes vulnerable to malicious attacks from cyberspace (Sturm et al., 2017). Some of the well-known attacks (e.g., Stuxnet, Shamoon, BlackEnergy, WannaCry, and TRITON) (Stouffer, 2020) created significant problems in recent decades.

The distributed manufacturing industry's critical issues are coordinating and controlling secure business information and its operational network. The application of cybersecurity controls in the operating environment demands the most significant attention and effort to ensure that appropriate security and risk mitigation are achieved. For example, manufacturing device spoofing and false authentication in information sharing (Kumar & Mallick, 2018) are significant problems for the industry.

However, disadvantages of the centralized IoT information system architecture issues have been reported by a group of researchers (Ali et al., 2019). A central point of failure could easily paralyze the whole data communication network. Besides, it is easy to misuse user-sensitive data in a centralized system; users have limited or no control over personal data. Centralized data can be tampered with or deleted by an intruder, and therefore the centralized system has lacks guaranteed traceability and accountability.

The vast popularity of IoT based information systems in the manufacturing industry also demands the appropriate protection of security and privacy-related issues to stop any system vulnerabilities and threats. Also, traditional security protections are not always problem-free. Hence, it is worth classifying different security problems classified based on objects of attack that are relevant to IoT based systems. This classification of security-related attacks would help industry-specific practitioners and researchers to understand which attacks are essential to their regular business operations. The additional layer-specific security-related research is shown in Table 1, Table 2, and Table 3.

Software attacks are launched by an attacker taking advantage of the associated software or security vulnerabilities presented by an IoT system is shown in Table 3. This way, a malicious code can attack IoT-based infrastructure applications and create disruption (e.g., repeating the request of a new connection until the IoT system reaches maximum level) of an existing service for global connectivity.

Table 1. Perception layer attacks

Type of attack	Description
Tampering	Physical damage is caused to the device (e.g., RFID tag, Tag reader) or communication network (Andrea et al., 2015).
Malicious Code Injection	The attacker physically introduces a malicious code onto an IoT system by compromising its operation. The attacker can control the IoT system and launch attacks (Ahemd et al., 2017).
Radio Frequency Signal Interference (Jamming)	The predator sends a particular type of radiofrequency signal to hinder communication in the IoT system, and it creates a denial of service (DoS) from the information system (Ahemd et al., 2017).
Fake Node Injection:	The intruder creates an artificial node and the IoT-based system network and access the information from the network illegally or control data flow (Ahemd et al., 2017).
Sleep Denial Attack	The attacker aims to keep the battery-powered devices awake by sending them with inappropriate inputs, which causes exhaustion of battery power, leading to shutting down of nodes (Ahemd et al., 2017).
Side-Channel Attack	In this attack, the intruder gets hold of the encryption keys by applying malicious techniques on the devices of the IoT-based information system (Andrea et al., 2015), and by using these keys, the attacker can encrypt or decrypt confidential information from the IoT network.
Permanent Denial of Service (PDoS)	In this attack, the attacker permanently damages the IoT system using hardware sabotage. The attack can be launched by damaging firmware or uploading an inappropriate BIOS using malware (Foundry, 2017).

Besides, the IoT based application system provides an innovative technology that has become a guiding technology behind the automation of the manufacturing industry and smart computing. The IoT application produces countless digitized services and applications that provide several advantages over existing solutions. The applications and services share some standard features, which include: (i) sensing capabilities, (ii) connectivity, (iii) extensive scale network, (iv) dynamic system, (v) intelligence capabilities, (vi) Big Data processing using traditional data analytics methods, (vii) unique identity of the objects to connect over the computer network, (viii) autonomous contextual and real-time decision making, and (ix) heterogeneity – the IoT system allows different devices and objects to be addressable and communicate with each other over the Internet. These devices come with heterogeneous characteristics, including platforms, operating systems, communication protocols, and other hardware and software components. Despite these heterogeneous characteristics, the IoT system allows all the devices to communicate efficiently and effectively in a manufacturing environment.

Table 2. Network layer attacks

Type of attack	Description
Traffic Analysis Attack	Confidential data flowing to and from the devices are sniffed by the attacker, even without going close to the network to get network traffic information and attacking purpose (Andrea et al., 2015).
RFID Spoofing	The intruder first spoofs an RFID signal to access the information imprinted on the RFID tag (Ahemd et al., 2017). Using the original tag ID, the intruder can then send its manipulated data, posing it as valid. In this way, the intruder can create a problem for the business operation.
RFID Unauthorized Access	An intruder can read, modify, or delete data present on RFID nodes because of the lack of proper authentication mechanisms (Andrea et al., 2015).
Routing Information Attacks	These are direct attacks where the attacker spoofs or alters routing information and makes a nuisance by creating routing loops and sending error messages (Andrea et al., 2015).
Selective Forwarding	In this attack, a malicious node may alter, drop, or selectively forward some messages to other nodes in the network (Varga et al., 2017). Therefore, the information that reaches the destination is incomplete.
Sinkhole Attack	In this attack, an attacker compromises a node closer to the sink (known as sinkhole node) and makes it look attractive to other nodes in the network, thereby luring network traffic towards it (Ahemd et al., 2017).
Wormhole Attack	In a wormhole attack, an attacker maliciously prepares a low-latency link and then tunnels packets from one point to another through this link (Varga et al., 2017).
Sybil Attack	Here, a single malicious node claims multiple identities (known as Sybil nodes) and locates itself at different places in the network (Andrea et al., 2015). It leads to colossal resource allocation unfairly. • Man in the Middle Attack (MiTM): Here, an attacker manages to eavesdrop or monitor the communication between two IoT devices and access their private data (Andrea et al., 2015).
Replay Attack	An attacker may capture a signed packet and resend the packet multiple times to the destination (Varga et al., 2017). It keeps the network busy, leading to a DoS attack.
Denial/Distributed Denial of Service (DoS/ DDoS) Attacks	Unlike DoS attack, multiple compromised nodes attack a specific target by flooding messages or connection requests to crash or slow down the system server/network resource (Rambus).

Table 3. Software layer attacks

Type of attack	Description
Virus, Worms, Trojan Horses, Spyware and Adware	Using this malicious software, an adversary can infect the system to tampering data or stealing information or even launching DoS (Andrea et al., 2015).
Malware	Data present in IoT devices may be affected by malware, contaminating the cloud or data centres (Varga et al., 2017).

The convergence of IoT with blockchain technology will have many advantages. The blockchain's decentralization model will have the ability to handle processing a vast number of transactions between IoT devices, significantly reducing the cost associated with installing and maintaining large, centralized data centres and distributing computation and storage needs across IoT devices networks. Working with blockchain technology will eliminate the single point of failure associated with the centralized IoT architecture. The convergence of Blockchain with IoT will allow the P2P messaging, file distribution, and autonomous coordination between IoT devices with no centralized computing model.

However, IoT-based applications' deployment results in an enlarged attack surface that requires end-to-end security mitigation. Blockchain technologies play a crucial role in securing many IoT-oriented applications by becoming security providing manufacturing application. Blockchain technology is based on a distributed database management system that keeps records of all business-related transactional information that have been executed and shared among participating business partners in the network. This distributed database system is known as a distributed ledger technology (DLT). Individual business exchange information is stored in the distributed ledger and must be verified by most network members. All business-related transactions that have ever made are contained in the block. Bitcoin, the decentralized peer-to-peer (P2P) digital currency, is the most famous example of blockchain technology (Nakamoto, 2008).

BACKGROUND OF BLOCKCHAIN TECHNOLOGY

Blockchain technology is based on a distributed database management system that keeps records of all business-related transactional information that have been executed and shared among participating business partners in the network. This distributed database system is known as a DLT. Individual business exchange information is stored in the distributed ledger and must be verified by most network members. All business-related transactions that have ever made are contained in the block. Bitcoin, the decentralized peer-to-peer (P2P) digital currency, is the most famous example of blockchain technology (Nakamoto, 2008).

The blockchain technology infrastructure has motivated many innovative applications in manufacturing industries. This technology's ideal blockchain vision is tamper evident and tamper resistant ledgers implemented in a distributed fashion, without a central repository. The central ideas guiding blockchain technology emerged in the late 1980s and early 1990s. A research paper (Lamport, 1998) published with the background knowledge of the Paxos protocol, which provided a consensus method for reaching an agreement resulting in a computer network. The central concepts of that research were combined and applied to the electronic cash-related research project by Satoshi Nakamoto (Nakamoto, 2008), leading to modern cryptocurrency or bitcoin-based systems.

Distributed Ledger Technology (DLT) Based Blockchain

The blockchain's initial basis is to institute trust in a P2P network bypassing any third managing parties' need. For example, Bitcoin started a P2P financial value exchange mechanism where no third-party (e.g., bank) is needed to provide a value-transfer transaction with anyone else on the blockchain community. Such a community-based trust is the main characteristic of system verifiability using mathematical modelling technique for evidence. The mechanism of this trust provision permits peers of a P2P network to transact with other community members without necessarily trusting each other. This behaviour is commonly known as the trustless behaviour of a blockchain system. The trustlessness also highlights that a blockchain network partner interested in transacting with another business entity on the blockchain does not necessarily need to know the real identity.

It permits users of a public blockchain system to be anonymous. A record of transactions among the peers is stored in a chain of a data structure known as blocks, the name blockchain's primary basis. Each block (or peer) of a blockchain network keeps a copy of this record. Moreover, a consensus, digital voting mechanism to use many network peers, is also decided on the blockchain state that all network stores' nodes. Hence, blockchain is often designed as distributed ledger-based technology. An individual instance of such a DLT, stored at each node (or peer) of the blockchain network and gets updated simultaneously with no mechanism for retroactive changes in the records. In this way, blockchain transactions cannot be deleted or altered.

Intelligent Use of Hashing

Intelligent techniques are used in hashing the blocks encapsulating transaction records together, which makes such records immutable. In other words, blockchain's transactions achieve validity, trust, and finality based on cryptographic proofs and underlying mathematical computation between different trading-peers (or partners), known as a hashing function. Encryption algorithms are used to provide confidentiality for creating hash function. These algorithmic solutions have the essential character that they are reversible in the sense that, with knowledge of the appropriate key, it must be possible to reconstruct the plaintext message from the cryptographic technique. This way hashing mechanism of a piece of data can be used to preserve the blockchain system's integrity. For example, Secure Hash Algorithm

256 (SHA256) is a member of the SHA2 hash functions currently used by many blockchain-based systems such as Bitcoin.

Figure 3. An overview of blockchain architecture

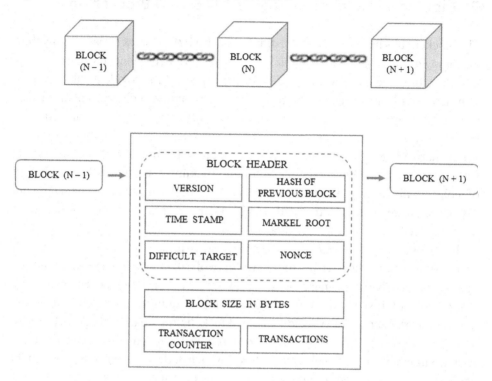

Terminologies in Blockchain

Some private blockchains provide read restrictions on the data within the blocks. Consortium blockchains are operated and owned by a group of organizations or a private community. Blockchain users use asymmetric key cryptography to sign on transactions. The trust factor maintenance within a distributed ledger technology (DLT) can be attributed to the consensus algorithms and the key desirable properties achieved thenceforth. Wüst and Gervais (2018) give a good description of these properties. Some of them are Public Verifiability, Transparency, Integrity. The main terminologies in blockchain have discussed below.

Terminologies in Blockchain:

Blocks: The transactions that occur in a peer-to-peer network associated with a blockchain are picked up from a pool of transactions and grouped in a block. Once a transaction has been validated, it basically impossible to be reverted. Transactions are pseudonymous as they are linked only to the user's public key and not to the user's real identity. A block may contain several hundreds of transactions. The block size limits the number of transactions that can be included in a block. Diagrammatic structure of a blockchain is shown in Figure 3. A block consists of version no., a hash of the previous block, the Merkle root tree to trace the transactions in the block, hash of the current block, timestamp, and nonce value. A blockchain starts with a genesis block.

Mining: Mining is when the designated nodes in the blockchain network called miners collect transactions from a pool of unprocessed transactions and combine them in a block. In mining, each miner competes to solve an equally tricky computational problem of finding a valid hash value with a particular no. of zeroes below a specific target. In Bitcoin mining, the number of zeroes indicates the difficulty of the computation. Many nonce values are tried to arrive at the golden nonce that hashes to a valid hash with the current difficulty level. When a miner arrives at this nonce value, we can say that he has successfully mined a block. This block then gets updated to the chain.

Consensus: The consensus mechanism serves two primary purposes, as given in Jesus et al. (2018): block validation and the most extensive chain selection. Proof-of-Work is the consensus algorithm used in Bitcoin Blockchain. The proof-of-stake algorithm is much faster than Proof-of-Work and demands less computational resources. The Ethereum blockchains use a pure proof-of-stake algorithm to ensure consensus. Besides Proof-of-Work, there are other consensus algorithms such as Proof of Byzantine Fault Tolerance (PBFT), proof- of activity, etc. Anwar(2018) presents a consolidated view of the different consensus algorithms. Proof-of-Work is a signature that indicates that the block has been mined after performing computation with the required difficulty level. The peers can easily verify this signature in the network to ensure a block's validity. The longest chain is always selected as the consistent one for appending the new block.

Smart Contracts: They are predefined rules deployed in the Blockchain network that two parties involved in a settlement must agree to priorly. Smart contracts were designed to avoid disagreement, denial, or violation of rules by the parties involved. They have triggered automatically in the blockchain on the occurrence of specific events mentioned in the rules.

Overall Functioning

Users connect to the blockchain and initiate a transaction signed with their private key. This transaction is sent to a pool of transactions where it resides 63 Securing IoT Applications Using Blockchain until it is fetched into a block by a miner. The miner then generates a new block after gathering transactions from the pool and computing the valid hash of the block. When a miner successfully generates a new block, the new block is broadcast to the nodes in the P2P network. All nodes in the network verify the block using a consensus algorithm, and upon successful validation, update it to their copy of the chain, and the transaction attains completion.

An overview of blockchain architecture is shown in Figure 2. In simple, blockchain can be of three different types: (i) public blockchain, (ii) private blockchain, and (iii) hybrid blockchain. A blockchain is permissionless when anyone is free to be involved in the process of authentication, verification and reaching consensus. A blockchain is permission one where its participants are pre-selected. A few different variables could apply to make a permissionless or permission system into some form of hybrid.

Ledger: One of the essential characteristics of blockchain-based operation is distributed ledger technology (DLT). It is a decentralized technology to eliminate the need for a central authority or intermediary to process, validate or authenticate transactions. Manufacturing businesses use DLT to process, validate or authenticate transactions or other types of data exchanges.

Secure: Blockchain technology produces a structure of data with inherent security qualities. It is based on principles of cryptography, decentralization, and consensus, which ensure trust in transactions. Blockchain technology ensures that the data within the network of blocks is not tampered.

Shared: Blockchain data is shared amongst multiple users of this network of nodes. It gives transparency across the node users in the network.

Distributed: Blockchain technology can be geographically distributed. The decentralization helps to scale the number of nodes of a blockchain network to ensure it is more resilient to predators' attacks. By increasing the number of nodes, a predator's capability to impact the blockchain network's consensus protocol is minimized.

Also, for blockchain-based system architectures that permit anyone to anonymously create accounts and participate (called *permissionless* blockchain networks), these capabilities produce a level of trust amongst collaborating business partners with no prior knowledge of one another. Blockchain technology provides decentralization with the collaborating partners across a distributed network. This decentralization means there is no single point of failure, and a single user cannot change the record of transactions.

Figure 4. Relationship between offering of blockchain and security requirements

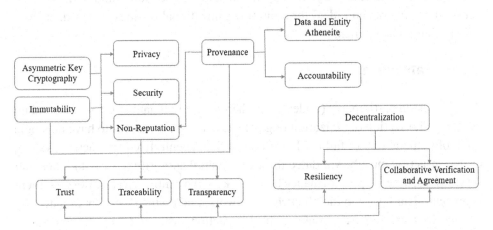

Figure 4 represents the outline of how one can manipulate blockchain to ensure security. The figure helps understand the relationship[between offerings such as immutability, province, and so on. Moreover, which aspect is needed to satisfy the specific security requirements in user specifications.

SECURING IoT APPLICATIONS USING BLOCKCHAIN

Blockchain technology uses a new way of managing trust in information systems and their transaction processing capabilities. A transaction processing system gathers and stores data regarding business activity (known as a transaction) and sometimes controls business decisions made as part of a transaction. The transaction is the activity that changes stored data. An individual transaction must succeed or fail as a complete unit; it can never be only partially complete. Since the introduction of the Bitcoin, blockchain technology has shown popularity in other business applications and attracted much attention from academia and industry. The blockchain's interest is its features that provide security, anonymity, and data integrity without any third-party involvement in the transaction control.

Primary Properties of Digital Blockchain

The information on the blockchain is digitized, getting rid of the requirement for manual documentation. Transactions are structured into blocks for information processing purposes, and standard data communication network protocol ensures that every node (i.e., business partner) receives every transaction in near real-time and uses the same rules. By design, blockchain is distributed and synchronized across the networks and ideal for a multi-organizational business network such as supply chain management.

Decentralization

All blockchain participants (nodes) have their copy of all data in the system and no central authorization organization (e.g., clearing bank). It ensures to have no single point of vulnerability or failure. In the conventional centralized transaction system, each transaction must be validated through a central authority (e.g., bank), needing service fees, time, and performance bottlenecks at the central servers. Besides, there is no central authority in the blockchain network, and no intermediary or authority service fees are required, making the transaction faster. Consensus algorithms maintain data consistency in a decentralized, distributed network (Zheng et al., 2017).

Immutability

The residing data on a blockchain is immutable. Once the participants agreed on a business transaction and recorded it, it is nearly impossible to change or delete or rollback transactions once they are included in the blockchain. If someone subsequently records another transaction about that asset to change its state, the participant cannot hide the original transaction. The provenance of assets deals with any asset, one can tell where it is, where it has been, and what has happened throughout its life (Pattison, 2017).

Consensus

There is a standard algorithm (or mechanism) used to make sure that all participants (or nodes) agree on the validity of transaction data in the system, replacing the requirement for a trusted third party (e.g., bank) for authorization purpose. There must be an agreement among all the participants that the transaction is valid before executing a transaction. The agreement process is known as "consensus", and it helps keep inaccurate or fraudulent transactions out of the blockchain. Blocks that include erroneous transactions could be revealed promptly.

Anonymity in Blockchain

Each participant can interact with the blockchain with a generated address, which does not reveal the user's real identity, but participants can see the transaction (Zheng et al., 2017). Arguably, the bitcoin blockchain cannot guarantee perfect privacy preservation due to its intrinsic constraints, but some other alternative blockchain protocols claim to provide a better privacy protection mechanism.

Traceability

The individual transaction included to a blockchain (i.e., public, or private) is digitally signed and timestamped that means that participant can trace- back to a specific time for an individual transaction and identify the appropriate party (through their public address) on the Blockchain (Swan, 2015). Therefore, every block is immutably and verifiably linked to the previous block. A complete history can always be reconstructed right back to the beginning (the genesis block).

Related Research on IoT Security and Privacy Using Blockchain

Leveraging the advantages of integrating blockchain in IoT, academics and practitioners have investigated how to handle critical issues, such as IoT device-level security, managing enormous volumes of data, maintaining user privacy, and keeping confidentiality and trust (Pal, 2020) (Dorri et al., 2019) (Shen et al., 2019). In research work, a group of researchers (Kim et al., 2017) have proposed a blockchain-based IoT system architecture to prevent IoT devices' hacking problems.

A group of researchers (Azzi et al., 2019) have introduced a blockchain integrated, IoT based information system for the supply chain management. It provides an example of a reliable, transparent, and secured system. Another group of researchers (Mondal et al., 2019) has reported a blockchain-based food supply chain that uses a proof-of-object (PoO) based authentication method. In this research, RFID tags are attached to the individual food products that are used for tracking purpose throughout their lifecycle within the supply chain network. All the real-time tracking and monitoring data produced are stored in a blockchain-based information system, which monitors food quality.

Francesco Longo and colleagues (Longo et al., 2019) have proposed that an information system consists of blockchain technology for the supply chain management. The system allows the supply chain business partners to share their information among peers with appropriate authentication and integrity.

Practitioners and academics (Pal, 2020) advocated three primary aspects of modern manufacturing: (i) integration of heterogeneous data along with the global operations, (ii) data collection, and (iii) analysis of collected data. Within heterogeneous data integration, service-oriented computing (SOC) plays a dominating role, given that intelligent perception and collection from the various computer networks of physical manufacturing resources and abilities. At the same time, new innovative technologies have emerged. They have wide use in different manufacturing applications, such as the IoT. The data collected by Radio Frequency Identification (RFID) tags and sensors for their underlying assets can help find the essential attributes (e.g., location, condition, availability) that form the essential ingredient for the modern manufacturing system.

Standard IoT systems are built on a centralized computing environment, which requires all devices to be connected and authenticated through the central server. This framework would not be able to provide the needs to outspread the IoT system in globalized operation. Therefore, moving the IoT system into the decentralized path may be the right decision. One of the popular decentralization platforms is blockchain technology.

Blockchain technology provides an appropriate solution to the security mentioned above challenges posed by a distributed IoT ecosystem. Blockchain technology offers an approach to storing information, executing transactions, performing functions, and establishing trust in secure computing without centralized authority in a networked environment. A blockchain is a chain of timestamped blocks connected by special mathematical techniques (i.e., cryptographic hashes) and behaves like a distributed ledger whose data are shared among a network of users. This paper emphasizes how the convergence of blockchain technology with IoT can provide a better manufacturing industry solution.

Blockchain in IoT

With the booming growth of IoT, the number of connected IoT devices and the data generated by them has become a massive bottleneck in meeting Quality-of-Service (QoS) (Ferrag et al., 2019). In this way, blockchain comes into the picture by supporting a decentralized way of storing data and trustful and anonymous transactions. Blockchain technology can thereby be used for tracking and coordinating the billions of connected devices. It can also enable the processing of transactions to allow significant savings for IoT industry manufacturers. This decentralized approach would further eliminate single points of failure, creating a more resilient ecosystem for devices to run on (Ali et al., 2019). The blockchains cryptographic algorithms would also help make consumer data privacy more robust (Makhdoom et al., 2019).

A blockchain is a distributed immutable, verifiable ledger. A typical design of a blockchain consists of a series of transactions that are put into one block. These blocks are then linked so that if a transaction is altered in one block, it must be updated in all the subsequent blocks (Makhdoom et al., 2019). Since the ledger is maintained with many peers, it is challenging to alter a transaction (Ferrag et al., 2019). All the blockchain peers need to agree or validate each transaction to get added to a block (Reyna et al., 2018). Once validated, the block gets updated in the blockchain.

This agreement is achieved with the help of consensus algorithms like Proof of Work (PoW), Proof of Stake (PoS), Delegated Proof-of-Stake (DPoS), Proof-of-Authority (PoA) etc. Blockchain technology is radically reshaping not only the modern IoT world but also the industries. Researchers of late have focused on integrating blockchain into the IoT ecosystem to include distributed architecture and security features. However, before this section discusses how blockchain is bringing about a significant paradigm shift in IoT, we explain the significant features of blockchain as follows (Ali et al., 2019):

- The decentralization offered by Blockchain technology enables two nodes to engage in transactions without a trusted third party. This eliminates the bottleneck of a single point of failure, thereby enhancing fault tolerance.
- All new entries made in the blockchain are agreed upon by nodes using a decentralized consensus algorithm. The design is such that all subsequent blocks in all the peers must be altered to modify an entry in a block. This ensures the immutability of blockchains.
- The audibility property of blockchains ensures transparency by allowing peers to look up and verify any transaction.
- The blockchain peers hold copies of identical replicas of ledger records. Blockchains, therefore, ensure fault tolerance. This property helps maintain data integrity and resiliency in the network.

The benefits of decentralizing IoT are numerous and notably superior to current centralized systems and are discussed below:

- Improved Trust and Security: The distributed and immutable nature of blockchain would eliminate the single point of entry/vulnerability for attackers/hackers. All transactions are cryptographically signed using unforgeable signatures, making them non-repudiable and resistant to attacks.
- More Robust: Decentralization will make IoT more accessible, and damage costs from hacks can be more easily prevented or avoided altogether. Intermediaries that operate for centralized IoT systems will be eliminated through decentralizing IoT, thereby reducing the associated costs.
- Autonomy: Blockchains enable smart devices to act independently according to the pre-determined logic (using Smart Contracts). This would altogether remove intermediary players and central authority.
- More trustworthy: The use of efficient Smart Contracts for communication amongst IoT devices and the decentralization offered by blockchain makes the entire system more trustworthy.

- Data provenance: Since all transactions are recorded on the ledger and signed by the devices/entities generating data, data provenance can be achieved.
- Fairness: By using native cryptocurrency in blockchain, parties can be incentivized. This makes the IoT system fair.

Despite the advantages (discussed above) that the integration of blockchain into the IoT platform will bring, the traditional blockchains (like Ethereum and Bitcoin) suffer from the following drawbacks too (Popov, 2018):

- Scalability: As the number of IoT devices increases, the amount of data generated will be huge, thereby leading to more storage space to keep the transactions updated in the ledger. This will further lead to high transaction and storage costs.
- Communication Overhead and Synchronization: Since each new transaction that is added to the blockchain needs to be broadcast to all the peers, it involves a lot of communication overhead. Further, all the blockchain peers need to synchronize and maintain the blockchain's duplicate copy, which further adds to the overhead.
- Efficiency: To get a transaction approved, it needs to be verified by all other peers. Thus, the verification algorithm is run multiple times at each of the peers, which drastically reduces operational efficiency.
- Energy Wastage: A majority of the popular blockchain technologies use Proof of Work (PoW) to achieve consensus and are thereby inefficient. They need to perform many computations, thereby leading to energy wastage.

Due to the disadvantages of the traditional blockchain technology, a challenging work direction is to design scalable, computable, and energy-efficient, secure blockchains for IoT applications. The IOTA Foundation has been provided with some examples of works in this direction (Popov, 2018).

The IOTA Foundation (As a distributed ledger technology, IOTA provides a trust layer for any devices connected to the global Internet) was specifically designed for the IoT. It differs from the existing blockchains as it does not use any traditional Blockchain at all. IOTA's main structure is the Tangle, a Directed Acyclic Graph (DAG) (Popov, 2018). The transactions (referred to as sites in Tangle) are stored in a graph format, where the nodes are entities that issue and validate transactions (Popov, 2018). Whenever a new transaction arrives, it is represented by directed edges and must be approved by two previous transactions.

For a node to validate a transaction, it must give Proof of Work, which is successfully executed registers the transaction. This functionality of Tangle allows us to eliminate the need for miners in the network as the node itself acts as a miner now, which further reduces the transaction costs to zero (Popov, 2018). To issue a transaction, users must work to approve other transactions. If a node realizes that a transaction conflicts with the Tangle history, the node will not approve the conflicting transaction, thereby ensuring network security (Popov, 2018). Despite all these, IOTA's Tangle has several advantages, as described below (Popov, 2018):

- Scalability: IOTA addresses this issue by not using a blockchain-based decentralized network instead of opting for their Tangle platform. With IOTA, as the transaction rate increases, scalability also increases, i.e., the more subscribers and transactions the system has, the faster it gets. More importantly, the latency, that is, the time between placing a transaction and validating it, also approaches zero as soon as a specific size is reached.
- Centralization of Control: For a transaction to occur in the Tangle, the previous two transactions must be validated by it. This makes the network faster with increasing use. Thus, IOTA allows each user who has initiated a transaction to act as a miner.
- Quantum Computing: IOTA uses 'exclusively quantum-resistant cryptographic algorithms, making it future-oriented and immune to brute force attacks. Moreover, Tangle holds power to decrease quantum consensus attacks by almost a million times.
- Micro Payments: In traditional blockchain platforms, the concept of mining involves transaction fees (i.e., financial rewards set by the transaction's sender). As a result, even the most minor payment amounts result in high transaction fees. However, in IOTA's Tangle, each site does its PoW to get added to the network, so the concept of transaction fees is completed eliminated.

However, Tangle also has the following disadvantages for which Ethereum, or Bitcoin is preferred over Tangle for commercial use in IoT (Popov, 2018).

REFERENCES

Abduvaliyev, A., Pathan, A. S. K., Zhou, J., Roman, R., & Wong, W. C. (2013). On the vital areas of intrusion detection systems in wireless sensor networks. *IEEE Communications Surveys and Tutorials*, *15*(3), 1223–1237.

Aberer, K., Hauswirth, H., & Salehi, A. (2006). *Middleware Support for the Internet of Things*. Available: www.manfredhauswirth.org/research/papers/WSN2006.pdf

Adat, V., & Gupta, B. B. (2017). A DDoS attack mitigation framework for Internet of things. *2017 International Conference on Communication and Signal Processing (ICCSP)*, 2036–2041.

Ahemd, M. M., Shah, M. A., & Wahid, A. (2017). IoT security: a layered approach for attacks and defenses. *2017 International Conference on Communication Technologies (ComTech)*, 104–110. 10.1109/COMTECH.2017.8065757

Airehrour, D., Gutierrez, J. A., & Ray, S. K. (2019). Sectrust-rpl: A secure trust-aware rpl routing protocol for the Internet of things. *Future Generation Computer Systems, 93*, 860–876.

Al-Turjman, F., & Alturjman, S. (2018). Context-sensitive access in industrial Internet of things (iiot) healthcare applications. *IEEE Transactions on Industrial Informatics, 14*(6), 2736–2744. doi:10.1109/TII.2018.2808190

Alaba, F. A., Othman, M., Hashem, I. A. T., & Alotaibi, F. (2017). Internet of things security: A survey. *Journal of Network and Computer Applications, 88*, 10–28.

Alccer, V., & Cruz-Machado, V. (2019). Scanning the industry 4.0: A literature review on technologies for manufacturing systems, Engineering Science and Technology. *International Journal (Toronto, Ont.), 22*(3), 899–919.

Ali, M. S., Vecchio, M., Pincheira, M., Dolui, K., Antonelli, F., & Rehmani, M. H. (2019). *Applications of blockchains in the Internet of things: A comprehensive survey. IEEE Commun. Surv. Tutorials.*

All, I. F. (2017). *The 5 Worst Examples of IoT Hacking and Vulnerabilities in Recorded History*. Academic Press.

Aman, M. N., Chua, K. C., & Sikdar, B. (2017). A lightweight mutual authentication protocol for IoT systems. *GLOBECOM 2017 - 2017 IEEE Global Communications Conference*, 1–6.

Andoni, M., Robu, V., Flynn, D., Abram, S., Geach, D., Jenkins, D., McCallum, P., & Peacock, A. (2019). Blockchain technology in the energy sector: A systematic review of challenges and opportunities. *Renewable & Sustainable Energy Reviews, 100*, 143–174. doi:10.1016/j.rser.2018.10.014

Andrea, I., Chrysostomou, C., & Hadjichristofi, G. (2015). Internet of things: security vulnerabilities and challenges. *2015 IEEE Symposium on Computers and Communication (ISCC)*, 180–187.

Araujo, J., Mazo, M., Anta, A. Jr, Tabuada, P., & Johansson, K. H. (2014, February). System Architecture, Protocols, and Algorithms for Aperiodic wireless control systems. *IEEE Transactions on Industrial Informatics, 10*(1), 175–184.

Ashibani, Y., & Mahmoud, Q. H. (2017). An efficient and secure scheme for smart home communication using identity-based encryption. *2017 IEEE 36th International Performance Computing and Communications Conference (IPCCC)*, 1–7.

Atlam, H. F., Alenezi, A., Alassafi, M. O., & Wills, G. B. (2018). Blockchain with Internet of things: Benefits, challenges, and future directions. *Int. J. Intell. Syst. Appl., 10*(6), 40–48.

Atlam, H. F., Azad, M. A., Alzahrani, A. G., & Wills, G. (2020). A Review of Blockchain in Internet of Things and AI. *Journal of Big Data and Cognitive Computing*, 1-27.

Azzi, R., Chamoun, R. K., & Sokhn, M. (2019). The power of a blockchain-based supply chain. *Computers & Industrial Engineering, 135*, 582–592.

Boyes, H., Hallaq, B., Cunningham, J., & Watson, T. (2018). The industrial Internet of things (iiot): An analysis framework. *Computers in Industry, 101*, 1–12.

Butun, I., Morgera, S. D., & Sankar, R. (2014). A survey of intrusion detection systems in wireless sensor networks. *IEEE Communications Surveys and Tutorials, 16*(1), 266–282.

Cervantes, C., Poplade, D., Nogueira, M., & Santos, A. (2015). Detection of sinkhole attacks for supporting secure routing on 6lowpan for Internet of things. *2015 IFIP/ IEEE International Symposium on Integrated Network Management (IM)*, 606–611.

Cha, S., Chen, J., Su, C., & Yeh, K. (2018). A blockchain connected gateway for ble-based devices in the Internet of things. *IEEE Access : Practical Innovations, Open Solutions, 6*, 24639–24649.

Chan, M. (2017). *Why Cloud Computing Is the Foundation of the Internet of Things.* Academic Press.

Chaudhary, R., Aujla, G. S., Garg, S., Kumar, N., & Rodrigues, J. J. P. C. (2018). Sdn-enabled multi-attribute-based secure communication for smart grid in riot environment. *IEEE Transactions on Industrial Informatics, 14*(6), 2629–2640.

Chen, G., & Ng, W. S. (2017). An efficient authorization framework for securing industrial Internet of things. *TENCON 2017 - 2017 IEEE Region 10 Conference*, 1219–1224.

Chen, L., Lee, W.-K., Chang, C.-C., Choo, K.-K. R., & Zhang, N. (2019). Blockchain-based searchable encryption for electronic health record sharing. *Future Generation Computer Systems*, *95*, 420–429.

Choi, J., & Kim, Y. (2016). An improved lea block encryption algorithm to prevent side-channel attack in the IoT system. *2016 Asia-Pacific Signal and Information Processing Association Annual Summit and Conference (APSIPA)*, 1–4.

Cirani, S., Ferrari, G., & Veltri, L. (2013). Enforcing security mechanisms in the IP-based internet of things: An algorithmic overview. *Algorithms*, *6*(2), 197–226.

Colema, L. (2006). Frequency of man-made disasters in the 20the century. *Journal of Contingencies and Crisis Management*, *14*(1), 3–11. doi:10.1111/j.1468-5973.2006.00476.x

De, S. J., & Ruj, S. (2017). *Efficient decentralized attribute-based access control for mobile clouds*. IEEE Transactions on Cloud Computing.

Dorri, A., Kanhere, S. S., Jurdak, R., & Gauravaram, P. (2019). *LSB: A Lightweight Scalable Blockchain for IoT Security and Privacy*. http://arxiv.org/ abs/1712.02969

Esfahani, A., Mantas, G., Matischek, R., Saghezchi, F. B., Rodriguez, J., Bicaku, A., Maksuti, S., Tauber, M. G., Schmittner, C., & Bastos, J. (2019). A lightweight authentication mechanism for m2m communications in industrial IoT environment. *IEEE Internet of Things Journal*, *6*(1), 288–296. doi:10.1109/JIOT.2017.2737630

Fernndez-Carams, T. M., & Fraga-Lamas, P. (2018). A review on the use of blockchain for the Internet of things. *IEEE Access : Practical Innovations, Open Solutions*, *6*, 32979–33001.

Ferran, M. A., Derdour, M., Mukherjee, M., Dahab, A., Maglaras, L., & Janicke, H. (2019). *Blockchain technologies for the Internet of things: research issues and challenges*. IEEE Internet Things J.

Forbes. (2019). Blockchain in healthcare: How it Could Make Digital Healthcare Safer and More Innovative. *Forbes*.

Frustaci, M., Pace, P., Aloi, G., & Fortino, G. (2018). *Evaluating critical security issues of the IoT world: present and future challenges*. IEEE Internet Things.

Gai, J., Choo, K., Qiu, K. R., & Zhu, L. (2018). Privacy-preserving content-oriented wireless communication in internet-of-things. *IEEE Internet Things Journal*, *5*(4), 3059–3067.

Gandino, F., Montrucchio, B., & Rebaudengo, M. (2014). *Key Management for Static Wireless Sensor Networks with Node Adding. IEEE Transaction Industrial Informatics.*

Gibbon, J. (2018). *Introduction to Trusted Execution Environment: Arm's Trust zone.* Academic Press.

Glissa, G., Rachedi, A., & Meddeb, A. (2016). A secure routing protocol based on rpl for Internet of things. *IEEE Global Communications Conference (GLOBECOM),* 1–7.

Gomes, T., Salgado, F., Tavares, A., & Cabral, J. (2017). Cute mote, a customizable and trustable end-device for the Internet of things. *IEEE Sensors Journal, 17*(20), 6816–6824. doi:10.1109/JSEN.2017.2743460

Gope, P., & Sikdar, B. (2018). *Lightweight and privacy-preserving two-factor authentication scheme for IoT devices.* IEEE Internet Things.

Granja, J., Silva, R., Monteiro, E., Silva, J. S., & Boavida, F. (2008). Why is IPSec a viable option for wireless sensor networks. *2008 5th IEEE International Conference on Mobile Ad Hoc and Sensor Systems,* 802–807.

Granville, K. (2018). *Facebook and Cambridge Analytica: what You Need to Know as Fallout Widens.* Academic Press.

Griggs, K. N., Osipova, O., Kohlios, C. P., Baccarini, A. N., Howson, E. A., & Hayajneh, T. (2018). Healthcare blockchain system using smart contracts for secure automated remote patient monitoring. *Journal of Medical Systems, 42*(7), 1–7.

Guan, Z., Si, G., Zhang, X., Wu, L., Guizani, N., Du, X., & Ma, Y. (2018). Privacy-preserving and efficient aggregation based on blockchain for power grid communications in smart communities. *IEEE Communications Magazine, 56*(7), 82–88.

Guin, U., Singh, A., Alam, M., Caedo, J., & Skjellum, A. (2018). A secure low-cost edge device authentication scheme for the Internet of things. *31st International Conference on VLSI Design and 17th International Conference on Embedded Systems (VLSID),* 85–90.

Hei, X., Du, X., Wu, J., & Hu, F. (2010). Defending resource depletion attacks on implantable medical devices. *2010 IEEE Global Telecommunications Conference GLOBECOM 2010,* 1–5.

Huang, J., Kong, L., Chen, G., Wu, M., Liu, X., & Zeng, P. (2019b). Towards secure industrial IoT: blockchain system with credit-based consensus mechanism. IEEE Trans. Ind.

Huang, X., Zhang, Y., Li, D., & Han, L. (2019a). An optimal scheduling algorithm for hybrid EV charging scenario using consortium blockchains. *Future Generation Computer Systems*, *91*, 555–562.

Huh, J.-H., & Seo, K. (2019). Blockchain-based mobile fingerprint verification and automatic log-in platform for future computing. *The Journal of Supercomputing*, *75*(6), 3123–3139.

Huh, S.-K., & Kim, J.-H. (2019). The blockchain consensus algorithm for viable management of new and renewable energies. *Sustainability*, *11*(3184), 3184.

IEEE. (2012). *IeEEE Standard for Local and metropolitan networks–Part 15.4: LowRate Wireless Personal Area Networks (LR-WPANs), 2012*. IEEE.

IoT-A. (2013). *Internet of Things–Architecture IoT-A Deliverable D1.5 –Final architectural reference model for the IoT v3.0, 2013*. http://iotforum.org/wpcontent/uploads/2014/09/D1.5-20130715-VERYFINAL.pdf

Islam, S. H., Khan, M. K., & Al-Khouri, A. M. (2015). Anonymous and provably secure certificateless multireceiver encryption without bilinear pairing. *Security and Communication Networks*, *8*(13), 2214–2231.

Kang, J., Xiong, Z., Niyato, D., Ye, D., Kim, D. I., & Zhao, J. (2019a). Toward secure blockchain-enabled Internet of vehicles: Optimizing consensus management using reputation and contract theory. *IEEE Transactions on Vehicular Technology*, *68*(3), 2906–2920.

Kang, J., Yu, R., Huang, X., Maharjan, S., Zhang, Y., & Hossain, E. (2017). Enabling localized peer-to-peer electricity trading among plug-in hybrid electric vehicles using consortium blockchains. *IEEE Transactions on Industrial Informatics*, *13*(6), 3154–3164.

Kang, J., Yu, R., Huang, X., Wu, M., Maharjan, S., Xie, S., & Zhang, Y. (2019b). Blockchain for secure and efficient data sharing in vehicular edge computing and networks. *IEEE Internet of Things Journal*, *6*(3), 4660–4670.

Karati, A., Islam, S. H., & Karuppiah, M. (2018). Provably secure and lightweight certificateless signature scheme for iiot environments. *IEEE Transactions on Industrial Informatics*, *14*(8), 3701–3711.

Khan, F. I., & Hameed, S. (2019). Understanding security requirements and challenges in the Internet of things (iots): a review. *Journal of Computer Networks and Communications*.

Khan, M. A., & Salah, K. (2018). IoT security: Review, blockchain solutions, and open challenges. *Future Generation Computer Systems, 82*, 395–411.

Kim, J.-H., & Huh, S.-K. (1973). A study on the improvement of smart grid security performance and blockchain smart grid perspective. *Energies, 11*.

Kim, S.-K., Kim, U.-M., & Huh, H. J. (2017). A study on improvement of blockchain application to overcome vulnerability of IoT multiplatform security. *Energies, 12*(402).

Konigsmark, S. T. C., Chen, D., & Wong, M. D. F. (2016). Information dispersion for trojan defense through high-level synthesis. *ACM/EDAC/IEEE Design Automation Conference (DAC)*, 1–6.

Kouicem, D. E., Bouabdallah, A., & Lakhlef, H. (2018). Internet of things security: A top-down survey. *Computer Networks, 141*, 199–221.

Li, C., & Palanisamy, B. (2019). Privacy in Internet of things: From principles to technologies. *IEEE Internet of Things Journal, 6*(1), 488–505. doi:10.1109/JIOT.2018.2864168

Li, R., Song, T., Mei, B., Li, H., Cheng, X., & Sun, L. (2019). Blockchain for large-scale Internet of things data storage and protection. *IEEE Transactions on Services Computing, 12*(5), 762–771.

Li, X., Niu, J., Bhuiyan, M. Z. A., Wu, F., Karuppiah, M., & Kumari, S. (2018a). A robust ECC-based provable secure authentication protocol with privacy-preserving for industrial Internet of things. *IEEE Transactions on Industrial Informatics, 14*(8), 3599–3609.

Li, Z., Kang, J., Yu, R., Ye, D., Deng, Q., & Zhang, Y. (2018b). Consortium blockchain for secure energy trading in industrial Internet of things. *IEEE Transactions on Industrial Informatics, 14*(8), 3690–3700.

Lin, C., He, D., Huang, X., Choo, K.-K. R., & Vasilakos, A. V. (2018). Basin: A blockchain-based secure mutual authentication with fine-grained access control system for industry 4.0. *Journal of Network and Computer Applications, 116*, 42–52.

Ling, Z., Liu, K., Xu, Y., Jin, Y., & Fu, X. (2017). An end-to-end view of IoT security and privacy. *IEEE Global Communications Conference*, 1–7.

Liu, C., Cronin, P., & Yang, C. (2016). A mutual auditing framework to protect iot against hardware trojans. *2016 21st Asia and South Pacific Design Automation Conference (ASP-DAC)*, 69–74.

Liu, C. H., Lin, Q., & Wen, S. (2019b). *Blockchain-enabled data collection and sharing for industrial IoT with deep reinforcement learning.* IEEE Transaction Industrial Informatics.

Liu, J., Zhang, C., & Fang, Y. (2018). Epic: A differential privacy framework to defend smart homes against internet traffic analysis. *IEEE Internet of Things Journal, 5*(2), 1206–1217.

Liu, Y., Guo, W., Fan, C., Chang, L., & Cheng, C. (2019a). A practical privacy-preserving data aggregation (3pda) scheme for smart grid. *IEEE Transactions on Industrial Informatics, 15*(3), 1767–1774.

Longo, F., Nicoletti, L., Padovano, A., d'Atri, G., & Forte, M. (2019). Blockchain-enabled supply chain: An experimental study. *Computers & Industrial Engineering, 136*, 57–69.

Lu, Y., & Li, J. (2016). A pairing-free certificate-based proxy re-encryption scheme for secure data sharing in public clouds. *Future Generation Computer Systems, 62*, 140–147.

Lukac, D. (2015). The fourth ICT-based industrial revolution "Industry 4.0": HMI and the case of CAE/CAD innovation with EPLAN. *23rd Telecommunications Forum Telfor (TELFOR)*, 835-838.

Machado, C., & Frhlich, A. A. M. (2018). IoT data integrity verification for cyber-physical systems using blockchain. *2018 IEEE 21st International Symposium on Real-Time Distributed Computing (ISORC)*, 83–90.

Makhdoom, I., Abolhasan, M., Abbas, H., & Ni, W. (2019). Blockchain's adoption in iot: The challenges, and a way forward. *Journal of Network and Computer Applications, 125*, 251–279.

Manditereza, K. (2017). *4 Key Differences between Scada and Industrial IoT.* Academic Press.

Manzoor, A., Liyanage, M., Braeken, A., Kanhere, S. S., & Ylianttila, M. (2019). Blockchain-Based Proxy Re-encryption Scheme for Secure IoT Data Sharing. *Clinical Orthopaedics and Related Research.*

Minoli, D., & Occhiogross, B. (2018). Blockchain mechanism for IoT security. *International Journal of Internet of Things*, 1-13.

Mitchell, R., & Chen, I. R. (2014). Review: A survey of intrusion detection in wireless network applications. *Computer Communications, 42*, 1–23.

Mondal, S., Wijewardena, K. P., Karuppuswami, S., Kriti, N., Kumar, D., & Chahal, P. (2019). Blockchain inspired RFID-based information architecture for food supply chain. *IEEE Internet of Things Journal*, 6(3), 5803–5813.

Mosenia, A., & Jha, N. K. (2017). A comprehensive study of security of internet-of-things. *IEEE Transactions on Emerging Topics in Computing*, 5(4), 586–602. doi:10.1109/TETC.2016.2606384

Naeem, H., Guo, B., & Naeem, M. R. (2018). A lightweight malware static visual analysis for IoT infrastructure. *International Conference on Artificial Intelligence and Big Data (ICAIBD)*, 240–244.

ObserveIT. (2018). *5 Examples of Insider Threat-Caused Breaches that Illustrate the Scope of the Problem*. Author.

Okorie, O., Turner, C., Charnley, F., Moreno, M., & Tiwari, A. (2017). A review of data-driven approaches for circular economy in manufacturing. *Proceedings of the 18th European Roundtable for Sustainable Consumption and Production*.

Oleshchuk, V. (2009). Internet of things and privacy preserving technologies. *2009 1st International Conference on Wireless Communication, Vehicular Technology, Information Theory and Aerospace Electronic Systems Technology*, 336–340.

Omar, A. A., Bhuiyan, M. Z. A., Basu, A., Kiyomoto, S., & Rahman, M. S. (2019). Privacy-friendly platform for healthcare data in cloud-based on blockchain environment. *Future Generation Computer Systems*, 95, 511–521.

OWASP. (2016). *Top IoT Vulnerabilities, 2016*. https://www.owasp.org/index.php/Top_IoT_Vulnerabilities

Oztemel, E., & Gusev, S. (2018). Literature review of industry 4.0 and related technologies. *Journal of Intelligent Manufacturing*.

Pal, K. (2017). Building High Quality Big Data-Based Applications in Supply Chains. IGI Global.

Pal, K. (2018). *Ontology-Based Web Service Architecture for Retail Supply Chain Management*. The 9th International Conference on Ambient Systems, Networks and Technologies, Porto, Portugal.

Pal, K. (2019). Algorithmic Solutions for RFID Tag Anti-Collision Problem in Supply Chain Management. *Procedia Computer Science*, 151, 929–934.

Pal, K. (2020). Information sharing for manufacturing supply chain management based on blockchain technology. In I. Williams (Ed.), *Cross-Industry Use of Blockchain Technology and Opportunities for the Future* (pp. 1–17). IGI Global.

Pal, K. (2021). Applications of Secured Blockchain Technology in Manufacturing Industry. In *Blockchain and AI Technology in the Industrial Internet of Things*. IGI Global Publication.

Pal, K., & Yasar, A. (2020). Internet of Things and blockchain technology in apparel manufacturing supply chain data management. *Procedia Computer Science, 170*, 450–457.

Park, N., & Kang, N. (2015). Mutual authentication scheme in secure Internet of things technology for comfortable lifestyle. *Sensors (Basel), 16*(1), 20.

Porambage, P., Schmitt, C., Kumar, P., Gurtov, A., & Ylianttila, M. (2014). Pauthkey: A pervasive authentication protocol and key establishment scheme for wireless sensor networks in distributed IoT applications. *International Journal of Distributed Sensor Networks, 10*(7), 357430.

Pu, C., & Hajjar, S. (2018). Mitigating forwarding misbehaviors in rpl-based low power and lossy networks. *2018 15th IEEE Annual Consumer Communications Networking Conference (CCNC)*, 1–6.

Rahulamathavan, Y., Phan, R. C., Rajarajan, M., Misra, S., & Kondoz, A. (2017). Privacy-preserving blockchain-based IoT ecosystem using attribute-based encryption. *IEEE International Conference on Advanced Networks and Telecommunications Systems (ANTS)*, 1–6.

Rambus. (n.d.). *Industrial IoT: Threats and countermeasures*. https://www.rambus.com/iot/ industrial-IoT/

Reyna, A., Martn, C., Chen, J., Soler, E., & Daz, M. (2018). On blockchain and its integration with iot. challenges and opportunities. *Future Generation Computer Systems, 88*, 173–190.

Roblek, V., Mesko, M., & Krapez, A. (2016). A complex view of Industry 4.0. *SAGE Open, 6*(2).

Roman, R., Lopez, J., & Mambo, M. (2016). Mobile edge computing, Fog et al.: A survey and analysis of security threats and challenges. *Future Gener. Comput. Syst.*

Sfar, A. R., Natalizio, E., Challal, Y., & Chtourou, Z. (2018). A roadmap for security challenges in the Internet of things. *Digital Communications and Networks., 4*(2), 118–137.

Shen, M., Tang, X., Zhu, L., Du, X., & Guizani, M. (2019). Privacy-preserving support vector machine training over blockchain-based encrypted IoT data in smart cities. *IEEE Internet of Things Journal,* 6(5), 7702–7712.

Shrestha, R., Bajracharya, R., Shrestha, A. P., & Nam, S. Y. (2019). *A new type of blockchain for secure message exchange in vanet.* Digital Communications and Networks.

Shukla, P. (2017). Ml-ids: A machine learning approach to detect wormhole attacks in the Internet of things. *Intelligent Systems Conference (IntelliSys),* 234–240.

Sicari, S., Rizzardi, A., Grieco, L., & Coen-Porisini, A. (2015). Security, privacy and trust in internet of things: The road ahead. *Computer Networks, 76*(Suppl. C), 146–164.

Sicari, S., Rizzardi, A., Miorandi, D., & Coen-Porisini, A. (2018). Reatoreacting to denial-of-service attacks in the Internet of things. *Computer Networks, 137,* 37–48.

Singh, M., Rajan, M. A., Shivraj, V. L., & Balamuralidhar, P. (2015). Secure MQTT for the Internet of things (IoT). *5th International Conference on Communication Systems and Network Technologies,* 746–751.

Song, T., Li, R., Mei, B., Yu, J., Xing, X., & Cheng, X. (2017). A privacy-preserving communication protocol for IoT applications in smart homes. *IEEE Internet of Things Journal, 4*(6), 1844–1852.

SOPHOS. (2015). *49 Busted in Europe for Man-In-The-Middle Bank Attacks.* https://nakedsecurity.sophos.com/2015/06/11/49-busted-in-europe-for-man-in-themiddle-bank-attacks/

Sreamr. (2017). *Streamr White Paper v2.0.* https://s3.amazonaws.com/streamr-public/streamr-datacoin-whitepaper-2017-07-25-v1_0.pdf

Srinivas, J., Das, A. K., Wazid, M., & Kumar, N. (2018). Anonymous lightweight chaotic map-based authenticated key agreement protocol for industrial internet of things. IEEE Trans. Dependable Secure Comput.

Su, J., Vasconcellos, V. D., Prasad, S., Daniele, S., Feng, Y., & Sakurai, K. (2018). Lightweight classification of IoT malware based on image recognition. *IEEE 42nd Annual Computer Software and Applications Conference (COMPSAC), 2,* 664–669.

Varga, P., Plosz, S., Soos, G., & Hegedus, C. (2017). Security Threats and Issues in Automation IoT. *2017 IEEE 13th International Workshop on Factory Communication Systems (WFCS),* 1–6.

Vasconcellos, V. D., Prasad, S., Daniele, S., Feng, Y., & Sakurai, K. (2018). Lightweight classification of IoT malware based on image recognition. *IEEE 42nd Annual Computer Software and Applications Conference (COMPSAC)*, *2*, 664–669.

Vechain Team. (2018). *Vechain White Paper.* https://cdn.vechain.com/vechain_ico_ideas_of_ development_en.pdf

Vogel-Heuser, B. & Hess, D. (2016). Guest editorial Industry 4.0 -prerequisites and vision. *IEEE Transactions, Autom. Sci. Eng.*, *13*(2).

Waltonchain. (2021). *Waltonchain white paper v2.0.* https://www.waltonchain.org/en/ Waltonchain_White_Paper_2.0_EN.pdf

Wan, J., Li, J., Imran, M., Li, D., & e-Amin, F. (2019). A blockchain-based solution for enhancing security and privacy in smart factory. *IEEE Transaction.*

Wan, J., Tang, S., Shu, Z., Li, D., Wang, S., Imran, M., & Vasilakos, A. V. (2016). Software-defined industrial Internet of things in the context of industry 4.0. *IEEE Sensors Journal*, *16*(20), 7373–7380.

Wang, Q., Zhu, X., Ni, Y., Gu, L., & Zhu, H. (2019b). *Blockchain for the IoT and industrial IoT: a review.* Internet Things.

Wang, X., Zha, X., Ni, W., Liu, R. P., Guo, Y. J., Niu, X., & Zheng, K. (2019a). Survey on blockchain for Internet of things. *Computer Communications*, *136*, 10–29.

Wang, Y., Uehara, T., & Sasaki, R. (2015). Fog computing: Issues and challenges in security and forensics. *2015 IEEE 39th Annual Computer Software and Applications Conference*, *3*, 53–59.

Wurm, J., Hoang, K., Arias, O., Sadeghi, A., & Jin, Y. (2016). Security analysis on consumer and industrial IoT devices. *21st Asia and South Pacific Design Automation Conference (ASP-DAC)*, 519–524.

Xiong, Z., Zhang, Y., Niyato, D., Wang, P., & Han, Z. (2018). When mobile blockchain meets edge computing. *IEEE Communications Magazine*, *56*(8), 33–39.

Xu, L. D., He, W., & Li, S. (2014). Internet of things in industries: A survey. *IEEE Transactions on Industrial Informatics*, *10*(4), 2233–2243.

Xu, L. D., Xu, E. L., & Li, L. (2018). Industry 4.0: State of the art and future trends. *International Journal of Production Research*, *56*(8), 2941–2962. doi:10.1080/00 207543.2018.1444806

Xu, Y., Ren, J., Wang, G., Zhang, C., Yang, J., & Zhang, Y. (2019). *A blockchain-based non-repudiation network computing service scheme for industrial IoT. IEEE Transaction Industrial Informatics.*

Yan, Q., Huang, W., Luo, X., Gong, Q., & Yu, F. R. (2018). A multi-level DDoS mitigation framework for the industrial Internet of things. *IEEE Communications Magazine, 56*(2), 30–36.

Yang, W., Wang, S., Huang, X., & Mu, Y. (2019a). On the Security of an Efficient and Robust Certificateless Signature Scheme for IIoT Environments. *IEEE Access : Practical Innovations, Open Solutions, 7,* 91074–91079.

Yang, Y., Wu, L., Yin, G., Li, L., & Zhao, H. (2017). A survey on security and privacy issues in internet-of-things. *IEEE Internet of Things Journal, 4*(5), 1250–1258.

Yang, Z., Yang, K., Lei, L., Zheng, K., & Leung, V. C. M. (2019b). Blockchain-based decentralized trust management in vehicular networks. *IEEE Internet of Things Journal, 6*(2), 1495–1505.

Yao, X., Kong, H., Liu, H., Qiu, T., & Ning, H. (2019). An attribute credential-based public-key scheme for fog computing in digital manufacturing. *IEEE Trans. Ind. Inf.*

Yi, S., Qin, Z., & Li, Q. (2015). Security and privacy issues of fog computing: A survey. *Wireless Algorithms, Systems, and Applications the 10th International Conference on,* 1–10.

Yin, D., Zhang, L., & Yang, K. (2018). A DDoS attack detection and mitigation with software-defined Internet of things framework. *IEEE Access : Practical Innovations, Open Solutions, 6,* 24694–24705.

Zhang, H., Wang, J., & Ding, Y. (2019b). Blockchain-based decentralized and secure keyless signature scheme for smart grid. *Energy, 180,* 955–967. doi:10.1016/j.energy.2019.05.127

Zhang, N., Mi, X., Feng, X., Wang, X., Tian, Y., & Qian, F. (2018). *Understanding and Mitigating the Security Risks of Voice-Controlled Third-Party Skills on Amazon Alexa and Google Home.* Academic Press.

Zhang, Y., Deng, R., Zheng, D., Li, J., Wu, P., & Cao, J. (2019a). *Efficient and Robust Certificateless Signature for Data Crowdsensing in Cloud-Assisted Industrial IoT.* IEEE Transaction Industry.

Zhang, Z. K., Cho, M. C. Y., Wang, C. W., Hsu, C. W., Chen, C. K., & Shieh, S. (2014). IoT security: Ongoing challenges and research opportunities. *Computer Applications, 2014,* 230–234.

Zheng, D., Wu, A., Zhang, Y., & Zhao, Q. (2018). Efficient and privacy-preserving medical data sharing in the Internet of things with limited computing power. *IEEE Access : Practical Innovations, Open Solutions*, 6, 28019–28027.

Zhou, J., Cao, Z., Dong, X., & Vasilakos, A. V. (2017). Security and privacy for cloud-based IoT: Challenges. *IEEE Communications Magazine*, *55*(1), 26–33.

Zhou, R., Zhang, X., Du, X., Wang, X., Yang, G., & Guizani, M. (2018). File-centric multi-key aggregate keyword searchable encryption for industrial Internet of things. *IEEE Transactions on Industrial Informatics*, *14*(8), 3648–3658.

Ziegeldorf, J. H., Morchon, O. G., & Wehrle, K. (2014). *Privacy in the Internet of Things: Threats and Challenges*. https://arxiv.org/abs/1505.07683

KEY TERMS AND DEFINITIONS

Block: A block is a data structure used to communicate incremental changes to the local state of a node. It consists of a list of transactions, a reference to a previous block and a nonce.

Blockchain: In simple, a blockchain is just a data structure that can be shared by different users using computing data communication network (e.g., peer-to-peer or P2P). Blockchain is a distributed data structure comprising a chain of blocks. It can act as a global ledger that maintains records of all transactions on a blockchain network. The transactions are time-stamped and bundled into blocks where each block is identified by its *cryptographic hash*.

Cryptography: Blockchain's transactions achieve validity, trust, and finality based on cryptographic proofs and underlying mathematical computations between various trading partners.

Decentralized Computing Infrastructure: These computing infrastructures feature computing nodes that can make independent processing and computational decisions irrespective of what other peer computing nodes may decide.

Immutability: This term refers to the fact that blockchain transactions cannot be deleted or altered.

Internet of Things (IoT): The internet of things (IoT), also called the internet of everything or the, is now a technology paradigm envisioned as a global network of machines and devices capable of interacting with each other. The IoT is recognized as one of the most important areas of future technology and is gaining vast attention from a wide range of industries.

Provenance: In a blockchain ledger, provenance is a way to trace the origin of every transaction such that there is no dispute about the origin and sequence of the transactions in the ledger.

Supply Chain Management: A supply chain consists of a network of *key business processes* and facilities, involving end-users and suppliers that provide products, services, and information.

Warehouse: A warehouse can also be called a storage area, and it is a commercial building where raw materials or goods are stored by suppliers, exporters, manufacturers, or wholesalers, they are constructed and equipped with tools according to special standards depending on the purpose of their use.

Compilation of References

ABB. (2020). *System 800xA Extended Automation.* https://new.abb.com/control-systems/system-800xa

Abbas, N., Andersson, J., & Löwe, W. (2010). Autonomic Software Product Lines (ASPL). *ACM International Conference Proceeding Series*, 324–331.

Abduvaliyev, A., Pathan, A. S. K., Zhou, J., Roman, R., & Wong, W. C. (2013). On the vital areas of intrusion detection systems in wireless sensor networks. *IEEE Communications Surveys and Tutorials*, *15*(3), 1223–1237.

Aberer, K., Hauswirth, H., & Salehi, A. (2006). *Middleware Support for the Internet of Things.* Available: www.manfredhauswirth.org/research/papers/WSN2006.pdf

Abuadlla, Y., Kvascev, G., Gajin, S., & Jovanovic, Z. (2014). Flow-based anomaly intrusion detection system using two neural network stages. *Computer Science and Information Systems*, *11*(2), 601–622.

Acceleo. (2020). *Obeo. Acceleo Generator.* Retrieved March 28, 2020 from http://www.eclipse.org/Acceleo/

Acerbis, R., Bongio, A., Brambilla, M., & Butti, S. (2015). *Model-Driven Development Based on OMG's IFML with WebRatio Web and Mobile Platform. In Engineering the Web in the Big Data Era* (Vol. 9114). Lecture Notes in Computer Science. Springer-Verlag.

Achtaich, A., Roudies, O., Souissi, N., Salinesi, C., & Mazo, R. (2019). Evaluation of the State-Constraint Transition Modeling Language: A Goal Question Metric Approach. *Software Product Line Conference Proceedings* - Volume B.

Adat, V., & Gupta, B. B. (2017). A DDoS attack mitigation framework for Internet of things. *2017 International Conference on Communication and Signal Processing (ICCSP)*, 2036–2041.

ADM. (2020). *Architecture-driven modernization task force.* Retrieved March 28, 2020 from http://www.adm.org

Afonso, C. (2017). *Competências de marketing digital: O que procura o mercado?* http://carolina-afonso.net/competencias-de-marketing-digital-o-que-procura-o-mercado-human-resources/

Ahemd, M. M., Shah, M. A., & Wahid, A. (2017). IoT security: a layered approach for attacks and defenses. *2017 International Conference on Communication Technologies (ComTech)*, 104–110. 10.1109/COMTECH.2017.8065757

Airehrour, D., Gutierrez, J. A., & Ray, S. K. (2019). Sectrust-rpl: A secure trust-aware rpl routing protocol for the Internet of things. *Future Generation Computer Systems*, *93*, 860–876.

Al Hinai, S., & Singh, A. V. (2018). Internet of things: Architecture, security challenges and solutions. In *2017 International Conference on Infocom Technologies and Unmanned Systems: Trends and Future Directions, ICTUS 2017* (Vol. 2018–January, pp. 1–4). Institute of Electrical and Electronics Engineers Inc.

Al Omar, A., Rahman, M. S., Basu, A., & Kiyomoto, S. (2017). Medibchain: A blockchain based privacy preserving platform for healthcare data. In *International conference on security, privacy and anonymity in computation, communication and storage* (pp. 534-543). Guangzhou, China: Springer. 10.1007/978-3-319-72395-2_49

Alaba, F. A., Othman, M., Hashem, I. A. T., & Alotaibi, F. (2017). Internet of things security: A survey. *Journal of Network and Computer Applications*, *88*, 10–28.

Alarcão, M., & Silva, S. (2013). *3.0: A evolução do paradigma do marketing.* https://www.hipersuper.pt/2013/12/18/3-0-a-evolucao-do-paradigma-do-marketing-por-susana-costa-e-silva-catolica-porto/

Alccer, V., & Cruz-Machado, V. (2019). Scanning the industry 4.0: A literature review on technologies for manufacturing systems, Engineering Science and Technology. *International Journal (Toronto, Ont.)*, *22*(3), 899–919.

Aleisa, N., & Renaud, K. (2017). Privacy of the Internet of Things: A Systematic Literature Review. *Proceedings of the 50th Hawaii International Conference on System Sciences*. 10.24251/HICSS.2017.717

Alexopoulos, N., Vasilomanolakis, E., Roux, S. L., Rowe, S., & Mühlhäuser, M. (2020). TRIDEnT: towards a decentralized threat indicator marketplace. In *35th Annual ACM Symposium on Applied Computing* (pp. 332–341). Brno Czech Republic: ACM. 10.1145/3341105.3374020

Al-Fuqaha, A., Guizani, M., Mohammadi, M., Aledhari, M., & Ayyash, M. (2015). Internet of Things: A survey on enabling technologies, protocols, and applications. *IEEE Communications Surveys and Tutorials*, *17*(4), 2347–2376. doi:10.1109/COMST. 2015.2444095

Ali, M. S., Vecchio, M., Pincheira, M., Dolui, K., Antonelli, F., & Rehmani, M. H. (2019). *Applications of blockchains in the Internet of things: A comprehensive survey. IEEE Commun. Surv. Tutorials.*

All, I. F. (2017). *The 5 Worst Examples of IoT Hacking and Vulnerabilities in Recorded History.* Academic Press.

Al-Sarawi, S., Anbar, M., Alieyan, K., & Alzubaidi, M. (2017). Internet of Things (IoT) communication protocols: Review. In *2017 8th International Conference on Information Technology (ICIT)* (pp. 685-690). doi: 10.1109/ICITECH.2017.8079928

Alshahrani, M., Traore, I., & Woungang, I. (2019). Design and Implementation of a Lightweight Authentication Framework for the Internet of Things (IoT). In *Sixth International Conference on Internet of Things: Systems, Management and Security (IOTSMS)* (pp. 185-194). Granada, Spain: IEEE. 10.1109/IOTSMS48152.2019.8939190

Al-Turjman, F., & Alturjman, S. (2018). Context-sensitive access in industrial Internet of things (iiot) healthcare applications. *IEEE Transactions on Industrial Informatics*, *14*(6), 2736–2744. doi:10.1109/TII.2018.2808190

Aman, M. N., Chua, K. C., & Sikdar, B. (2017). A lightweight mutual authentication protocol for IoT systems. *GLOBECOM 2017 - 2017 IEEE Global Communications Conference*, 1–6.

Ambika, N. (2019). Energy-Perceptive Authentication in Virtual Private Networks Using GPS Data. In Security, Privacy and Trust in the IoT Environment (pp. 25-38). Springer.

Ambika, N. (2020). Methodical IoT-Based Information System in Healthcare. In c. Chakraborthy (Ed.), Smart Medical Data Sensing and IoT Systems Design in Healthcare (pp. 155-177). Bangalore, India: IGI Global.

Ambika, N. (2019). Energy-Perceptive Authentication in Virtual Private Networks Using GPS Data. In *Security, Privacy and Trust in the IoT Environment* (pp. 25–38). Springer. doi:10.1007/978-3-030-18075-1_2

Ambika, N. (2020). Diffie-Hellman Algorithm Pedestal to Authenticate Nodes in Wireless Sensor Network. In B. K. Bhargava, M. Paprzycki, N. C. Kaushal, P. K. Singh, & W. C. Hong (Eds.), *Handbook of Wireless Sensor Networks: Issues and Challenges in Current Scenario's* (Vol. 1132, pp. 348–363). Springer Nature. doi:10.1007/978-3-030-40305-8_17

Ambika, N. (2020). Encryption of Data in Cloud-Based Industrial IoT Devices. In S. Pal & V. G. Díaz (Eds.), *IoT: Security and Privacy Paradigm* (pp. 111–129). CRC Press, Taylor & Francis Group.

Améndola, F., & Favre, L. (2013). Adapting CRM Systems for Mobile Platforms: An MDA Perspective. *International Journal of Computer & Information Science*, *14*(1), 31–40. doi:10.1109/SNPD.2013.25

Andoni, M., Robu, V., Flynn, D., Abram, S., Geach, D., Jenkins, D., McCallum, P., & Peacock, A. (2019). Blockchain technology in the energy sector: A systematic review of challenges and opportunities. *Renewable & Sustainable Energy Reviews*, *100*, 143–174. doi:10.1016/j.rser.2018.10.014

Andrea, I., Chrysostomou, C., & Hadjichristofi, G. (2015). Internet of things: security vulnerabilities and challenges. *2015 IEEE Symposium on Computers and Communication (ISCC)*, 180–187.

Antao, L., Pinto, R., Reis, J. P., & Gonçalves, G. (2018). ̃ Requirements for testing and validating the industrial Internet of Things. In *2018 IEEE International Conference on Software Testing, Verification and Validation Workshops (ICSTW)* (p. 110-115). doi: 10.1109/ICSTW.2018.00036

Antonino, P. O., Morgenstern, A., Kallweit, B., Becker, M., & Kuhn, T. (2018). Straightforward Specification of Adaptation-Architecture-Significant Requirements of IoT-enabled Cyber-Physical Systems. In *Proceedings - 2018 IEEE 15th International Conference on Software Architecture Companion, ICSA-C 2018*, 19–26. IEEE. 10.1109/ICSA-C.2018.00012

Araujo, J., Mazo, M., Anta, A. Jr, Tabuada, P., & Johansson, K. H. (2014, February). System Architecture, Protocols, and Algorithms for Aperiodic wireless control systems. *IEEE Transactions on Industrial Informatics*, *10*(1), 175–184.

Ari, A.A., Ngangmo, O.K., Titouna, C., Thiare, O., Mohamadou, A., & Gueroui, A.M. (2019). Enabling privacy and security in Cloud of Things: Architecture, applications, security & privacy challenges. *Applied Computing and Informatics*.

Arrington, B., Barnett, L., Rufus, R., & Esterline, A. (2016). Behavioral modeling intrusion detection system (bmids) using internet of things (iot) behavior-based anomaly detection via immunity-inspired algorithms. In *25th International Conference on Computer Communication and Networks (ICCCN)* (pp. 1-6). Waikoloa, HI: IEEE. 10.1109/ICCCN.2016.7568495

Ashibani, Y., & Mahmoud, Q. H. (2017). An efficient and secure scheme for smart home communication using identity-based encryption. *2017 IEEE 36th International Performance Computing and Communications Conference (IPCCC)*, 1–7.

ASM. (2017). *ASM*. http://www.asmconsortium.net

ASTM. (2011). *Abstract Syntax Tree Metamodel*, version 1.0, OMG Document Number: formal/2011-01-05. Retrieved March 28, 2020 from https://www.omg.org/spec/ASTM

ATL. (2020). *Atlas Transformation Language Documentation*. Retrieved March 28, 2020 from http://www.eclipse.org/atl/documentation/

Atlam, H. F., & Wills, G. B. (2019). Technical aspects of blockchain and IoT. In Role of Blockchain Technology in IoT Applications (Vol. 115). doi:10.1016/bs.adcom.2018.10.006

Atlam, H. F., Azad, M. A., Alzahrani, A. G., & Wills, G. (2020). A Review of Blockchain in Internet of Things and AI. *Journal of Big Data and Cognitive Computing*, 1-27.

Atlam, H. F., Alenezi, A., Alassafi, M. O., & Wills, G. B. (2018). Blockchain with Internet of things: Benefits, challenges, and future directions. *Int. J. Intell. Syst. Appl.*, *10*(6), 40–48.

Atzori, L., Iera, A., & Morabito, G. (2010). 10). The Internet of Things: A survey. *Computer Networks*, 2787–2805. doi:10.1016/j.comnet.2010.05.010

Atzori, L., Iera, A., & Morabito, G. (2017). Understanding the Internet of Things: Definition, potentials, and societal role of a fast evolving paradigm. *Ad Hoc Networks*, *56*, 122–140. doi:10.1016/j.adhoc.2016.12.004

Azzi, R., Chamoun, R. K., & Sokhn, M. (2019). The power of a blockchain-based supply chain. *Computers & Industrial Engineering, 135*, 582–592.

Babu, S. S., & Balasaubadra, K. (2018). Chronic Privacy Protection from Source to Sink in Sensor Network Routing. *International Journal of Applied Engineering Research, 13*(5), 2798-2808.

Baccelli, E., Gundogan, C., Hahm, O., Kietzmann, P., Lenders, M. S., Petersen, H., Schleiser, K., Schmidt, T. C., & Wahlisch, M. (2018). RIOT: An Open Source Operating System for Low-End Embedded Devices in the IoT. *IEEE Internet of Things Journal, 5*(6), 4428–4440. doi:10.1109/JIOT.2018.2815038

Balaji, B. S., Shivakumara, M. C., Sunil, Y. S., Yamuna, A. S., & Shruthi, M. (2018). Smart Phone Operated Multipurpose Agricultural Robot. *International Journal of Engineering Research & Technology (Ahmedabad), 7*(5), 478–481.

Balandina, E., Balandin, S., Koucheryavy, Y., & Mouromtsev, D. (2015). IoT use cases in healthcare and tourism. *IEEE 17th Conference on Business Informatics, 2*, 37-44.

Banerjee, M., Lee, J., & Choo, K. K. (2018). A blockchain future for internet of things security: A position paper. *Digital Communications and Networks, 4*(3), 149–160. doi:10.1016/j.dcan.2017.10.006

Baouya, A., Chehida, S., Bensalem, S., & Bozga, M. (2020). Fog computing and blockchain for massive IoT deployment. In *2020 9th Mediterranean Conference on Embedded Computing (MECO)* (p. 14). doi: 10.1109/MECO49872.2020.9134098

Basha, S., & S. A. K., J. (2016, 03). An intelligent door system using raspberry pi and amazon web services IoT. *International Journal of Engineering Trends and Technology, 33*, 84-89. doi:10.14445/22315381/IJETT-V33P217

Basu, S., Karuppiah, M., Selvakumar, K., Li, K. C., Islam, S. K. H., Hassan, M. M., & Bhuiyan, M. Z. A. (2018). An intelligent/cognitive model of task scheduling for IoT applications in cloud computing environment. *Future Generation Computer Systems, 88*(June), 254–261. doi:10.1016/j.future.2018.05.056

Behl, A., & Behl, K. (2012). An Analysis of Cloud Computing Security Issues. *Information and Communication Technologies (WICT), 2012 World Congress on,* 109-114. 10.1109/WICT.2012.6409059

Bertino, E. (2016). Data Security and Privacy in the IoT. *Proc. 19th International Conference on Extending Database Technology (EDBT)*.

Bezerra, V. H., da Costa, V. G. T., Martins, R. A., Junior, S. B., Miani, R. S., & Zarpelao, B. B. (2018). Providing IoT host-based datasets for intrusion detection research. In Anais do XVIII Simpósio Brasileiro em Segurança da Informação e de Sistemas Computacionais (pp. 15–28). Academic Press.

Bianco, A., Birke, R., Giraudo, L., & Palacin, M. (2010). Openflow switching: Data plane performance. In *International Conference on Communications* (pp. 1-5). Cape Town, South Africa: IEEE.

Boehm, B. W. (1984). Verifying and Validating Software Requirements and Design Specifications. *IEEE Software*, *1*(1), 75–88. doi:10.1109/MS.1984.233702

Borgohain, T., Kumar, U., & Sanyal, S. (2015). Survey of Security and Privacy Issues of Internet of Things. *Int. J. Advanced Networking and Applications*, *6*(4), 2372–2378.

Bostani, H., & Sheikhan, M. (2017). Hybrid of anomaly-based and specification-based IDS for Internet of Things using Unsupervised OPF based on Map-Reduce Approach. *Computer Communications*, *98*, 52–71.

Botta, A., Donato, W. D., Persico, V., & Pescape, A. (2016). Integration of Cloud computing and Internet of Things: A survey. In *Future Generation Computer Systems*. Elsevier.

Boussard, M., Papillon, S., Peloso, P., Signorini, M., & Waisbard, E. (2019). STewARD: SDN and blockchain-based Trust evaluation for Automated Risk management on IoT Devices. In *INFOCOM 2019-IEEE Conference on Computer Communications Workshops (INFOCOM WKSHPS)* (pp. 841-846). Paris, France: IEEE.

Bowen, J. P., & Hinchey, M. G. (1999). *High-Integrity System Specification and Design. High-Integrity System Specification and Design.* Springer London. doi:10.1007/978-1-4471-3431-2

Boyes, H., Hallaq, B., Cunningham, J., & Watson, T. (2018). The industrial Internet of things (iiot): An analysis framework. *Computers in Industry*, *101*, 1–12.

Brambilla, M., Cabot, J., & Wimmer, M. (2017). Model-Driven Software Enginneering in Practice. Morgan & Claypool Publishers.

Branco, F. M.-Y.-O. (2019). *Conceptual Approach for an Extension to a Mushroom Farm Distributed Process Control System: IoT and Blockchain. In WorlCIST. A Toxa.* AISTI. doi:10.1007/978-3-030-16181-1_69

Breibvold, H. P. (2010). El Operario eficaz. *Revista ABB*, 6-11.

Bruneliere, N., Cabot, J., Dupé, G., & Madiot, F. (2014). MoDisco: A Model-driven Reverse Engineering Framework. *Information and Software Technology*, *56*(8), 1012–1032. doi:10.1016/j.infsof.2014.04.007

Brush, A. B. (2013). Lab of Things: A Platform for Conducting Studies with Connected Devices in Multiple Homes. *Proc. 2013 ACM Conf. Pervasive and Ubiquitous Computing*, 35–38. 10.1145/2494091.2502068

Bucchiarone, A., & Cabot, J. (2020). Grand Challenges in model-driven engineering: An analysis of the state of the research. *Software & Systems Modeling*, (January), 1–12.

Buhalis, D., & Foerste, M. (2015). SoCoMo marketing for travel and tourism: Empowering co-creation of value. *Journal of Destination Marketing & Management, 4*(3), 151–161. doi:10.1016/j.jdmm.2015.04.001

Burhan, M., Rehman, R. A., Khan, B., & Kim, B. S. (2018). IoT Elements, Layered Architectures, and SecurityIssues: A Comprehensive Survey. *Mdpi Sensors*.

Butun, I., Morgera, S. D., & Sankar, R. (2014). A survey of intrusion detection systems in wireless sensor networks. *IEEE Communications Surveys and Tutorials, 16*(1), 266–282.

Cámara de Ópticos. (2013). *Salud y tendencias visuales de los españoles.* https://camaraopticos.com/salud-visual-y-tendencias-de-los-espanoles/

Camenisch, J., Shelat, A., Sommer, D., Hubner, F., Hansen, M., Krasemann, H., Lacoste, G., Leenes, R., & Tseng, J. (2005). Privacy and identity management for everyone. In *Proceedings of the 2005 workshop on Digital identity management, DIM '05*. ACM. 10.1145/1102486.1102491

Cannasse, N. (2014). *Haxe. Too good to be True?* GameDuell Tech Talk. Retrieved March 28, 2020 from http://www.techtalk-berlin.de/news/read/nicolas-cannasse-introducing-Haxe/

Cao, J. (2011). CASTLE: Continuously anonymizing data streams. *IEEE Transactions on Dependable and Secure Computing, 8*(3), 337–352. doi:10.1109/TDSC.2009.47

Cave, J. (2011). *Does It Help or Hinder? Promotion of Innovation on the Internet and Citizens' Right to Privacy. Economic and Scientific Policy report.* European Parliament.

Celdran, A. H. (2014). A semantic aware policy framework for developing privacy-preserving and context-aware smart applications. *IEEE Systems Journal*.

Cervantes, C., Poplade, D., Nogueira, M., & Santos, A. (2015). Detection of sinkhole attacks for supporting secure routing on 6LoWPAN for Internet of Things. In *2015 IFIP/IEEE International Symposium on Integrated Network Management* (pp. 606–611). IEEE.

Cervantes, C., Poplade, D., Nogueira, M., & Santos, A. (2015). Detection of sinkhole attacks for supporting secure routing on 6lowpan for Internet of things. *2015 IFIP/IEEE International Symposium on Integrated Network Management (IM)*, 606–611.

Chaabouni, N., Mosbah, M., Zemmari, A., Sauvignac, C., & Faruki, P. (2019). Network intrusion detection for IoT security based on learning techniques. *IEEE Communications Surveys and Tutorials, 21*(3), 2671–2701. doi:10.1109/COMST.2019.2896380

Chakraborty, A., Kanti Baowaly, M., Arefin, A., & Newaz Bahar, A. (2012). The Role of Requirement Engineering in Software Development Life Cycle. *Journal of Emerging Trends in Computing and Information Sciences, 3*(5), 723–729.

Chang, V., Sharma, S., & Li, C. S. (2020). Smart cities in the 21st century. *Technological Forecasting and Social Change*, 153.

Chan, M. (2017). *Why Cloud Computing Is the Foundation of the Internet of Things*. Academic Press.

Chaparro-Peláez, J. P.-R.-M. (n.d.). Inter-organizational information systems adoption for service innovation in building sector. *Journal of Business Research*, 673-679. doi:10.1016/j. jbusres.2013.11.026

Cha, S., Chen, J., Su, C., & Yeh, K. (2018). A blockchain connected gateway for ble-based devices in the Internet of things. *IEEE Access : Practical Innovations, Open Solutions, 6*, 24639–24649.

Chaudhary, R., Aujla, G. S., Garg, S., Kumar, N., & Rodrigues, J. J. P. C. (2018). Sdn-enabled multi-attribute-based secure communication for smart grid in riot environment. *IEEE Transactions on Industrial Informatics, 14*(6), 2629–2640.

Chen, G., & Ng, W. S. (2017). An efficient authorization framework for securing industrial Internet of things. *TENCON 2017 - 2017 IEEE Region 10 Conference*, 1219–1224.

Chen, K., Zhang, S., Li, Z., Zhang, Y., Deng, Q., Ray, S., & Jin, Y. (2018). Internet-of-Things Security and Vulnerabilities: Taxonomy, Challenges, and Practice. *Journal of Hardware and Systems Security, 2*, 97–110.

Chen, L., Lee, W.-K., Chang, C.-C., Choo, K.-K. R., & Zhang, N. (2019). Blockchain-based searchable encryption for electronic health record sharing. *Future Generation Computer Systems, 95*, 420–429.

Cherian, M., & Chatterjee, M. (2018). Survey of security threats in iot and emerging countermeasures. In *International Symposium on Security in Computing and Communication* (pp. 591-604). Bangalore: Springer.

Choi, J., & Kim, Y. (2016). An improved lea block encryption algorithm to prevent side-channel attack in the IoT system. *2016 Asia-Pacific Signal and Information Processing Association Annual Summit and Conference (APSIPA)*, 1–4.

Chouhan, P., & Singh, R. (2016). Security Attacks on Cloud Computing With Possible Solution. *International Journal of Advanced Research in Computer Science and Software Engineering, 6*(1).

Christin, D., & Reinhardt, A. (2011). A survey on privacy in 1245 mobile participatory sensing applications. *Journal of Systems and Software, 84*(11), 1928–1946. doi:10.1016/j.jss.2011.06.073

Ciccozzi, F., Crnkovic, I., Di Ruscio, D., Malavolta, I., Pelliccione, P., & Spalazzese, R. (2017, January-February). Model-Driven Engineering for Mission-Critical IoT Systems. *IEEE Software, 34*(1), 46–53. doi:10.1109/MS.2017.1

Cirani, S., Ferrari, G., & Veltri, L. (2013). Enforcing security mechanisms in the IP-based Internet of things: An algorithmic overview. *Algorithms*, 197–226.

Cirani, S., Ferrari, G., & Veltri, L. (2013). Enforcing security mechanisms in the IP-based internet of things: An algorithmic overview. *Algorithms, 6*(2), 197–226.

Colema, L. (2006). Frequency of man-made disasters in the 20the century. *Journal of Contingencies and Crisis Management, 14*(1), 3–11. doi:10.1111/j.1468-5973.2006.00476.x

Costa, B., Pires, P. F., & Delicato, F. C. (2016). Modeling IoT Applications with SysML4IoT. *Proceedings - 42nd Euromicro Conference on Software Engineering and Advanced Applications, SEAA 2016*, 157–164. 10.1109/SEAA.2016.19

Cristian García, E. (2018). A Review of Artificial Intelligence in the Internet of Things. *International Journal of Interactive Multimedia and Artificial Intelligence, 5*(4), 9–20. doi:10.9781/ijimai.2018.03.004

D'Ippolito, N., Braberman, V., Kramer, J., Magee, J., Sykes, D., & Uchitel, S. (2014). Hope for the Best, Prepare for the Worst: Multi-tier Control for Adaptive Systems. *Proceedings of the 36th International Conference on Software Engineering*. 10.1145/2568225.2568264

Dasnois, B. (2011). *Haxe 2 Beginner's Guide*. Packt Publishing.

de C Henshaw, M. J. (2016). Systems Of Systems, Cyber-Physical Systems, The Internet-Of-Things...Whatever Next? *Insight (American Society of Ophthalmic Registered Nurses), 19*(3), 51–54.

Dehlinger, J., & Dixon, J. (2011). Mobile application software engineering: Challenges and research directions. In *Proceedings of the Workshop on Mobile Software Engineering* (pp. 29-32). Berlin: Springer-Verlag.

Deogirikar, J., & Vidhate, A. S. (2017). Security Attacks in IoT: A Survey. *International Conference on I-SMAC (IoT in Social, Mobile, Analytics, and Cloud, 32-37*.

Derhab, A., Guerroumi, M., Gumaei, A., Maglaras, L., Ferrag, M. A., Mukherjee, M., & Khan, F. A. (2019). Blockchain and Random Subspace Learning-Based IDS for SDN-Enabled Industrial IoT Security. *Sensors (Basel), 19*(3119), 3119. doi:10.339019143119 PMID:31311136

De, S. J., & Ruj, S. (2017). *Efficient decentralized attribute-based access control for mobile clouds*. IEEE Transactions on Cloud Computing.

Diaz Bilotto, P. (2015). *Software development for mobile applications through an integration of MDA and Haxe* (Undergraduate Thesis). Computer Science Department, Universidad Nacional del Centro de la Provincia de Buenos Aires, Argentina.

Diaz Bilotto, P., & Favre, L. (2016). Migrating JAVA to Mobile Platforms through HAXE: An MDD Approach. In A. M. Cruz & S. Paiva (Eds.), *Modern Software Engineering Methodologies for Mobile and Cloud Environments* (pp. 240–268). IGI Global. doi:10.4018/978-1-4666-9916-8.ch013

Donno, M. D., Giaretta, A., Dragoni, N., Bucchiarone, A., & Mazzara, M. (2019). *Cyber-Storms Come from Clouds: Security of Cloud Computing in the IoT Era*. Future Internet.

Dorri, A., Kanhere, S. S., Jurdak, R., & Gauravaram, P. (2019). *LSB: A Lightweight Scalable Blockchain for IoT Security and Privacy*. http://arxiv.org/ abs/1712.02969

Draqui. (2017). *Smart Helmet.* https://daqri.com/products/smart-helmet: https://daqri.com/products/smart-helmet

Duan, R., Chen, X., & Xing, T. (2011). A QoS Architecture for IoT. *IEEE International Conferences on Internet of Things, and Cyber, Physical and Social Computing.*

Dubovitskaya, A., Xu, Z., Ryu, S., Schumacher, M., & Wang, F. (2017). *Secure and trustable electronic medical records sharing using blockchain. In AMIA annual symposium proceedings.* American Medical Informatics Association.

Duthey, M., & Spina, C. (2016). *Migrating C/C++ to mobile platforms through MDD* (Undergraduate Thesis). Computer Science Department, Universidad Nacional del Centro de la Provincia de Buenos Aires, Argentina.

Dutta, M., & Granjal, J. (2020). Towards a secure Internet of Things: A comprehensive study of second line defense mechanisms. *IEEE Access: Practical Innovations, Open Solutions, 8,* 127272–127312.

Dwivedi, A. D., Srivastava, G., Dhar, S., & Singh, R. (2019). A decentralized privacy-preserving healthcare blockchain for IoT. *Sensors (Basel), 19*(2), 326. doi:10.339019020326 PMID:30650612

Eclipse. (2020). *Eclipse-The Eclipse Foundation open source community.* http://eclipse.org/

Ejarque, J., Micsik, A., & Badia, R. (2015). Towards Automatic Application Migration to Clouds. *Proceedings IEEE 8th Int. Conf. on Cloud Computing, 25-32.*

Ekblaw, A., Azaria, A., Halamka, J. D., & Lippman, A. (2016). A Case Study for Blockchain in Healthcare:"MedRec" prototype for electronic health records and medical research data. *OBD 2016: The 2nd International Conference on Open and Big Data, 13, 1-13.*

El Khateeb, S. (2018). IoT architecture a gateway for smart cities in Arab world. *15th Learning and Technology Conference (L&T), 153–160.* 10.1109/LT.2018.8368500

Emerson. (2020). *Delta V.* https://www.emerson.com/en-us/automation/deltav: https://www.emerson.com/en-us/automation/deltav

EMF. (2020). *Eclipse Modeling Framework (EMF).* Retrieved March 28, 2020 from http://www.eclipse.org/modeling/emf/

EMFText. (2020). *EMFText Document.* Retrieved March 28, 2020 from www.emftext.org

Epson. (2017). *Epson Moverio BT-300.* https://epson.com/moverio-augmented-reality-smart-glasses?pg=3#sn

Esfahani, A., Mantas, G., Matischek, R., Saghezchi, F. B., Rodriguez, J., Bicaku, A., Maksuti, S., Tauber, M. G., Schmittner, C., & Bastos, J. (2019). A lightweight authentication mechanism for m2m communications in industrial IoT environment. *IEEE Internet of Things Journal, 6*(1), 288–296. doi:10.1109/JIOT.2017.2737630

Euromonitor International. (2015). *From the online to the mobile travel era*. http://www.euromonitor.com/from-the-online-to-the-mobile-travel-era/report

European Commission. (2016). *Smart regions conference*. https://ec.europa.eu/regional_policy/en/conferences/smart-regions/

European Commission. (2017). *The digital economy and society index (DESI)*. https://ec.europa.eu/digital-single-market/en/desi

Evans, D., & Eyers, D. (2012). Efficient data tagging for managing privacy in the internet of things. Conf. on Internet of Things, iThings 2012 and Conf. on Cyber, Physical and Social Computing, CPSCom 2012, 244–248. doi:10.1109/GreenCom.2012.45

Farooq, M., Waseem, M., Khairi, A., & Mazhar, P. (2015). 02). A critical analysis on the security concerns of Internet of Things (IoT). *International Journal of Computers and Applications, 111*, 1–6.

Favre, L., & Duarte, D. (2016). Formal MOF Metamodeling and Tool Support. In *Proceedings of the 4th International Conference on Model-Driven Engineering and Software Development. MODELSWARD 2016.* (pp. 99-110). Roma, Italy: SCITEPRESS (Science and Technology Publications).

Favre, L. (2009). A Formal Foundation for Metamodeling. In *Proceedings of 14th Ada-Europe International Conference. Lecture Notes in Computer Science* (Vol 5570, pp.177-191). Berlin: Springer-Verlag. 10.1007/978-3-642-01924-1_13

Favre, L. (2010). *Model-driven Architecture for Reverse Engineering Technologies: Strategic Directions and System Evolution*. IGI Global. doi:10.4018/978-1-61520-649-0

Favre, L. (2018). A Framework for Modernizing Non-Mobile Software: A Model-Driven Engineering Approach. In *Protocols and Applications for the Industrial Internet of Things* (pp. 192–224). IGI Global. doi:10.4018/978-1-5225-3805-9.ch007

Feng, H., & Fu, W. (2010). Study of recent development about privacy and security of the internet of things. *Web Information Systems and Mining (WISM), 2010 International Conference on, 2*, 91–95. 10.1109/WISM.2010.179

Fernndez-Carams, T. M., & Fraga-Lamas, P. (2018). A review on the use of blockchain for the Internet of things. *IEEE Access : Practical Innovations, Open Solutions, 6*, 32979–33001.

Ferran, M. A., Derdour, M., Mukherjee, M., Dahab, A., Maglaras, L., & Janicke, H. (2019). *Blockchain technologies for the Internet of things: research issues and challenges*. IEEE Internet Things J.

Feynman, R., & Objectives, C. (2016). *EBNF A Notation to Describe Syntax*. Academic Press.

Finextra. (2019). *What is the role of IoT in Smart Cities?* https://www.finextra.com/blogposting/17931/what-is-the-role-of-iot-in-smart-cities

Forbes. (2019). Blockchain in healthcare: How it Could Make Digital Healthcare Safer and More Innovative. *Forbes.*

Freire, M. (2017). *Especialistas em digital marketing e data analytics são das profissões mais procuradas pelas empresas.* https://www.bit.pt/especialistas-em-digital-marketing-e-data-analytics-sao-as-profissoes-que-as-empresas-mais-procuram/?inf_by=59cba655671db80f3d8b46cb

Frustaci, M., Pace, P., Aloi, G., & Fortino, G. (2018). *Evaluating critical security issues of the IoT world: present and future challenges.* IEEE Internet Things.

Fu, Y., Yan, Z., Cao, J., Koné, O., & Cao, X. (2017). An automata based intrusion detection method for internet of things. *Mobile Information Systems*, 1-14.

Fu, Y., Yan, Z., Cao, J., Kone, O., & Cao, X. (2017). An automata-based intrusion detection method for Internet of Things. *Mobile Information Systems, 2017.*

Gai, J., Choo, K., Qiu, K. R., & Zhu, L. (2018). Privacy-preserving content-oriented wireless communication in internet-of-things. *IEEE Internet Things Journal, 5*(4), 3059–3067.

Galitiello, E., & Rolandi, B. (2015). *Reverse engineering of Object-Oriented Code. System engineering* (Thesis). Computer Science Department. Universidad Nacional del Centro de la Provincia de Buenos Aires, Argentina.

Gandino, F., Montrucchio, B., & Rebaudengo, M. (2014). *Key Management for Static Wireless Sensor Networks with Node Adding. IEEE Transaction Industrial Informatics.*

Gartner. (2020). *IoT Adoption Trends.* Retrieved June 23, 2020, from https://www.gartner.com/en/innovation-strategy/trends/iot-adoption-trends

Gessner, D. (2012). Trustworthy Infrastructure Services for a Secure and Privacy-Respecting Internet of Things. *International Conference on Trust, Security and Privacy in Computing and Communications*, 998-1003.

Gheisari, M., Pham, Q. V., Alazab, M., Zhang, X., Fernández-Campusano, C., & Srivastava, G. (2019). ECA: An Edge Computing Architecture for Privacy-Preserving in IoT-Based Smart City. *IEEE Access: Practical Innovations, Open Solutions, 7*, 155779–155786. doi:10.1109/ACCESS.2019.2937177

Gheisari, M., Wang, G., Chen, S., & Ghorbani, H. (2018). IoT-SDNPP: A Method for Privacy-Preserving in Smart City with Software Defined Networking. In *International Conference on Algorithms and Architectures for Parallel Processing* (pp. 303-312). Guangzhou, China: Springer. 10.1007/978-3-030-05063-4_24

Giannikos, M. (2013). Towards secure and context-aware information lookup for the Internet of Things. *Computing, Networking and Communications (ICNC). Proceedings of the IEEE*, 632–636.

Gibbon, J. (2018). *Introduction to Trusted Execution Environment: Arm's Trust zone.* Academic Press.

Gigli, M., & Koo, S. (2011). 01). Internet of Things: Services and applications categorization abstract. *Adv. Internet of Things*, *1*, 27–31. doi:10.4236/ait.2011.12004

Glissa, G., Rachedi, A., & Meddeb, A. (2016). A secure routing protocol based on rpl for Internet of things. *IEEE Global Communications Conference (GLOBECOM)*, 1–7.

Golomb, T., Mirsky, Y., & Elovici, Y. (2018). Ciota: Collaborative iot anomaly detection via blockchain. In *Workshop on Decentralized IoT Security and Standards (DISS) of the Network and Distributed Systems Security Symposium (NDSS)* (pp. 1-6). San Diego, CA: NDSS.

Gomes, M., & Kury, G. (2013). *A evolução do marketing para o marketing 3.0: O marketing de causa*. XV Congresso de Ciências da Comunicação na Região Nordeste. Intercom - Sociedade Brasileira de Estudos Interdisciplinares da Comunicação, Mossoró, Brasil.

Gomes, T., Salgado, F., Tavares, A., & Cabral, J. (2017). Cute mote, a customizable and trustable end-device for the Internet of things. *IEEE Sensors Journal*, *17*(20), 6816–6824. doi:10.1109/JSEN.2017.2743460

González García, C., & Espada, J. (2015). MUSPEL: Generation of Applications to Interconnect Heterogeneous Objects Using Model-Driven Engineering. In V. G. Díaz, J. M. C. Lovelle, & B. C. P. García-Bustelo (Eds.), *Handbook of Research on Innovations in Systems and Software Engineering* (pp. 365–385). IGI Global. doi:10.4018/978-1-4666-6359-6.ch015

González García, C., Meana-Llorián, D., Pelayo G-Bustelo, C., & Cueva-Lovelle, J. M. (2017). A review about Smart Objects, Sensors, and Actuators. *International Journal of Interactive Multimedia and Artificial Intelligence*, *4*(3), 7–10. doi:10.9781/ijimai.2017.431

González García, C., Zhao, L., & García-Díaz, V. (2019, April). A User-Oriented Language for Specifying Interconnections between Heterogeneous Objects in the Internet of Things. *IEEE Internet of Things Journal*, *6*(2), 3806–3819. doi:10.1109/JIOT.2019.2891545

Google. (2017). *Google Glass*. https://developers.google.com/glass/

Gope, P., & Sikdar, B. (2018). *Lightweight and privacy-preserving two-factor authentication scheme for IoT devices*. IEEE Internet Things.

Gordon, W. J., & Catalini, C. (2018). Blockchain technology for healthcare: Facilitating the transition to patient-driven interoperability. *Computational and Structural Biotechnology Journal*, *16*, 224–230. doi:10.1016/j.csbj.2018.06.003 PMID:30069284

Gowrishankar & Venkatachalam. (2018). IoT Based Precision Agriculture using Agribot. *GRD Journals-Global Research and Development Journal for Engineering, 3*(5), 98-101.

Granja, J., Silva, R., Monteiro, E., Silva, J. S., & Boavida, F. (2008). Why is IPSec a viable option for wireless sensor networks. *2008 5th IEEE International Conference on Mobile Ad Hoc and Sensor Systems*, 802–807.

Granville, K. (2018). *Facebook and Cambridge Analytica: what You Need to Know as Fallout Widens*. Academic Press.

Gretzel, U. (2011). Intelligent systems in tourism: A social science perspective. *Annals of Tourism Research*, *38*(3), 757–779. doi:10.1016/j.annals.2011.04.014

Griggs, K. N., Ossipova, O., Kohlios, C. P., Baccarini, A. N., Howson, E. A., & Hayajneh, T. (2018). Healthcare blockchain system using smart contracts for secure automated remote patient monitoring. *Journal of Medical Systems*, *42*(7), 1–7. doi:10.100710916-018-0982-x PMID:29876661

GSMA. (2016a). *AirQ Internet of Things Case Study*. https://www.gsma.com/iot/airq-internet-things-case-study/

GSMA. (2016b). *Smart Cities Guide: Crowd Management*. https://www.gsma.com/iot/gsma-smart-cities-guide-crowd-management/

Guan, Z., Si, G., Zhang, X., Wu, L., Guizani, N., Du, X., & Ma, Y. (2018). Privacy-preserving and efficient aggregation based on blockchain for power grid communications in smart communities. *IEEE Communications Magazine*, *56*(7), 82–88.

Gubbi, J., Buyya, R., Marusic, S., & Palaniswami, M. (2013). Internet of Things (IoT): A vision, architectural elements, and future directions. *Future Generation Computer Systems*, *29*(7), 1645–1660. doi:10.1016/j.future.2013.01.010

Guin, U., Singh, A., Alam, M., Caedo, J., & Skjellum, A. (2018). A secure low-cost edge device authentication scheme for the Internet of things. *31st International Conference on VLSI Design and 17th International Conference on Embedded Systems (VLSID)*, 85–90.

Guizzo, E. (2011). Robots with their Heads in the Clouds. *IEEE Spectrum*, *48*(3), 17–18. doi:10.1109/MSPEC.2011.5719709

Gupta, M., & Abdelsalam, M. (2020). *Security and Privacy in Smart Farming: Challenges and Opportunities* (Vol. 8). IEEE Access.

Gupta, R., Tanwar, S., Tyagi, S., Kumar, N., Obaidat, M. S., & Sadoun, B. (2019). HaBiTs: Blockchain-based telesurgery framework for healthcare 4.0. In *International Conference on Computer, Information and Telecommunication Systems (CITS)* (pp. 1-5). Beijing, China: IEEE. 10.1109/CITS.2019.8862127

Gyory, M., & Chuah, M. (2017). IoT One: Integrated Platform for Heterogeneous IoT Devices. *International Conference on Computing, Networking, and Communications (ICNC): Workshop*.

Hameed, S., Khan, F.I., & Hameed, B. (2019).Understanding Security Requirements and Challenges in The Internet of Things (IoT): A Review. *Hindawi, Journal of Computer Networks and Communication*.

Hamza, A., Gharakheili, H. H., & Sivaraman, V. (2018). Combining MUD policies with SDN for IoT intrusion detection. In *Proceedings of the 2018 Workshop on IoT Security and Privacy* (pp. 1-7). ACM. 10.1145/3229565.3229571

Hany, F. A., & Gary, B. W. (2019). *IoT security, Privacy, Safety, and Ethics*. Springer Nature Switzerland.

Harini, S., Jothika, K. & Jayashree, K. (2017). A Survey on Privacy and Security in Internet of Things. *International Journal of Innovations in Engineering and Technology, 8*(1).

Haxe. (2020). *The Haxe Language*. Retrieved March 28, 2020 from https://haxe.org/

Hei, X., Du, X., Wu, J., & Hu, F. (2010). Defending resource depletion attacks on implantable medical devices. *2010 IEEE Global Telecommunications Conference GLOBECOM 2010*, 1–5.

Hemalatha, Dhanalakshmi, Matilda, & Bala Anand. (2018). Farmbot- A Smart Agriculture Assistor Using Internet of Things. *International Journal of Pure and Applied Mathematics, 119*(10), 557-566.

Henze, M. (2013). *The Cloud Needs Cross-Layer Data Handling Annotations. In 2013 IEEE Security and Privacy Workshops (SPW)*. IEEE.

He, Y., Han, G., Wang, H., Ansere, J. A., & Zhang, W. (2019). A Sector Based Random Routing Scheme for Protecting the Source Location Privacy in WSNs for the Internet of Things. *Elsevier Future Generation Computer Systems*.

Hodo, E., Bellekens, X., Hamilton, A., Dubouilh, P. L., Iorkyase, E., Tachtatzis, C., & Atkinson, R. (2016). Threat analysis of IoT networks using artificial neural network intrusion detection system. In *International Symposium on Networks, Computers and Communications (ISNCC)* (pp. 1-6). IEEE. 10.1109/ISNCC.2016.7746067

Honeywell Corporation. (2006). *TotalPlant Alcont and Printa. Configuration Manual & Application planning guide*. Author.

Honeywell Corporation. (2020). *Honeywell Experion*. https://www.honeywellprocess.com/en-US/pages/default.aspx

Hosseinpour, F., Vahdani Amoli, P., Plosila, J., Hämäläinen, T., & Tenhunen, H. (2016). An intrusion detection system for fog computing and IoT based logistic systems using a smart data approach. *International Journal of Digital Content Technology and its Applications, 10*, 34-48.

Hu, C., Zhang, J., & Wen, Q. (2011). An identity-based personal location system with protected privacy in IoT. In *2011 4th IEEE International Conference on Broadband Network and Multimedia Technology* (pp. 192-195). doi: 10.1109/ICBNMT.2011. 6155923

Huang, J., Kong, L., Chen, G., Wu, M., Liu, X., & Zeng, P. (2019b). Towards secure industrial IoT: blockchain system with credit-based consensus mechanism. IEEE Trans. Ind.

Huang, X., Fu, R., Chen, B., Zhang, T., & Roscoe, A. (2012). User interactive internet of things privacy preserved access control. *7th International Conference for Internet Technology and Secured Transactions, ICITST 2012*, 597–602.

Huang, X., Zhang, Y., Li, D., & Han, L. (2019a). An optimal scheduling algorithm for hybrid EV charging scenario using consortium blockchains. *Future Generation Computer Systems*, *91*, 555–562.

Hu, G., Tay, W., & Wen, Y. (2012). Cloud Robotics: Architecture, Challenges and Applications. *IEEE Network*, *26*(3), 21–28. doi:10.1109/MNET.2012.6201212

Huh, J.-H., & Seo, K. (2019). Blockchain-based mobile fingerprint verification and automatic log-in platform for future computing. *The Journal of Supercomputing*, *75*(6), 3123–3139.

Huh, S.-K., & Kim, J.-H. (2019). The blockchain consensus algorithm for viable management of new and renewable energies. *Sustainability*, *11*(3184), 3184.

Husak, M., Velan, P., & Vykopal, J. (2015). Security monitoring of HTTP traffic using extended flows. In *2015 10th International Conference on Availability, Reliability and Security* (pp. 258–265). Academic Press.

Hussain, F., Hussain, R., Hassan, S. A., & Hossain, E. (2019). *Machine Learning in IoT Security: Current Solutions and Future Challenges.* Arxiv: 1904.05735v1 [cs.CR].

Hussain, F., Hussain, R., Hassan, S. A., & Hossain, E. (2020). Machine learning in IoT security: Current solutions and future challenges. *IEEE Communications Surveys and Tutorials*, *22*(3), 16861721. doi:10.1109/COMST.2020.2986444

Hussein, M., Li, S., & Radermacher, A. (2019). Model-driven development of adaptive IoT systems. *CEUR Workshop Proceedings*, 17–23.

Hwang, K., & Chen, M. (2017). *Big-Data Analytics for Cloud, IoT and Cognitive Computing.* John Wiley & Sons.

IEEE. (2009). *830-1998 - IEEE Recommended Practice for Software Requirements Specifications.* Retrieved March 1, 2020, from https://standards.ieee.org/standard/830-1998.html

IEEE. (2012). *IeEEE Standard for Local and metropolitan networks–Part 15.4: LowRate Wireless Personal Area Networks (LR-WPANs), 2012.* IEEE.

INCOSE. (2018). Systems Engineering Handbook. *Insight, 1*(2), 20–20. Retrieved February 9, 2020, from http://doi.wiley.com/10.1002/inst.19981220

International Telecommunication Union — ITU-T Y.2060. (2012). *Overview of the Internet of things. Next Generation Networks — Frameworks and functional architecture models.*

IoT-A. (2013). *Internet of Things–Architecture IoT-A Deliverable D1.5 –Final architectural reference model for the IoT v3.0, 2013.* http://iotforum.org/wpcontent/uploads/2014/09/D1.5-20130715-VERYFINAL.pdf

Iqbal, D., Abbas, A., Ali, M., Khan, M. U. S., & Nawaz, R. (2020). Requirement Validation for Embedded Systems in Automotive Industry through Modeling. *IEEE Access: Practical Innovations, Open Solutions*, *8*, 8697–8719. doi:10.1109/ACCESS.2019.2963774

Islam, N., & Want, R. (2014). Smarthphones: Past, present and future. *IEEE Pervasive Computing*, *13*(4), 82–92. doi:10.1109/MPRV.2014.74

Islam, S. H., Khan, M. K., & Al-Khouri, A. M. (2015). Anonymous and provably secure certificateless multireceiver encryption without bilinear pairing. *Security and Communication Networks*, *8*(13), 2214–2231.

Ivor, D. (2014). Reference Architectures For Privacy Preservation In Cloud-Based Iot Applications. *International Journal of Services Computing*, *2*, 65–78.

J., E. (2005). *Establishing Human Performance Improvements an Economic Benefit for Human-Centered Operator Interface.* Human Factors and Ergonomic Society.

Jafari, J. (2019). Closing gaps in tourism intelligence for creative destination development. Creatour Conference, UAlg, Faro.

Jara, A. J., Sun, Y., Song, H., Bie, R., Genooud, D., & Bocchi, Y. (2015). Internet of Things for Cultural Heritage of Smart Cities and Smart Regions. *IEEE 29th International Conference on Advanced Information Networking and Applications Workshops*, 668-675. 10.1109/WAINA.2015.169

Jia, X., Feng, O., Fan, T., & Lei, Q. (2012). RFID technology and its applications in internet of things (IoT). *Proc. 2nd IEEE Int. Conf. Consum. Electron. Commun. Netw. (CECNet)*, 1282–1285. 10.1109/CECNet.2012.6201508

Jiang, S., Cao, J., Wu, H., Yang, Y., Ma, M., & He, J. (2018). *Blochie: a blockchain-based platform for healthcare information exchange. In International Conference on Smart Computing (SMARTCOMP).* IEEE.

Jones, C. B. (1995). *Systematic software development using VDM.* Prentice Hall International.

Joshi, P., Nivangune, A., Kumar, R., Kumar, S., Ramesh, R., Pani, S., & Chesum, A. (2015). Understanding the Challenges in Mobile Computation Offloading to Cloud through Experimentation. *2nd ACM Int. Conf. on Mobile Software Engineering and Systems*, 158-159. 10.1109/MobileSoft.2015.43

Kalkan, K., & Zeadally, S. (2017). Securing internet of things with software defined networking. *IEEE Communications Magazine*, *56*(9), 186–192. doi:10.1109/MCOM.2017.1700714

Kandi, M. A., Lakhlef, H., Bouabdallah, A., & Challal, Y. (2019). An Efficient Multi-Group Key Management Protocol for Heterogeneous IoT Devices. In *Wireless Communications and Networking Conference (WCNC)* (pp. 1-6). Marrakesh, Morocco: IEEE. 10.1109/WCNC.2019.8885613

Kang, J., Xiong, Z., Niyato, D., Ye, D., Kim, D. I., & Zhao, J. (2019a). Toward secure blockchain-enabled Internet of vehicles: Optimizing consensus management using reputation and contract theory. *IEEE Transactions on Vehicular Technology*, *68*(3), 2906–2920.

Kang, J., Yu, R., Huang, X., Maharjan, S., Zhang, Y., & Hossain, E. (2017). Enabling localized peer-to-peer electricity trading among plug-in hybrid electric vehicles using consortium blockchains. *IEEE Transactions on Industrial Informatics, 13*(6), 3154–3164.

Kang, J., Yu, R., Huang, X., Wu, M., Maharjan, S., Xie, S., & Zhang, Y. (2019b). Blockchain for secure and efficient data sharing in vehicular edge computing and networks. *IEEE Internet of Things Journal, 6*(3), 4660–4670.

Kapoor, S., Suchetha, & Mehra. (2016). Implementation of IoT (Internet of Things) and Image processing in Smart Agriculture. *International Conference on Computation System and Information Technology for Sustainable Solutions (CSITSS),* 21-26.

Karakostas, B. (2016). Event Prediction in an IoT Environment Using Naïve Bayesian Models. *Procedia Computer Science, 83*(Ant), 11–17. doi:10.1016/j.procs.2016.04.093

Karati, A., Islam, S. H., & Karuppiah, M. (2018). Provably secure and lightweight certificateless signature scheme for iiot environments. *IEEE Transactions on Industrial Informatics, 14*(8), 3701–3711.

KDM. (2016). *Knowledge Discovery Meta-Model* (KDM), OMG Document Number: formal/2016-09-01. Retrieved April, 25, 2017 from https://www.omg.org/spec/KDM/1.4

Khan, F. I., & Hameed, S. (2019). Understanding security requirements and challenges in the Internet of things (iots): a review. *Journal of Computer Networks and Communications.*

Khan, R., Khan, S. N., Zaheer, R., & Khan, S. (2012). Future Internet: The Internet of Things Architecture, Possible Applications, and Key Challenges. *10th International Conference on Frontiers of Information Technology (FIT): Proceedings.*

Khan, Z. A., & Herrmann, P. (2017). A trust based distributed intrusion detection mechanism for internet of things. In *IEEE 31st International Conference on Advanced Information Networking and Applications (AINA)* (pp. 1169-1176). Taipei, Taiwan: IEEE.

Khan, M. A., & Salah, K. (2018). IoT security: Review, blockchain solutions, and open challenges. *Future Generation Computer Systems, 82,* 395–411. doi:10.1016/j.future.2017.11.022

Khan, S., Dulloo Aruna, B., & Verma, M. (2014). Systematic Review of Requirement Elicitation Techniques. *International Journal of Information and Computation Technology, 4*(2), 133–138. Retrieved February 12, 2020, from http://www.irphouse.com/ijict.htm

Kim, D., & Kim, S. (2017). The role of mobile technology in tourism: Patents, articles, news, and mobile tour app reviews. *Sustainability, 9*(11), 1–45. doi:10.3390u9112082

Kim, J.-H., & Huh, S.-K. (1973). A study on the improvement of smart grid security performance and blockchain smart grid perspective. *Energies, 11.*

Kim, S.-K., Kim, U.-M., & Huh, H. J. (2017). A study on improvement of blockchain application to overcome vulnerability of IoT multiplatform security. *Energies, 12*(402).

Knauss, E., Boustani, C. E. I., & Flohr, T. (2009). Investigating the impact of software requirements specification quality on project success. In *International Conference on Product-Focused Software Process Improvement* (Vol. 32, pp. 28–42). Springer Verlag. 10.1007/978-3-642-02152-7_4

Koch, R. (2011). Towards next-generation intrusion detection. In *2011 3rd International Conference on Cyber Conflict* (pp. 1–18). Academic Press.

Konigsmark, S. T. C., Chen, D., & Wong, M. D. F. (2016). Information dispersion for trojan defense through high-level synthesis. *ACM/EDAC/IEEE Design Automation Conference (DAC)*, 1–6.

Körner, S. J., & Brumm, T. (2009). Natural language specification improvement with ontologies. *International Journal of Semantic Computing*, *3*(4), 445–470. doi:10.1142/S1793351X09000872

Kotler, P., Kartajaya, H., & Setiawan, I. (2015). *Marketing 3.0 - Do produto e do consumidor até ao espírito humano*. Actual Editora.

Kouicem, D. E., Bouabdallah, A., & Lakhlef, H. (2018). Internet of things security: A top-down survey. *Computer Networks*, *141*, 199–221.

Kramer, D., Clark, T., & Oussena, S. (2010). MobDSL: A domain specific language for multiple mobile platform deployment. *Proceedings of IEEE Int. Conf. on Networked Embedded Systems for Enterprise Applications*, 1-7. 10.1109/NESEA.2010.5678062

Kshetri, N. (2017). Can blockchain strengthen the Internet of Things? *IT Professional*, *19*(4), 68–72. doi:10.1109/MITP.2017.3051335

Kumar, J. S., & Patel, D. R. (2014). A Survey on Internet of Things: Security and Privacy Issues. *International Journal of Computers and Applications*, *90*(11), 20–25. doi:10.5120/15764-4454

Kumar, & Kumar Raja, & Karthik. (2020). Agriculture based on Robot Using Raspberry Pi. *International Journal of Engineering Research & Technology (Ahmedabad)*, *8*(7), 1–3.

Kuo, T. T., & Ohno-Machado, L. (2018). Modelchain: Decentralized privacy-preserving healthcare predictive modeling framework on private blockchain networks. *Cryptography and Security*, 1-13.

Lahboube, F., Haidrar, S., Roudies, O., Souissi, N., & Adil, A. (2014). Systems of Systems Paradigm in a Hospital Environment: Benefits for Requirements Elicitation Process. *International Review on Computers and Software*, *9*(10), 1798–1806.

Lamsfus, C., Wang, D., Alzua-Sorzabal, A., & Xiang, Z. (2015). Going mobile: Defining context for on-the-go travelers. *Journal of Travel Research*, *54*(6), 691–701. doi:10.1177/0047287514538839

Latha, Reddy, & Kumar. (2014). Image Processing in Agriculture. *International Journal of Innovative Research in Electrical, Electronics. Instrumentation and Control Engineering*, *2*(6), 1562–1565.

Lee, G. M., & Kim, J. Y. (2010). The internet of things: A problem statement. *Information and Communication Technology Convergence (ICTC), 2010 International Conference on*, 517–518. 10.1109/ICTC.2010.5674788

Leite, J., Batista, T., & Oquendo, F. (2017). Architecting IoT applications with SysADL. *2017 IEEE International Conference on Software Architecture Workshops, ICSAW 2017: Side Track Proceedings*, 92–99. 10.1109/ICSAW.2017.57

Liang, X., Zhao, J., Shetty, S., Liu, J., & Li, D. (2017). Integrating blockchain for data sharing and collaboration in mobile healthcare applications. In *IEEE 28th annual international symposium on personal, indoor, and mobile radio communications (PIMRC)* (pp. 1-5). Montreal, Canada: IEEE.

Liao, H.-J., Lin, C.-H. R., Lin, Y.-C., & Tung, K.-Y. (2013). Intrusion detection system: A comprehensive review. *Journal of Network and Computer Applications*, *36*(1), 16–24.

Li, C., & Palanisamy, B. (2019). Privacy in Internet of things: From principles to technologies. *IEEE Internet of Things Journal*, *6*(1), 488–505. doi:10.1109/JIOT.2018.2864168

Lin, J., Yuy, W., Zhangz, N., Yang, X., Zhangx, H., & Zhao, W. (2016). *A Survey on Internet of Things: Architecture, Enabling Technologies, Security and Privacy, and Applications*. Academic Press.

Lin, C., He, D., Huang, X., Choo, K.-K. R., & Vasilakos, A. V. (2018). Basin: A blockchain-based secure mutual authentication with fine-grained access control system for industry 4.0. *Journal of Network and Computer Applications*, *116*, 42–52.

Ling, Z., Liu, K., Xu, Y., Jin, Y., & Fu, X. (2017). An end-to-end view of IoT security and privacy. *IEEE Global Communications Conference*, 1–7.

Lin, J., Yu, W., Zhang, N., Yang, X., Zhang, H., & Zhao, W. (2017). A survey on internet of things: Architecture, enabling technologies, security and privacy, and applications. *Internet of Things Journal*, *4*(5), 1125–1142. doi:10.1109/JIOT.2017.2683200

Li, Q., Wang, Z. Y., Li, W. H., Li, J., Wang, C., & Du, R. (2013). Applications integration in a hybrid cloud computing environment: Modelling and platform. *Enterprise Information Systems*, *7*(3), 237–271. doi:10.1080/17517575.2012.677479

Li, R., Song, T., Mei, B., Li, H., Cheng, X., & Sun, L. (2019). Blockchain for large-scale Internet of things data storage and protection. *IEEE Transactions on Services Computing*, *12*(5), 762–771.

Li, S. (2017). Security Requirements in IoT Architecture. In S. Li & L. D. Xu (Eds.), *Securing the internet of things* (pp. 97–108). Syngress. doi:10.1016/B978-0-12-804458-2.00005-6

Li, S., Xu, L., Wang, X., & Wang, J. (2012). Integration of hybrid wireless networks in cloud services oriented enterprise information systems. *Enterprise Information Systems*, *6*(2), 165–187. doi:10.1080/17517575.2011.654266

Liu, C., Cronin, P., & Yang, C. (2016). A mutual auditing framework to protect iot against hardware trojans. *2016 21st Asia and South Pacific Design Automation Conference (ASP-DAC)*, 69–74.

Liu, A., Liu, X., Tang, Z., Yang, L. T., & Shao, Z. (2017). Preserving Smart Sink-Location Privacy with Delay Guaranteed Routing Scheme for WSNs. *ACM Transactions on Embedded Computing Systems*, *16*(3), 68.

Liu, B., Yu, X. L., Chen, S., Xu, X., & Zhu, L. (2017). Blockchain based data integrity service framework for IoT data. In *IEEE International Conference on Web Services (ICWS)* (pp. 468-475). IEEE. 10.1109/ICWS.2017.54

Liu, C. H., Lin, Q., & Wen, S. (2019b). *Blockchain-enabled data collection and sharing for industrial IoT with deep reinforcement learning.* IEEE Transaction Industrial Informatics.

Liu, J., Zhang, C., & Fang, Y. (2018). Epic: A differential privacy framework to defend smart homes against internet traffic analysis. *IEEE Internet of Things Journal, 5*(2), 1206–1217.

Liu, Y., Guo, W., Fan, C., Chang, L., & Cheng, C. (2019a). A practical privacy-preserving data aggregation (3pda) scheme for smart grid. *IEEE Transactions on Industrial Informatics, 15*(3), 1767–1774.

Li, W., Tug, S., Meng, W., & Wang, Y. (2019). Designing collaborative blockchained signature-based intrusion detection in IoT environments. *Future Generation Computer Systems, 96*, 481–489. doi:10.1016/j.future.2019.02.064

Li, X., Niu, J., Bhuiyan, M. Z. A., Wu, F., Karuppiah, M., & Kumari, S. (2018a). A robust ECC-based provable secure authentication protocol with privacy-preserving for industrial Internet of things. *IEEE Transactions on Industrial Informatics, 14*(8), 3599–3609.

Li, Z., Kang, J., Yu, R., Ye, D., Deng, Q., & Zhang, Y. (2018b). Consortium blockchain for secure energy trading in industrial Internet of things. *IEEE Transactions on Industrial Informatics, 14*(8), 3690–3700.

Logeswari, S., & Subhashini, R. (2015). Cloud Robot with Agriculture Using Raspberry Pi. *International Journal of Engineering Research & Technology (Ahmedabad), 3*(4), 1–5.

Longo, F., Nicoletti, L., Padovano, A., d'Atri, G., & Forte, M. (2019). Blockchain-enabled supply chain: An experimental study. *Computers & Industrial Engineering, 136*, 57–69.

Lopez-Martin, M., Carro, B., Sanchez-Esguevillas, A., & Lloret, J. (1967). Conditional variational autoencoder for prediction and feature recovery applied to intrusion detection in iot. *Sensors (Basel), 17*(9), 2017. PMID:28846608

Lubetkin, M. (2016). *Tourism and the internet of things- IoT.* https://medium.com/3baysover-tourism-networking/tourism-and-the-internet-of-things-iot-e41b125e7ddd#.3prmu1rb8

Lukac, D. (2015). The fourth ICT-based industrial revolution "Industry 4.0": HMI and the case of CAE/CAD innovation with EPLAN. *23rd Telecommunications Forum Telfor (TELFOR)*, 835-838.

Lunardi, G. M., Al Machot, F., Shekhovtsov, V. A., Maran, V., Machado, G. M., Machado, A., & Mayr, H. C. (2018). IoT-based human action prediction and support. *Internet of Things, 3–4*, 52–68. doi:10.1016/j.iot.2018.09.007

Lu, Y., & Li, J. (2016). A pairing-free certificate-based proxy re-encryption scheme for secure data sharing in public clouds. *Future Generation Computer Systems, 62*, 140–147.

M.R., D. (2015). *How Google Glass Will Revolutionize 9 Industries.* https://www.businessinsider.com/google-glass-will-totally-disrupt-these-tktk-industries-2013-3?op=1

Maalem, S., & Zarour, N. (2016). Challenge of validation in requirements engineering. *Journal of Innovation in Digital Ecosystems, 3*(1), 15–21. doi:10.1016/j.jides.2016.05.001

Machado, C., & Frhlich, A. A. M. (2018). IoT data integrity verification for cyber-physical systems using blockchain. *2018 IEEE 21st International Symposium on Real-Time Distributed Computing (ISORC),* 83–90.

Mahya, P., & Tahayori, H. (2016). IoT is SoS. *Int'l Conf. Internet Computing and Internet of Things,* 38–42.

Makhdoom, I., Abolhasan, M., Abbas, H., & Ni, W. (2019). Blockchain's adoption in iot: The challenges, and a way forward. *Journal of Network and Computer Applications, 125,* 251–279.

Maloney, M., Reilly, E., Siegel, M., & Falco, G. (2019). *Cyber Physical IoT Device Management Using a Lightweight Agent. In IEEE Green Computing and Communications (GreenCom).* IEEE.

Malý, I. E. A. (2016, July). Augmented reality experiments with industrial robot in industry 4.0 environment. In *IEEE 14th International Conference on Industrial Informatics (INDIN)* (pp. 19-21). Pointiers, France: IEEE.

Mamoshina, P., Ojomoko, L., Yanovich, Y., Ostrovski, A., Botezatu, A., Prikhodko, P., Izumchenko, E., Aliper, A., Romantsov, K., Zhebrak, A., Ogu, I. O., & Zhavoronkov, A. (2018). Converging blockchain and next-generation artificial intelligence technologies to decentralize and accelerate biomedical research and healthcare. *Oncotarget, 9*(5), 5665–5690. doi:10.18632/oncotarget.22345 PMID:29464026

Manditereza, K. (2017). *4 Key Differences between Scada and Industrial IoT.* Academic Press.

Manzoor, A., Liyanage, M., Braeken, A., Kanhere, S. S., & Ylianttila, M. (2019). Blockchain-Based Proxy Re-encryption Scheme for Secure IoT Data Sharing. *Clinical Orthopaedics and Related Research.*

Mao, B., Kawamoto, Y., Liu, J., & Kato, N. (2019). Harvesting and threat aware security configuration strategy for IEEE 802.15.4 based IoT networks. *IEEE Communications Letters, 23*(11), 2130–2134. doi:10.1109/LCOMM.2019.2932988

Martella, C., Li, J., Conrado, C., & Vermeeren, A. (2017). On current crowd management practices and the need for increased situation awareness, prediction, and intervention. *Safety Science, 91,* 381–393. doi:10.1016/j.ssci.2016.09.006

Martinez, L., Pereira, C., & Favre, L. (2017). Migrating C/C++ Software to Mobile Platforms in the ADM Context. *International Journal of Interactive Multimedia and Artificial Intelligence, 4*(3), 34–44. doi:10.9781/ijimai.2017.436

Mayer, C. P. (2009). *Security and Privacy Challenges in the Internet of Things.* Workshops on Scientific Conf. Communication in Distributed Systems.

Mayzaud, A., Badonnel, R., Chrisment, I. (2016) A Taxonomy of Attacks in RPL-based Internet of Things. *International Journal of Network Security, 18*(3), 459 - 473.

Mazo, R. (2018). Software Product Lines, from Reuse to Self Adaptive Systems. Université Paris 1 Panthéon - Sorbonne.

Mazo, R., Salinesi, C., Djebbi, O., Diaz, D., & Lora-Michiels, A. (2012). Constraints: the Heart of Domain and Application Engineering in the Product Lines Engineering Strategy. *International Journal of Information System Modeling and Design, 3*(2).

McMahon. (2015). *Three decades of DCS technology.* https://www.controlglobal.com/articles/2005/227.html

MDA. (2020). *The Model-Driven Architecture.* Retrieved March 28, 2020 from www.omg.org/mda/

Mehra, P. (2012). Context-Aware Computing: Beyond Search and Location-Based Services. *IEEE Internet Computing, 16*(2), 12–16. doi:10.1109/MIC.2012.31

Meng, W. (2018). Intrusion detection in the era of IoT: Building trust via traffic filtering and sampling. *Computer, 51*(7), 36–43. doi:10.1109/MC.2018.3011034

Menn, J. (2012). *Social networks scan for sexual predators, with uneven results.* Reuters. http://reut.rs/Nnejb7

Menzies, A. (2016). *Co-creation for successful customer engagement.* https://www.summa.com/blog/successful-customer-engagement-with-co-creation

Metavision. (2017). *Meta 2.* https://www.metavision.com

Microsoft Corporation. (2020). *Hololens.* https://www.microsoft.com/en-us/hololens/

Mikula, T., & Jacobsen, R. H. (2018). Identity and access management with blockchain in electronic healthcare records. In *21st Euromicro conference on digital system design (DSD)* (pp. 699-706). Prague, Czech Republic: IEEE. 10.1109/DSD.2018.00008

Minoli, D., & Occhiogross, B. (2018). Blockchain mechanism for IoT security. *International Journal of Internet of Things*, 1-13.

Miranda, J., Makitalo, N., Garcia-Alonso, J., Berrocal, J., Mikkonen, T., Canal, C., & Murillo, J. (2015). From the Internet of Things to the Internet of People. *IEEE Internet Computing, 19*(2), 40–47. doi:10.1109/MIC.2015.24

Mitchell, R., & Chen, I. R. (2014). Review: A survey of intrusion detection in wireless network applications. *Computer Communications, 42*, 1–23.

MoDisco. (2020). *Model Discovery.* Retrieved March 28, 2020 from https://eclipse.org/MoDisco/

MOF. (2016). *Meta Object Facility (MOF) Core Specification*, Version 2.5, OMG Document Number: formal/2016-11-01. Retrieved March 28, 2020 from https://www.omg.org/spec/MOF/2.5.1/

Mohammadi, M., Al-Fuqaha, A., Sorour, S., & Guizani, M. (2018, October 1). Deep learning for IoT big data and streaming analytics: A survey. In *IEEE Communications Surveys and Tutorials*. Institute of Electrical and Electronics Engineers Inc.

Molugu, S. V., Bindu, S. M., Aishwarya, B., Dhanush, B. N., & Manjunath, R. K. (2018). Security and Privacy Challenges in Internet of Things. *Proceedings of the 2nd International Conference on Trends in Electronics and Informatics.*

Mondal, S., Wijewardena, K. P., Karuppuswami, S., Kriti, N., Kumar, D., & Chahal, P. (2019). Blockchain inspired RFID-based information architecture for food supply chain. *IEEE Internet of Things Journal, 6*(3), 5803–5813.

Mosenia, A., & Jha, N. K. (2017). A comprehensive study of security of internet-of-things. *IEEE Transactions on Emerging Topics in Computing, 5*(4), 586–602. doi:10.1109/TETC.2016.2606384

Moustafa, N., & Slay, J. (2015). UNSW-NB15: a comprehensive data set for network intrusion detection systems (UNSW-NB15 network data set). In 2015 Military Communications and Information Systems Conference (pp. 1–6). Academic Press.

Muñoz-Fernández, J. C., Mazo, R., Salinesi, C., & Tamura, G. (2018). 10 Challenges for the specification of self-adaptive software. *Proceedings - International Conference on Research Challenges in Information Science, 1*–12.

Naeem, H., Guo, B., & Naeem, M. R. (2018). A lightweight malware static visual analysis for IoT infrastructure. *International Conference on Artificial Intelligence and Big Data (ICAIBD),* 240–244.

Nagaraj, A. (2021). *Introduction to Sensors in IoT and Cloud Computing Applications.* Bentham Science Publishers.

Necstour. (2019). *Roadmap 2019-2021: The 5 "S" of the tourism of tomorrow.* http://www.necstour. eu/system/files/NECSTouR%20Roadmap%202019-2021%20-Tourism%20of%20Tomorrow

Neeraj & Singh, A. (2016). Internet of Things and Trust Management in IOT – Review. *International Research Journal of Engineering and Technology, 3*(6).

Neisse, R., Steri, G., Baldini, G., Tragos, E., Nai Fovino, I., & Botterman, M. (2015). *Dynamic context-aware scalable and trust-based IoT security, privacy framework.* River Publishers.

Ngu, A. H., Gutierrez, M., Metsis, V., Nepal, S., & Sheng, Q. Z. (2017). IoT Middleware: A Survey on Issues and Enabling Technologies. *IEEE Internet of Things Journal, 4*(1), 1–20.

Nikolopoulos, B., Dimopoulos, A. C., Nikolaidou, M., Dimitrakopoulos, G., & Anagnostopoulos, D. (2019). *A System of Systems Architecture for the Internet of Things exploiting Autonomous Components.* Int. J. System of Systems Engineering.

Nitti, M., Girau, R., & Atzori, L. (2014). Trustworthiness management in the social Internet of Things. *IEEE Transactions on Knowledge and Data Engineering, 26*(5), 1253–1266. doi:10.1109/ TKDE.2013. 105

Nobakht, M., Sivaraman, V., & Boreli, R. (2016). A host-based intrusion detection and mitigation framework for smart home IoT using OpenFlow. In *11th International conference on availability, reliability and security (ARES)* (pp. 147-156). Salzburg, Austria: IEEE. 10.1109/ARES.2016.64

Nolle, T. (2016). *Enterprise architecture model helps to maximize mobile empowerment.* http://searchsoa.techtarget.com/tip/Enterprise-architecture-model-helps-to-maximize-mobile-empowerment?utm_medium=EM&asrc=EM_NLN_65809390&utm_campaign=20161007_Enterprise%20architecture%20holds%20the%20secret%20to%20mobile_fchurchville&utm_source=NLN&track=NL-1806&ad=910397&src=910397

ObserveIT. (2018). *5 Examples of Insider Threat-Caused Breaches that Illustrate the Scope of the Problem.* Author.

OCL. (2014). *OMG Object constraint language* (OCL), version 2.4. OMG Document Number: formal/2014-02-03. Retrieved March 28, 2020 from https://www.omg.org/spec/OCL/2.4

OECD. (2018). *OECD tourism trends and policies.* OECD Publishing. doi:10.1787/tour-2018-

Ogonji, M. M., Okeyo, G., & Wafula, J. M. (2020). A survey on privacy and security of Internet of Things. *Computer Science Review*, *38*, 100312. doi:10.1016/j.cosrev.2020.100312

Okorie, O., Turner, C., Charnley, F., Moreno, M., & Tiwari, A. (2017). A review of data-driven approaches for circular economy in manufacturing. *Proceedings of the 18th European Roundtable for Sustainable Consumption and Production.*

Olausson M., L. M. (2012). Colaborando en una nueva dimensión. *Revista ABB*, 6-11.

Oleshchuk, V. (2009). Internet of things and privacy preserving technologies. *2009 1st International Conference on Wireless Communication, Vehicular Technology, Information Theory and Aerospace Electronic Systems Technology*, 336–340.

Oleshchuk, V. (2009). Internet of Things and Privacy Preserving Technologies. *International Conference on Wireless Communication, Vehicular Technology, Information Theory and Aerospace & Electronic Systems Technology*, 336-340. 10.1109/WIRELESSVITAE.2009.5172470

Omar, A. A., Bhuiyan, M. Z. A., Basu, A., Kiyomoto, S., & Rahman, M. S. (2019). Privacy-friendly platform for healthcare data in cloud-based on blockchain environment. *Future Generation Computer Systems*, *95*, 511–521.

Omerth. (2017). *C-Thru.* http://www.omerh.com/c-thru#0

OMG. (2017). *Unified Modeling Language Specification.* Retrieved February 12, 2020, from https://www.omg.org/spec/UML/About-UML/

OPEN FL. (2020). *OPEN FL 4.7.* Retrieved March 28, 2020 from https://www.openfl.org/

Otim, S. D. (2012). The Impact of Information Technology Investments on Downside Risk of the Firm: Alternative Measurement of the Business Value of IT. *Journal of Management Information Systems*, 159-194. doi:10.2753/MIS0742-1222290105

OWASP. (2016). *Top IoT Vulnerabilities, 2016.* https://www.owasp.org/index. php/Top_IoT_ Vulnerabilities

Ozay, M., Esnaola, I., Yarman Vural, F. T., Kulkarni, S. R., & Poor, H. V. (2016). Machine learning methods for attack detection in the smart grid. *IEEE Transactions on Neural Networks and Learning Systems, 27*(8), 1773–1786. doi:10.1109/TNNLS.2015.2404803

Oztemel, E., & Gusev, S. (2018). Literature review of industry 4.0 and related technologies. *Journal of Intelligent Manufacturing.*

Pajouh, H. H., Javidan, R., Khayami, R., Ali, D., & Choo, K. K. (2016). A two-layer dimension reduction and two-tier classification model for anomaly-based intrusion detection in IoT backbone networks. *IEEE Transactions on Emerging Topics in Computing.*

Pal, K. (2017). Building High Quality Big Data-Based Applications in Supply Chains. IGI Global.

Pal, K. (2018). *Ontology-Based Web Service Architecture for Retail Supply Chain Management.* The 9th International Conference on Ambient Systems, Networks and Technologies, Porto, Portugal.

Pal, K. (2019). Algorithmic Solutions for RFID Tag Anti-Collision Problem in Supply Chain Management. *Procedia Computer Science, 151*, 929–934.

Pal, K. (2020). Information sharing for manufacturing supply chain management based on blockchain technology. In I. Williams (Ed.), *Cross-Industry Use of Blockchain Technology and Opportunities for the Future* (pp. 1–17). IGI Global.

Pal, K. (2021). Applications of Secured Blockchain Technology in Manufacturing Industry. In *Blockchain and AI Technology in the Industrial Internet of Things.* IGI Global Publication.

Pal, K., & Yasar, A. (2020). Internet of Things and blockchain technology in apparel manufacturing supply chain data management. *Procedia Computer Science, 170*, 450–457.

Palos-Sanchez, P., Saura, J., Reyes-Menendez, A., & Esquivel, I. (2018). Users acceptance of location-based marketing apps in tourism sector: An exploratory analysis. *Journal of Spatial and Organizational Dynamics, 6*(3), 258–270.

Park, N., & Kang, N. (2015). Mutual authentication scheme in secure Internet of things technology for comfortable lifestyle. *Sensors (Basel), 16*(1), 20.

Parr, T. (2013). *The Definitive ANTLR 4 Reference* (2nd ed.). Pragmatic Bookshelf.

Patel, K. K., & Patel, S. M. (2016). Internet of Things-IOT: Definition, Characteristics, Architecture, Enabling Technologies, Application & Future Challenges. *International Journal of Engineering Science and Computing, 6*(5).

Pearson, S. (2009). Taking Account of Privacy when Designing Cloud Computing Services. *2009 ICSE Workshop on Software Engineering Challenges of Cloud Computing*, 44–52. 10.1109/CLOUD.2009.5071532

Peeters, P., Gössling, S., Klijs, J., Milano, C., Novelli, M., Dijkmans, C., Eijgelaar, E., Hartman, S., Heslinga, J., Isaac, R., Mitas, O., Moretti, S., Nawijn, J., Papp, B., & Postma, A. (2018). *Research for TRAN Committee - Overtourism: impact and possible policy responses*. Policy Department for Structural and Cohesion Policies. https://www.europarl.europa.eu/RegData/etudes/STUD/2018/629184/IPOL_STU(2018)629184_EN.pdf

Peng, L.B. Ru-Chuan, W.B. Xiao-Yu, S., & Long, C. (2014). Privacy protection based on key-changed mutual authentication protocol in internet of things. *Commun. Comput. Inf. Sci., 418*, 345–355.

Peppard, J. (2018). Rethinking the concept of the IS organization. *Information Systems Journal, 28*(1), 76–103. doi:10.1111/isj.12122

Perera, C., Liu, C.H., Jayawardena, S., & Chen, M. (2014). A Survey on Internet of Things From Industrial Market Perspective. *IEEE Access, 2*.

Perera, C., Zaslavsky, A., Christen, P., & Georgakopoulos, D. (2013). Context Aware Computing for The Internet of Things: A Survey. Communications Surveys Tutorials, IEEE, 16(1), 414-454.

Pérez Castillo, R., García Rodriguez, I., Gómez Cornejo, R., Fernández Ropero, M., & Piattini, M. (2013). ANDRIU. A Technique for Migrating Graphical User Interfaces to Android. In *Proceedings of The 25th International Conference on Software Engineering and Knowledge Engineering*. Boston: Knowledge Systems Institute.

Pérez-Cota, M., & González-Castro, M. R. (2011). Interfaz avanzado de operador de DCS. In *6º CISTI* (pp. 37-41). Chaves, Portugal: AISTI.

Pérez-Cota, M., & González-Castro, M. R. (2013). DCS 3D Operators in Industrial Environments: New HCI Paradigm for the Industry. In Virtual, Augmented and Mixed Reality. Systems and Applications (pp. 271-280). Springer.

Pérez-Cota, M., & González-Castro, M. R. (2013). Usability in a new DCS interface. In Human-Computer Interaction. Design Methods, tools and interaction Techniques for inclusion (pp. 87-96). Academic Press.

Pérez-Cota, M., González-Castro, M. R., & Díaz-Rodríguez, M. (2018). Advanced Visualization Systems in Industrial Environments: Accessible Information in Any Factory Place. In *C. G. García, V. García-Díaz, B. C. García-Bustelo, & J. M. Lovelle (Eds.), Protocols and Applications for the Industrial Internet of Things (pp. 1-34)*. IGI Global. doi:10.4018/978-1-5225-3805-9.ch001

Pinto, I., & Castro, C. (2019). Online travel agencies: Factors influencing tourist purchase decision. *Tourism & Management Studies, 15*(2), 7–20. doi:10.18089/tms.2019.150201

Ploennigs, J., Cohn, J., & Stanford-Clark, A. (2018, Sept.). The Future of IoT. IEEE Internet of Things Magazine, 28-33.

Pohl, K. (2016). Requirements Engineering Fundamentals (2nd ed.). Rocky Nook.

Pohl, K., Böckle, G., & van der Linden, F. J. (2005). *Software Product Line Engineering. Foundations, Principles, and Techniques. Uwplatt.Edu* (Vol. 49). Academic Press.

Pohl, K. (2010). *Requirements engineering: fundamentals, principles, and techniques.* Springer Publishing Company, Incorporated. doi:10.1007/978-3-642-12578-2

Polonetsky, J., & Wolf, C. (2012). *Spring Privacy Series: Mobile Device Tracking.* Retrieved from https://fpf.org/wp-content/uploads/Comments-of-the-Future-of-Privacy-Forum-on-Mobile-Device-Tracking.pdf

Porambage, P., Schmitt, C., Kumar, P., Gurtov, A., & Ylianttila, M. (2014). Pauthkey: A pervasive authentication protocol and key establishment scheme for wireless sensor networks in distributed IoT applications. *International Journal of Distributed Sensor Networks, 10*(7), 357430.

Potoczny-JonesI. (2015). www.networkcomputing.com/internet-things/iot-security-privacy-reducing vulnerabilities /807681850

Prajapati, V. (2014). *Mobile technology advancements speed up the growth of tourism worldwide.* https://www.techprevue.com/mobile-technology-advancements-speed-up-the-growth-of-tourism/

Pu, C., & Hajjar, S. (2018). Mitigating forwarding misbehaviors in rpl-based low power and lossy networks. *2018 15th IEEE Annual Consumer Communications Networking Conference (CCNC),* 1–6.

QVT. (2016). *QVT: MOF 2.0 query, view, transformation: Version 1.3.* OMG Document Number: formal/2016-06-03 Retrieved March 28, 2020 https://www.omg.org/spec/QVT/1.3

Radomirovic, S. (2010). Towards a Model for Security and Privacy in the Internet of Things. *1st International Workshop on the Security of the Internet of Things,* 1-6.

Rahman, M. A., Rashid, M. M., Hossain, M. S., Hassanain, E., Alhamid, M. F., & Guizani, M. (2019). Blockchain and IoT-based cognitive edge framework for sharing economy services in a smart city. *IEEE Access: Practical Innovations, Open Solutions, 7,* 18611–18621. doi:10.1109/ACCESS.2019.2896065

Rahulamathavan, Y., Phan, R. C., Rajarajan, M., Misra, S., & Kondoz, A. (2017). Privacy-preserving blockchain-based IoT ecosystem using attribute-based encryption. *IEEE International Conference on Advanced Networks and Telecommunications Systems (ANTS),* 1–6.

Rahul, D. S., Sudarshan, S. K., Meghana, K., Nandan, K., & Kirthana, R. (2018). IoT based Solar Powered Agribot for Irrigation and Farm Monitoring. *2nd International Conference on Inventive Systems and Control (ICISC),* 826- 831.

Raibulet, C., Arcelli Fontana, F., & Zanoni, M. (2017). Model-Driven Reverse Engineering Approaches: A Systematic Literature Review. *IEEE Access: Practical Innovations, Open Solutions, 5,* 14516–14542. doi:10.1109/ACCESS.2017.2733518

Ramani, V., Kumar, T., Bracken, A., Liyanage, M., & Ylianttila, M. (2018). Secure and efficient data accessibility in blockchain based healthcare systems. In *IEEE Global Communications Conference (GLOBECOM)* (pp. 206-212). Abu Dhabi, UAE: IEEE. 10.1109/GLOCOM.2018.8647221

Rambus. (n.d.). *Industrial IoT: Threats and countermeasures.* https://www.rambus.com/iot/industrial-IoT/

Ramirez, E. (2014). *Privacy and security in the internet of things: Challenge or Opportunity.* Academic Press.

Rayes, A., & Salem, S. (2019). *Internet of Things from Hype to Reality: The Road to digitization.* Springer.

Raza, S., Wallgren, L., & Voigt, T. (2013). Real-time intrusion detection in the Internet of Things. *Ad Hoc Networks*, *11*(8), 2661–2674. doi:10.1016/j.adhoc.2013.04.014

Razzaq, M. A., Habib, M. Q. S., & Ullah, G. S. (2017). Security Issues in the Internet of Things (IoT): A Comprehensive Study. *International Journal of Advanced Computer Science and Applications*, *8*(6), 383–388.

Rehman, A. (2016). Security and Privacy Issues in IoT. *International Journal of Communication Networks and Information Security*, *8*(3), 147–157.

Reising D. V. L. J. (2010). Supporting Operator Sitation Awareness With Overview Displays: A Series of Studies on Information vs. Vitualization Requeriments. In *ICOCO*, (pp. 188-198). Academic Press.

Reyna, A., Martn, C., Chen, J., Soler, E., & Daz, M. (2018). On blockchain and its integration with iot. challenges and opportunities. *Future Generation Computer Systems*, *88*, 173–190.

Riahi Sfar, A., Natalizio, E., Challal, Y., & Chtourou, Z. (2018). A roadmap for security challenges in the Internet of Things. *Digital Communications and Networks*, *4*(2), 118–137. doi:10.1016/j.dcan.2017.04.003

Robertson, S., & Robertson, J. (2012). *Mastering the Requirements Process: Getting Requirements Right.* Addison-Wesley.

Roblek, V., Mesko, M., & Krapez, A. (2016). A complex view of Industry 4.0. *SAGE Open*, *6*(2).

Roman, R., Lopez, J., & Mambo, M. (2016). Mobile edge computing, Fog et al.: A survey and analysis of security threats and challenges. *Future Gener. Comput. Syst.*

Rose, K., Eldridge, S., & Chapin, L. (2015). *The Internet of Things: An Overview Understanding the Issues and Challenges of a More Connected World.* The Internet Society (ISOC).

Sadier, G., & Sabri, F. (2017). *Nanosatellite Communications: A Market Study for IoT/M2M applications.* London Economics, Market Sizing, and Requirements Report.

Saeed, A., Ahmadinia, A., Javed, A., & Larijani, H. (2016). Intelligent intrusion detection in low-power IoTs. *ACM Transactions on Internet Technology*, *16*(4), 1–25. doi:10.1145/2990499

Sahay, R., Meng, W., & Jensen, C. D. (2019). The application of Software Defined Networking on securing computer networks: A survey. *Journal of Network and Computer Applications, 131,* 89–108. doi:10.1016/j.jnca.2019.01.019

Salinesi, C., Kusumah, I., & Rohleder, C. (2018). New Approach for Supporting Future Collaborative Business in Automotive Industry. In *2018 IEEE International Conference on Engineering, Technology and Innovation, ICE/ITMC 2018 - Proceedings.* Institute of Electrical and Electronics Engineers Inc. 10.1109/ICE.2018.8436382

Salinesi, C., Mazo, R., Djebbi, O., Diaz, D., & Lora-Michiels, A. (2011). Constraints: The core of product line engineering. In *Fifth International Conference On Research Challenges In Information Science* (pp. 1–10). IEEE. 10.1109/RCIS.2011.6006825

Salman, O., Chaddad, L., Elhajj, I. H., Chehab, A., & Kayssi, A. (2018). Pushing intelligence to the network edge. In *Fifth International Conference on Software Defined Systems (SDS)* (pp. 87-92). Barcelona, Spain: IEEE. 10.1109/SDS.2018.8370427

Salman, O., Elhajj, I. H., Chehab, A., & Kayssi, A. (2019). A machine learning based framework for IoT device identification and abnormal traffic detection. *Transactions on Emerging Telecommunications Technologies,* 3743. doi:10.1002/ett.3743

Samsung Corporation. (2017). *Gear VR.* https://www.samsung.com/global/galaxy/gear-vr/

Sánchez Cuadrado, J., Cánovas, J., & García Molina, J. (2014). Applying model-driven engineering in small software enterprises. *Science of Computer Programming, 89,* 176–198. doi:10.1016/j.scico.2013.04.007

Sánchez-Arias, G., & García, C. G. (2017). Midgar: Study of communications security among Smart Objects using a platform of heterogeneous devices for the Internet of Things. *Future Generation Computer Systems, 74,* 444–466. doi:10.1016/j.future.2017.01.033

Sánchez-González, G., & Herrera, L. (2014). Effects of customer cooperation on knowledge generation activities and innovation results of firms. *Business Research Quarterly, 17*(4), 292–302. doi:10.1016/j.brq.2013.11.002

Sankar, L. S., Sindhu, M., & Sethumadhavan, M. (2017). Survey of consensus protocols on blockchain applications. In *4th International Conference on Advanced Computing and Communication Systems (ICACCS)* (pp. 1-5). Coimbatore, India: IEEE. 10.1109/ICACCS.2017.8014672

Santa Moreno, M. V., Zamora, J., & Skarmeta, A.F. (2014). A Holistic IoT-based Management Platform for Smart Environments. *IEEE International Conference on Communications (ICC),* 3823-3828.

Santos, L., Rabadão, C., & Gonçalves, R. (2019). Flow monitoring system for IoT networks. In *World conference on information systems and technologies* (pp. 420–430). Academic Press.

Sapre, K., Savekar, S., Sharma, R., & Chougule, M. (2018). IoT Based Agribot for Backyard Farming. *International Research Journal of Engineering and Technology, 5*(4), 1647–1651.

Sarkar, C., Nambi, A.U., Prasad, S. N., Rahim, A., Neisse, R., & Baldini, G. (2014). A Scalable Distributed Architecture for IoT. IEEE Internet of Things Journal.

SC. (2019). *The GSMA smart cities guide: Crowd management.* https://www.thesmartcityjournal. com/en/news/1301-gsma-smart-cities-guide-crowd-management

Schindler, H. R. (2012). *Europe's policy options for a dynamic and trustworthy development of the Internet of Things.* RAND Europe.

Schmidt. (2013). *Context-aware computing.* https://www.interaction-design.org/literature/book/ the-encyclopedia-of-human-computer-interaction-2nd-ed/context-aware-computing-context-awareness-context-aware-user-interfaces-and-implicit-interaction

Schneier, B. (2012). When It Comes to Security, We're Back to Feudalism. *Wired.* https://www. wired.com/opinion/2012/11/feudal-security/

Schneier, E. (2006). *Updating the Traditional Security Model.* https://www.schneier.com/blog/ archives/ 2006/08/updating the tr.html

Sehrawat, D., & Gill, N. S. (2019). Smart sensors: Analysis of different types of IoT sensors. In *2019 3rd International Conference on Trends in Electronics and Informatics* (pp. 523-528). doi: 10.1109/ICOEI.2019.8862778

Sezer, O. B., Dogdu, E., & Ozbayoglu, A. M. (2018). Context-Aware Computing, Learning, and Big Data in Internet of Things: A Survey. *IEEE Internet of Things Journal, 5*(1), 1–27. doi:10.1109/JIOT.2017.2773600

Sfar, A. R., Natalizio, E., Challal, Y., & Chtourou, Z. (2018). A roadmap for security challenges in the Internet of things. *Digital Communications and Networks., 4*(2), 118–137.

Sforzin, A., Mármol, F. G., Conti, M., & Bohli, J. M. (2016). RPiDS: Raspberry Pi IDS—A fruitful intrusion detection system for IoT. In *Intl IEEE Conferences on Ubiquitous Intelligence & Computing, Advanced and Trusted Computing, Scalable Computing and Communications, Cloud and Big Data Computing, Internet of People, and Smart World Congress (UIC/ATC/ ScalCom/CBDCom/IoP/SmartWorld)* (pp. 440-448). IEEE.

Sharma, R., Pandey, N., & Khatri, S. K. (2017). Analysis of IoT Security at Network Layer. *Proceedings of 6th International Conference on Reliability, Infocom Technologies and Optimization (ICRITO) (Trends and Future Directions),* 585-590.

Shatat, A. S. (2015). Critical success factors in enterprise resource planning (ERP) system implementation: An exploratory study in Oman. Academic Press.

Shaw, G., Bailey, A., & Williams, A. (2011). Aspects of service-dominant logic and its implications for tourism management: Examples from the hotel industry. *Tourism Management, 32*(2), 207–214. doi:10.1016/j.tourman.2010.05.020

Shen, B., Guo, J., & Yang, Y. (2019). MedChain: Efficient healthcare data sharing via blockchain. *Applied Sciences (Basel, Switzerland), 9*(6), 1207. doi:10.3390/app9061207

Shen, M., Tang, X., Zhu, L., Du, X., & Guizani, M. (2019). Privacy-preserving support vector machine training over blockchain-based encrypted IoT data in smart cities. *IEEE Internet of Things Journal*, 6(5), 7702–7712.

Shrestha, R., Bajracharya, R., Shrestha, A. P., & Nam, S. Y. (2019). *A new type of blockchain for secure message exchange in vanet*. Digital Communications and Networks.

Shukla, P. (2017). Ml-ids: A machine learning approach to detect wormhole attacks in the Internet of things. *Intelligent Systems Conference (IntelliSys)*, 234–240.

Sicari, S. (2014). A security-and quality-aware system architecture for internet of things. *Information Systems Frontiers*, 1–13.

Sicari, S., Rizzardi, A., Grieco, L., & Coen-Porisini, A. (2015). Security, privacy and trust in internet of things: The road ahead. *Computer Networks*, 76(Suppl. C), 146–164.

Sicari, S., Rizzardi, A., Grieco, L., & Coen-Porisini, A. (2015). Security, privacy and trust in Internet of Things: The road ahead. *Computer Networks*, 76, 146–164. doi:10.1016/j.comnet.2014.11.008

Sicari, S., Rizzardi, A., Miorandi, D., & Coen-Porisini, A. (2018). Reatoreacting to denial-of-service attacks in the Internet of things. *Computer Networks*, *137*, 37–48.

Siemens, G. M. B. H. (2017). *Simatic PCS7*. https://w3.siemens.com/mcms/process-control-systems/en/distributed-control-system-simatic-pcs-7/Pages/distributed-control-system-simatic-pcs-7.aspx

Siemens, G. M. B. H. (2020). *Siemens Comos-Walkinside*. https://new.siemens.com/global/en/products/automation/industry-software/plant-engineering-software-comos-virtual-reality-training.html

Sigala, M., & Chalkiti, K. (2014). Investigating the exploitation of web 2.0 for knowledge management in the Greek tourism industry: An utilisation–importance analysis. *Computers in Human Behavior*, *30*, 800–812. doi:10.1016/j.chb.2013.05.032

Sikder, A. K., Petracca, G., Aksu, H., Jaeger, T., & Uluagac, S. (2018). *A survey on sensor-based threats to internet-of-things (IoT) devices and applications*. arXiv preprint arXiv:1802.02041.

Silva, B. N. (2017). Internet of Things: A Comprehensive Review of Enabling Technologies, Architecture, and Challenges. *IETE Technical Review*, 1–16.

Silva, M. F. (2014). Glassist: Using Augmented Reality on Google Glass as an Aid to Classroom Management. In *XVI Symposium on Virtual and Augmented Reality (SVR)* (pp. 37-44). IEEE. 10.1109/SVR.2014.41

Singh, J., Gimekar, A., & Venkatesan, S. (2019). An efficient lightweight authentication scheme for human-centered industrial Internet of Things. *International Journal of Communication Systems*, 4189. doi:10.1002/dac.4189

Singh, M., Rajan, M. A., Shivraj, V. L., & Balamuralidhar, P. (2015). Secure MQTT for the Internet of things (IoT). *5th International Conference on Communication Systems and Network Technologies*, 746–751.

Sivanathan, A., Sherratt, D., Gharakheili, H. H., Radford, A., Wijenayake, C., Vishwanath, A., & Sivaraman, V. (2017). Characterizing and classifying IoT traffic in smart cities and campuses. In *2017 IEEE Conference on Computer Communications Workshops (Infocom Wkshps)* (pp. 559–564). IEEE.

Soares, M., Jéssyka, V., Guedes, G., Silva, C., & Castro, J. (2017). Core Ontology to Aid the Goal Oriented Specification for Self-Adaptive Systems. *Advances in Intelligent Systems and Computing, 571*, V–VI.

Sodhro, A. H., Pirbhulal, S., & de Albuquerque, V. H. C. (2019). Artificial intelligence-driven mechanism for edge computing-based industrial applications. *IEEE Transactions on Industrial Informatics, 15*(7), 4235–4243. doi:10.1109/TII. 2019.2902878

Solove, D. J. (2006). A Taxonomy of Privacy. *University of Pennsylvania Law Review, 154*(3), 477. doi:10.2307/40041279

Song, T., Li, R., Mei, B., Yu, J., Xing, X., & Cheng, X. (2017). A privacy-preserving communication protocol for IoT applications in smart homes. *IEEE Internet of Things Journal, 4*(6), 1844–1852.

SOPHOS. (2015). *49 Busted in Europe for Man-In-The-Middle Bank Attacks*. https://nakedsecurity.sophos.com/2015/06/11/49-busted-in-europe-for-man-in-themiddle-bank-attacks/

Souza, V. E. S., Lapouchnian, A., Robinson, W. N., & Mylopoulos, J. (2013). Awareness requirements. Lecture Notes in Computer Science, 7475, 133–161.

Souza, V. E. S., Lapouchnian, A., & Mylopoulos, J. (2012). (Requirement) evolution requirements for adaptive systems. *ICSE Workshop on Software Engineering for Adaptive and Self-Managing Systems*, 155–164.

Spivey, J. M. (1989). *The Z notation: a reference manual | Guide books*. Prentice-Hall, Inc.

Sreamr. (2017). *Streamr White Paper v2.0*. https://s3.amazonaws.com/streamr-public/ streamr-datacoin-whitepaper-2017-07-25-v1_0.pdf

Srinivas, J., Das, A. K., Wazid, M., & Kumar, N. (2018). Anonymous lightweight chaotic map-based authenticated key agreement protocol for industrial internet of things. IEEE Trans. Dependable Secure Comput.

Stankovic, J. (2014). Research Directions for the Internet of Things. *IEEE Internet of Things Journal, 1*(1), 1, 3–9. doi:10.1109/JIOT.2014.2312291

Stefanick, L. (2011). *Controlling Knowledge: Freedom of Information and Privacy Protection in a Networked World*. DOAB Directory of Open Access Books. AU Press.

Steinberg, D., Budinsky, F., Paternostro, M., & Merks, E. (2009). *EMF: Eclipse Modeling Framework* (2nd ed.). Addison-Wesley.

Su, J., Vasconcellos, V. D., Prasad, S., Daniele, S., Feng, Y., & Sakurai, K. (2018). Lightweight classification of IoT malware based on image recognition. *IEEE 42nd Annual Computer Software and Applications Conference (COMPSAC), 2*, 664–669.

Sundmaeker, H. (2010). *Vision and Challenges for Realizing the Internet of Things*. Cluster of European Research Projects on the Internet of Things.

Sun, Y., Zhang, R., Wang, X., Gao, K., & Liu, L. (1-9). A decentralizing attribute-based signature for healthcare blockchain. In *International conference on computer communication and networks (ICCCN)* (p. 2018). Hangzhou, China: IEEE. 10.1109/ICCCN.2018.8487349

Surendar, M., & Umamakeswari, A. (2016). InDReS: An Intrusion Detection and response system for Internet of Things with 6LoWPAN. In *International Conference on Wireless Communications, Signal Processing and Networking (WiSPNET)* (pp. 1903-1908). Chennai, India: IEEE. 10.1109/WiSPNET.2016.7566473

Suryawanshi, S. R. (2016). A Study on Privacy and Security concerns in Internet of Things. *International Journal of Innovative Research in Computer and Communication Engineering, 4*(9).

Swamy, S. N., Jadhav, D., & Kulkarni, N. (2017). Security threats in the application layer in IoT applications. In *2017 International Conference on I-SMAC (IoT in social, mobile, analytics and cloud) (I-SMAC)* (p. 477-480). doi: 10.1109/I-SMAC.2017. 8058395

Tanwar, S., Parekh, K., & Evans, R. (2020). Blockchain-based electronic healthcare record system for healthcare 4.0 applications. *Journal of Information Security and Applications, 50*, 1–13. doi:10.1016/j.jisa.2019.102407

Teixeira, J., & Ferreira, R. E. (2014). Teleoperation Using Google Glass and AR, Drone for Structural Inspection. In *XVI Symposium on Virtual and Augmented Reality (SVR)* (pp. 28-36). IEEE. 10.1109/SVR.2014.42

Thramboulidis, K., Bochalis, P., & Bouloumpasis, J. (2017). A Framework for MDE of IoT-based Manufacturing Cyber-Physical System. In *Proceedings of the Seventh International Conference on the Internet of Things*. ACM. 10.1145/3131542.3131554

Tonella, P., & Potrich, A. (2005). *Reverse engineering of Object-Oriented Code. Monographs in Computer Science*. Springer-Verlag.

Tukur, Y. M., Thakker, D., & Awan, I. (2019). Ethereum blockchain-based solution to insider threats on perception layer of IoT systems. In *2019 IEEE Global Conference on Internet of Things (GCIoT)* (p. 1-6). doi: 10.1109/GCIoT47977.2019.9058395

Ullah, Z., Ahmad, S., & Ahmad, M. Ata-ur-Rehman, & Junaid, M. (2019). A preview on Internet of Things (IoT) and its applications. In *2019 2nd International Conference on Computing, Mathematics and Engineering Technologies (iCoMet)* (p. 1-6). doi: 10.1109/ICOMET.2019.8673468

Umuhoza, E., & Brambilla, M. (2016). Model-driven Development Approaches for Mobile Applications: A Survey. In *Proceedings of Mobile Web and Intelligent Information Systems - 13th International Conference, MobiWIS 2016* (pp. 93-107). Berlin: Springer.

Uthariaraj, V. R., & Florence, P. M. (2011). *QoS With Reliability And Scalability In Adaptive Service-Based Systems.* Academic Press.

Van Lamsweerde, A. (2009). Requirements Engineering: From System Goals to UML Models to Software Specifications. *Change.*

Varga, P., Plosz, S., Soos, G., & Hegedus, C. (2017). Security Threats and Issues in Automation IoT. *2017 IEEE 13th International Workshop on Factory Communication Systems (WFCS),* 1–6.

Vasconcellos, V. D., Prasad, S., Daniele, S., Feng, Y., & Sakurai, K. (2018). Lightweight classification of IoT malware based on image recognition. *IEEE 42nd Annual Computer Software and Applications Conference (COMPSAC),* 2, 664–669.

Vassev, E. (2015). Requirements Engineering for Self-Adaptive Systems with ARE and KnowLang. *EAI Endorsed Transactions on Self-Adaptive Systems, 1*(1), e6. doi:10.4108as.1.1.e6

Vechain Team. (2018). *Vechain White Paper.* https://cdn.vechain.com/vechain_ico_ideas_of_development_en.pdf

Verdouw, C., Robbemond, R. M., Verwaart, T., Wolfert, J., & Beulens, A. J. (2018). A reference architecture for IoT-based logistic information systems in agri-food supply chains. *Enterprise Information Systems,* 755-779.

Verma, A., & Ranga, V. (2019). Evaluation of network intrusion detection systems for rpl based 6LoWPAN networks in IoT. *Wireless Personal Communications, 108*(3), 1571–1594.

Videira, C., & Da Silva, A. R. (2005). Patterns and metamodel for a natural-language-based requirements specification language. *CAiSE, 05,* 189–194.

Vogel-Heuser, B. & Hess, D. (2016). Guest editorial Industry 4.0 -prerequisites and vision. *IEEE Transactions, Autom. Sci. Eng., 13*(2).

Vuzix. (2017). *Smart Glasses.* https://www.vuzix.com/Products/Series-3000-Smart-Glasses

Waltonchain. (2021). *Waltonchain white paper v2.0.* https://www.waltonchain.org/en/Waltonchain_White_Paper_2.0_EN.pdf

Wan, J., Li, J., Imran, M., Li, D., & e-Amin, F. (2019). A blockchain-based solution for enhancing security and privacy in smart factory. *IEEE Transaction.*

Wang, Y., Uehara, T., & Sasaki, R. (2015). Fog computing: Issues and challenges in security and forensics. *2015 IEEE 39th Annual Computer Software and Applications Conference, 3,* 53–59.

Wang, F. (2016). Recent Advances in the Internet of Things: Multiple Perspectives. *IETE Technical Review,* 1–11.

Wangi, N. I. C., Prasad, R. V., Jacobsson, M., & Niemegeers, I. (2008 Address autoconfiguration in wireless ad hoc networks: Protocols and techniques. *Wireless Communications, IEEE, 15*(1), 70–80. doi:10.1109/MWC.2008.4454707

Wang, L., Da-Xu, L., Bi, Z., & Xu, Y. (2014). Data cleaning for RFID and WSN integration. *Ind. Inform. IEEE Trans, 10*(1), 408–418. doi:10.1109/TII.2013.2250510

Wang, Q., Zhu, X., Ni, Y., Gu, L., & Zhu, H. (2019b). *Blockchain for the IoT and industrial IoT: a review*. Internet Things.

Wang, S., Wang, J., Wang, X., Qiu, T., Yuan, Y., Ouyang, L., Guo, Y., & Wang, F.-Y. (2018). Blockchain-powered parallel healthcare systems based on the ACP approach. *IEEE Transactions on Computational Social Systems, 5*(4), 942–950. doi:10.1109/TCSS.2018.2865526

Wang, X., Zha, X., Ni, W., Liu, R. P., Guo, Y. J., Niu, X., & Zheng, K. (2019a). Survey on blockchain for Internet of things. *Computer Communications, 136*, 10–29.

Wang, Y., & Wen, Q. (2011). A privacy enhanced dns scheme for the internet of things. *IET International Conference on Communication Technology and Application*, 699–702.

Wan, J., Tang, S., Shu, Z., Li, D., Wang, S., Imran, M., & Vasilakos, A. V. (2016). Software-defined industrial Internet of things in the context of industry 4.0. *IEEE Sensors Journal, 16*(20), 7373–7380.

Washburn, D., Sindhu, U., Balaouras, S., Dines, R. A., Hayes, N., & Nelson, L. (2010). *Helping CIOs understand 'smart city' initiatives*. http://www.uwforum.org/upload/board/forrester_help_cios_smart_city.pdf

Weyns. (2017). Software Engineering of Self-Adaptive Systems: An Organised Tour and Future Challenges. Handbook of Software Engineering, 1–41.

Weyrich, M., & Ebert, C. (2016). Reference architectures for the Internet of Things. *IEEE Software, 33*(1), 112–116. doi:10.1109/MS.2016.20

Whittle, J., Sawyer, P., Bencomo, N., Cheng, B. H. C., & Bruel, J. M. (2010). RELAX: A language to address uncertainty in self-adaptive systems requirement. *Requirements Engineering, 15*(2), 177–196. doi:10.100700766-010-0101-0

Witchey, N. J. (2019). *Patent No. 10,340,038*. Washington, DC: U.S.

World Health Organization. (2020). *Coronavirus disease 2019 (COVID-19) Situation Report-72 highlights*. Author.

Wu, L., & Shao, P. (2011). Research on the Protection Algorithm and Model of Personal Privacy Information in Internet of Thing. *International Conference on E-Business and E-Government*, 1-4.

Wurm, J., Hoang, K., Arias, O., Sadeghi, A., & Jin, Y. (2016). Security analysis on consumer and industrial IoT devices. *21st Asia and South Pacific Design Automation Conference (ASP-DAC)*, 519–524.

Wurm, J., Jin, Y., Liu, Y., Hu, S., Heffner, K., Rahman, F., & Tehranipoor, M. (2016). *Introduction to cyber-physical system security: A cross-layer perspective. IEEE Transactions on Multi-Scale Computing Systems.*

Xiong, Z., Zhang, Y., Niyato, D., Wang, P., & Han, Z. (2018). When mobile blockchain meets edge computing. *IEEE Communications Magazine, 56*(8), 33–39.

XMI. (2015). *XML Metadata Interchange (XMI) Specification*, OMG Document Number: formal/2015-06-07. Retrieved March 28, 2020 from https://www.omg.org/spec/XMI/2.5.1

XText. (2020) *XText Documentation*. Retrieved March 28, from https//www.eclipse.org/Xtext

Xu, L. D., He, W., & Li, S. (2014). Internet of things in industries: A survey. *IEEE Transactions on Industrial Informatics, 10*(4), 2233–2243.

Xu, L. D., Xu, E. L., & Li, L. (2018). Industry 4.0: State of the art and future trends. *International Journal of Production Research, 56*(8), 2941–2962. doi:10.1080/00207543.2018.1444806

Xu, L., He, S., & Li, S. (2014). Internet of Things in Industries: A Survey. *IEEE Transactions on Industrial Informatics, 10*(4), 2233–2243. doi:10.1109/TII.2014.2300753

Xu, Y., Ren, J., Wang, G., Zhang, C., Yang, J., & Zhang, Y. (2019). *A blockchain-based non-repudiation network computing service scheme for industrial IoT. IEEE Transaction Industrial Informatics.*

Yadav, M., Kamboj, S., & Rahman, Z. (2016). Customer co-creation through social media: The case of 'Crash the Pepsi IPL 2015'. *Journal of Direct, Data and Digital Marketing Practice, 17*(4), 259–271. doi:10.1057/dddmp.2016.4

Yang, J., & Fang, B. (2011). Security model and key technologies for the internet of things. *Journal of China Universities of Posts and Telecommunications, 8*(2), 109–112. doi:10.1016/S1005-8885(10)60159-8

Yang, Q. L., Lv, J., Tao, X. P., Ma, X. X., Xing, J. C., & Song, W. (2013). Fuzzy self-adaptation of mission-critical software under uncertainty. *Journal of Computer Science and Technology, 28*(1), 165–187. doi:10.100711390-013-1321-9

Yang, W., Wang, S., Huang, X., & Mu, Y. (2019a). On the Security of an Efficient and Robust Certificateless Signature Scheme for IIoT Environments. *IEEE Access : Practical Innovations, Open Solutions, 7*, 91074–91079.

Yang, Y., Li, X., Ke, W., & Liu, Z. (2019). Automated Prototype Generation From Formal Requirements Model. *IEEE Transactions on Reliability*, 1–25. doi:10.1109/TR.2019.2934348

Yang, Y., Wu, L., Yin, G., Li, L., & Zhao, H. (2017). A survey on security and privacy issues in internet-of-things. *IEEE Internet of Things Journal, 4*(5), 1250–1258.

Yang, Z., Yang, K., Lei, L., Zheng, K., & Leung, V. C. M. (2019b). Blockchain-based decentralized trust management in vehicular networks. *IEEE Internet of Things Journal, 6*(2), 1495–1505.

Yan, Q., Huang, W., Luo, X., Gong, Q., & Yu, F. R. (2018). A multi-level DDoS mitigation framework for the industrial Internet of things. *IEEE Communications Magazine, 56*(2), 30–36.

Yao, X., Kong, H., Liu, H., Qiu, T., & Ning, H. (2019). An attribute credential-based public-key scheme for fog computing in digital manufacturing. *IEEE Trans. Ind. Inf.*

Yi, S., Qin, Z., & Li, Q. (2015). Security and privacy issues of fog computing: A survey. *Wireless Algorithms, Systems, and Applications the 10th International Conference on*, 1–10.

Yifan & Wang. (2011). The Application of Cloud Computing and the Internet of Things in Agriculture and Forestry. *International Joint Conference on Service Sciences,* 168-172.

Yin, D., Zhang, L., & Yang, K. (2018). A DDoS attack detection and mitigation with software-defined Internet of things framework. *IEEE Access : Practical Innovations, Open Solutions, 6,* 24694–24705.

Yue, X., Wang, H., Jin, D., Li, M., & Jiang, W. (2016). Healthcare data gateways: Found healthcare intelligence on blockchain with novel privacy risk control. *Journal of Medical Systems, 40*(10), 1–8. doi:10.100710916-016-0574-6 PMID:27565509

Zanella, A., Bui, N., Castellani, A., Vangelista, L., & Zorzi, M. (2014). Internet of Things for Smart Cities. *IEEE Internet of Things Journal, 1*(1), 22–32.

Zaslavsky, A., Perera, C., & Georgakopoulos, D. (2012). Sensing as a Service and Big Data. *Proc. Int'l Conf. Advances in Cloud Computing,* 21–29.

Zhang, P., White, J., Schmidt, D. C., & Lenz, G. (2017). Applying software patterns to address interoperability in blockchain-based healthcare apps. *24th Pattern Languages of Programming conference,* 1-17.

Zhang, H., Wang, J., & Ding, Y. (2019b). Blockchain-based decentralized and secure keyless signature scheme for smart grid. *Energy, 180,* 955–967. doi:10.1016/j.energy.2019.05.127

Zhang, N., Mi, X., Feng, X., Wang, X., Tian, Y., & Qian, F. (2018). *Understanding and Mitigating the Security Risks of Voice-Controlled Third-Party Skills on Amazon Alexa and Google Home.* Academic Press.

Zhang, Y., Deng, R., Zheng, D., Li, J., Wu, P., & Cao, J. (2019a). *Efficient and Robust Certificateless Signature for Data Crowdsensing in Cloud-Assisted Industrial IoT.* IEEE Transaction Industry.

Zhang, Z. K., Cho, M. C. Y., Wang, C. W., Hsu, C. W., Chen, C. K., & Shieh, S. (2014). IoT security: Ongoing challenges and research opportunities. *Computer Applications, 2014,* 230–234.

Zhao, S., Li, W., Zia, T., & Zomaya, A. Y. (2017). A dimension reduction model and classifier for anomaly-based intrusion detection in internet of things. In *IEEE 15th Intl Conf on Dependable, Autonomic and Secure Computing* (pp. 836-843). IEEE.

Zheng, D., Wu, A., Zhang, Y., & Zhao, Q. (2018). Efficient and privacy-preserving medical data sharing in the Internet of things with limited computing power. *IEEE Access : Practical Innovations, Open Solutions*, *6*, 28019–28027.

Zhou, J., Cao, Z., Dong, X., & Vasilakos, A. V. (2017). Security and privacy for cloud-based IoT: Challenges. *IEEE Communications Magazine*, *55*(1), 26–33.

Zhou, R., Zhang, X., Du, X., Wang, X., Yang, G., & Guizani, M. (2018). File-centric multi-key aggregate keyword searchable encryption for industrial Internet of things. *IEEE Transactions on Industrial Informatics*, *14*(8), 3648–3658.

Ziegeldorf, J. H., Morchon, O. G., & Wehrle, K. (2014). *Privacy in the Internet of Things: Threats and Challenges*. https://arxiv.org/abs/1505.07683

Ziegeldorf, J. H., Viol, N., Henze, M., & Wehrle, K. (2014). Privacy preserving Indoor Localization. *7th ACM Conference on Security and Privacy in Wireless and Mobile Networks*, 1–2.

Ziegeldorf, H., Morchon, O. G., & Wehrle, K. (2014). Privacy in the Internet of Things: Threats and challenges. *Security and Communication Networks*, *7*(12), 2728–2742. doi:10.1002ec.795

About the Contributors

Cristian González García is a Technical Engineer in Computer Systems, M.Sc. in Web Engineering, and a Ph.D. in Computer Science graduated from School of Computer Engineering of Oviedo in 2011, 2013, and 2017 (University of Oviedo, Spain). He has been a visiting Ph.D. candidate in the University of Manchester, United Kingdom. Besides, he has been working in different national and regional projects, in projects with private companies, and in the University of Oviedo as a professor. His research interests are in the field of the Internet of Things, Web Engineering, Mobile Devices, and Modelling Software with DSL and MDE.

Vicente García-Díaz is an associate professor in the Computer Science Department of the University of Oviedo. He has a PhD from the University of Oviedo in computer engineering. His research interests include model-driven engineering, domain specific languages, technology for learning and entertainment, project risk management, software development processes and practices. He has graduated in Prevention of Occupational Risks and is a Certified Associate in Project Management through the Project Management Institute.

* * *

Asha Ambhaikar is Professor & Dean Students Welfare at Kalinga University, New Raipur, Chhattisgarh. She is Ph.D. in Computer Science & Engineering, M. Tech and B.E. She has 25 years of Academic experience and has Guided 3 Ph. D. scholars. She has published more than 75 Research Papers in reputed National and International Journals. Dr. Prof. Asha Ambhaikar has conducted various National and International Conferences (CGCOST), Seminars, Workshops and FDP's at Institute/University level. She was a member of Selection Committee as a Subject Chairman and Expert. She is a Member of Editorial Board and Reviewer of various reputed International Journals and Conferences. Dr. Prof. Asha Ambhaikar has also received Awards like Bharat Excellence 2015, Personality of India at New Delhi, etc.

Bivin Biju is pursuing his final year Bachelor's degree in Instrumentation Engineering from APJ Abdul Kalam Technological University, India.

Rogério Luís de Carvalho Costa received a PhD in Computer Engineering from the University of Coimbra (UC), Portugal, in 2011, and an MSc in Informatics from the Pontifícia Universidade Católica do Rio de Janeiro (PUC-Rio), Brazil, in 2002. He has over 15 years of teaching experience. He participated in research projects in Brazil and Portugal and published papers at international conferences and leading journals. Rogério also held technical and managerial positions in software development companies. He is currently a researcher at the Polytechnic of Leiria, Portugal. His research interests include big data, machine learning, data integration, and data quality.

Liliana Favre is a full professor of Computer Science at Universidad Nacional del Centro de la Provincia de Buenos Aires in Argentina. She is also a researcher of CIC (Comisión de Investigaciones Científicas de la Provincia de Buenos Aires). Her current research interests are focused on model driven development, model driven architecture and formal approaches, mainly on the integration of algebraic techniques with MDA-based processes. She has been involved in several national research projects about formal methods and software engineering methodologies. Currently she is research leader of the Software Technology Group at Universidad Nacional del Centro de la Provincia de Buenos Aires. She has published several book chapters, journal articles and conference papers. She has acted as editor of the book UML and the Unified Process. She is the author of the book Model Driven Architecture for Reverse Engineering Technologies: Strategic Directions and System Evolution.

Silvia Fernandes is Assistant Professor at the Faculty of Economics of the University of Algarve. She holds a PhD from this university and is member of the Cinturs (Research Centre for Tourism, Sustainability and Well-being). She lectures Information Technology, Innovation Economics and Entrepreneurship in undergraduate and master courses. She has several publications in books, journals, and communications in national/international conferences in themes such as: information systems, tourism development, innovation, emergent technologies, etc.

Miguel González Castro is a PhD from the University of Vigo, Telecommunications Engineer and Computer Engineer, with more than 15 years of experience in positions of responsibility in the area of technologies and information systems. Extensive experience in leadership of multidisciplinary teams responsible for the design, management, and programming of advanced computer systems (ERP, 3D, artificial vision, databases, neural networks, security policies, web applications,

DCS, industry 4.0); as well as extensive experience in the management of critical IT-Industrial systems projects.

Dominik Hromada is currently a student of Master's degree study program Information Management at Brno University of Technology, Czech Republic.

Jerin Geo Jacob received his Master's degree in Instrumentation Engineering from Hindustan University, Tamil Nadu, India in 2017 and Bachelor's degree in Instrumentation Engineering from Mahatma Gandhi University, Kerala, India in 2014. He is currently an Assistant Professor in Department of Applied Electronics and Instrumentation Engineering at Mount Zion College of Engineering, Pathanamthitta, Kerala, India. He has worked in the field of Automation, signal processing, Robotics and Internet of Things. His research interests include Robotics and Automation, Smart Farming, Video Processing, Neural Networks, Deep Learning and Internet of Things (IoT).

Richarld John is pursuing his final year Bachelor's degree in Instrumentation Engineering from APJ Abdul Kalam Technological University, India.

Jayashree K. is an Engineer by qualification, having completed her Doctorate in the area of Web services Fault Management from Anna University, Chennai and Masters in Embedded System Technologies from Anna University and bachelor's in computer science and Engineering from Madras University. She is presently working as Professor in the Department of Computer Science and Engineering at Rajalakshmi Engineering College, affiliated to Anna University Chennai. Her areas of interest include Web services, Cloud Computing, Data Mining and distributed computing. She is a member of ACM, CSI.

Sunil Kumar is a Professor in school of Electrical & Electronics Engineering at Kalinga University, New Raipur, Chhattisgarh and has 25 years of Teaching & Administrative experience. He has published 40 Research Papers in highly reputed Journals and organized Conferences, Seminar, Workshops and Chaired Technical Sessions. He has written a book for CSIR & GATE Examinations. Dr. Kumar is Chairman of Board of Study and Member of Academic Council of various Universities. He is Advisory Board member of 2 reputed Universities of Rajasthan.He is also Editor of 20 reputed International Journals and reviewed number of papers of National and International authors.

Kamalendu Pal is with the Department of Computer Science, School of Mathematics, Computer Science and Engineering, City University London. Kamalendu received his BSc (Hons) degree in Physics from Calcutta University, India, Post-graduate Diploma in Computer Science from Pune, India; MSc degree in Software Systems Technology from Sheffield University, Postgraduate Diploma in Artificial Intelligence from Kingston University, MPhil degree in Computer Science from University College London, and MBA degree from University of Hull, United Kingdom. He has published dozens of research papers in international journals and conferences. His research interests include knowledge-based systems, decision support systems, computer integrated design, software engineering, and service oriented computing. He is a member of the British Computer Society, the Institution of Engineering and Technology, and the IEEE Computer Society.

Manuel Pérez Cota is Professor and Researcher at the University of Vigo (UVIGO) in Vigo, Spain. He has a degree in Electrical Engineering (Universidad La Salle) and Electronics and Communications Engineering (Universidad Nacional Autónoma de México – UNAM, 1980), a PhD in Industrial Engineering (Universidad de Santiago de Compostela, 1990). He is the director of the international research group SI1-GEAC (http://cuautla.uvigo.es/si1-geac/). He was the first director and developer of the Computer Department (Computer Science School of the University of Vigo). He collaborates in different Master and PhD programs in Spain, Portugal, Germany, Argentina and Bolivia, and has been supervisor of several PhDs. He has been involved in different European and International projects. He has published quite extensively and has many publications (including books, book chapters, Scientific Citation Index journal articles, and international journal articles, as well as publications in refereed conference proceedings). He is a member of different international committees and associations (ACM, IEEE, AISTI, AIPO, ANALCT).

Abhilash R. is pursuing his final year Bachelor's degree in Instrumentation Engineering from APJ Abdul Kalam Technological University, India.

Babu R. is a Research Scholar in Anna University. He has completed his Masters in Software Engineering with a merit of 2nd rank in the University and Bachelors in Computer Science and Engineering from Rajalakshmi Engineering College affiliated to Anna University. His areas of interest include Web Services, Service Oriented Architecture, Cloud Computing, Big Data Analytics and Internet of Things. He is a life member of CSI and served as a Management Committee Member for three years. He has received Active Participation Award – Youth from CSI. He also received Faculty Excellence Award from Infosys in Faculty Enablement Program for three successive years.

Carlos Rabadão is Coordinator Professor at Department of Computer Science Engineering at School of Technology and Management of Polytechnic of Leiria (ESTG). He is the Head of Computer Science and Communication Research Centre (CIIC) of Polytechnic of Leiria and Chair of the Technical-Scientific Council of ESTG. He received his PhD degree in Computer Science Engineering from University of Coimbra, Portugal, in 2007, his MSc degree in Electronics and Telecommunications Engineering, from University of Aveiro, Portugal, in 1996 and his BSc degree in Electrical Engineering, specialization in Telecommunications and Electronics, from University of Coimbra, Portugal, in 1989. He has more than 24 years of teaching and research experience in Computer Engineering, namely in the areas of Cybersecurity and Computer Networks. He has published around 50 papers in international conferences and journals in the areas of Cybersecurity, Computer Science and Data Communications. He has participated in more than 20 national and international R&D projects, having coordinated 5 of these. His major research interests include Information and Networks Security, Information Security and Privacy Management, Security Incident Response Systems for Industry 4.0, Next Generation Networks and Services and Wireless Networks.

Leonel Santos is an Assistant Professor at the Computer Science Engineering Department at Superior School of Technology and Management, Polytechnic of Leiria (Portugal). He is a researcher, collaborator member of the Computer Science and Communication Research Centre - CIIC, at Polytechnic of Leiria. He is a forensic computer expert, collaborator member of the Cybersecurity and Computer Forensics Laboratory – LabCIF, at Polytechnic of Leiria. He received is PhD degree in University of Trás-os-Montes e Alto Douro (Portugal) and received his BSc degree in Computer Science Engineering, from Polytechnic of Leiria (Portugal) in 2006. Outside the education system, has worked as a Coordinator Professor at Senhor dos Milagres School (Portugal). His major research interests include Cybersecurity, Information and Networks Security, Internet of Things, Intrusion Detection Systems and Computer Forensics.

Anjum Sheikh is working as Assistant Professor at Rajiv Gandhi College of Engineering Research & Technology, Chandrapur and has a teaching experience of 13 years. She received her M.Tech degree in Electronics and Communication Engineering from RTM Nagpur university and currently pursuing Ph.D degree from Kalinga Univeristy, Raipur. She has published 8 research papers in National and International conferences. Her areas of interests are Internet of Thing and wireless communication.

Nissrine Souissi is a fulltime professor at the MINES-RABAT School, Morocco. She obtained a PhD in computer science in 2006 from the University of Paris XII, France and an engineer degree in computer engineering in 2001 from Mohammadia Engineers School, Morocco. Her research interests include process engineering, business process management, databases, data lifecycle, smart data, hospital information system, and information system.

Siji A. Thomas received her Master's degree in Communication Engineering from APJ Abdul Kalam Technological University, India in 2019 and Bachelor's degree in Instrumentation Engineering from Mahatma Gandhi University, Kerala, India in 2016. She is currently an Assistant Professor in Department of Applied Electronics and Instrumentation Engineering, Mount Zion College of Engineering, Pathanamthitta, Kerala, India. She has worked in the field of Instrumentation Maintenance, Medical Image Processing, Internet of Things and Robotics. Her research interests include Image Processing, Neural Networks, Deep Learning, Robotics, Smart Farming and Internet of Things (IoT).

Index

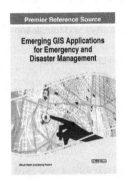
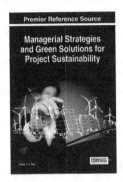